TEACHING THROUGH TEXT

A Content
Literacy
Approach
to
Content
Area
Reading

Michael C. McKenna
Georgia Southern University
Richard D. Robinson
University of Missouri-Columbia

Longman
New York & London

Teaching through Text: A Content Literacy Approach to Content Area Reading

Longman, 10 Bank Street, White Plains, N.Y. 10606

Associated companies:
Longman Group Ltd., London
Longman Cheshire Pty., Melbourne
Longman Paul Pty., Auckland
Copp Clark Pitman, Toronto

Senior acquisitions editor: Laura McKenna
Sponsoring editor: Raymond T. O'Connell
Development editor: Virginia L. Blanford
Production editor: Ann P. Kearns
Text design: Kevin C. Kall
Cover design: Kevin C. Kall
Text art: Publication Services
Production supervisor: Anne P. Armeny

Library of Congress Cataloging-in-Publication Data

McKenna, Michael C.
   Teaching through text : a content literacy approach to content
area reading / Michael C. McKenna, Richard D. Robinson.
      p.   cm.
   Includes bibliographical references (p.) and index.
   ISBN 0-8013-0584-5
   1. Reading (Higher education)   2. Content area reading.
3. English language—Rhetoric.   4. Interdisciplinary approach in
education.   I. Robinson, Richard David, Date.   II. Title.
LB2365.R4M35   1992
428.4'071'1—dc20   92-27870
                                                                          CIP

1 2 3 4 5 6 7 8 9 10—HA—9695949392

To our wives, Beverly and Alice

CONTENTS

v

FOREWORD

It is my pleasure to introduce *Teaching through Text: A Content Literacy Approach to Content Area Reading,* by Michael C. McKenna and Richard D. Robinson. I must confess that when my colleagues heard that I was writing the Foreword for this new textbook several of them commented, "What? Another content area reading book!" I was happy to respond to these individuals that "this isn't *just another* content area reading textbook." McKenna and Robinson's text is unique in many ways. First, it is clear to me that the authors have considered the perspectives of practicing and prospective teachers as they compiled the information for this book. McKenna and Robinson have considered the arguments put forth by researchers who have worked to understand *why* content area teachers typically resist adopting reading and writing strategies as an integral part of learning content material. The authors have acknowledged these participants' beliefs and attitudes and then used these as a basis for the selection and presentation of material in their textbook. Let me provide several examples. In the Title and Preface of the book the authors use the term *content literacy* as opposed to the terms *reading* or *writing* only. Because content teachers traditionally do not believe that teaching reading or writing skills is part of their responsibility, they tend to be put off by the idea that they should learn information to help them accomplish this goal. However, helping students become more literate tends to be a holistic goal shared by all educators. In addition, McKenna and Robinson base their text on the idea that "an important (and virtually unassailable) priority of most content area teachers is the acquisition of content." As one who has spent considerable time working with content area teachers, I can attest that this is their overriding concern. Literacy educators will be successful "selling" the idea of content literacy only by acknowledging this content-centered goal and using it to ground the ideas we present to teachers. McKenna and Robinson work toward this goal by offering "content literacy techniques...[that] are likely to enhance such learning (rather than merely improve general reading skills)." Thus, the authors of this text are not paying lip service to the resistance research; rather, they have used these data to prepare literacy materials that represent information content teachers will find acceptable—strategies that will help students learn content. Once preservice and inservice teachers who read this book are aware of this position, they may be more likely to find the ideas presented amenable to their specific content area teaching goals.

A further strength of this text is the careful selection of strategies and information included. Unlike many content area textbooks, this text does not contain every prereading, during-reading, and postreading activity ever devised. Instead, McKenna and Robinson have selected for inclusion only those ideas that have been supported by research and that have been found to be effective by teachers in classroom settings. Again, this type of care in the information included (and excluded) from this text reflects a concern for participants' (both practicing and prospective teachers) needs and a good sense of what ideas these individuals will find credible as they search to select appropriate teaching strategies.

As educators we share the common concern of motivating students to want to learn while providing them with the strategies to help them learn. Our goal is to provide experiences through which students learn content but more importantly learn how to work through difficult material with their teacher and peers. McKenna and Robinson consider this goal carefully by devoting an entire chapter to the social dynamics of postreading discussions and how teachers and students can engage in conversations where active and meaningful thinking and learning occur. They have also considered this goal by practicing what they preach. Specifically, they have included effective literacy guides to accompany each chapter of the text and to enhance discussion over the ideas presented.

I have highlighted but a few of the strengths of this text. Some readers will be happy to also find the familiar topics many educators believe are essential for inclusion in a book of this nature. However, to *avoid* writing yet another content area reading book, authors must be willing to try something different—to move beyond what researchers think is important for inclusion in a text and to think about what our stakeholders in preservice and inservice courses find important and relevant. I believe that McKenna and Robinson have worked toward this goal and I find their efforts commendable.

DEBORAH R. DILLON
PURDUE UNIVERSITY

PREFACE

We have brought to the planning of this text certain beliefs about students, about teachers, and about learning through text. This book inevitably reflects these beliefs, which we regard as mainstream views based defensibly on available research and informed opinion. Specifically, we contend that

- the most effective content area teachers know their materials and their students and purposefully acquire information about both;
- an important (and virtually unassailable) priority of most content area teachers is the acquisition of content;
- content literacy techniques must therefore be included only insofar as they are likely to enhance such learning (rather than merely improve general reading skills);
- the best learners from text actively engage in a process of constructing, verifying, and extending meaning as they read;
- content area teachers are ideally placed to maximize such interaction between their students and their materials; and
- this result is most likely to be achieved when both reading and writing (the two domains of literacy) are integrated.

Our goal is to produce a book that provides you with a wide variety of suggestions for instructional practice that is consistent with these beliefs. We have tried very hard to include only those recommendations that have been validated through research and that teachers tend to regard as practical. This task has not been easy because of the multitude of ideas now in the literature. Rather than offer a comprehensive review of these ideas, we have sifted through them in a search for those that have proved both practical and effective.

TO THE TEACHER

A New Approach to the Topic. As a matter of conjecture, we suspect that the authors of other content area reading texts subscribe to the beliefs outlined above. While some of these authors may qualify and prioritize them differently, the dissimilarities among existing titles are less a matter of guiding philosophy than of conclusions about how that philosophy is best translated into recommendations for teachers. Our perspective for making such recommendations is that literacy skills are vital for adequately assimilating and accommodating disciplinary knowledge. We have therefore defined *content literacy* as the condition of possessing those skills needed for constructing subject matter knowledge through the processes of reading and writing (McKenna & Robinson, 1990). Such skills include the prior knowledge and technical vocabulary needed in these processes. While we believe that the most effective teaching techniques tend to transcend disciplinary boundaries and are useful in a majority of content area settings, we suggest that virtually any conceptualization of literacy, beyond its most basic applications, is best viewed from a content-specific perspective. It has been our hope to produce a book that instills within content teachers the conviction that literacy is a tool uniquely defined by their disciplines, a tool whereby knowledge is used to acquire more knowledge.

We began by building a profile of the "ideal" content area text, one that we could adopt ourselves without reservation and that optimally reflects the philosophical perspectives detailed above. In our view, such a text should include the following characteristics:

1. It should continually emphasize how the recommended techniques will enhance achievement (that is, the acquisition of content).

2. It should serve to broaden the reader's perspective on the very nature of achievement, to include not merely the acquisition of facts but also higher-order processes such as inference, analysis, synthesis, application, and critical evaluation, once facts are understood.

3. It should underscore the notion of content literacy, which involves both reading and writing about content, as a means to improved understanding of content.

4. In this respect, it should underscore the interconnectedness of reading and writing *throughout the text,* not in a segregated chapter devoted to writing.

5. It should be based on current research, especially findings in the areas of (1) effective teaching, (2) the effectiveness of specific content area reading techniques, and (3) the reading process.

6. It should stress the universal applicability of most content area techniques by integrating numerous examples from a variety of content areas throughout the text, not by devoting entire chapters to each of several core content areas.

7. Its organization should facilitate the reader's assimilation of the many methods and techniques discussed by first presenting global lesson designs (i.e., comprehensive lesson formats that involve prereading, reading, and postreading phases). Only then should it present

techniques useful *within* each of these phases. In this way, the reader will first be given an overall structure followed by specifics.

8. It should provide a practical treatment of how teachers can encourage reading of *content-specific* materials beyond textbooks. We suggest that this is a more effective approach to motivational issues than that of stressing how content teachers can make their students more inclined to read *general* materials, those not necessarily related to their disciplines.

9. It should discuss the changing nature of text (and consequently literacy) brought about by technology. Classroom computer applications that involve reading and writing as means to enhanced content understanding should be presented.

A New Approach to College Teaching. This book is accompanied by 14 content literacy guides, one for every chapter. They appear in the Instructor's Manual and may be duplicated and distributed as frequently as desired. The guides are designed to serve two purposes. First, they can model for students some of the most important techniques described in this text, including the use of such guides to assist reading and to plan postreading discussions. Second, the guides can help to ensure adequate independent study of any chapters that may receive limited attention in class due to time constraints and instructional priorities.

TO ALL READERS

This text is organized into five sections, each containing two or more chapters. Section 1 provides background in literacy and addresses unit planning. Section 2 takes a closer look at planning, focusing on activities that might precede a reading assignment, such as introducing vocabulary. Section 3 presents ways of guiding students' reading in order to ensure that what they derive from an assignment corresponds with teacher expectations. Section 4 discusses methods of following up assigned reading in such a way that learning is reinforced and extended. Section 5 provides more techniques for helping students use literacy for developing an understanding of course content; special learners are discussed, as well as ways of enhancing attitudes and of using technology. Issues related to special learners are discussed in Chapter 12 by Belinda D. Lazarus.

Each chapter begins with an organizing diagram that visually summarizes the chapter's main features. Chapter content is summarized verbally at the end of the chapter. Students are encouraged to become active readers by means of sections entitled "Getting Involved," which follow the summary of each chapter. Here, activities are suggested for applying chapter content and for making it specific to the student's teaching area.

We have attempted to make the ideas presented in this book thoroughly understandable and enjoyable by two means. One is the inclusion of numerous graphic aids, including diagrams, charts, definitions, illustrations, and "concept bridges," indicated by the bridge symbol, which link certain ideas. The other feature, perhaps unique to this text, is the use of quotations from noted writers who, through the years, have addressed the very topics we examine.

If we have succeeded in creating a tool for moving content teachers to consider, actively and openly, both the problems and the potential of using literacy in their classrooms, then the labors of constructing this book will have been rewarded.

We gratefully acknowledge the efforts of our reviewers in offering detailed and insightful comments at several stages of development. These individuals include

Deborah R. Dillon, Purdue University;

Lawrence Erickson, Southern Illinois University/Carbondale;

Jill Fitzgerald, University of North Carolina/Chapel Hill;

Mary Ann Gray-Schlegel, Millersville University;

Douglas K. Hartman, University of Pittsburgh;

Martha Kinney, Eastern Michigan University;

John Shefelbine, Utah State University;

Cheryl Spaulding, Syracuse University; and

Elaine Stephens, Saginaw Valley State University.

Their input has strengthened the book in many ways and has been very much appreciated.

Section . . . . one

Teaching and Learning through Text

Never before have educators so actively discussed and so extensively researched the development of literacy. Reading and writing are no longer isolated issues but touch all areas of learning, including content subjects. The goal of this section is to provide the groundwork you will need to understand exactly how literacy can enhance (or limit) the learning of your students.

Chapter 1 defines literacy and describes its relationship to the oral language processes of speaking and listening. We then introduce four important aspects of literacy, one of which is its potential in content area classrooms. This fourth aspect we call *content literacy*.

Chapter 2 describes reading and writing as mental processes. We examine how an individual's purposes and background greatly influence what is learned through reading. We then look at writing as a process guided by intentions, a process of great usefulness as a means of refining and clarifying what we know about a subject.

Chapter 3 compares ways of gathering information about the needs of students. We look at three areas: (1) the reading ability of students, (2) the demands of reading materials, and (3) the suitability of instructional practices.

Chapter 4 lays the groundwork of lesson planning. We present and contrast four global lesson designs useful in planning entire units or major portions of units. Many of the details of "filling in" these global plans with specific activities are a matter of daily planning. These activities will be described in Chapters 5 through 10.

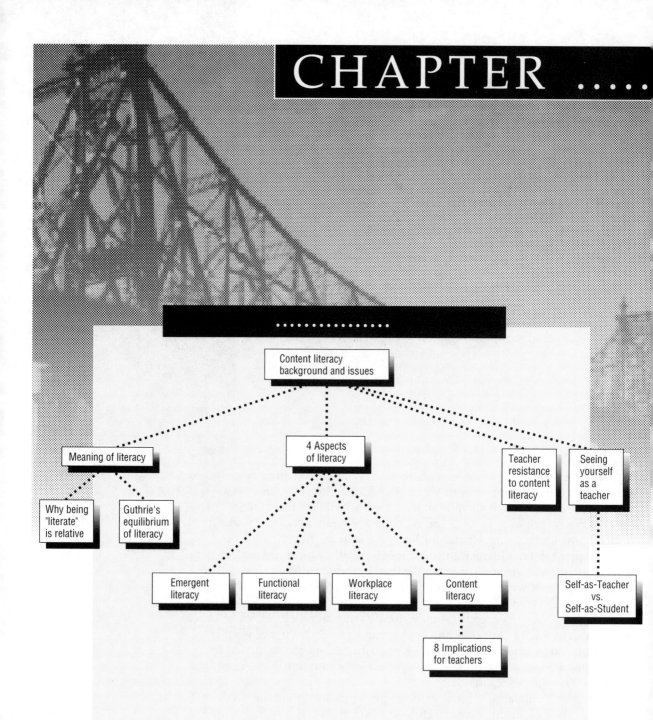

ONE

The Importance of Literacy in Content Areas

The mass of every people must be barbarous where there is no printing.
                                                                    Samuel Johnson

Why should content area teachers be concerned with literacy? In the words of one, "Isn't it enough to know about my teaching speciality without having to worry about reading and writing as well?" This important question will be addressed in various ways throughout this book.

This chapter is devoted to the term *literacy* and its implications for how students acquire content knowledge and skills. We begin with a discussion of what it means to be a literate person, because your eventual answer to this question (and it is *you* who must answer it!) will determine in large part your decisions concerning the role of literacy in your classes.

OBJECTIVES

After reading this chapter you should be able to

1. discuss the question, Should content teachers be teachers of reading? noting the principal reasons for and against this position;

2. define the various aspects of literacy, including emergent, developmental, functional, and content literacy;

3. describe how content literacy facilitates greater content achievement;

4. note some of the false assumptions many teachers believe about reading and writing in the content fields; and

5. develop the beginnings of a philosophy toward content literacy in regard to the eventual role it will play in your own teaching.

THE MEANING OF LITERACY

While we might all agree on the importance of being literate, defining *literacy* is a difficult and divisive task. Past definitions have often entailed the measurement of a few narrowly selected abilities (*Bottom line*, 1988; Stedman & Kaestle, 1987; Wedman & Robinson, 1990). At one time, a literate person was one who was able to sign his or her name, or who had reached a certain grade level in school, or who had scored above a predetermined point on a test. Often the application of these definitions of literacy was handled in an arbitrary and prejudicial manner, as with the infamous "literacy tests" that once determined which individuals were qualified to vote.

Today, literacy is typically thought of in much broader terms and is seen as one of the avenues by which individuals interact in social contexts (Robinson & Good, 1987). The literate are defined not simply as those who have attained a certain level of proficiency in language ability but rather as those who are able to use written materials effectively in the environment in which they live and work (Mikulecky, 1990).

For the concept of literacy to be meaningful, you must think of it in relation to the unique requirements of the context in which it is to be used (Langer, 1986a, 1986b). This context may be as large as a nation or as small as a classroom. Each situation presents unique requirements; adequate language proficiency in one situation might be inadequate in another.

Guthrie (1983) uses a graphic representation to suggest how situational demands interact with the level of individual literacy. (See Figure 1.1.) The horizontal axis of the graph describes environmental demands, and the vertical axis describes personal literacy levels. Our consideration is limited to the demands placed on students in content area classrooms. Think of the reading and writing demands of a variety of teachers as ranging from low to high across the bottom of the graph. Students on the diagonal line demonstrate a general proficiency roughly equal to classroom demands. Hill, who is above the diagonal, demonstrates a personal literacy level significantly exceeding what is expected in class. Students like Marino and Compton, on the other hand, whose literacy development is unequal to the demands of their classrooms, will undoubtedly struggle—and this is true even though Compton's proficiency is superior to Marino's—because the key variable is the demands of their respective classrooms. Far more is expected of Compton.

The horizontal line labeled Z represents the traditional view that one definable level of literacy is adequate for all individuals in all settings within a society. The fallacy of this idea as it relates to content area instruction is evident from the examples of the graph. Compton, for instance, is well above the Z line but is nonetheless unequal to the expectations of a specific teacher; Jones is below the line but will experience no difficulty in a class where demands are

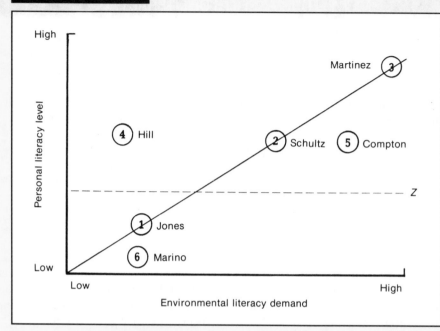

Equilibrium of literacy

SOURCE: From "Equilibrium of Literacy" by John T. Guthrie, April 1983, *Journal of Reading*, *26*(7), p. 670. Copyright 1983 by the International Reading Association. Reprinted by permission of John Guthrie and the International Reading Association.

modest. The idea that content teachers establish varying literacy demands that may render some students "illiterate" is one to which we will return presently.

In 1985 the National Assessment of Educational Progress completed a landmark study of 3,600 young people between the ages of 21 and 25 using a wide variety of literacy tasks (Kirsch & Jungeblut, 1986). The definition of literacy used in this study is the following:

> Using printed and written information to function in society, to achieve one's goals, and to develop one's knowledge and potential. (p. xiii)

This definition of literacy is important because it does not measure literacy success by identifying a specific set of skills. Instead of limiting literacy as being able to sign one's name or pass a given grade level, this literacy definition emphasizes performance *in relation to* the requirements of the society in which that performance occurs. Beginning with the work of Gray (1969) and extending through five national assessments of reading, *literacy* has come to mean a person's performance in relation to the need to use literacy skills in a particular social setting (Robinson & Good, 1987; Searfoss & Readence, 1989).

FOUR ASPECTS OF LITERACY

Recent research has led to a new appreciation for the complexity of literacy processes. One important consequence has been an abandonment of the notion that literacy is a single state or set of skills. In this section, we develop this notion by discussing four diverse aspects of literacy: *emergent, functional, workplace,* and *content.* It will become clear that these aspects, while distinct in many respects, are nevertheless highly interconnected and interdependent.

Emergent Literacy

An outmoded view of learning to read and write holds that a child begins to acquire these abilities only upon entry into the formal settings of school instruction. The kindergarten teacher's job was to prepare children for actual literacy instruction (to begin in first grade) by undertaking an extensive regimen of "readiness" training.

A view that squares more accurately with the results of research is that literate behavior and experiences begin long before schooling and that there is really no magic moment in the life of a child at which readiness for instruction occurs. Literacy acquisition is now seen instead as a gradual process beginning in the home. Literate behavior has been observed to *emerge* slowly in young children, a process described by Teale and Sulzby (1989) as follows:

> Even during the first months of life, children come in contact with written language as parents place soft alphabet blocks in their environments or read them books. These early contacts with print can be thought of as the beginning of a lifelong process of learning to read and write. By the time they are two or three, many children can identify signs, labels, and logos they see in their homes and communities. (p. 3)

The task of primary teachers is now increasingly perceived as a matter of building on this groundwork. In short, their job is to take children at their individual points of development and help literacy continue to emerge.

Functional Literacy

The notion of *functional literacy* is one of the most complex, dynamic, and elusive concepts encountered by educators. One reason for this difficulty is the political significance of the term. When functional literacy is defined broadly, large numbers of people are classified as illiterate; narrower definitions result in rosier pictures (Levine, 1982). In general, the term denotes the ability to use reading and writing to function adequately in one's environment, including in one's job; functional literacy includes the more specific concept of workplace literacy, which we will discuss presently. Because functional literacy varies with an individual's environment (including the demands of employment), no single level of literacy can possibly suffice to make everyone functional—unless, of course, we use the highest standard of proficiency for all individuals.

In one popular though misguided conceptualization, functional literacy has been separated from workplace demands, so that the functionally literate person is sometimes seen as one who is able to read a newspaper, street signs, and other "public" information and who can write a check or fill out an application when the need arises. It is difficult, however, to see how persons who are able to do these things and who are yet unequal to the literacy demands of their jobs can possibly be regarded as functionally literate.

Hunter and Harman (1979) described functional literacy as

> the possession of skills *perceived as necessary by particular persons and groups* to fulfill their own self-determined objectives as family and community members, citizens, consumers, job holders, and members of social, religious, or other associations of their choosing. This includes the ability to obtain information they want and to use that information for their own and others' well-being; the ability to read and write adequately to satisfy the requirements *they set for themselves* as being important for their own lives; the ability to deal positively with demands made on them by society; and the ability to solve the problems they face in their daily lives. (pp. 7–8, original emphasis)

Such a description serves to make clear how functional literacy has at last come to be viewed as a concept relative not just to everyday uses of print but to the demands of the workplace as well.

Workplace Literacy

In recent years, literacy demands in the workplace have drawn increased attention. At one time the assumption was that traditional education would provide the necessary language abilities for most jobs, but this belief has changed as the realities of occupational demands have changed. The need for increasingly higher levels of literacy in particular jobs, as well as the general shifts from industrial to service occupations, has made workplace literacy a growing concern (see *Countdown 2000*, 1988).

In the past, a prospective office worker needed to know only basic keyboarding skills. In today's world, however, this level of literacy knowledge is not sufficient in most business settings. Skills in programming, logic, and problem solving are necessary for all but the most elementary work positions. By one estimate, approximately 70 percent of today's jobs require some degree of literacy (Howie, 1990). This figure is probably low, however; the true proportion may exceed 90 percent (Diehl & Mikulecky, 1980)! In contrast with the past, workplace literacy today requires individuals who can apply general learning strategies in a wide variety of situations.

How do workers acquire these skills? While some skills are developed on the job, the foundations of literacy ability are formed in school, and in numerous ways the foundation may be a weak one. Reading and writing have traditionally been taught in academic settings primarily as a means of acquiring and transmitting information via print. This policy is defensible, as far as it goes, but it stops short of what many students will need in the world of work. Students have been graded on what they are able to remember from their reading rather than on how they can apply this knowledge. Formal writing instruction tends to be limited in scope, receiving far less attention that reading. Yet the literacy demands of today's workplace go far beyond simply being able to read and recall specific information and to convey it to others through writing. Workers must be skilled in knowing how to set their own specific purposes for reading and how to choose reading strategies for achieving these purposes. In writing, they must often be able to analyze, synthesize, predict, and persuade rather than simply inform.

In many ways, the content classroom is comparable to the workplace: It places specific literacy demands on students as they attempt to accomplish the day-to-day tasks of the course. What has been called *workplace literacy* in the industrial world has a counterpart in the world of education. We call this counterpart *content literacy.*

Content Literacy

We define content literacy as *the ability to use reading and writing for the acquisition of new content in a given discipline* (McKenna & Robinson, 1990). Such ability includes three principal cognitive components: (1) general literacy skills, (2) prior knowledge of content, and (3) content-specific literacy skills (such as map reading in the social studies). (See Figure 1.2.) The first two of these—overall literacy ability and content knowledge—are clearly the two factors with the greatest influence on learning through text (Perfetti, 1991).

Obvious connections exist between the content area classroom and a place of employment: Both require knowledge in specific areas, and both make special demands on participants that may change dramatically as they move to a new setting. Finally, both may involve highly specialized literacy requirements germane to that setting and to few others. Content literacy differs considerably from workplace literacy in purpose, however; it is primarily a tool for learning, not job performance.

The potential of *writing* for the purpose of learning has only recently been realized. Researchers now recognize that both reading and writing are constructive processes in which information is organized and accommodated into memory structures. Accordingly, the writing-to-learn movement stresses that writing, like reading, is a means of clarifying, refining, and extending one's internalization of content (Myers, 1984). Writing, like reading, becomes a tool for acquiring content.

FIGURE 1.2

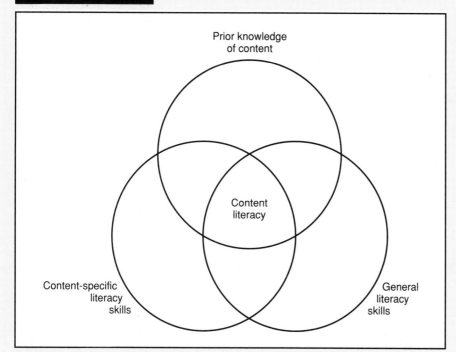

Prior knowledge
of content

Content
literacy

Content-specific
literacy
skills

General
literacy
skills

Cognitive components
of content literacy

THE IMPLICATIONS OF CONTENT LITERACY

The concept of content literacy has a number of important implications for content area teachers, and we believe that these implications lead to a single, inescapable conclusion: By engaging students in appropriate content literacy activities, teachers can optimize learning. We recently suggested the following specific implications (McKenna & Robinson, 1990).

1. *Content literacy is not the same as content knowledge.* The term *literacy* is often used to mean "having knowledge" of a particular area. A person who is *computer literate*, for example, is assumed to *know* about computers. Unfortunately, this kind of usage gets us dangerously far from reading and writing. The term *content literacy* is not merely a synonym for *content knowledge*. Instead, it represents skills needed to acquire knowledge of content. Nor is content literacy a prerequisite for content knowledge, for one can certainly acquire knowledge of content without recourse to reading or writing. On the other hand, content knowledge *is* a prerequisite of content literacy. In a cyclical

pattern, the more prior knowledge one possesses, the more such knowledge will facilitate reading and writing as activities leading to the integration of still more knowledge, and so forth. In short, the more you know about a given area, the easier it is to learn new material in the same area.

2. *Teaching content automatically makes students more content literate.*

What's a book? Everything or nothing.
The eye that sees it is all.
Ralph Waldo Emerson

Whether they know it or not, content area teachers enhance their students' ability to read and write about content simply by teaching it. Ironically, even those teachers who refuse to embrace the ideas of "reading in the content areas" and "writing to learn" improve their students' ability to read and write within their disciplines whenever their instruction is successful. Enchanced prior knowledge always enhances subsequent reading and writing germane to that knowledge. Unfortunately, many teachers, by providing high-quality direct instruction, set the stage for even greater levels of content acquisition (through reading and writing) but never realize this potential with appropriate assignments.

3. *Content literacy is content specific.* To be literate, for example, in mathematics is not a matter of merely "knowing" mathematics. It is being able to read and write about the subject as effective means of knowing still more about it. While the general ability to read and write obviously bears on one's success in reading and writing about a specific subject, prior knowledge of the specific topics involved is a vital variable of content literacy. Thus, an individual who is highly literate in math may have a far lower level of literacy in history or economics. This circumstance is largely the result of differences in prior knowledge and occurs even though the individual brings the same *general* literacy skills to all reading and writing tasks.

4. *In content literacy, reading and writing are complementary tasks.* While reading and writing can serve well enough as alternative means of enhancing content learning, the greatest gains can be expected when the two are used in tandem. When printed materials are assigned to be read and when written responses are also required, students are placed in the position first of constructing an internal representation of the content they encounter in print and next of refining that representation through such processes as synthesis, evaluation, and summarization.

5. *Content literacy is germane to all subject areas, not just those relying heavily on printed materials.* Teachers of subjects such as art, music, physical education, and others tending to involve little use of prose materials have frequently objected that content area reading coursework, now compulsory in at least 36 states (Farrell & Cirrincione, 1986), does not apply to their instructional situations. Certain states have in fact excluded such groups from these course requirements. The notion of content literacy, however, suggests that students' understanding of the content presented in all subjects could be substantially enhanced through appropriate writing assignments. While the primary presentation may comprise lecture and demonstration rather than reading, and while the principal domain involved may be psychomotor rather than

cognitive, content acquisition nevertheless invariably includes understanding of key concepts and their interrelationships. Such understanding can always be fostered through writing.

6. *Content literacy does not require content area teachers to instruct students in the mechanics of writing.* A long-standing misinterpretation that has hampered the effort to encourage content area *reading* techniques is that such techniques call for subject matter specialists to teach the minutiae of decoding—to master a new and very different curriculum, in other words, and, worse, to take class time away from subject matter instruction. This false notion has lingered tenaciously despite widespread efforts to overcome it. We need to make clear, then, in elaborating the idea of content literacy (which embraces writing as well as reading), that the concept includes no responsibility for developing the mechanical skills of writing. As Myers put it, "Writing to learn is not learning to write" (1984, p. 7). Mechanical problems severe enough to distort meaning may require a teacher's attention, especially in subjects like mathematics where precise usage is an absolute necessity (Orr, 1987), but the focus of such follow-up should be meaning, not mechanics.

7. *Content literacy is relative to the tasks expected of students.* The literacy requirements of a classroom, like those of a workplace or of an entire culture, readily define who is literate and who is not (Guthrie, 1983; Mikulecky, 1990; Wedman & Robinson, 1990). In an effort to reduce or eliminate the "illiterate" subpopulation in their classes, teachers all too frequently resort to slashing literacy requirements. Reading assignments may be circumvented or minimized while writing may never be seriously considered. Students consequently meet the literacy demands of the instructional setting—so that all are technically "literate"—but the opportunity to enhance content learning through reading and writing is lost. Students at even a rudimentary level of general literacy are equipped to advance their understanding through literacy activities. This is possible whenever (1) reading materials are commensurate with ability (or steps are taken to facilitate comprehension of more difficult material) and (2) writing assignments are within the range of student sophistication.

8. *Content literacy has the potential to maximize content acquisition.* While reading content materials may introduce new ideas into a student's knowledge base, and while writing about content may help the student organize and store that information more effectively, some argue that similar results may also be accomplished without reliance on reading and writing. Instructors may indeed "spoon-feed" new content in carefully organized curricular designs using direct oral instruction. This argument has been strong enough to persuade some teachers to avoid literacy activities altogether. There are, however, at least four good reasons for not depending exclusively on direct instruction:

1. The products of literacy activities will never precisely match those of oral instruction. They therefore serve to complement such instruction and broaden student perspectives.

2. Individualized extension is made possible through such activities as a natural follow-up to direct instruction. Students are in a position to pursue content on their own, following in some measure their personal predilections, needs, and interests.

3. Present-day models of direct instruction incorporate practice phases that follow up the presentation of content for the purpose of reinforcing it (e.g., Rosenshine, 1986). Such practice could certainly incorporate literacy activities, which seem ideally suited to these models. (We consider direct instruction in more detail in Chapter 4.)

4. Students who have received opportunities to become content literate will be better able to use content literacy as a means of extending their knowledge of a discipline even after they have completed a given course.

TEACHER RESISTANCE TO CONTENT LITERACY

Even though research has shown the effectiveness of many content area teaching techniques involving reading (Alvermann & Swafford, 1989) and writing (Myers, 1984), teachers of content subjects frequently do not employ them. In a recent national survey, for example, Irvin and Connors (1989) found that no more than 14 percent of the respondents employed such techniques as an important part of their programs. If content literacy strategies are effective at increasing content learning, why do teachers resist their use? Stewart and O'Brien (1989) have observed that teachers offer numerous answers to this question, though three reasons in particular stand out.

First, many teachers feel inadequate to handle reading problems in their classrooms. Certainly students experiencing severe reading difficulties present special problems that may exceed the expertise of most subject matter specialists. These individuals are relatively few in number, however, and strategies for meeting their needs are readily available. (See Chapter 12.) Moreover, content literacy strategies are designed to assist *all* students, the poorest readers included, by facilitating their use of text while reading and by extending their thinking through writing. The techniques involved are remarkably simple. No specialized training in how to teach the skills of word recognition and comprehension are needed.

Second, teachers often feel that literacy activities infringe on subject matter time. We are not in any way suggesting that a portion of the daily instructional time in content classes be set aside for general reading development. The literacy activities recommended in this book require no "time out" from content instruction. Instead they involve rearranging (rather than shortening) discussion time and merging reading and writing with content acquisition. It will be important to remember that the point of the strategies we will discuss in this book is to increase content learning, *not* to improve reading and writing ability (though this may follow as a by-product).

Last, many teachers deny the need for content area reading and writing techniques. As we have mentioned, some have eliminated this need by reducing the literacy requirements of their courses, creating an atmosphere in which writing and reading have no place. While literacy may not be a liability in such classrooms, neither will it be an asset. Other teachers find that the majority of their students are capable of mastering the material assigned when they apply themselves. While this may be true, as far as it goes, there are three problems with such a view: (1) It wastes students' time as they struggle unnecessarily with difficult material, (2) it dampens their attitude toward the subject matter, and (3) it results in inferior comprehension even though they have "read" the material.

SEEING YOURSELF AS A TEACHER

Teaching is possibly the only profession with which newcomers have great familiarity before they are trained. You may never have taught, but you have watched others do so for literally thousands of hours. In your many experiences as a student, you have had a chance to evaluate numerous teaching practices, primarily in terms of the effects they may have had on your own learning.

> Teachers, who educate children, deserve more honor than parents, who merely gave them birth; for the latter provided mere life, while the former ensure a good life.
>
> *Aristotle*

Now, as you are introduced to teaching methods you may not have experienced as a student, it will probably seem natural to think back to your own days as a student in middle- and secondary-level classrooms. Diane Holt-Reynolds (1991) found that preservice teachers tend to evaluate the usefulness of a new method by imagining themselves as a student in a class where the method is practiced. They then attempt to project how they might have reacted to the method. If they suspect their experience would not have been a productive one, they reject the new method as unsuitable to their future instructional practice. In other words, undergraduates tend to make a distinction between *Self-As-Teacher* and *Self-As-Student*. Because they lack actual classroom experience on which to base their judgments, any proposed new method is put to the only test available to them: their experience as students. The result is a kind of dialogue between Self-As-Teacher and Self-As-Student. Holt-Reynolds (1991) describes the process this way:

> Almost simultaneously switching roles, they imagined participating in the activity themselves as a student. If Self-As-Student reacted to the imaginary scenario in ways that Self-As-Teacher has already decided are valuable, then these preservice teachers report making favorable decisions about that activity. If, however, Self-As-Student reacted in ways that Self-As-Teacher already sees as undesirable, the preservice teacher made a negative decision. (n.p.)

A difficulty with this very natural process is that preservice teachers' observations of the teachers they themselves have had (numerous as the observations were) have revealed little about how those teachers thought and planned. Nor does this process account for the variety of students one is likely to encounter in a typical classroom. Moreover, it relies on vague and distant impressions made long ago and fails to provide any basis for comparing the methods actually experienced with those a teacher *might* have used but did not.

Our wish is to make you aware, at this early point, of the tendency to use your own background in classrooms (Self-As-Student) to judge the worth of instructional techniques to your teaching (to Self-As-Teacher). We hope that by becoming aware of the process and its limitations you can defer a final judgment until you try a technique for yourself and witness its actual effects on your own students.

SOURCE: Courtesy Christopher Wagner

We close this chapter with a request and a challenge. If you are skeptical about the potential of literacy activities for improving learning in your classes, we ask that you keep an open mind as you read on and that you carefully consider our previous discussion of how content teachers often rationalize their way out of literacy activities. Should you still be skeptical at the conclusion of the course, we challenge you to give the techniques we will present a fair trial in the classroom. Conduct an action research study in which comparable classes are exposed to the same unit with and without the use of literacy activities. Use your own unit test, or some similar performance measure, as the yardstick by which you compare the classes. We're confident that your own evidence will satisfy your doubts.

SUMMARY

Literacy is a concept that has changed considerably over the years. A recent insight has been that the question of whether an individual is literate or not is relative to the demands of the individual's environment (classroom, workplace, society, etc.). To some extent classroom teachers control whether students are literate through the assignments they make.

Four aspects of literacy are important. Emergent literacy is the developing ability among young children to read and write. Functional literacy is the ability to function within one's environment insofar as reading and writing are concerned. While this concept was once limited to "public" tasks, such as reading signs and completing forms, it now embraces demands of the workplace as well. Workplace literacy is therefore a part of functional literacy—the part that concerns an individual's ability to use reading and writing successfully on the job. Content literacy is the ability to use reading and writing to acquire new content within a given subject area. It requires general literacy skills, skills related to reading and writing in the specific area of study, and existing content knowledge within that area.

This definition of content literacy has important implications for teachers. It suggests that knowing content is not the same as being able to read and write about it. Instead, content knowledge is one requirement of content literacy. This means that by teaching content, teachers automatically make students more content literate simply by adding to their knowledge base. It also means that content literacy is not a general skill since specific knowledge within the area of study is needed. The content literate student is one who can add new knowledge through reading, and refine and reorganize that knowledge through writing. These are not processes that are limited to certain subjects; they pertain to all areas. Because learning content is the only relevant goal of literacy activities, teachers do not have to be concerned with the fine points of teaching writing. Rather, by establishing reasonable literacy demands, teachers can extend students' understanding of new materials without presenting tasks that are beyond their abilities.

Even though the methods for using and developing content literacy have an extensive research base, teachers have often resisted using them. They have argued that they lack the training to contend with students having special needs, that literacy activities infringe on time needed to teach content, and that such activities are not really needed to teach content. The idea of content literacy and its implications refute these arguments. Literacy activities within content classrooms tend to maximize and reinforce learning when they are appropriately matched to student abilities.

G E T T I N G   I N V O L V E D

1. A colleague tells you she plans to revise her science course so that reading and writing are not required, except for objective tests. She will rely on lecture, demonstrations, and discussion to convey content. She estimates impressive savings for the district in textbook purchases, and she looks forward to fewer papers to grade and no interference with instruction caused by reading problems. Do you think her plan is likely to result in acceptable learning by students? Would you support her in her efforts? Suppose the idea began to catch on among teachers in other content areas. Would you support a district policy to severly limit reading and writing in all subjects but language arts? Defend your position.

2. In the 1985 movie *Teachers*, starring Nick Nolte, a social studies instructor made the following complaint to a colleague in the lounge:

"I signed a contract to teach social studies, not reading. I don't see why I should have to spend my time dealing with students who can't read the text. I'm a history teacher, not a reading teacher."

Her friend looked at her thoughtfully.

"But you are a *teacher*, aren't you?" he asked.

The woman had nothing to say. How would you have responded? Does being a teacher imply a duty to do whatever may be needed to ensure learning?

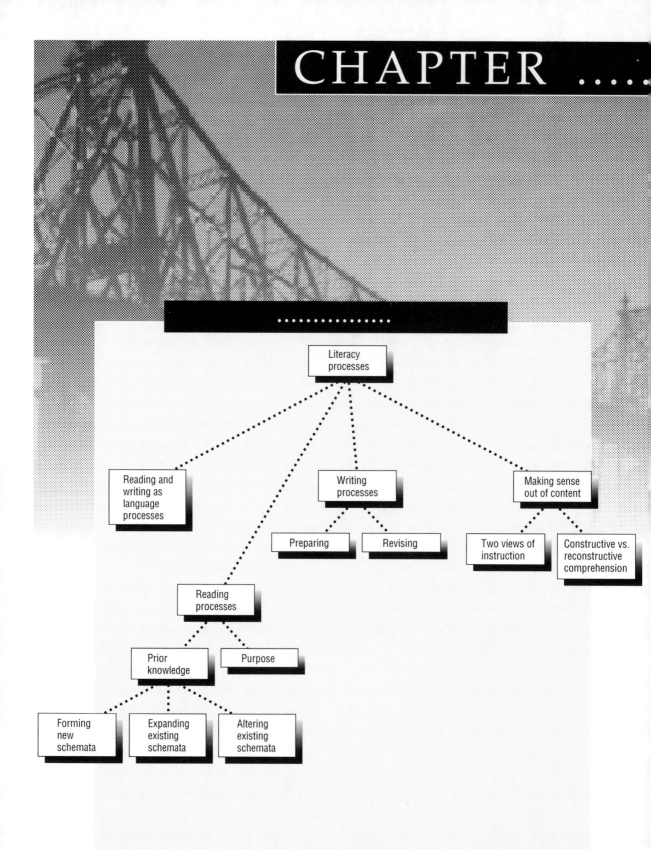

TWO

Literacy Processes

There is in writing the constant joy of sudden discovery, happy accident.
H. L. Mencken

It is probably natural to think of reading and writing as two vastly different processes, linked only by a mutual dependence on printed language. Yet we now know that writing and reading share numerous similarities. For our purposes, the most important of these common traits is the potential of each process to enhance learning. To better understand this potential, it is necessary to appreciate in general terms how the two processes work.

OBJECTIVES

Your study of this chapter should enable you to

1. relate reading and writing to their oral language counterparts;

2. describe the sequence of key events in the process of written communication;

3. explain the role of prior knowledge and purpose in reading and the role of intention in writing; and

4. list important similarities shared by reading and writing and explain their implications for content instruction.

READING AND WRITING AS LANGUAGE PROCESSES

Imagine a world without language. To convey even the simplest thoughts would require the use of gestures, facial expressions, drawings, physical objects, and other contrivances. Even then, precise communication would seldom be assured, while expressing—or even thinking about—abstract ideas would be extremely difficult. Assume, for example, that as a cave dweller in prelinguistic antiquity you happen to shatter a stone chisel while working. In examining the broken fragments, it might occur to you that each one of them could be broken in turn into still smaller fragments, and so on. You wonder if there is some limit beyond which the fragments cannot under any circumstances be further subdivided. How would you communicate this thought to a friend? You could show your friend the pieces and break one of them a second time and gesticulate and pantomime and perhaps paint wordless diagrams on the wall of your cave, but these efforts would in no way guarantee that you would be understood.

If, however, you had developed a collection of spoken sounds to symbolize concepts and a system of rules for combining those sounds as a means of expressing ideas, your task would be far simpler. These spoken symbols are of course *words*, while the set of all available words is called the *lexicon*. The rules for combining words are together referred to as *grammar*, or *syntax*. Thus, the lexicon and syntax are the two primary components of any language.

So far we have been discussing *oral* language. Consider now a second set of symbols, this time visual, designed to represent spoken words. These symbols (written words) can be combined largely according to the grammatical rules governing oral language, though written communication has nuances all its own. Historically, two principal methods have been used to represent spoken words with visual symbols. One method is to use letters to symbolize the smallest, most basic speech sounds, called *phonemes*. The advantage of this approach is that the letters are interchangeable and relatively few are needed to depict virtually any word. Written languages formulated through this method are described as *alphabetic*. These include most Western languages, including English. Certain other languages, such as Chinese, employ an *ideographic* method, in which a unique symbol is used to represent an entire word. While in some cases complex ideographs can be constructed from simpler forms, component speech sounds are not symbolically represented. Thus, thousands of individual symbols must be learned by the language user. Because there is little relationship between print and sound, the same visual word may have entirely different pronunciations in two localities. Thus, speakers of the Mandarin and Cantonese dialects of Chinese cannot converse with one another even though they read and write the same language!

Whatever the method of visually symbolizing spoken language, the result is a second system of symbols (written ones) superimposed on the first. Reading and writing are therefore the more recent counterparts of the much older processes of speaking and listening.

Because communication involves the transmission of ideas and feelings from one individual to another, a complete model of the process, as it relates to literacy, must begin in the mind of the writer and end in that of the reader. Figure 2.1 starts with the thoughts a writer may wish to convey. These intentions tend to be somewhat fluid and independent of language until they are given linguistic form. This process, whether oral or written, is sometimes described as *encoding* since the language itself is made up of arbitrary, cipherlike symbols that differ from one language to the next. Because the reader cannot directly access the writer's thoughts, the written product must be used

FIGURE 2.1

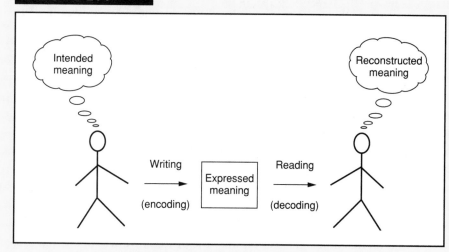

Transformations of meaning from writing to reading

in an effort to *reconstruct* those thoughts. The success of this effort depends on the reader's ability to *decode* the printed symbols. The degree to which the ideas the writer initially intended to convey were eventually reconstructed in the reader's mind is the degree to which communication was successful.

It is important to make clear that this model sidesteps some of the other reasons an individual might choose to write: to evoke an emotion in the reader, to persuade or move the reader to action, to mislead or distract the reader, and so on (see Smith, 1988, for a discussion). The purpose of *informing* the reader is, however, the chief reason writers write in content subjects and the chief reason their writing is assigned to students. Depicting the reading and writing processes from an information-processing perspective is therefore well suited to the topics we will explore in the coming chapters.

THE READING PROCESS

What happens when we read? This "simple" question has intrigued researchers for decades and is yet to be satisfactorily answered. For our purposes, we will not be concerned with a detailed description of the subprocesses that underlie reading. We can, however, offer the following capsule description based on the conclusions that reading researchers have reached:

1. Reading is an interactive process in which a reader's prior knowledge of the subject and purpose for reading operate to influence what is learned from text.

2. The visual structure of printed words and the system by which letters represent the sounds of speech together define subprocesses used to identify words.

3. These word identification processes are applied rapidly by fluent readers, but they may hamper readers with problems.

4. As visual word forms are associated with word meanings, a mental reconstruction of overall textual meaning is created. This reconstruction is subject to continual change and expansion as the reader progresses.

5. In the end, the nearer the reconstructed meaning is to the writer's originally intended meaning, the more successful will be the act of communication (McKenna, 1977a).

6. The reader's purpose may deliberately limit the scope of the reconstruction, however, as when one reads an article for its main points or consults an encyclopedia for a specific fact.

Based on this nutshell description of the process, we will define reading as *the reconstruction in the mind of meaning encoded in print*. From the perspective of the content teacher, two points are important to note. First, it is not the content specialist's role to *teach* the process we have outlined here but to *facilitate* students as they try to use that process to learn through written materials. Second, the best way to achieve this facilitation is to focus on two factors in the reading process that are most easily influenced by the teacher who assigns the materials: (1) the prior knowledge of the students and (2) the purposes for which the students will read. In the chapters that follow, we will present many techniques for addressing these two factors. For now, let's examine the role each of these factors plays in the process of reading.

The Role of Prior Knowledge

Figure 2.2 presents a passage written to demonstrate exactly how limiting prior knowledge can be when it is not adequate for making sense of new information. Read the passage now if you have not already done so. Did you become vaguely (perhaps openly) frustrated as you read? We suspect you may have, even though you knew it was part of a planned demonstration. Imagine the plight of your students when unplanned shortcomings in prior knowledge make the material they must read just as frustrating. Especially ironic is the fact that limitations in prior knowledge are often easily overcome if an instructor is aware they exist and takes a few simple steps to address them. How much better your comprehension would have been a moment ago, for example, had we bothered to provide you in advance with the simple fact that the passage deals with washing clothes!

Knowledge is the true organ of sight, not the eyes.

Panchatantra, *5th century*

Let's look a little further at how prior knowledge can wield such power over comprehension. It is helpful to think of the underlying knowledge needed

FIGURE 2.2

The procedure is actually quite simple. First you arrange things into different groups. Of course, one pile may be sufficient depending on how much there is to do. If you have to go somewhere else due to lack of facilities, that is the next step, otherwise you are pretty well set. It is important not to overdo things. That is, it is better to do too few things rather than too many. In the short run this may not seem important but complications can easily arise. A mistake can be expensive as well. At first the whole procedure will seem complicated. Soon, however, it will become just another facet of life. It is difficult to foresee any end to the necessity for this task in the immediate future, but then one can never tell. After the procedure is completed one arranges the materials in groups again. Then they can be put into their appropriate places. Eventually they will be used once more and the whole cycle will have to be repeated. However, this is part of life.

(8.2)

An example of how prior knowledge can help or hinder comprehension

SOURCE: From "Contextual Prerequisites for Understanding: Some Investigations of Comprehension and Recall" by J. D. Bransford and M. K. Johnson, 1972, *Journal of Verbal Learning and Verbal Behavior, 11*, p. 722.

to comprehend what we read as being stored in interconnected categories within memory. These categories are called *schemata* (plural of *schema*). Think of a schema as all you know about a given concept. You have a schema for "contracts," for example, that may differ considerably from the extensive schema for this same concept that exists in the mind of an attorney. In the same way, the schemata for "contracts" that individual students might bring to the reading of a business law chapter are likely to vary considerably from one student to the next.

Schemata are not stored in isolation but are connected by intricate networks of associations. As you read, various schemata are "activated" and that portion of your prior knowledge is brought to bear on the task of bringing meaning to the print before you. Connections among schemata are also activated as you attempt to reconstruct the author's expressed meaning.

Comprehending what we read is thus highly dependent on prior knowledge. As Pearson and Johnson put it, *"Comprehension is building bridges between the new and the known"* (1978, p. 24, original emphasis). When a student's existing knowledge of the content to be covered by a reading assignment is scant, comprehension is poor. Accordingly, some of the techniques we shall introduce involve building background knowledge before the students begin to read. This effort entails a rearrangement of discussion time and takes nothing from the presentation of content. Rather, it is merely an alternative way of introducing the content, and it pays tangible dividends in student understanding.

As the reader progresses through print, schemata for the concepts discussed by the writer will be changed in one or more of three basic ways.

New schemata may be formed, existing schemata may be expanded, or existing schemata may be fundamentally altered.

Formation of New Schemata   The introduction of new concepts is a frequent occurrence in content learning and calls for the establishment of new schemata. This involves forming associations with existing schemata so that the new knowledge is meaningfully linked to the old.

Consider the language arts student who has just read a selection on haiku, complete with definition, examples, writing guidelines, and so on. Let us assume that the reading serves to introduce the concept of haiku for the first time. The student will already possess knowledge structures relevant to the creation of a new schema for this type of poetry. Figure 2.3(a) depicts how a portion of these structures might be diagrammed prior to the student's exposure to the new concept. Poetic genres already familiar to the student are stored in association with the general concept of "poems," which is in turn related to the larger notion of "written forms," and so forth. Figure 2.3(b) illustrates how the memory structures might look after the new concept has been learned. The learning has not involved the alteration of existing schemata, other than by the addition of a new schema for "haiku." This new schema fits conveniently into what the student already knows.

Expansion of Existing Schemata   You may have had occasion as a high school biology student to dissect a frog. Your laboratory manual and the actual experience itself doubtless served to introduce many new facts about frogs, facts that greatly complemented your prior knowledge. These new facts are not likely to have contradicted any of the assumptions you may previously have made: that frogs are usually green, that they have a certain size and shape, webbed feet, slick skin, and so forth. Rather, the new information tended to amplify, extend, and supplement what you already knew. You were not compelled to "unlearn" anything in order to make room for the new facts. Piaget (1952) described the process by which existing schemata are extended in this fashion as *assimilation*. This is likely to occur whenever one's background knowledge is relatively broad so that new information fits rather well into existing cognitive structures. In such cases, the new information is largely congruent with the old.

Alteration of Existing Schemata   What happens when new facts are encountered that do not square with what an individual believes to be true? Two things can occur: The person can reject the information or can *accommodate* it by altering prior knowledge accordingly. Piaget's notion of accommodation (like that of assimilation) was not limited to reading but extended to all learning situations. Imagine, for example, that you were told something shocking about a close friend, someone you'd known for years. You might question your source, dismissing the new information as false since it was so

FIGURE 2.3

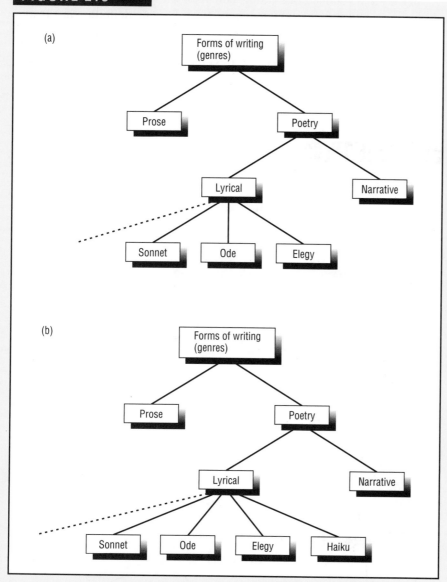

(a)

Forms of writing (genres)
- Prose
- Poetry
  - Lyrical
    - Sonnet
    - Ode
    - Elegy
  - Narrative

(b)

Forms of writing (genres)
- Prose
- Poetry
  - Lyrical
    - Sonnet
    - Ode
    - Elegy
    - Haiku
  - Narrative

Example of the assimilation of a new schema

out of character for your friend. If you were to accept the new information, however, it would not be possible to maintain your friend's schema unaltered. The new fact would need to be accommodated by changing the way you think about your friend. "Well," you might conclude, "this adds a whole new dimension to my friend's character."

In the circumstances of reading, comparable events occur. Let's return to our business law student, who may read the following definition in a textbook: "A contract is a promise, or set of promises, for the breach of which the law prescribes a remedy." Like so many technical vocabulary terms, the word *contract* has many meanings beyond the precise usage of the text, and some of these may be known to the reader in advance. A portion of a typical student's schema for "contracts" might be diagrammed as shown in Figure 2.4(a). Here the concept of "contracts" has been stored in association with the broader

FIGURE 2.4

Example of how new information may be accommodated into memory structures

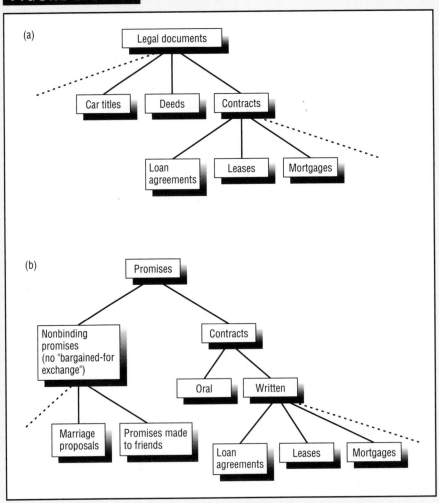

notion of "documents." It is also stored with numerous examples, personal experiences, and so on, all of which might comprise a typical individual's nontechnical knowledge of contracts. The new information, however, suggests that contracts are incorrectly classed as documents, for in fact many enforceable contracts are oral in nature. Further reading and discussion might leave the student's schemata in the substantially altered condition approximated by Figure 2.4(b). As we will see in later chapters, new ideas that require us to "unlearn" some of our previous beliefs are among the most difficult to teach.

The Role of Purpose in Reading

As we read, it is vital that relevant schemata be activated, or "switched on," so that new information can be integrated with existing knowledge. Assume, for example, that a friend had agreed to meet you for lunch but that the place and time had not been decided. You then receive the following note from your friend:

Meat me at the Union around 12. If that's not good, call me before 10.

As you begin to read, your focus is limited to certain elements in the message according to your purposes for reading. Overall, you expect your friend to specify the time and place of your meeting. In the first sentence, you look for and find these facts. While the number 12 can have many meanings, your purpose and prior knowledge assist you in knowing precisely what meaning to give it. Likewise, the Union may contain a myriad of shops, meeting rooms, commons, and so forth, but you automatically limit the meaning of the term *Union* to eating areas. Since the time and place are both specified in the first sentence, you create a new expectation with regard to the second sentence and a refined purpose for reading it. You may suspect that it probably conveys some further specification, or clarification.

In the course of reading, your purposes have caused appropriate schemata to come into play. (Note that this is usually an unconscious process.) At the broadest level, you have a schema for "notes," and perhaps even for those written by your friend. Your schemata for "lunch" and "Union" are also helpful. The former, in fact, prevented you from even considering that *12* might have meant midnight! At the lowest, most local levels, your expectations also shaped what you consciously attended to in terms of individual words and letters. Even though you are likely to have processed every letter of every word (Adams, 1990), your purposes for reading helped determine what information you eventually considered, interpreted, and remembered. For example, you probably noticed the spelling error in the first word of the message but were quickly able to determine that it *was* an error.

THE WRITING PROCESS

Think back to a recent writing task: a letter to a relative, an essay exam question, or a memo to a colleague. It is likely that you began with relatively general ideas about what you wished to convey through writing. Even if you had a wealth of information from which to choose, as might have been the case with an exam question, it is highly unlikely that this information existed in a form anything like complete sentences ready for transcription. Rather, your task was one of selecting, organizing, and finally encoding your thoughts into coherent prose form. Your own experiences may cause you to empathize with Johnson's comment on just how laborious this process can be when it is done well. However, the benefits of writing more than justify the effort required, for the writer's thoughts are clarified, extended, and reorganized in ways only writing can accomplish.

> *Composition is, for the most part, an effort of slow diligence, to which the mind is dragged by necessity or resolution.*
> *Samuel Johnson*

Thus, while we think of writing chiefly as a means by which one individual communicates with another, it is also a process by which writers communicate with themselves. As you rely on your overall (global) intentions to help you compose the first sentence of a paragraph, the ensuing sentence will depend not only on the global intentions with which you began, but also on what you expressed in the preceding sentence. In this way, global intentions help shape "local" intentions as each new sentence is written (Smith, 1988).

The writer's relationship to print is an interactive one. Intentions (from global to local) help in formulating sentences, but their very formulation causes changes in the writer's thinking. Ideas become crystallized in print, "visible" in a sense, encoded for close inspection, not only by the reader but by the writer as well. The act of committing ideas to print tends to refine and revise one's own intentions in writing.

Let's compare this process with that of reading. While reading each new sentence, an individual alters slightly the overall reconstruction of meaning that is mentally forming. While writing, an individual also alters, with each new sentence, his or her inner conceptualization of the content. This happens because writing forces us to clarify and organize our own thinking before we can put it into words (encode it) for others. For this reason, reading and writing are remarkably similar as ways of enhancing our understanding.

It is true that writing is a slower and less fluent process. Writing, it has been said, "because its very slowness makes it more deliberately self-conscious, enhances our sense of details and choices" (Connolly, 1989, p. 10). Nevertheless, the similarities are striking. For both the reader and the writer, meaning is constructed through processes in which printed language is used as the primary tool (Squire, 1983).

The emerging view that writing, like reading, is a constructive process has been long realized by skilled writers, as Forster's remark suggests. This view has a major implication for teaching content, one we have already stressed in Chapter 1: Writing can be utilized as a means through which students can clarify, analyze, and integrate their own thoughts about, and knowledge of, subject matter (Myers, 1984). A colleague of ours recently confided that the experience of writing a textbook on the teaching of reading helped him to clarify his own thinking on the subject. While we may tend to regard the knowledge possessed by authorities as being at all times precisely organized and articulated, this is simply not the case. For novice and expert alike, writing is a wonderfully illuminating experience.

> How can I know what I think till I see what I say?
>
> *E. M. Forster*

Before and After Writing

The writing process we have just described must now be placed in a larger context if we are to appreciate its potential for content instruction. Current recommendations suggest more than a single step in the process of writing (e.g., Graves, 1983). While such models differ as to the number and nature of steps, all include (1) planning activities carried out in advance of writing and (2) revising activities undertaken afterward.

Preparing to Write   Britton and his colleagues (1975) offered a distinction between *transactional writing,* which targets a particular readership and is undertaken to inform, persuade, or instruct, and *expressive writing,* which amounts to "thinking on paper" and is intended for the writer's own use. The notes one makes prior to formulating the actual sentences of connected discourse are apt to be expressive in nature. They tend to be "messy, exploratory" (Rose, 1989, p. 16), and their goal is to assist the writer in selecting and organizing ideas *before* they are encoded into English sentences. The notes might be as thoroughly delineated as a formal outline or as cryptic as a mere word or phrase per intended paragraph, depending on the experience and sophistication of the writer.

Skinner (1981) recommended that this pre-prose stage be extended as long as possible, both because the writer's thoughts tend to remain fluid and because once the effort is expended to compose sentences and paragraphs, there is a powerful resistance to dismantling them, even when the need to do so becomes clear. Despite these reasons, there is usually an impatient rush to get past the planning phase and on to the writing itself. Students must be trained to be deliberate in their planning, which, when done properly, actually tends to *reduce* the time spent "writing."

The sense of readership needed for transactional writing is vital to good planning and is frequently ignored by students. After all, they know they are writing for the teacher, whose knowledge base is assumed to be extensive enough for accurate interpretation of anything they might say. The result can be highly assumptive, "inconsiderate" writing that fails to express ideas

> Bad authors are those who write with reference to an inner context which the reader cannot know.
>
> *Albert Camus*

adequately (even for a teacher!). The observation of the French novelist Camus is an insightful one. It suggests that students, from the planning stage on, be encouraged to monitor their writing carefully to avoid assumptions about knowledge the reader may not possess. An increasingly popular way to provide such encouragement is to arrange for situations in which students write not for the teacher alone but for other students, whose prior knowledge of a topic may be minimal.

Revising What Is Written Capable writers are rarely satisfied with first drafts. Revision represents a second chance to bring expressed meaning into closer alignment with the writer's intentions. The need for

> Nothing you write, if you hope to be good, will ever come out as you first hoped.
>
> *Lillian Hellman*

targeting a specific readership is never more important than when revising, for the writer now becomes a reader—not in the ordinary sense but with the purpose of role-playing the sort of reader eventually targeted. Sentences are reconsidered in the complete context of the draft, awkward expressions are corrected, prose rhythms are tested, mechanics are mended.

MAKING SENSE OUT OF CONTENT

Consider the following two statements about how students acquire knowledge. Which one is closer to your own perspective?

1. The student's mind is like a vessel, to be filled by the teacher with specific knowledge.
2. The student constructs an individual representation of knowledge by interacting with the world.

These statements represent markedly different views of how knowledge develops. The first suggests that the process is a passive one and that the result is the "transmission" of knowledge, more or less intact, from teacher to learner. The second suggests that knowledge building is an active process resulting in a unique conceptualization of content in the mind of each student. Our experience is that many content specialists prefer the former view. Research, on the other hand, very clearly supports the latter.

The result, however, is not a hopeless impasse. While different, the two viewpoints are not contradictory. A teacher may engage students in active encounters with content and nevertheless ensure that particular concepts, ideas, and skills have in fact been the result of such encounters. Students will construct their own ideas about content, to be sure, but teachers can guide the process so that the result, while unique to each student, nevertheless meets desirable curricular standards.

What we hope to show is that reading and writing are tools a student can use in the process of constructing content knowledge. In the case of reading, the student attempts to *reconstruct* what an author intends, of course, but this is not the same as transmitting the author's message unaltered into the reader's preexisting memory and beliefs. The student does not stop at reconstructing what one author intends but uses the experience to further *construct* a more global knowledge of content. Our point is that while many educators tend to view the two statements above as offering an "either/or" choice, there is in fact a middle ground that we believe offers the best results.

SUMMARY

Language consists primarily of symbols (written and oral) and rules for combining those symbols into meaningful relationships. Most languages have both oral and written forms, and most written forms are alphabetic. In alphabetic languages, a small number of letters are used to represent basic speech sounds. Written language developed after oral language and involves a second system of symbols (visual) that overlies the first (acoustic).

Writing is a language process by which one attempts to "construct" with words a document that conveys an intended message. A mental construction of the message also occurs during writing as the writer's own thoughts are sharpened and clarified. Reading is a process by which one attempts to mentally "reconstruct" such a message from its printed representation. The extent to which the reconstructed message matches the one originally intended by the writer is the extent to which communication occurs.

In reading, new information encountered in print is integrated into existing knowledge structures called schemata (plural of *schema*). Schemata are best described as categories of knowledge corresponding to concepts. Schemata are interconnected in memory by associational links. As one reads, new schemata might be formed or existing schemata might be expanded or altered. Because new information is always learned in relation to previous knowledge, it is important for a reader to have certain purposes and expectations about what a reading selection contains so that appropriate prior knowledge can be brought to bear.

While reading is guided by what one seeks and expects, writing is guided by what one intends. Intentions guide the writer's choice of words, sentence structures, organizational patterns, and so on. Writing is now recognized as a powerful learning tool by virtue of its help in clarifying, refining, and organizing what one knows about a topic. Prior to writing, it is important to make brief notes as one examines one's own prior knowledge. It is at this point vital not to worry about forming complete sentences and paragraphs. In this way, thoughts remain fluid longer as one actively considers, manipulates, and rearranges them. After writing, it is important to revise. The object is for the writer to role-play the targeted reader and to read for the purpose of determining whether the intended meaning has been successfully incorporated into print.

GETTING INVOLVED

1. Imagine yourself in an airplane heading due south over downtown Detroit. If you continued on this course, what is the first foreign country over which you would pass? A group of our students produced such well-reasoned guesses as Mexico, Cuba, Guatemala, and so on. They were wrong. The correct answer is Canada, because an arm of Ontario extends just to the south of Detroit. If this fact surprised you as much as it did our students, you have just experienced an alteration in your geographical schemata as the new information was accommodated. Unusual facts, and their resulting accommodation, can be interest arousing as well as instructional. Can you think of such a fact in your own subject area, a fact that might be used to evoke surprise and encourage student engagement at the beginning of a lesson?

2. Consider the concept of "book." In memory, you already have an extensive schema for book, and this schema involves many meaningful associations with other concepts. For example, what concept would include book as an example? That is to say, a book is a type of *what*? By the same token, name a specific kind of book—a member of the category called "books." Figure 2.5 shows how these relationships can be diagrammed to produce a depiction of part of your schema for books. Note that, similar to the examples of Figures 2.3 and 2.4, larger concepts appear higher in the diagram. Do you think constructing and discussing such diagrams with students as they encounter new vocabulary might be productive? Research has been positive, and we explore this method in detail in Chapter 6.

FIGURE 2.5

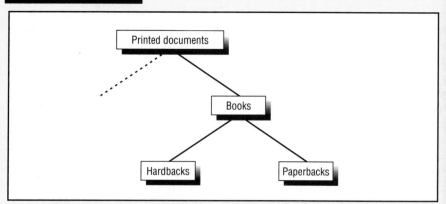

Diagramming the concept of "books" as it relates to larger and smaller concepts

3. In the meantime, free associate from the concept of book. Make a mental list of 10 other words suggested by the word *book*. In so doing, you've exposed more of your vast schema for books, and, we suspect, demonstrated that it includes much more than the simple category memberships outlined in Figure 2.5. Now imagine having gone through a similar process for each of the 10 related concepts you listed. If you continued in this way, you would soon have included thousands of concepts arranged in a vast network of hubs and spokes, similar to a highway map. And like a map it would be possible to "travel" from any given concept to any other concept by means of associative links. Conceptualizing memory in this way suggests that new concepts are best learned when key associations with known concepts are emphasized. Think of a technical term from your own discipline. What concepts do you suppose might have been previously taught that your students should associate with the new term? Do you think a review of these prior concepts would be helpful before introducing the new one?

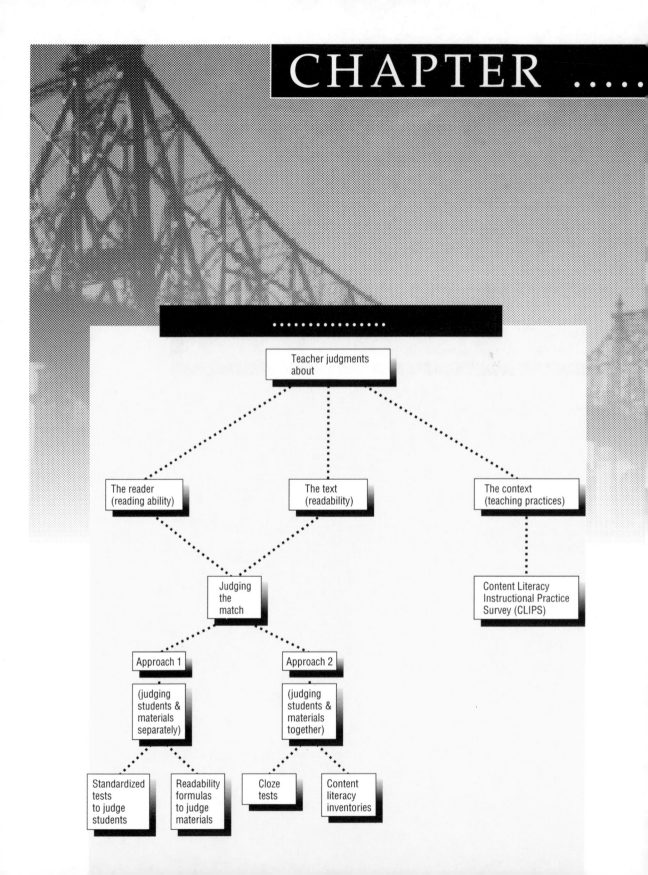

Teacher judgments about

The reader (reading ability)

The text (readability)

The context (teaching practices)

Judging the match

Content Literacy Instructional Practice Survey (CLIPS)

Approach 1

Approach 2

(judging students & materials separately)

(judging students & materials together)

Standardized tests to judge students

Readability formulas to judge materials

Cloze tests

Content literacy inventories

THREE

Getting to Know Your Students, Your Materials, and Your Teaching

We can attempt nothing great, but from a sense of the difficulties we have to encounter.

William Hazlitt

Have you ever been asked to perform a task that was too difficult? It might have involved solving a math problem, taking part in a certain sport, attempting an advanced musical piece, or responding to an essay exam question. It might also have involved reading an especially difficult book. You may still recall feelings of anxiety, frustration, and failure as you attempted the task. Depending on a host of factors—the assistance and encouragement you may have received, your determination, and the amount of time available to you—you might eventually have succeeded in performing the task.

When teachers in content subjects ask their students to read specific materials or to undertake written work, some of these students may feel a similar kind of frustration. This book offers a variety of techniques aimed at minimizing such frustration: Some of them are devoted to helping *all* students learn through reading and writing, and some are designed to help special learners in particular. Before teachers can knowledgeably choose among such techniques, however, they must know something about the reading and writing abilities of their students. They must judge whether these abilities are equal to the demands that planned literacy activities are likely to involve. In this chapter we offer relatively quick, informal methods of gathering such information.

OBJECTIVES

When you finish reading this chapter, you should be able to

1. describe the three dimensions of assessment necessary to content literacy–based instruction;

2. define the independent, instructional, and frustration reading levels;

3. identify the strengths and limitations of readability formulas;

4. apply the Raygor formula (1977) to a prose selection;

5. state the guidelines for constructing cloze tests;

6. interpret cloze scores in terms of approximate reading levels;

7. describe the components of a content literacy inventory;

8. interpret the results of such an inventory; and

9. describe an approach to assessing your own teaching and the literacy demands it places on your students.

THREE DIMENSIONS OF CLASSROOM ASSESSMENT

Historically, a common assumption among teachers has been that if a student experiences problems, the source of the difficulty must lie within the student. This *deficit model* is now being replaced with a more realistic view—that problems can sometimes be traced to the match between a given student and the materials and methods used for instruction. Lipson and Wixson (1991) speak of the need to assess not only the reader but the text and context as well. Kinney and Harry (1991) have recommended extending this three-dimensional approach to assessment to content classrooms as well as the reading clinic.

This idea is consistent with the notion discussed in Chapter 1 that the adequacy of a student's literacy skills is relative to the literacy demands made by a particular class. In this chapter we present ways of acquiring information about all three dimensions of your students' literacy performance: student ability, instructional materials, and teaching methods. The remaining chapters describe ways of achieving a balance among the three dimensions so that content literacy becomes a powerful asset.

WHAT IS READING ABILITY?

A reading clinician typically devotes many pages to describing the reading ability of a given student, especially a student with problems. Such a description would entail a report of the many subskills that underlie reading ability, as well as other factors bearing on school performance. While debate continues over how best to teach reading, few experts would deny that *reading ability* involves the capacity to coordinate a number of mental processes that enable the reader to form a reasonable idea of the meaning represented by print. A description of these processes is beyond the scope of this book, but we must nevertheless consider the sorts of behaviors we would accept as evidence of reading ability. Which of the following, for example, would you be inclined to accept?

1. Ability to answer questions after reading
2. Ability to summarize what has been read
3. Ability to decide which of two statements is aligned with an author's views
4. Ability to guess missing words periodically deleted from a passage
5. Ability to choose from among several pictures the one that best represents the content of a selection
6. Ability to "retell" the information or events of the selection
7. Ability to apply the information contained in a selection to some new problem or situation

All of these tasks have been used as yardsticks of a reader's ability to comprehend. While they differ in what they demand, all appear to tap comprehension in some manner. Moreover, all can be quantified, if desired, so that we can describe reading ability in numerical terms. Just as a coach might describe an athlete's sprinting ability by referring to average speed in the 100-meter dash, a teacher might gauge a student's reading ability in terms of the percentage of questions answered, the thoroughness of a retelling, or the number of key points contained in a written summary.

This process is not as simple as it sounds, however. Let's consider just a few of the factors that might influence your own performance on a test over this textbook. To begin with, if this is the first reading-related course you've taken, you're not likely to do as well as the student who has had prior coursework in reading. The effects of background knowledge on reading comprehension are enormous. Second, assume that your instructor has given you highly detailed objective tests over Chapters 1 and 2 and then, without warning, asks for a written summary and critique of this chapter. Your expectations would have ill prepared you for such a task. Third, consider two classmates of equivalent background who differ in terms of their motivation to learn from this book. Would you predict higher comprehension scores for the more highly motivated student? You should. Our point is that reading ability is not easy to measure because a host of factors affect it. Even under the best of circumstances reading ability cannot be reduced to a single number or test score. Scores can help us gain rather crude impressions of reading ability, but we must resist the notion that they represent precise measurements.

Even though we must face severe limitations in measuring reading ability, we can still make some fairly accurate quantitative statements about it. We know that it typically increases with a student's age, as the student becomes more skilled and acquires more and more knowledge of the world to bring to

FIGURE 3.1

Some ways of describing the extent of reading ability

(a)

Low   High

(b)

Rudimentary   Basic   Intermediate   Adept   Advanced

(c)

K   1   2   3   4   5   6   7   8   9   10   11   12   College

bear while reading. When we say that reading ability *increases,* we are actually suggesting a numerical scale, or continuum, beginning at zero (no ability whatever) and progressing upward. We can describe points on this scale in various ways. Figure 3.1(a) is perhaps the simplest system, characterizing ability as ranging from low to high. This approach is hard to fault in general, but unless we carefully define these terms, the system is not very useful. Figure 3.1(b) uses the terms adopted in the National Assessment of Educational Progress to describe comprehension ability. These terms are defined in Figure 3.2 and make it possible to place readers of different ages on the same continuum. Perhaps the most common way of demarcating our scale of reading ability is by using grade levels, as in Figure 3.1(c), where the 3 represents the ability of the average third grader, and so on.

Many teachers have trouble thinking about reading ability in grade-level terms because of difficulties inherent in the grade-equivalent scores produced by standardized tests. Indeed, these difficulties are so grave that in 1980 the International Reading Association formally condemned the use of such scores. We wish to make clear, however, that our depiction in Figure 3.1(c) is an abstract one and merely portrays the typical progression of ability as students move through school. Figure 3.1(c) has nothing to do with grade-equivalent scores, which amount to crude estimates of a given student's position on the scale. We stress that such a position can *never* be determined precisely. However, the notion of a grade-level continuum has been a useful one in conceptualizing what is meant by reading ability.

LEVELS OF READING ABILITY

Our grade-level depiction of reading ability is helpful in making an important point. To suggest that, given accurate measurements, a student can be placed at a particular point along the scale is actually an oversimplification.

FIGURE 3.2

Rudimentary

Readers who have acquired rudimentary reading skills and strategies can follow brief written directions. They can also select words, phrases, or sentences to describe a simple picture and can interpret simple written clues to identify a common object. *Performance at this level suggests the ability to carry out simple, discrete reading tasks.*

Basic

Readers who have learned basic comprehension skills and strategies can locate and identify facts from simple informational paragraphs, stories, and news articles. In addition, they can combine ideas and make inferences based on short, uncomplicated passages. *Performance at this level suggests the ability to understand specific or sequentially related information.*

Intermediate

Readers with the ability to use intermediate skills and strategies can search for, locate, and organize the information they find in relatively lengthy passages and can recognize paraphrases of what they have read. They can also make inferences and reach generalizations about main ideas and author's purpose from passages dealing with literature, science, and social studies. *Performance at this level suggests the ability to search for specific information, interrelate ideas, and make generalizations.*

Adept

Readers with adept reading comprehension skills and strategies can understand complicated literary and informational passages, including material about topics they study at school. They can also analyze and integrate less familiar material and provide reactions to and explanations of the text as a whole. *Performance at this level suggests the ability to find, understand, summarize, and explain relatively complicated information.*

Advanced

Readers who use advanced reading skills and strategies can extend and restructure the ideas presented in specialized and complex texts. Examples include scientific materials, literary essays, historical documents, and materials similar to those found in professional and technical working environments. They are also able to understand the links between ideas even when those links are not explicitly stated and to make appropriate generalizations even when the texts lack clear introductions or explanations. *Performance at this level suggests the ability to synthesize and learn from specialized reading materials.*

Definitions of terms used by the National Assessment of Educational Progress to describe reading ability

SOURCE: Mullis, I. V. S., & Jenkins, L. B. (1990). *The Reading report card, 1971–88.* Washington, DC: U.S. Department of Education.

FIGURE 3.3

Definitions of the three reading ability levels

Independent Level	The highest level at which there is good comprehension without assistance
Instructional Level	Any level at which there is good comprehension as long as assistance is available
Frustration Level	The lowest level at which comprehension is inadequate even when assistance is available

Reading specialists work under the useful assumption that individuals typically possess not one level of reading ability but three!

At the *independent level,* materials are easily understood by the reader without outside assistance. A popular novel you might read for pleasure is likely to be at this level, for example. At the *instructional level,* materials are more difficult so that the help of a teacher may be needed for the reader to comprehend them adequately. Reading is challenging but not prohibitive. At the *frustration level,* as the phrase suggests, materials are apt to be so trying that the reader gives up. Even the help of an instructor cannot make the reading sufficiently comprehensible.

It is important to realize that these levels differ from one individual to another. The same novel that might fall at your independent level would frustrate a young child. It is also important to note that our caution about measurement applies here also. Though we can speak about John's independent level or Susan's instructional level in the abstract, these levels cannot be precisely measured—only estimated.

The definitions provided in Figure 3.3 are conventional ways of dealing with the fact that John might have, for example, more than a single independent level. After all, if he can read third-grade materials independently, he can read comparable materials of second- or first-grade difficulty. To avoid confusion,

FIGURE 3.4

Depiction of the three reading ability levels

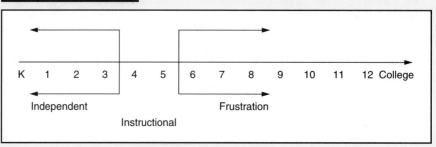

the independent level is therefore taken to be the *highest* level of independent performance. Likewise, the frustration level is assumed to be the *lowest* level at which comprehension breaks down and frustration occurs. We assume that still more difficult materials would have a similar effect. We have depicted this relationship for a particular, hypothetical child in Figure 3.4. Between the independent level of third grade and the frustration level of sixth lie two instructional levels (fourth and fifth grades), sometimes called the instructional range.

READING ABILITY AND READABILITY

We have spoken not only of placing *students,* theoretically, on a grade-level continuum but also of placing *materials* on the same scale. The more difficult the reading, the higher will be the placement. The same continuum can thus serve as a frame of reference (though an admittedly imperfect one) for placing students *and* materials. When grade-level designations are applied to students, we speak of reading ability; when they are applied to materials, we speak of *readability.*

We use the term to refer to the overall difficulty level of a book (or some other unit of text) and admit that the choice of terms is unfortunate. This is because the word *readable* is also used to denote such ideas as how legible the print is or how enjoyable the writing proves to be (Klare, 1988). For our purposes, however, the term refers in a general way to difficulty and can be thought of as synonymous with *comprehensibility* or *understandability* (terms that are more cumbersome but less ambiguous).

An advantage of using the same scale to characterize both students and materials is that it enables us to judge whether the two are suitably matched. When the reading ability of a student falls significantly below the readability of the materials that student is asked to read, as in Figure 3.5, the match is clearly unsuitable and the results can be disastrous. Again, remember that our placement of materials and students along the continuum is theoretical. Precise measurements of this kind are not possible. Moreover, we confess

FIGURE 3.5

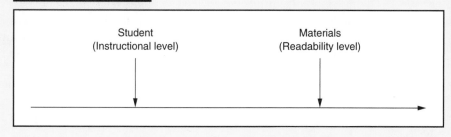

Example of a poor match between a student and materials

to oversimplifying the notion of readability for purposes of our illustration. (Some of the factors that affect readability lie within the *reader*.) However, the depiction of Figure 3.5 is a defensible one for our purposes and makes clear the need to determine whether the match between students and reading materials is a viable one. We now examine ways teachers can make such a determination.

JUDGING THE MATCH BETWEEN STUDENTS AND MATERIALS

Let's consider Mr. Ross, a tenth-grade biology teacher who will use a textbook adopted by his school district. He is free to modify or even abandon the text if he chooses, but he lacks the funds to use an alternate text. Mr. Ross must determine whether his class will be able to read the typical assignments he plans to make from the book. In the process he will identify those students who are likely to have substantial problems with the text.

Mr. Ross has two choices. He can estimate the students' reading ability and the readability of the text and then compare the two measures. Or, he can construct a brief reading and writing task based on the text itself and judge the students' success with this task. Each of these approaches has distinct advantages and drawbacks. Keep in mind that the two approaches are not mutually exclusive. It is possible to do both!

Approach 1: Assessing Students and Materials Separately

Mr. Ross can evaluate his students and his text independently by examining test scores on file for his pupils and by applying any of several common measures of readability to his book. The chief advantage of this approach is that it can be accomplished outside of class, even before the start of a school year. The disadvantages, however, are formidable. The measures available to Mr. Ross are relatively crude estimates of the information he needs. Moreover, he can never really be certain about the suitability of the text until his students actually begin to interact with it. Below, we look briefly at the measures Mr. Ross would use in this approach.

Standardized Tests   In most American schools, standardized tests are administered once a year. These measurements are designed to assess groups rather than individual students, and yet because of their availability teachers often attempt to use such tests in making tentative decisions about their students. Up to a point this practice can be beneficial, but we stress the word *tentative.* The following guidelines will help you to arrive at reasonable conclusions about the reading ability of your students based on standardized tests.

1. Refer only to the reading comprehension subtest.
2. Ignore all norms but the percentile rank. (Ignore in particular the grade-equivalent score.)
3. Tentatively classify students as average, above average, or below average using the following guide:

0–22	Below average
23–39	Borderline
40–59	Average
60–76	Borderline
77–99	Above average

When Mr. Ross finds that Richard has scored at the 47th percentile rank on a standardized subtest of reading comprehension, he can reasonably assume that Richard's reading ability is roughly commensurate with his grade level. Since Richard is a sophomore, his ability level is likely to be near tenth grade. This, however, is as far as Mr. Ross can proceed in translating Richard's score into a grade level. If the score were higher—perhaps at the 80th percentile rank—Mr. Ross could say only that Richard's ability level was probably higher than tenth grade.

   If these restrictions seem overly prohibitive, remember that they are based on sound psychometric principles. Remember, too, that the test has already been given. Mr. Ross need only consult a roster of results (usually generated by a computer) in order to make these tentative judgments about his students.

   Measures of Readability   Mr. Ross's next step would be to estimate the text's level of difficulty. Think for a moment about what makes a reading selection easy or difficult. As we noted earlier, some of the factors we might list lie within the reader rather than the selection (the familiarity of the topic, for example). If we limit ourselves to the writing itself, the factors we might list would include at least the following (Miller & McKenna, 1989):

sentence length
vocabulary
grammatical complexity
organization
cohesion
abstractness
clarity
assumptions about prior knowledge

   Attempting to arrive at an overall estimate of difficulty level by considering these factors is not an easy task. As you might expect, some teachers are better than others at doing so (Frager, 1984). In an effort to make the process of estimating readability more systematic, researchers have offered several methods. The oldest involves the use of numerical formulas that account for a few of the factors just mentioned. A second approach involves comparing a selection with a sequence of passages of progressive difficulty (Singer, 1975). The third and newest alternative entails structured (though subjective) considerations of numerous textual factors (Binkley, 1988; Zakaluk & Samuels, 1988). Currently, we believe that formulas offer teachers the most practical alternative, one that will result in defensible estimates of text difficulty (Fry, 1989).

Readability formulas typically account for only the first two of the eight factors we listed previously: sentence length and vocabulary. This is a severe limitation indeed, and yet formulas succeed in predicting a remarkable amount of the variance in student comprehension performance on different prose materials. While there are newer formulas that attempt to account for more factors, they are quite time-consuming (unless computerized). Our experience is that teachers may be willing to apply a formula only if it is sufficiently simple to use. We will consider only one such formula, that developed by Raygor (1977).

Raygor's formula has the advantages of being extremely quick to administer and of correlating well with more complex formulas, as well as with student performance measures. The steps of the formula and its accompanying chart appear in Figure 3.6. As you can see, the formula requires first computing the average length of sentences in three representative selections of 100 words each and next determining the proportion of words with six or more letters in these selections. These two numbers are then used to plot a point on the graph. For most selections the point will fall in one of the numbered sections. The number is the grade-level estimate.

Let's assume that Mr. Ross applies the Raygor formula to his textbook and produces a twelfth-grade estimate. Comparing this estimate with Richard's tenth-grade reading ability level might lead Mr. Ross to predict that Richard will have difficulties with the book. This may be the case, but there are two problems with Mr. Ross's reasoning. One is that both the estimate of Richard's ability and the estimate of the book's readability are highly suspect. Either or both may be off the mark. The other is that the difference between grade levels in the secondary years is smaller than at the elementary level. No one, for example, could fail to note the difference between first- and second-grade materials, but the difference between eleventh- and twelfth-grade materials is quite small.

What we are suggesting is that a large difference between our estimate of (1) a student's reading level and (2) the readability of assigned materials is necessary before serious difficulty can be predicted. If Richard's percentile rank on the standardized test were below the average for tenth graders, and if the Raygor formula had placed the text at the college level, Mr. Ross would have had a better foundation for his fears. Because of the availability of standardized

FIGURE 3.6

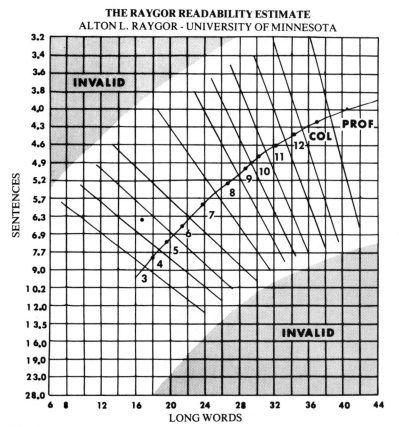

THE RAYGOR READABILITY ESTIMATE
ALTON L. RAYGOR - UNIVERSITY OF MINNESOTA

The Raygor
readability estimate

SOURCE: From "The Raygor Readability Estimate: A Quick and Easy Way to Determine Difficulty" by Alton L. Raygor, 1977, *Reading: Theory, Research, and Practice: Twenty-Sixth Yearbook of the National Reading Conference,* p. 261. Copyright 1977 by the National Reading Conference, Inc. Reprinted by permission of the National Reading Conference.

Directions:

Count out three 100-word passages at the beginning, middle, and end of a selection or book. Count proper nouns, but not numerals.

1. Count sentences in each passage, estimating to nearest tenth.
2. Count words with six or more letters.
3. Average the sentence length and word length over the three samples and plot the average on the graph.

Example:

	Sentences	6+ Words
A	6.0	15
B	6.8	19
C	6.4	17
Total	19.2	51
Average	6.4	17

Note mark on graph. Grade level is about 5.

test results and the quickness of applying the Raygor formula, Approach 1 can be useful in obtaining an "early warning" about those students most likely to have difficulty.

Approach 2: Assessing Students and Materials Together

Knowledge must come through action; you can have no test which is not fanciful, save by trial.

Sophocles

In this section we examine the second approach to judging the match between assigned materials and student ability. This approach involves constructing a short exercise over a brief portion of the material in order to appraise student performance. A disadvantage of this approach is that it requires class time. However, because the time is spent on materials the instructor has decided to assign anyway, few teachers object to such assessment. Moreover, basing reading evaluation on the materials to be read can lead to far more accurate predictions than those arrived at through Approach 1.

There are two principal methods of constructing such exercises: the cloze test and the content literacy inventory—two vastly different techniques that yield surprisingly similar information.

Cloze Testing   The cloze procedure has been used to assess reading comprehension for nearly four decades, and it is extraordinarily well researched (McKenna & Robinson, 1980). In a cloze test, some of the words in a passage are replaced with blanks. The student is asked to infer them—to "close" the gaps—on the basis of context.

Many cloze formats have been used, but the extensive research studies done to determine scoring guidelines have nearly all used the same format. It is therefore essential to follow these same guidelines when constructing your own cloze tests. These guides are summarized by Miller and McKenna (1989, p. 321):

1. Instructions emphasize that the object is to supply the word actually deleted, the word the author used—not just any word that makes sense and not the word the student might personally have chosen.
2. Blanks are of equal length.
3. Although the placement of the first blank does not matter, the following blanks occur at intervals of every fifth word.
4. Blanks may be numbered, if a separate answer sheet is to be used, or made long enough to accommodate a student's written answers. The latter practice is perhaps a good idea in the upper elementary grades.
5. The total number of blanks is 50. This number is a minimum for good reliability and has the advantage of permitting scores to be easily converted to percentages.

6. A sentence or two at the beginning and end of the passage is left intact. This practice is customary, but research suggests it is optional.

Surprisingly, the point in the text at which the passage is selected makes little difference. Cloze items are not very dependent on preceding material. Try to choose a passage that is (1) largely typical of the material presented in the text and (2) relatively free of non-English inclusions, such as formulas and equations.

In administering the test, acquaint students in advance with the idea of a cloze exercise. Examples should be provided and thoroughly discussed. Inform students that a good score is much lower than one that would be considered good on more traditional tests. Also, make it clear that scores will not affect their grades. The testing itself is untimed.

Scoring is simple: Correct answers must be the exact words deleted, with the exception of minor misspellings. Resist the temptation to give credit for synonyms and other reasonable responses. Otherwise, scoring becomes subjective and time-consuming, and results can no longer be evaluated on the basis of research—all of which has credited verbatim responses only. Moreover, studies have clearly shown that counting synonyms adds nothing to the discriminating power of the test (Henk, 1981; McKenna, 1976; Miller & Coleman, 1967) and increases the subjectivity of scoring (Henk & Selders, 1984). The scoring guide established through criterion studies is as follows:

• •

independent level	60% or higher
instructional level	40%–59%
frustration level	39% or lower

• •

These guidelines should not be applied too rigorously. Scores in the vicinity of 40 percent or 60 percent should be regarded as borderline. As a general rule, however, these criteria are quite useful and have shown remarkable stability across populations. Investigations of upper-elementary students have resulted in similar findings (Bormuth, 1967; Rankin & Culhane, 1969), as have studies of high school students (Peterson, Paradis, & Peters, 1973), vocational-technical students and college students (Peterson, Peters, & Paradis, 1972), and reading-disabled students (Peterson & Carroll, 1974).

An example of a cloze test appears in Figure 3.7. If you are unfamiliar with the technique, we suggest you try your hand at cloze completion. Check your answers at the end of the chapter. (See Figure 3.11.)

FIGURE 3.7

Sample cloze test

SOURCE: From *Scott Foresman Earth Science* by Timothy M. Cooney et al., pp. 213–214. Copyright ©1990 by Scott, Foresman and Company. Reprinted by permission of HarperCollins Publishers.

WARNING—EARTHQUAKE AHEAD

Where and when will the next major earthquake happen? How strong will it be? Some scientists _____ trying to answer these _____ , but at present, their _____ to predict the time, _____ , and size of earthquakes _____ limited.

Progress has been _____ in calculating the likelihood _____ an earthquake of a _____ magnitude will occur in _____ region within a general _____ period. Such predictions have _____ made for seismic gaps, _____ are areas along plate _____ that have had regular _____ activity in the past _____ are currently overdue for _____ . In the gray areas _____ the map, quakes within _____ last forty years have _____ stress. But in the _____ seismic gaps, no large _____ have taken place recently, _____ stress must still be _____ . Some scientists predict major _____ will occur in these _____ before the end of _____ century.

The seismic gap _____ greatest interest in the _____ States includes the San _____ Fault, which separates the _____ and North American Plates. _____ have set up equipment _____ various places along this _____ to record some of _____ known warning signs of _____ .

At certain seismic stations, _____ beams are shot across _____ San Andreas Fault and _____ back to measure the _____ movement of the two _____ plates. Observe the laser _____ in Figure 9–22. Any _____ from a normal pattern _____ movement might mean a _____ is coming. Other instruments _____ bulges or tilts in _____ ground near a fault— _____ indicator of a coming _____ . Some measure the rise _____ fall of underground water _____ wells. A sudden change _____ the water level is a warning sign. Another sign of a major earthquake is a sharp increase in the number of small earthquakes, or tremors. Seismographs constantly record these tremors and geologists keep busy interpreting them.

Content Literacy Inventories   An alternative to cloze testing is the content literacy inventory, a more traditional, question-and-answer approach to assessment. At its core is a series of questions posed over a small section of the textbook. The student's success at answering these questions after reading the section is used to predict probable performance on the text as a whole, including writing tasks related to it. Two optional supplements to this component are (1) a subtest composed of questions related to the book's parts and how to use them (the table of contents, index, glossary, and other components) and (2) a second subtest containing questions related to a knowledge of resources beyond the text (card catalogue, encyclopedias, etc.) if these are considered important to the subject area.

An example of a content literacy inventory appears in Figure 3.8 and is based on the same selection as the cloze test of Figure 3.7. The portion on using parts of the book is, of course, based on the text as a whole.

When you construct a content literacy inventory, observe the following guidelines:

1. Choose a two-to-four page selection that is (a) typical of the material presented in the text and (b) not highly dependent for comprehension on previous sections of the text. The first chapter is often a good source.
2. Write 10 to 15 questions based on the passage, stressing the comprehension skills you intend to emphasize. Be sure to include several questions on understanding of technical vocabulary terms.
3. Make sure the last few questions require written responses by the students. These might target the ability to summarize the passage, the application of inferential or mathematical reasoning, or a critique of some aspect of the content.
4. Write three to five questions requiring the use of important parts of the book.
5. Write three to five questions requiring a knowledge of outside resources important to the subject area (if any).

The inventory should be given as an untimed, open-book experience. We suggest that each component be evaluated separately and that a judgment of the book's suitability be based solely on the student's score on the comprehension section. Ideally, the percentage of correct answers on this section should fall between 75 and 90, but you should be lenient in applying these criteria. Scores as low as 65 percent may indicate the instructional level (Bormuth, 1969).

FIGURE 3.8

Sample content
literacy inventory

Part 1: LEARNING FROM THIS TEXT

Read the section in your book entitled "Warning—Earthquake Ahead" on pages 213–214. Then answer the following questions. Refer back to the text as much as you wish.

1. Scientists can now predict the time and place of earthquakes with fairly good accuracy. (true/false)
2. An area that has just experienced a major earthquake is called a seismic gap. (true/false)
3. During the time since the last earthquake in a seismic gap, stress
   a. is relatively stable.
   b. builds.
   c. declines.
   d. changes unpredictably.
4. What is the name of the seismic gap that lies along the western edge of the North American plate?_____
5. In addition to lasers, what other equipment do you suspect scientists may have set up near the San Andreas Fault?

6–9. Write one sentence each to describe the four ways of gaining information about coming earthquakes.

10. Discuss how you think the lasers might be used to "measure the slightest movement of the two crustal plates." The authors don't really say.

11–12. Based on the selection, write a definition for each of these terms:

seismic gap:

tremor:

Part 2: BOOK PARTS

13. On which page would you find a discussion of granite?_____
14. On which page would you find the start of a section that gives definitions of all the key words in the book?_____
15. How many sections is the entire book divided into?_____

JUDGING THE CONTEXT OF INSTRUCTION

Knowing the match between the reading ability of students and the readability of materials is an important first step. There is another dimension to students' literacy performance in content classes, however. This is the context in which literacy is used. Context is often broadly defined to include socioeconomic background, cultural considerations, and similar factors (Lipson & Wixson, 1991). Our approach is narrower, however. We limit our discussion of context to the instructional methods a teacher uses and to the literacy demands that these methods make on students.

This idea may suggest a kind of assessment quite new to you, for it requires taking stock of your own instructional practice. This is not an empty exercise in matters that are self-evident. Many teachers fail to reflect adequately on the effects their day-to-day classroom behaviors may have on student performance. To assist you, we have constructed a self-administered survey, the Content Literacy Instructional Practice Inventory, which appears in Figure 3.9. If you have not yet begun to teach, you can still take the survey on the basis of your intentions as a future teacher.

The survey touches on many issues that we examine in detail later in this book. We encourage you to respond to all the items, however, and to return to the survey at the conclusion of the course. At that time, you may discover areas in which your philosophy has changed.

Note that there is no provision for arriving at a total score. Each aspect of your teaching practice is considered independently, and the result is not a number but a profile you can use to modify your instruction, if need be, in order to achieve a better balance among the three dimensions—students, materials, and methods. In short, the survey allows you to become a little more reflective about your teaching and the extent to which it influences your students' ability to use reading and writing to learn content.

As a brief example, let's assume that Mr. Ross responds to the survey and that his profile reveals the following traits. We note first that his reading assignments are made daily and over a semester will include his entire biology text. His average daily reading assignment will be more than 30 pages. Moreover, Mr. Ross does not introduce technical vocabulary, nor does he ensure that students have specific purposes for which to read. From these responses alone, Mr. Ross might begin to think about some possibilities for improving his students' reading performance (and consequently the amount of biology they learn). He might, for example, become more selective in his assignments, using other means (such as lecture, discussion, and demonstration) to introduce some of the material. He might also try some of the techniques outlined in Chapters 5 through 8 in preparing his students for the assignments he does make. But Mr. Ross may never reach these conclusions unless his idea of assessment includes his own instructional practice and unless he occasionally reflects on that practice in a more or less structured way. The inventory presented in Figure 3.9 may help you achieve this kind of reflective practice.

FIGURE 3.9

Self-assess your
own teaching

CONTENT LITERACY INSTRUCTIONAL PRACTICE SURVEY (CLIPS)

Frequency of Reading (Check one.)

_____ No reading
_____ Occasional reading (much reliance on lecture, demonstration)
_____ Frequent reading (most textbook chapters assigned)
_____ Daily or near-daily reading (all or nearly all textbook chapters assigned)

Amount of Reading (Check one.)

_____ No reading
_____ Average less than 10 pages per week (per course or subject)
_____ Average between 10 and 30 pages per week
_____ Average between 30 and 50 pages per week
_____ Average over 50 pages per week

Frequency of Writing (Check one.)

_____ No writing
_____ Occasional writing (once a week or less per course or subject)
_____ Frequent writing (more than once a week per course or subject)
_____ Daily or near-daily writing

Amount of Writing (Check one.)

_____ No writing
_____ Average less than 1 page per week (per course or subject)
_____ Average between 1 and 3 pages per week
_____ Average between 3 and 5 pages per week
_____ Average over 5 pages per week

Instructional Practice (Check all that apply to your teaching.)

_____ 1. I judge whether students' background is adequate before they read.
_____ 2. I try to refresh or add to students' knowledge before they read.
_____ 3. I introduce new technical terms before students read about them.
_____ 4. I stress the relationships among technical vocabulary terms.
_____ 5. I ensure that students have specific purposes for reading before they begin.
_____ 6. I relate postreading discussions to the original purposes students read to achieve.
_____ 7. I involve all students in class discussions.
_____ 8. I sometimes allow students to question and respond to one another during discussions.

_____ 9. I interact with students through journals or other forms of written interchange.

_____ 10. I provide opportunities for students to reinforce and extend their vocabulary knowledge after they read about new terms.

_____ 11. I provide opportunities for extended writing after some reading assignments.

_____ 12. I constantly look for ways to relate new material to previous material.

_____ 13. I occasionally assist students in developing good study habits and note-taking skills.

_____ 14. I occasionally discuss test-taking strategies with my students.

_____ 15. I talk with special educators in my school about students with special needs.

_____ 16. I modify reading assignments and other tasks, where appropriate, for special students.

_____ 17. I attempt to modify my teaching where possible to accommodate students with special needs.

_____ 18. I use alternative means of testing for special students when appropriate.

_____ 19. I attempt to discover which aspects of my subject specialty students would like to read more about.

_____ 20. My classroom is filled with examples of print materials related to my subject.

_____ 21. I occasionally apportion some time for free reading by students.

_____ 22. Whenever possible I point out links between course material and students' everyday lives.

_____ 23. I vary my teaching methods occasionally to avoid boredom.

_____ 24. I occasionally read aloud to my students.

_____ 25. When I can, I point out to students how course material is connected to other subject areas.

_____ 26. I try to provide students with choices as often as possible.

_____ 27. I find ways to integrate microcomputers into my teaching.

SUMMARY

In order to make instructional decisions that turn content literacy into an asset, a teacher must have three types of information. These involve the proficiency of the students, the nature of the written materials, and the literacy-related demands made by the teacher. A balance of the three should be an important goal.

Reading ability is a concept that has proved very difficult to measure. Many formats have been used in testing it, and many scales have been devised for describing the extent of an individual's proficiency at reading. One of the most common is the use of grade levels. All attempts to measure or describe reading ability are imprecise.

A useful idea in conceptualizing an individual's reading ability is to speak of three distinct levels based on a grade-level frame of reference. The independent level is the highest at which comprehension is good and no assistance is necessary. In contrast, the frustration level is the lowest at which comprehension is poor even when help is available. The instructional level lies between these two and represents materials that are challenging but not frustrating—materials that are neither too easy nor too difficult and that are therefore appropriate for instructional purposes. Like reading ability in general, these three levels are never precisely measurable, but they can be estimated.

The word *readability* refers to the overall difficulty of text and is often estimated in grade-level terms. A useful method is to think of a student's reading ability and an assignment's readability on the same scale so that the two can be compared and a judgment reached as to whether the match is a good one.

There are two approaches to making such a judgment. The first is to judge students and materials separately. The advantage of such an approach is that these assessments can be made without the use of regular class time. Students' reading levels can be estimated from standardized test results, typically available at the beginning of school. The readability of materials can be estimated through the use of formulas designed for this purpose. The difficulties with this approach are numerous, however. One problem is that standardized test results are not designed for use with readability formulas, yielding crude and misleading estimates. Another is that readability formulas tend to ignore a host of factors that influence the difficulty of text.

The second approach solves these problems by assessing students and materials together. A brief test is made from the actual materials students will be using, and the results can provide an instructor with useful information about whether the match between students and text will be a good one. A cloze test is one exercise of this sort. It involves systematically deleting words from a representative passage and then asking students to guess the missing words based on context. A more traditional approach to developing such a test is the content literacy inventory. This device consists of a set of questions based on a brief selection to which the students are free to refer during the testing. The questions should be of a type that the teacher will typically ask and should also require in their responses writing tasks of a kind expected by the teacher.

In addition to assessing students' abilities and the difficulty of assigned readings, it is also important for teachers to assess their instructional practices. An individual profile of such practices may assist teachers in recognizing which teaching behaviors may help and which may hinder students as they attempt to use literacy to learn content. Self-assessment can be organized through the Content Literacy Instructional Practice Survey, presented in Figure 3.9.

GETTING INVOLVED

1. Apply the Raygor formula to samples you choose from this text. Do the results reinforce your own insights about its difficulty level? Do different portions of the text vary markedly in estimated readability or are they relatively similar?

2. Figure 3.10 contains the information Mr. Ross might have collected about his tenth-grade biology students. Based on these data, which students, in your opinion, are most at risk of doing poorly on the literacy activities Mr. Ross may plan? For which students is the profile information unclear or contradictory? How might you explain these ambiguities? How might you deal with the contradictions?

3. Remember that Figure 3.11 presents the answers to the cloze test in Figure 3.7, for you to use in checking your own answers to the cloze test.

FIGURE 3.10

| Student | Cloze Percentage | Content Literacy Inventory | | | | |
| | | Reading (1–12) | Writing (5–12) | Book Parts | | |
				Index (10)	Glossary (11)	Contents (12)
1	56	12/12	S	+	+	+
2	40	6/12	A	+	+	+
3	46	9/12	A	+	+	+
4	42	9/12	W	−	+	+
5	30	3/12	W	−	−	−
6	22	4/12	A	+	+	+
7	66	12/12	A	+	+	+
8	70	12/12	W	+	+	+
9	68	10/12	S	+	−	+
10	36	5/12	A	+	+	+
11	10	1/12	W	−	−	−
12	50	9/12	A	+	+	+
13	48	11/12	S	+	+	+
14	40	11/12	S	+	+	+
15	60	5/12	W	+	+	−

Note: S = Strong   A = Adequate   W = Weak

FIGURE 3.11

WARNING—EARTHQUAKE AHEAD

Where and when will the next major earthquake happen? How strong will it be? Some scientists _____are_____ trying to answer these _____questions_____ , but at present, their _____ability_____ to predict the time, _____place_____ , and size of earthquakes _____is_____ limited.

Progress has been _____made_____ in calculating the likelihood _____that_____ an earthquake of a _____given_____ magnitude will occur in _____a_____ region within a general _____time_____ period. Such predictions have _____been_____ made for seismic gaps, _____which_____ are areas along plate _____boundaries_____ that have had regular _____seismic_____ activity in the past _____but_____ are currently overdue for _____earthquakes_____ . In the gray areas _____on_____ the map, quakes within _____the_____ last forty years have _____relieved_____ stress. But in the _____red_____ seismic gaps, no large _____earthquakes_____ have taken place recently, _____so_____ stress must still be _____building_____ . Some scientists predict major _____earthquakes_____ will occur in these _____gaps_____ before the end of _____this_____ century.

The seismic gap _____of_____ greatest interest in the _____United_____ States includes the San _____Andreas_____ Fault, which separates the _____Pacific_____ and North American Plates. _____Scientists_____ have set up equipment _____at_____ various places along this _____fault_____ to record some of _____the_____ known warning signs of _____earthquakes_____ .

At certain seismic stations, _____laser_____ beams are shot across _____the_____ San Andreas Fault and _____reflected_____ back to measure the _____slightest_____ movement of the two _____crustal_____ plates. Observe the laser _____light_____ in Figure 9–22. Any _____change_____ from a normal pattern _____of_____ movement might mean a _____quake_____ is coming. Other instruments _____measure_____ bulges or tilts in _____the_____ ground near a fault— _____another_____ indicator of a coming _____quake_____ . Some measure the rise _____and_____ fall of underground water _____in_____ wells. A sudden change _____in_____ the water level is a warning sign. Another sign of a major earthquake is a sharp increase in the number of small earthquakes, or tremors. Seismographs constantly record these tremors and geologists keep busy interpreting them.

Answers to cloze test in Figure 3.7

SOURCE: From *Scott Foresman Earth Science* by Timothy M. Cooney et al., pp. 213–214. Copyright ©1990 by Scott, Foresman and Company. Reprinted by permission of HarperCollins Publishers.

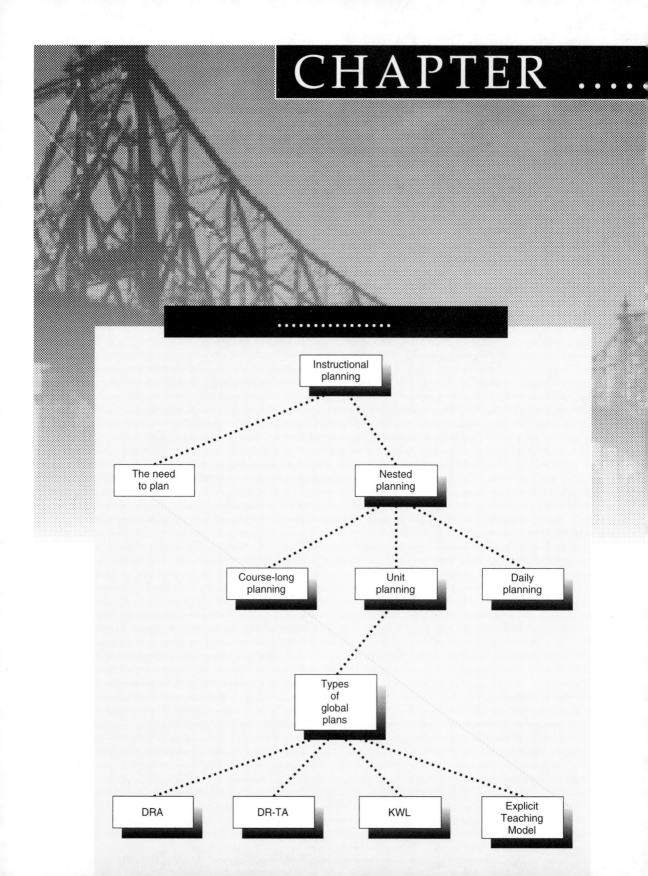

FOUR

Global Lesson Planning

There is always a best way of doing everything, if it be to boil an egg.
Ralph Waldo Emerson

In this chapter we discuss lesson planning in relatively broad terms, involving an entire unit of instruction. Our assumption is always that writing, reading, or both will play some role in the activities planned for students. Such literacy activities may come early or late in the unit or may be infused throughout, depending on the nature of the content and on the instructional objectives determined by the teacher.

We make an important distinction in this and subsequent chapters. By *global* planning, we refer to an overall plan of instruction covering as much as an entire unit. A unit may correspond to a textbook chapter, to an essay or article, to a novel or short story, to an important concept or set of related concepts, or to a specific skill or cluster of skills. The global plan offers the teacher a general framework in which to select and arrange various specific activities.

A military analogy may be helpful. In planning military actions, a distinction is made between *strategy* and *tactics*. Strategic considerations are broadly based and grow out of the overall goals to be sought. Tactical considerations follow from the strategy and involve short-range objectives, some of which may not be known very far in advance. Our notion of global planning therefore entails the selection of a long-range strategy for a particular unit of instruction. In this chapter we present various "strategic" plans along with a discussion of the types of units for which they are best suited. In Chapters 5 through 10, we introduce specific instructional techniques ("tactics") that may be incorporated at various points *within* the global framework.

OBJECTIVES

When you finish this chapter, you should be able to make effective decisions about global planning. You should be able to

1. define nested planning;

2. describe several frequently used global plans;

3. contrast these plans in terms of their advantages and shortcomings; and

4. select among them based on the specific content you are likely to teach.

WHY PLAN?

It is a bad plan that admits no modification.

Publilius Syrus

The process of writing out detailed daily lesson plans is a tedious prospect for most teachers. A popular myth contends that teaching is more art than science and that good teachers reject specific, preconceived plans that might limit their flexibility. According to this myth, good teaching is above all spontaneous, and teachers should be attuned to the occurrence of "teachable moments," during which students are optimally receptive to learning about a given concept or topic. Some have argued that because such moments cannot be easily predicted in advance, teachers must formulate their plans as their class sessions proceed. (For a discussion of this issue, see Robinson, 1991.)

Because preplanning is demanding, both in terms of the out-of-class time involved and the effort required, the above line of reasoning has a certain appeal. Research evidence, however, clearly suggests that the most effective teachers are those who plan their instruction in advance (Baumann, 1984; Brophy & Evertson, 1974; Brown, 1988). We are not suggesting that lesson plans be rigidly adhered to without regard to their effects on students. In fact, an equally compelling body of research indicates that the best teachers are able to make on-the-spot adjustments in lesson plans whenever these plans prove to be inappropriate (Hunter & Russell, 1977; Rosenshine, 1986). However, such adjustments occur within the framework of an overall plan developed *prior* to the lesson.

Another challenge to the necessity of planning stems from the debate between child-centered and curriculum-centered instruction. In the former, the needs and interests of individual students are central to the decision of what will be taught. In the latter, educators determine a more or less universal curriculum that will be taught to all students who lack mastery of it. It is probably better to think of these extreme positions as the endpoints of a philosophical continuum. In reality, most teachers are likely to place their own positions somewhere in-between.

Let's consider, for the sake of argument, a largely child-centered point of view in which all that is taught is selected on the basis of what the child needs and desires. Even in this case, teachers are not absolved from the necessity of planning. This is because students' interests and/or their deficiencies do not often demand *immediate* action on the part of the teacher. As needs become known, time is available for carefully selecting strategies that might best teach what is desired, regardless of how the content is determined.

In summary, planning instruction pays substantial dividends in terms of student growth. The question is not *whether* to plan but *how*, and it is to a discussion of this important question that we now turn.

NESTED PLANNING

Nearly half a century ago, Tyler (1950) recommended that teachers begin their planning by formulating specific objectives and then selecting activities aimed at accomplishing these objectives. Studies of how teachers actually plan, however, have revealed that this objectives-first model is rarely used in practice (Brown, 1988; McLeod, 1981; Zahorik, 1975). Instead, teachers tend to begin by broadly considering (1) the content to be taught, (2) their general goals (rather than specific objectives), (3) their past experiences with teaching similar content, and (4) the time available for instruction (Brown, 1988; Clark & Yinger, 1979; Leinhardt, 1983; Morine, 1976; Yinger, 1980; Zahorik, 1975).

In considering these four factors, experienced teachers often make notes to themselves about techniques that have been particularly effective in the past. These notes are usually compiled at the unit level and may include information about materials needed, time required, lecture content to be included, textbook assignments, practice activities, and so forth. The result is a *unit notebook* (Brown, 1988) that will then be used, and perhaps revised, each time a particular unit is taught.

Because most units require more than a single class session to complete, teachers must plan at a day-to-day level as well. Unit planning is central, but it does not eliminate the need to make daily plans, depending on how the unit plan has proceeded during each class session. By the same token, units should be planned in the context of a school year or specific course. In this manner, the daily lesson can be viewed in the context of a unit plan, which in turn is constructed in the context of an entire course. Yinger (1980) has referred to planning of this kind as "nested." That is, the plan for any given day is nested (contained within and dependent upon) the plan developed for a unit, which is nested in turn within the course plan. Figure 4.1 depicts this relationship with regard to a single day's planning. Figure 4.2 portrays the way nested planning actually proceeds across time.

> *P*lans get you into things but you got to work your way out.
>
> *Will Rogers*

Because course-long planning is given little time by accomplished secondary teachers (Brown, 1988), and because it tends to vary with subject matter and to depend on curricular decisions made in part by others, our chief concern in this chapter is with unit planning. Our goal is to present several well-researched global plans and to discuss the merits and drawbacks of each. All involve literacy activities, and it is likely that some will prove more compatible than others with the nature of a particular unit to be taught.

FIGURE 4.1

How a single daily lesson plan is nested within unit and course planning

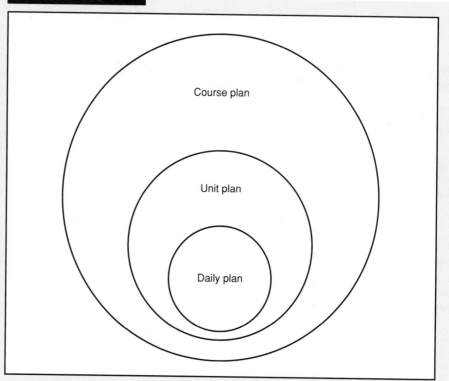

FIGURE 4.2

Nested planning across time

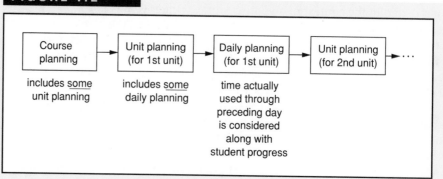

Note that we prefer the term *global* to *unit* in characterizing these plans because they are not necessarily designed to "cover" a particular unit of content. While a global plan may often correspond to a single unit, a unit may sometimes comprise more than one global plan. That is, the amount of content taught by means of a global plan may sometimes fall between the unit and daily levels.

GLOBAL PLAN 1: THE DIRECTED READING ACTIVITY (DRA)

The Directed Reading Activity (DRA) has long been a staple of elementary teachers (Betts, 1946) and remains the format of choice in organizing basal reader lessons. However, its great flexibility and breadth of application make it an effective plan for content area teachers as well (Tierney, Readence, & Dishner, 1990). The DRA is appropriate whenever a reading assignment is to be a focal point of instruction. When a biology teacher assigns a textbook chapter, when a literature teacher assigns a poem or short story, or when a social studies teacher assigns a historical novel are all occasions suitable to a DRA.

The chief assumption of the DRA is that the comprehension of students can be increased by building their background knowledge in advance and by giving them specific purposes for which to read. Once they complete the reading, the students engage in class discussion and then in activities designed to extend their understanding still further. The DRA therefore has components that come before and after reading. A five-step process is usually recommended, and in the following description we follow the outline provided by Robinson and Good (1987), though with slight modifications for the content area setting.

• •

Step 1: *Develop readiness for the reading activity.*
   A. Develop background needed for good comprehension. Begin by introducing the new topic and relating it to what students have already studied and, where pertinent, to their personal experiences. An effort may also be made to stimulate student questioning and to set an appropriate mood or tone for what is to be read. Writing activities may be initiated at this point.
   B. Develop special reading abilities if they are needed. If the selection contains unusual features that might cause difficulties, review them with students in advance. Such features might include charts, maps, diagrams, and the organizational pattern employed.
   C. Develop new vocabulary introduced in the material to be read. Present technical terms and the names of people and relevant places. The discussion should link the new terms with those previously introduced.

Step 2: *Set purpose/s for silent reading.*

A. Determine the objective/s for reading. Decide what knowledge, impressions, and understandings you want students to come away with. If the selection is lengthy and/or contains subdivisions, analyze each section separately.

B. Convey the purpose/s to the students. Tell students what you expect of them. Outline questions to be answered, information to be obtained, and so on. One means of accomplishing this goal is the content literacy guide, which is discussed in Chapter 8.

Step 3: *Arrange for students to read the selection silently.*

Decide how much class time will be apportioned for silent reading and how much out-of-class time. Set clear expectations that the material *will* be read—not necessarily word for word but with sufficient care to accomplish the purpose/s set forth in Step 2.

Step 4: *Discuss what has been read.*

A. Respond to purposes set prior to reading. Lead a class discussion, using as a "blueprint" the purpose provided to students in advance. The text (or whatever the students have read) should be used as a resource during the discussion. Portions may be reread orally to review or underscore certain points.

B. Develop oral reading for a purpose. In certain classes, though not in all, the teacher may wish to encourage oral reading. In the study of literature, for example, students may be asked to read a poem aloud for rhetorical effect, or to choose characters in a conversation-rich short story and read aloud their statements in a classroom version of "reader's theatre."

Step 5: *Extend students' understanding of the material.*

A. Use collateral materials where appropriate. Select additional sources that may be used to stretch your students' grasp of what has been read. These might include library materials, reference books, treatments of the same topic by different authors, and other works by the same author.

B. Stimulate student thinking through writing activities. Select an activity well matched to the initial purposes for reading. Such activities can vary widely in nature, from writing out a step-by-step problem-solving process in an algebra class to writing a personal response to a poem read as a literature assignment.

• •

A basic strength of the DRA is that it is easily adapted to a wide range of content reading situations. The DRA can be thought of as a framework within which the content teacher determines the specific details of what is to

---

The Directed Reading Activity (DRA)

Description: A five-step plan based on a particular reading assignment. The goal is to improve comprehension by preparing students for the assigned reading and by then following up with discussion and other activities.

Steps:
1. Building background
2. Setting purposes for reading
3. Silent reading
4. Discussion
5. Extension activities, skill development, and so on

Uses: With any reading material that may be challenging

Advantages: Flexible in terms of time devoted to each step
Useful with any assigned reading
Purposeful, as it assumes teacher will determine purposes for reading

Drawbacks: Risk of being overly teacher directive
Risk of overrelying on teacher-supplied purposes

---

be taught. It should be emphasized that the DRA does not dictate what is to be included in a particular lesson but only how to organize the instruction.

GLOBAL PLAN 2: THE DIRECTED READING–THINKING ACTIVITY (DR–TA)

The Directed Reading–Thinking Activity (DR–TA) is a popular variation of the Directed Reading Activity. First suggested by Stauffer (1969), the DR–TA is designed to help readers determine their own purposes for reading a selection and then to decide on the most appropriate strategies for achieving these purposes. A strength of the DR–TA is the emphasis placed on reading as a thinking activity and on the need for students to determine their own purposes for reading.

Stauffer originally intended the DR–TA as a strategy for elementary teachers to use while teaching from basal readers. Shepherd (1982), Manzo and Manzo (1990), and other writers have since made a case for using the DR–TA in content area courses. We believe the plan does have a viable role in such courses, but it is limited by several shortcomings. First, Stauffer (1969) suggested that a prereading discussion of vocabulary was unnecessary due to the careful vocabulary control in the basals of that era. This suggestion clearly does not apply to content courses, in which the introduction of new technical vocabulary is often of central importance. Fortunately, Stauffer's own modification of the strategy (1980) includes discussion of new vocabulary. Second, this strategy places a premium on *prediction* as readers proceed through a selection. There are two difficulties with this perspective. One is that prediction is more appropriate to narrative materials than to the expository writing most content area teachers rely on. The other is that research has indicated quite persuasively that fluent adult readers rarely take the time to predict as they read (Rayner & Pollatsek, 1989).

There are circumstances, however, under which prediction is an important ability. Consider:

- a chemistry chapter discussing how certain laws govern the outcome of various chemical reactions;
- a history chapter detailing policy considerations during a crisis and how policy decisions affected the eventual resolution of the crisis;
- a health pamphlet on cardiopulmonary resuscitation (CPR) outlining what to do and what to avoid under certain circumstances;
- a lesson based on interactive fiction software, in which students make decisions on behalf of the protagonist and then learn the consequences of their choices (see Chapter 14);
- a literature unit based on an entire novel, to be discussed chapter by chapter as the class follows the actions of principal characters.

Given this range of possibilities, it makes sense to examine the process of the DR–TA and to consider specific applications of this global plan in your own discipline. We have presented an adaptation of Stauffer's revised (1980) format.

• •

Step 1: *Assist students in developing purposes for reading.*
   A. Determine students' background related to the material to be read. Ask questions that assess the knowledge of students in an effort to determine whether their prior understanding will be equal to the demands of the reading. In reality, past experiences with a group of students will often provide a teacher with a fair appraisal of whether their existing knowledge is adequate.
   B. Provide appropriate teaching, when needed, to address lack of information or misconceptions about the reading. Many of the activities to be presented in the coming chapters are appropriate here.

C. Discuss new vocabulary relative to the reading material. This process is likely be an essential part of background building.

D. Help students set purposes for reading the material. As we have mentioned, this is largely a predictive process. Ask the students what they *suspect* will be presented in the material to be read. Encourage class members to critique one another's projections in an effort to explore a variety of possibilities and, in many cases, to get competing predictions into the open simultaneously.

Step 2: *Facilitate reasoning as reading proceeds.*

A. Circulate as students read, offering assistance where needed. Respond to specific questions about vocabulary first by encouraging students to make use of context, glossaries, and other aids available to them.

B. Break down longer assignments into manageable segments. Predictions can be checked at the end of each section and new ones formed. (See Step 3.)

Step 3: *Help students test their predictions.*

A. After students have read a selection (or a specified section of an entire selection), remind them of their predictions; have the students examine the predictions to decide whether they were supported by what was encountered in print.

B. Require proof based on the reading. Ask students to locate and share aloud supporting material. When predictions are not borne out, require students to cite information that refutes their original assumptions.

• •

We have suggested that the DR–TA offers an important alternative to guiding students through certain kinds of reading materials. Stauffer (1980) has argued that the plan will work for any reading selection, but this is true only if the idea of "prediction" is broadly assumed to mean any speculation about what the material contains and not the usual time-related notion of "what happens next."

DRA VERSUS DR–TA

Both of the global plans we have discussed have their own distinct advantages, and Stauffer clearly succeeded in giving teachers a real alternative in the DR–TA. When you choose between the two, it is important to keep in mind the points at which the two plans are most different. We have summarized these differences as follows:

● ●

DRA	DR–TA
1. Generally more teacher directed.	1. Generally more student centered.
2. Relies on teacher to analyze material and determine what the purposes for reading should be.	2. Encourages students to set their own purposes based on what they already know and what they think the material may tell them.
3. Postreading discussion based on prereading purposes set by the teacher.	3. Postreading discussion based on whether students' predictions were borne out by reading.
4. Useful with all selections.	4. More useful with narrative than with expository selections.
5. Useful with relatively unfamiliar topics.	5. Most useful with relatively familiar topics.

● ●

The Directed Reading–Thinking Activity (DR–TA)

Description: A three-step plan designed to assist readers in setting their own purposes for reading. The teacher's role is to help students form predictions about a selection and later to help them test their predictions.

Steps:
1. Assist students in developing purposes
2. Facilitate reasoning as students read
3. Help students test their predictions

Uses: Works best with narrative materials and with topics that are fairly familiar to students already

Advantages: Stresses the need to think actively while reading
Emphasizes the need to set one's own purposes

Drawbacks: Limited usefulness with expository materials
Not well suited to unfamiliar new topics
Role of prediction in good reading has been questioned

GLOBAL PLAN 3: KWL

We have mentioned two limitations of the DR–TA as an alternative to the traditional DRA: (1) it is better suited to narrative than to expository material, and (2) it works best with topics already rather familiar to the students (Spiegel, 1981). Ogle (1986) has proposed a DRA alternative designed to remedy these shortcomings. While Ogle's method can serve as a study strategy whenever students are working independently, it is also useful as a global lesson design into which numerous specific techniques can be employed.

Ogle's strategy involves three steps: (1) a discussion designed to determine what students already know prior to reading, (2) group and individual decisions about what they would like to learn from the material, and (3) a postreading appraisal of what they did in fact learn. From these three steps—what the students already *know*, what they *want* to learn, and what they do *learn*—comes the acronym KWL. Let's examine these steps in greater detail.

· ·

Step 1: *Determine what students know.*

A. Begin by leading a brainstorming session with the students about the topic to be addressed by the reading. Use a word or brief phrase to sum up the principal topic—crustaceans, sonnets, the legislative branch, and so on. Be as specific as possible. (If a social studies chapter deals with the legislative branch of government, don't say the topic is "government.") Ask what students know about the topic. If you draw a blank with your topic label, try becoming a little more general. For example, you might ask what they know about the "branches of government." Write responses on the board or use the overhead projector. Be receptive to student input without close regard to its appropriateness. As you write, abbreviate and condense where necessary.

B. With the students' help, identify categories that can be used to group the information you've listed. You may need to model this process until students become familiar with KWL. In our legislature example, you may note that several items supplied by students have to do with passing bills into law. You would suggest this as a category, write it on the board as a heading, and list the items below it.

Step 2: *Help students determine what they want to learn.*

A. As you proceed through Step 1, gaps and uncertainties in students' preexisting knowledge will begin to become clear. Your goal is to translate these into reasons for reading. Ask students what they wish to learn from the material, and in the ensuing discussion attempt to steer them toward their deficiencies. Attempt to arouse their curiosity about these points by asking questions (e.g., "I wonder what happens if the vote on a bill is a tie?").

B. Ask students to decide on purpose questions individually. They should write these out. Expect overlap in the questions but some divergence as well. Tolerate individual interests but shepherd students toward obvious shortcomings in their knowledge base.

Step 3: *Assess what students have learned.*

A. Request that students jot down, at least in abbreviated form, the answers to their questions as they read. Caution them in advance that they might not find the answers to all the questions.

B. Conduct a discussion comparing what students wished to learn with what they actually gained from the reading. Stress points at which the selection did not address their needs, pointing out that what an author chooses to include is not the beginning and end of a topic. Indicate other sources where students might have their questions answered and provide opportunities for using them.

• •

Although KWL is relatively specific about the activities to be included, there are many points at which a teacher can insert literacy activities designed to facilitate learning. For example, the process of categorizing student input in Step 1 can be accomplished through the use of a graphic organizer or semantic map, techniques we explore in Chapter 6. Carr and Ogle (1987) recommended this modification in what they termed KWL Plus. This variation, however, is just one additional example of how KWL can serve as a global, start-to-finish structure for organizing many activities.

KWL	
Description:	A three-step plan in which the teacher helps the students locate gaps in their existing knowledge of the topics covered by a selection and turn these gaps into purposes for reading.
Steps:	1. Determine what students *know* (K) 2. Help students determine what they *want* to learn (W) 3. Assess what students have *learned* (L)
Uses:	Designed primarily for expository materials, such as textbooks
Advantages:	Stresses the need to link old learning with new Provides for the activation of prior knowledge Lends itself well to the goal of acquiring knowledge
Drawbacks:	May not be sufficiently teacher centered for some

GLOBAL PLAN 4: THE EXPLICIT TEACHING MODEL

One of the most popular lesson designs used in recent years is based on the Explicit Teaching Model. (See Figure 4.3.) This model is appropriate when the teacher has a very clear idea of what is to be taught, in terms of new knowledge to be instilled and/or new skills to be developed. Because what will be taught can be clearly specified in advance, such teaching is said to be *explicit.* The teacher using this model should have a clear notion of what the specific objectives for a lesson will be.

An important strength of the Explicit Teaching Model is its research base. The steps of the plan come from careful observation of how effective teachers actually carry out instruction, and in many cases cause-and-effect links have been documented between teaching behaviors and student achievement. For these reasons, the Explicit Teaching Model now constitutes the basis of teacher evaluation systems in a number of states and in many districts. Popular systems, such as the Madeline Hunter model, are derived from this research base.

Two cautions should be raised in considering the Explicit Teaching Model. One is that the notion of *effectiveness* has often been equated by researchers with gains on standardized achievement measures. If you harbor philosophical problems with this definition, you may be disenchanted with the model, which is highly teacher directed in nature. Second, the model is more appropriate for some objectives than others. Objectives that are clear-cut and easily definable in nature, such as acquiring a specific skill or learning a given set of facts, are well suited to explicit teaching. Objectives that tend to be more elusive and vague, such as improving students' attitudes or increasing their reading comprehension, are not as well suited to the model (Rosenshine, 1986).

The effectiveness research literature is vast and is cited again in subsequent chapters. While the teaching models that have arisen from it vary to some degree, what they possess in common is reflected in the following outline.

FIGURE 4.3

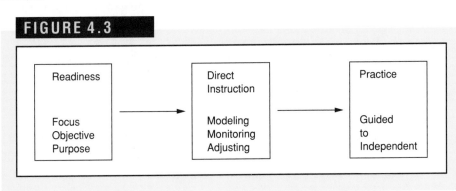

The explicit teaching model

● ●

Step 1: *Create readiness for the lesson.*

   A. Gain students' attention and focus it on the content of the lesson. Attempt to link what will be learned to past learning—for example, by conducting a brief review, asking a provocative question, and so on.

   B. State the objectives of the lesson. In the explicit model, it is not enough to *have* objectives. They must be communicated to students. You can explain the objectives by telling students what they will be able to do at the end of the lesson or unit. Where feasible, you should attempt to suggest for each objective a motivational purpose for achieving it. For example, a science teacher, after identifying an objective related to learning about cholesterol, might add that this substance is known to be an important contributor to circulatory disease and that we therefore need to know about it.

Step 2: *Conduct direct instruction.*

   A. Introduce new concepts and skills by using numerous examples. When teaching skills, you should *model* them carefully and repeatedly for students. As the teacher, you should provide the initial examples, later eliciting additional ones from students.

   B. Continually monitor student understanding as you teach. Ask questions and watch as students work. If it becomes clear that students are not catching on, make on-the-spot adjustments in your lesson plan. Do not hesitate to reteach material you thought students had previously mastered.

Step 3: *Provide opportunities to practice.*

   A. When students appear ready, permit them to practice what they have learned while you are available to offer guidance and feedback. If you are teaching skills, the notion of practice is self-evident. If the objective requires students to acquire factual information, their practice might be to answer questions or apply the knowledge gained in a structured situation, such as solving problems, writing compositions, and so forth.

   B. When students appear to have achieved the objective/s so long as guidance is available, let them practice on their own. Students' progression from guided to independent practice again requires the teacher to make a judgment concerning their readiness. Independent practice can take the form of homework, tests, and any other task in which guidance is deliberately removed in order to determine whether the student can function independently.

● ●

The Explicit Teaching Model

Description: A three-phase plan based on teacher effectiveness research and designed to accomplish specific, clear-cut objectives by means of direct instruction followed by practice.

Steps:
1. Create readiness for the lesson
2. Conduct direct instruction
3. Provide opportunities to practice

Uses: Not centered around a specific reading selection, but is suitable whenever objectives are clear and a strongly teacher-centered approach is desired

Advantages: Broad research base
Conducive to clear-cut sequential planning

Drawbacks: Not well suited to cases in which objectives are vague
May be too teacher centered for some educators
May encourage overreliance on teacher for direction
May encourage avoidance of literacy activities

It is perhaps easy to see why the Explicit Teaching Model is so appealing to many content area teachers. It is well suited to conveying knowledge and skills in a highly structured, workable, and repeatable manner. A danger of the model is that teachers may tend to minimize literacy activities. In fact, however, reading and writing can be built into the model at many points. During the readiness step, students might be asked to write about their current understanding of the topic to be addressed. In the direct instruction phase, you can incorporate guided note taking and read or create written examples. During practice, students can be asked to read specific materials or to produce written evidence of content acquisition. These are only a few examples; many more are offered in Chapters 5 through 10.

SUMMARY

Planning for instruction occurs at several levels, from course-long planning to unit planning to daily planning. The planning process is therefore a "nested" one in which one level of planning occurs within other, broader levels. Some

Pause a moment to think about your reactions to the four global plans presented. Does one of them seem more "like you" than the others? You may have made your judgment based on visualizing yourself as a student in each of the four settings. In Chapter 1 we discussed this tendency and we encourage you now to keep an open mind as we explore how each plan might be used to achieve different purposes.

educators have suggested a minimal need for detailed planning because it may infringe on a teacher's flexibility in reacting to students' needs and because it may place too great an emphasis on the curriculum and too little on the child. However, research indicates that relatively careful planning results in higher levels of learning regardless of subject area. These studies also suggest that the most effective teachers are those who pay particular attention to planning at a unit level as well as at a daily level. Our focus in this chapter has therefore been on the development of global plans, which involve units or major portions of units, usually longer than a single class period.

Four major global formats were introduced. The Directed Reading Activity (DRA) comprises five steps: (1) establishing readiness for reading, (2) setting purposes for reading, (3) reading assigned materials silently, (4) discussing what has been read, and (5) doing activities designed to extend and reinforce what has been learned. The Directed Reading–Thinking Activity (DR–TA) is a major modification of the DRA based largely on the use of prediction as a means of setting purposes for reading. Its three steps include (1) assisting students to set their own purposes for reading based on what they expect the selection to contain, (2) assisting students to reason as they read, and (3) helping students to test their predictions following reading. The DRA tends to be more teacher directed than the DR–TA largely because the teacher, rather than the students, is responsible for setting the purposes. Consequently, the postreading discussion in a DRA is also more teacher directed because it centers around teacher-determined purposes rather than those set by individual students. An advantage of the DRA is its applicability to virtually all reading materials, while the DR-TA tends to be better suited to narrative than to expository selections and to topics that are relatively familiar to students so that predictions can be reasonably made.

A third global format is KWL. This plan begins with the teacher helping students survey what they already *know* (K) about a topic. The teacher then assists students in determining what they *want* (W) to know by helping them turn gaps in their knowledge into reasons for reading. Finally, the teacher follows the reading of the selection with a discussion of what the students have actually *learned* (L). A fourth global format is the Explicit Teaching Model. Its three major phases include (1) creating readiness for the new instruction by building an appropriate mental set and by communicating the objectives and purposes of the lesson; (2) the direct instruction itself, in which examples are frequent and careful monitoring is conducted by the teacher to ensure that students grasp the new material; (3) a practice phase, which provides students the opportunity to perform skills first in a guided and later in an independent setting. The Explicit Teaching Model, unlike the other three global plans presented in this chapter, is not centered around a single reading selection but affords instead many opportunities for the incorporation of literacy activities.

GETTING INVOLVED

1. Figure 4.4 presents a chart comparing the four global formats described in this chapter. Across the top are characteristics that may or may not apply to each format. Test your understanding by writing a plus (+) if a format possesses a characteristic or a zero (0) if it lacks it. Refer to the discussion to check your judgments but note that not all of them have been specifically addressed. You will need to infer some of your conclusions, and even then some may involve an element of discretion.

2. Locate a brief reading selection that has future potential for use with your students. A stand-alone selection (an article, essay, story, poem, etc.) is better for this task than a textbook chapter because you will be able to incorporate it into your instruction regardless of the text that is in use. Choose any one of the first three global plans (DRA, DR–TA, or KWL) and outline a lesson plan for your selection. Make notes about what you would generally do to guide students at each step, but do not be overly detailed in your planning because these formats allow for many additional "tactical" devices to be incorporated. You will read about these devices in Chapters 5 through 10, and you will be asked to implement some of them in your plan. So choose well! We'll revisit this selection in the future.

FIGURE 4.4

For each of the characteristics listed below, place a plus (+) under the heading of each of the plans to which it applies. Place a zero wherever the characteristic does not apply.

Characteristic	DRA	DR–TA	KWL	Explicit Teaching
Highly teacher directed				
Purposes for reading are set by students				
More useful with expository than narrative selections				
Useful with relatively unfamiliar topics				
Not based on a major reading assignment				
Emphasizes the ability to predict				

An exercise in contrasting the four global plans

SECTION . . . . two

Prereading Strategies

Whenever a teacher requires students to read, it is vital to prepare them for the task. This is true regardless of how extensive their background may be or whether the selection to be read is a textbook chapter or outside reading. Simply assigning the material, by identifying the pages to be read or by distributing an extra selection with the warning to "read with care," is totally inadequate. In this section we examine methods by which teachers can facilitate students' reading by ensuring that their background is adequate for the task. We might have approached this topic in one lengthy chapter but chose instead to separate activities for building background into those directly concerned with introducing new vocabulary and those that are more general in nature.

Chapter 5 examines why it is vital first to take stock of prior knowledge, by comparing what an author assumes students already know with what they actually do know. We then present numerous activities designed either to "activate" (that is, "switch on") relevant background knowledge or to add to students' background specific information they will need to comprehend.

Chapter 6 continues the topic of prereading activities by presenting those useful in introducing new vocabulary. We describe a great variety of techniques that have proved effective for presenting terminology and other vocabulary. An important distinction is that most of the methods described in this chapter are especially designed for content area teachers because they rely on the knowledge that new words are neither taught nor learned one at a time in isolation but are often closely interrelated, making them best approached in clusters.

STEP 1

- Judging whether prior knowledge is adequate
  - What the writer assumes
  - What the reader knows

STEP 2

- Activating and adding prior knowledge
  - Activating
    - Review
    - PReP
    - Writing
  - Adding
    - Organizational walk-throughs
    - Advance organizers
    - Facts
    - Anecdotes
    - Analogies
    - Marginalia
    - Props

Vocabulary methods (Chapter 6)

FIVE

Building Prior Knowledge

I suggest that the only books that influence us are those for which we are ready, and which have gone a little further down our particular path than we have yet got ourselves.

E. M. Forster

If you have not already done so, take a moment to examine the cartoon in Figure 5.1. We suspect that your reaction was either one of amusement (you "got" it) or mystification (you knew there was some point to it but were unable to discover just what the point was). The cartoon depends heavily on the reader's background. The cartoonist assumes in particular that the reader is familiar with *Psycho*, a 1960 motion picture directed by Alfred Hitchcock. If you are not familiar with the film, the cartoon could not have had the desired effect because you could not make the necessary connection between events in the film and the scene depicted in the cartoon.

The fact is, you needed a host of connections to interpret the cartoonist's idea properly. You needed the striking visual image from the movie of the hilltop house with the silhouette of the psychotic Norman Bates at the window. You needed to catch the subtle substitution of a fishing rod for Norman's knife, and you needed to relate this switch to the realization that the unsuspecting victims in the cartoon are worms. Finally, you needed to perceive the pun created by re-spelling the name of the Bates Motel. If you failed to make any one of these connections, the humor was weakened or lost.

In much the same way the artist conceived his cartoon, an author writing for students makes assumptions about their previous familiarity with certain topics, concepts, and ideas. In making these assumptions, the author is handicapped by two limitations. First, the author's knowledge considerably exceeds that of students, making it difficult to identify with student readers and to predict what they might or might not be likely to know already. Second, the background knowledge of individual students tends to vary widely so that generalizations about what the "typical" student may know are impossible. Writing that is appropriate for the background of some students is sure to be inappropriate for others.

Additional factors can make the issue of background even worse. Some writers, for example, are less sensitive than others to the limits of their readers'

FIGURE 5.1

An example of the need for prior knowledge

"Say, Anthony, this looks like a pleasant little place."

prior knowledge. In addition, teachers sometimes find it useful to assign reading selections not expressly written for students—articles, essays, short stories, and so on. In these cases the authors were obviously in no position to consider the needs of students.

OBJECTIVES

In Chapter 2 we examined the role of prior knowledge in assisting readers as they attempt to make written materials meaningful. In this chapter we look at methods of determining differences in what students need to know before they read a given selection and what they actually do know. We suggest techniques useful in filling gaps in prior knowledge and present ways of "activating" relevant knowledge that already exists. When you have completed this chapter, you should be able to

> Information's pretty thin stuff, unless mixed with experience.
>
> *Clarence Day*

1. know what is meant by considerate and inconsiderate text;

2. assess the prior knowledge demands of reading assignments;

3. assess the adequacy of students' prior knowledge;

4. select and use appropriate techniques of building background; and

5. select and use appropriate techniques of activating existing prior knowledge.

JUDGING WHETHER PRIOR KNOWLEDGE IS ADEQUATE

All authors make assumptions about what their readers are likely to know before they read. This is true regardless of the type of writing, as the following two examples plainly show. First, when writing the second chapter of a textbook, the author may well assume that the student has understood the content of the first chapter. Because of this assumption, knowledge of the initial chapter's content may be necessary for the reader to grasp the facts and concepts introduced in the second chapter. Likewise, an eighteenth-century English novelist might expect a reader to be rather familiar with life and customs in England during the 1700s. The novelist would therefore not bother to provide detailed accounts of these subjects, and consequently, a modern reader unfamiliar with them will have difficulties whenever such knowledge is assumed.

Considerate and Inconsiderate Text

We have suggested that some writers are more sensitive than others to the prior knowledge of students. Such writers make an effort to review or reference earlier material whenever its content is needed to comprehend new information. They are careful to define new concepts clearly and, where possible,

Remember the "laundry" example of Chapter 2 (Figure 2.2)? That was surely an example of inconsiderate text—for any reader!

to relate abstract ideas to the everyday experiences of students. These writers have a well-developed *sense of readership,* an idea of what sorts of readers are likely to read what they've written. Writing of this kind is said to be "considerate" (Alvermann & Boothby, 1983) in that the author carefully considers the limitations of what students are likely to know and writes with these limitations in mind.

Inconsiderate writing, on the other hand, is the result of a poor sense of readership so that too much reliance is placed on the reader's background. This can and does happen in content area texts, but the issue is rather complicated. First, a given selection may be considerate of some readers and inconsiderate of others. This is because of differences in their prior knowledge. Moreover, some portions of the same textbook may be considerate, others inconsiderate. This may be the result of multiple authors each contributing different portions to the book or of a single author's being less cognizant about student knowledge in some areas than in others.

When reading materials are assigned that were not written with students in mind, the chances of inconsiderate writing are especially high because the author's sense of readership may be off target. As an extreme example, consider a health instructor who asks students to read an article appearing in the *Journal of the American Medical Association.* Because the author anticipated a readership made up of physicians, the writing would not be considerate of the needs of secondary school students. This example is admittedly exaggerated to illustrate our point, but similar results can befall the language arts teacher who assigns a Shakespearean play, the biology teacher who duplicates an article from *Scientific American,* or the government teacher who distributes a column by George Will.

Our point is that teachers must be aware of the assumptions writers make about prior knowledge. Such awareness can occur only if a teacher inspects the material to be assigned.

Judging What the Writer Assumes

Regardless of how considerate a writer attempts to be, there is always some reliance on the reader's background. We know of no precise way to itemize that dependence, but the following guidelines are useful for identifying major instances of reliance.

1. *Look for references to previous material.*   Examine the selection for references to earlier chapters. If the selection is a stand-alone (that is, an article, poem, essay, etc.), look for references to other sources with which the author may assume the reader is familiar.
2. *Examine the new vocabulary introduced.*   We say much more about this subject in Chapter 6, but for now it is important to note that newly introduced terms offer a major hint as to the background a reader will need. This is because

words are not learned in isolation but by association with word concepts previously learned. The point of listing new words is to gain a perspective on which words must be known in advance in order to make sense of them. Often teachers' editions of textbooks list new words in advance so that the only real task confronting the teacher is to decide which previously introduced words the new terms build on.

3. *Look for references that are not adequately explained.* An author may refer to facts or ideas that were not previously introduced and that may require additional explanation. This happens frequently in literature but can occur in textbooks as well. The issue is whether the reference is critical to an understanding of the content. When a biology text mentions that fossils of ancient fish were studied by Agassiz, a famous nineteenth-century scientist, the teacher must ask whether the time needed to explain who Agassiz was would substantially improve the students' understanding of a chapter on fossils.

Judging What the Reader Knows

The relationship between a reader's prior knowledge of a topic and the prior knowledge actually needed for adequate comprehension is depicted in Figure 5.2. The left-hand circle represents all that a given reader knows about the topic, the right-hand circle all that the author assumes the reader knows. Region 1 contains information known to the reader but not essential to understanding the selection. Region 2 also comprises information known in advance to the reader but information crucial to

> *A book, like a landscape, is a state of consciousness varying with readers.*
> *Ernest Dimnet*

FIGURE 5.2

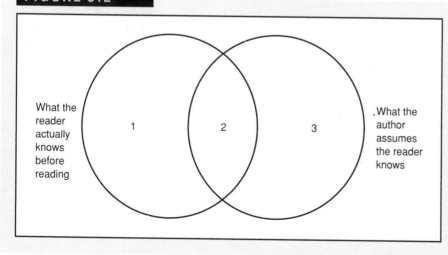

Prior knowledge needs: What the author assumes versus what the reader knows

What the reader actually knows before reading

1   2   3

What the author assumes the reader knows

comprehension. Region 3 represents information assumed to be known in advance to the reader but in fact not known.

In the previous section we examined guidelines for determining a selection's demands on prior knowledge. We now look at methods of determining whether students' prior knowledge is equal to these demands. Answering this question gives a teacher a good notion of what Region 3 contains. Answering it need not be involved, and a variety of quick and simple techniques is possible. Holmes and Roser (1987) offer the following.

1. *Free recall.* The teacher suggests a topic and asks students to brainstorm, saying anything they suspect a treatment of that topic might contain.

2. *Word associations.* Using a list of topics or subtopics, the teacher tells students they are to react with whatever association occurs to them. Then each topic is read aloud.

3. *Structured questions.* The teacher begins by asking a relatively simple question concerning the content of a reading selection. If students successfully answer it, the teacher proceeds to a second question that is an outgrowth of the first and that is slightly more difficult. Sequences of carefully crafted, progressively more difficult questions can tell a teacher a great deal about the limits of prior knowledge.

4. *Recognition questions.* The teacher prepares and distributes a number of multiple-choice questions about the topic. The idea is to assess misinformation as well as prior knowledge.

5. *Unstructured discussion.* Here the teacher attempts to elicit from students their own experiences as they relate to the upcoming topic. This technique seems especially well suited to fiction.

To these we can add structured writing assignments as a means of assessment. Any task that calls on students to summarize what they know about a topic, categorize key concepts, and so forth will provide useful information. It may be natural to think of time as a limiting factor in using writing tasks in this way—time to write and time, subsequently, for the teacher to read the written products. There are ways around this limitation, however. First, students could be asked to work on a task collaboratively, thus producing less for the teacher to scrutinize. Second, the teacher can inspect student work as it is being written by circulating about the room. Third, writing tasks need not produce full-blown compositions but can involve single paragraphs, even sentences, and can include categorization tasks in which only a few words are used. Last, writing often has the effect of clarifying and organizing prior knowledge as well as activating it. The writing task can therefore be designed to do double duty. It is for this reason that we will revisit writing techniques in the next section.

Approaches such as these serve a variety of functions. Their main role, of course, is to allow the teacher to plan and modify how background is to be built for a reading assignment. They also serve to focus attention on the topic/s to be covered and are therefore appropriate to the initial steps of the DRA and the Explicit Teaching Model. When discussion is involved, they fit quite well within the framework of the DR–TA and KWL. Finally, they give the teacher a benchmark by which to gauge the extent of student comprehension and learning.

WAYS TO ADD AND ACTIVATE BACKGROUND KNOWLEDGE

Comprehension can be improved when a reader's relevant prior knowledge is "activated" before reading. By assisting students to recall knowledge needed for a given reading assignment, teachers help them in "building bridges from the new to the known" (Pearson & Johnson, 1978, p. 24). Prince (1987) found that comprehension was even improved by conducting certain enrichment activities before reading rather than afterward (the usual practice). Comprehension can also be enhanced by adding important background knowledge that students lack. When background is *activated*, Region 2 of Figure 5.2 is involved. When background is *added*, Region 3 is involved. We now present a variety of methods useful in adding or in activating background knowledge.

Activating Prior Knowledge

The notion of activating, or "switching on," appropriate background knowledge is an important one because new knowledge, if it is to be well learned and understood, must be integrated into existing knowledge. The teacher's job is to help students bring relevant facts, concepts, and experiences to consciousness. While the methods for doing so are probably limitless, we offer three that are broadly useful, and we discuss more in relation to vocabulary in Chapter 6.

Review Whenever an upcoming reading assignment builds on information previously provided, review can be an effective first step in introducing the new material. This circumstance is true, for example, of a mathematics textbook chapter introducing a more advanced version of a problem type. It is not as relevant, however, to a chapter (perhaps a chapter in the same textbook) in which a major shift in topics occurs.

PReP Langer (1981) has suggested a PreReading Plan (PReP), which can be used to activate prior knowledge and at the same time provide the teacher with an idea of problem areas. PReP has three goals: (1) to determine the extent of students' prior knowledge and how that knowledge is organized,

(2) to ascertain how well students can express their understanding of the topic/s to be studied, and (3) to discover what additional background students might need in order to understand the new material.

PReP has two steps, the first involving a three-part class discussion. In the second step, the teacher analyzes the responses given by students.

• •

Step One: Class Discussion

   1. Initial Associations with the Concept

      Questions such as the following are asked during this first phase of PReP:

      "What do you first think of when you hear this word, see this picture, and so on?"

      "What do you associate with this idea based on your past experiences?"

      The teacher records the student responses to this initial presentation of the new word on the chalkboard.

   2. Reflection on Initial Associations

      The teacher then asks the students to reflect on why they said what they did in phase one. Questions might be similar to the following, though phrased more specifically in an actual classroom setting:

      "What are some reasons for your suggestions in our initial discussion?"

      "Why do you think others in class made the suggestions they did?"

   3. Reformulation of Associations

      The third phase of the PReP reading strategy gives students the opportunity to reflect on the various ideas that have been presented to this point. The teacher could ask the class to discuss the following:

      "Based on our discussion to this point, do you have any new ideas or feelings on our topic of discussion?"

      "What do you think of the ideas presented by your classmates?"

      The teacher summarizes the class discussion in this step as well as the others without commenting or making a critical judgment of what was said.

Step Two: Analysis

      Langer suggested that the teacher then evaluate the total responses of the group on the basis of the following guidelines:

   1. Students with a high level of prior knowledge about a particular subject will answer using definitions, analogies, linkages, and superordinate concepts.

2. Students with some prior knowledge will most often respond by noting examples, attributes, or defining characteristics of the idea.

3. Students with little prior knowledge show this lack of information by answering with low-level associations, words that sound like the primary word, and not quite relevant experiences.

• •

Analyzing the discussion provides the teacher with an idea of which students may have inadequate prior knowledge. It also helps in making decisions about how best to add to that knowledge.

Writing   We have stated repeatedly that writing can be used as a means of clarifying one's thoughts about a subject. By confronting students with a brief writing task, a teacher compels prior knowledge to be activated and applied. Moreover, the teacher who circulates among students as they write, or who collects their written products for inspection, has a good means of assessing prior knowledge as well as activating it. Writing tasks can be used for these purposes in virtually all content areas as the following examples show:

- A math teacher asks students to write out the proof of a theorem based on previous material—a theorem used in the upcoming chapter.

- A language arts teacher, about to assign a short story about a wilderness expedition, asks students to write about an experience they may have had while camping.

- A chemistry teacher, prior to a chapter describing a particular experiment, tells the students to formulate a hypothesis based on what they have already learned.

- A history teacher invites students to work in groups to prepare a possible scenario for the Battle of Waterloo. The students do not know the outcome of the battle but have read an account of events *up to* the point of the conflict. They then read to contrast their scenarios with what actually happened.

Writing, as these examples indicate, not only provokes thinking based on prior knowledge but lends itself to collaborative activities. Such activities can also be linked to setting purposes for reading, a topic we address in Chapter 7.

> *There are many virtues in books, but the essential value is the adding of knowledge to our stock by the record of new facts, and, better by the record of intuitions which distribute facts.*
> *Ralph Waldo Emerson*

Adding to Prior Knowledge

Whenever a reader's background is inadequate for the task of reading a particular selection, the teacher can improve comprehension by enhancing background knowledge. There are numerous methods for achieving this goal, and they vary widely depending on what kind of information the teacher wants to supply. Some techniques deal with how the author has organized a selection, others with providing specific knowledge the author may have assumed on the part of students. Still others are concerned primarily with vocabulary. These last are examined in the next chapter.

Organizational Walk-Throughs   It is often helpful (especially with expository writing) for students to know in advance how material is organized (Holbrook, 1984). One way of accomplishing this is to "walk through" the selection in a teacher-led discussion, noting subheadings and reasoning aloud about how the subtopics are organized. This technique has acquired a very consistent basis in research (Alvermann & Swafford, 1989) and deserves our close attention.

We begin by considering the various types of organizing patterns used by authors. Fortunately, the number of effective patterns is relatively limited. The first five of the following were suggested by Readence, Bean, and Baldwin (1989). The sixth is an additional pattern we view as equally important.

1. *Time order.*   Topics are arranged chronologically. A history text chapter on the Civil War might be organized as follows in terms of *major* headings:
     I. Precursors of War
    II. Early Phases of Conflict
   III. The Tide Turns
    IV. Appomattox and After

2. *Comparison–contrast.*   Major viewpoints, theories, concepts, or ideas are contrasted and compared. The same history chapter might have been organized alternatively as follows:
     I. What the Confederacy Believed
    II. What the Union Believed
   III. Irreconcilable Differences

3. *Cause–effect.*   Writing about an event, phenomenon, or process, an author may focus on causal relationships. Our Civil War chapter might have been handled like this:
    I. Why the War Was Fought
       A. The Slavery Issue
       B. States' Rights
   II. Changes Brought about by the War
       A. Emancipation
       B. Civil Rights Movement
       C. Reconstruction

4. *Problem–solution.*   The author's principal focus is on a major problem with a view to possible solutions. Our hypothetical chapter

would certainly be an appropriate candidate for this pattern. For example:

I. The Impasse in 1860
II. Solutions That Failed
   A. Negotiation and Diplomacy
   B. Missouri Compromise Continued
   C. Influence of Great Britain
   D. Congressional Initiatives

5. *Simple listing.* Subtopics are ordered at random in the absence of any rationale for determining their order. A portion of the Civil War chapter might have been organized this way:

I. Portraits of Generalship
   A. Hood
   B. Grant
   C. Sherman
   D. Lee

6. *Systematic listing.* As in simple listing, the author wishes to enumerate several relatively unconnected subtopics but chooses to arrange them in some systematic way, such as by importance, location, or some other criterion. For example, the generals in the previous illustration might have been listed in terms of how the author viewed their skills or eminence:

I. Portraits of Generalship
   A. Lee
   B. Grant
   C. Sherman
   D. Hood

Discussing the organizational pattern is a good way to ensure that students have in mind the proper skeletal framework into which details will eventually be fitted. The process is usually not lengthy and can easily be combined with other background-building techniques.

We offer three specific observations before considering these additional methods. First, selections are rarely organized around a single pattern. Rather, authors tend to employ nested schemes, in which the overall organizational pattern is of one kind while subsections are organized differently. A good example is the outline just discussed for the problem–solution pattern. The four alternative solutions mentioned follow a simple-listing format.

Second, it is a good idea to mention the organizational patterns by name as you discuss them. Students will soon develop a schema for each that will assist them both in comprehending subsequent reading selections and in organizing their writing. Finally, two authorities have recommended specific guidelines for discussing organizational patterns.

Stein's (1978) Visual Reading Guide (VRG) is a strategy designed to call students' attention to visual aids located in a selection. The teacher first decides which of the aids are central to the instructional goals of reading. The teacher then proceeds from graphic to graphic and does the following:

1. tells why each is important or optional;
2. for those deemed important, analyzes what they offer the reader; and
3. discusses the information they convey and conclusions or applications they make possible.

It is a good idea to become consciously aware of the types of graphic aids used in the text. Examples from two present-day textbooks, one from science and the other from language arts, are presented in Figures 5.3 and 5.4. They offer an idea of the many devices now used in an effort to help students comprehend.

Aukerman (1972) suggested a simple overall method of sequencing a discussion of organizational patterns. His steps comprise a time frame for much of what we have introduced:

1. Analyze the chapter title.
2. Analyze the subtitles.
3. Analyze the visual aids.
4. Read the introductory paragraph.
5. Read the concluding paragraph.
6. Derive the main idea.

While the teacher guides the students through these steps, they can also serve as an independent study technique.

Advance Organizers   Ausubel (1960) introduced an effective technique for preparing readers for a selection likely to prove challenging. An advance organizer is a brief prose introduction to the topic/s presented in the actual selection. It is similar to the abstract of a journal article or the blurb located on the inside of a book jacket.

We suggest four sources of advance organizers. First, authors and editors of content area textbooks are more likely now than in previous years to provide an introduction or abstract to each chapter. Check the selection to see whether such a device is already available. Then discuss it with students as you read it together. Second, chapter summaries offer another good source. While their primary function is to synthesize and review chapter content, they can also serve as a focal point of prereading discussion, provided the teacher elaborates on the extremely condensed and cryptic treatment of the content. (After all, the author assumes the students have completed the chapter when they reach the summary.) Third, you can write your own organizers. While this prospect is a little demanding, it does afford the chance of organizing your own thoughts about a topic and of deciding what's vitally important to emphasize at the

FIGURE 5.3

Photograph

Key words in boldface

Italics for figure references

Pronunciation aid

Notice in *Figure 19-15* the lining of the stomach is very rough. Thousands of tiny gastric glands pit the stomach lining. These glands produce gastric juice and mucus. **Gastric** (gas′trik) **juice** contains hydrochloric acid, digestive enzymes, and water. The acid kills most bacteria in the food and activates the digestive enzymes. The digestive enzymes in gastric juice break large protein molecules into smaller molecules. Mucus is secreted by the gastric glands. A thick layer of mucus coats the inside of the stomach. This mucus prevents the acid from digesting the stomach lining.

Figure 19-15 Thousands of tiny glands dot the stomach lining. These glands produce mucus and gastric juices. 3×

Digestion and Absorption in the Small Intestine

After a few hours, the soupy chyme leaves the stomach in small squirts, approximately 50 milliliters at a time. Chyme enters the small intestine through an opening at the base of the stomach.

The small intestine is a long, narrow, coiled tube. If the small intestine were uncoiled, it would be more than 6 meters long. *Figure 19-16* shows the upper one-third of the small intestine. This upper part of the small intestine is where most of the chemical digestion takes place. Observe this section collects many juices from the nearby digestive glands.

Applying Science

A stomach ulcer results when too much gastric juice is produced or too little mucus coats the stomach. Hydrochloric acid in the gastric juice eats a sore in the stomach wall. Doctors treat ulcers with medications that reduce the production of acid in the stomach.

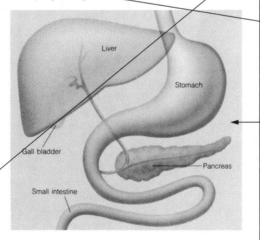

Figure 19-16 Most digestion occurs in the upper third of the small intestine; the liver, gall bladder, and pancreas supply the digestive juices needed for chemical digestion.

424

Embedded aids in a present-day science text

SOURCE: From *Life Science* (p. 424) by L. Balzer, L. A. Berne, P. L. Goodson, L. Lauer, & I. L. Slesnick. Copyright ©1990 by Scott, Foresman. Reprinted by permission of Scott, Foresman.

Subheading

Figure caption

Marginal gloss

Labeled diagram

91

FIGURE 5.4

Embedded aids in
a contemporary
language arts text

SOURCE: From
Houghton Mifflin English
by Haley-James, et
al., pp. 456–457.
Copyright ©1990
by Houghton Mifflin
Company. Reprinted by
permission of Houghton
Mifflin Company.

Color-accented
chapter title

Section title

Applying Research Reports

Literature and Creative Writing

"The Eagle" described the majestic bird standing over the
world. "Geography Lesson" took you higher and higher in a
jet plane as you watched the world become smaller and
smaller. "Early Theories of Flight" reported on ways people
first tried to get themselves into the air.

You have already practiced writing a research report. Now
use what you have learned to do one or more of the following
activities.

1. Report on the early theories of . . . . You read about some of
   people's first attempts to fly. Now find out about the first
   attempts to do something else, such as heating homes, keeping food cold, recording music, or performing surgery.
   Write a research report about it.

2. Report on something that flies. What are some of the things
   that fly? There are birds, bats, insects, gliders, and model
   planes, for example. Write a research report about something that flies. Be sure to tell how it flies.

3. Report on a symbolic animal. The eagle is a symbol for
   strength and majesty. Other animals, such as the lion and
   the dove, have become symbols for other qualities. Write a
   research report on one of these animals to tell why it sym-
   bolizes what it does.

Boxed reminder

Running unit title

Remember these things ☑
- Be sure your topic is narrow enough.
- Plan and organize your report.
- Present your ideas clearly.
- Use transitional words and phrases.

Writing Across the Curriculum
Space Exploration

Few fields of study have developed as rapidly as astronautics, the science and technology of space flight. Scientists hope that their research in space may have many useful applications to life on Earth.

Choose one or more of the following activities.

Color-coded section guide

Repeated section title

Subheading relations keyed by size

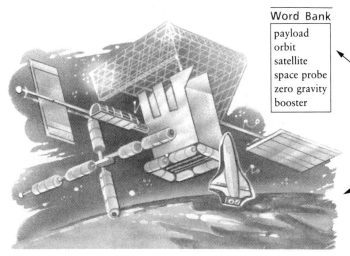

Word Bank

payload
orbit
satellite
space probe
zero gravity
booster

Key word box

Stimulus drawing

1. **Research space stations.** In the future, space stations (manned satellites that orbit Earth) will become more common. Research to find out what the major purposes of space stations are and will be. What effect will these space stations have on life on Earth? Illustrate your report.
2. **Travel with Voyager 2.** In 1977 Voyager 2 was launched to probe and study the distant planets. During its travels it made numerous discoveries. Research these discoveries. You might want to include a map of Voyager 2's journey through the solar system.
3. **Research the spin-offs.** Many space-related inventions have been modified for use on Earth through NASA's Technology Utilization Program. Research to find at least five of these technological spin-offs. Find out how they are being used. What has been their effect on our lives on Earth?

outset. Last, you can ask students to compose such an organizer after they read. This is an excellent writing activity in which the students' task is to prepare the next group of students for what lies ahead in the selection. Exemplary organizers can be saved for future use.

Factual Information   For some reading selections, specific facts are needed for adequate comprehension. As we have mentioned, there are two principal reasons that such information was not included in the selection. One is that the author is unable to anticipate the prior knowledge limitations of students. The second is that the selection may have been originally intended for a different readership. It is up to the teacher to determine which information is likely to be needed.

As an illustration of how a single fact, provided in advance, can significantly enhance comprehension, read the following maxims written by La Rochefoucauld, a French nobleman of the seventeenth century. See if you can discern his single guiding principle.

- If you judge love by most of its results, it seems more akin to hate than to friendship.
- For most of mankind, love of justice is nothing more than the fear of suffering injustice.
- To refuse praise means that you want to be praised twice.
- For most of mankind, gratitude is no more than a secret wish to receive even greater benefits.
- Moderation has been made a virtue in order to curb the ambition of the great, and also to console those who are mediocre in either fortune or merit.
- We admit our small failings only in order to persuade others that we have no greater ones.
- We would often be ashamed of our finest acts if the world were aware of the motives behind them.

It is easy enough to recognize that La Rochefoucauld was a cynic, but it is more difficult to summarize his philosophy. Actually, one of his maxims formed the entire basis of his book of such sayings, which he expanded several times during his life:

Most frequently, our virtues are but vices in disguise.

If you will reexamine the maxims introduced previously, you will note that each is in reality a special case of this statement. How much easier your initial reading would have been had we informed you of this fact beforehand!

Anecdotes   Occasionally a reading selection can be made more engaging, more personal, and more comprehensible when the teacher offers a brief story in advance. The story might involve the author, it might represent some historical oddity not in itself very important, or it might concern the teacher's experiences. The benefits of anecdotes in terms of motivation and comprehension easily outweigh the short time needed to tell them. Their use requires teachers to draw on their own knowledge of the content, which is likely to be much more extensive and diverse than what is included in a given reading selection.

Anecdotes can be used with virtually any topic, even one as dry (in our opinion) as the rectangular coordinate system used to plot points on a graph. In the seventeenth century, this system was invented one morning by the French philosopher Descartes, who was lying in bed watching a fly crawl across the ceiling of his room. "No matter where that fly is on the ceiling," Descartes remarked to himself, "I can describe its position with two numbers." He proceeded to develop the Cartesian coordinate system, which forms the basis of analytic geometry and calculus. All because of a fly! Such a story could do much to enliven a topic that students might otherwise find uninspiring.

Analogies   Abstract ideas are often so far removed from the experiences of students that they prove difficult to grasp. This may even be so when the writing itself is competent and considerate. An effective strategy can be the introduction of an analogy to enable students to compare a new, abstract idea with one that is familiar and concrete (Hayes & Tierney, 1982).

Imagine, for example, that a biology teacher is about to begin a unit on the digestive system. A good way of prefacing what the students will read is to compare this system with an automobile. (Gasoline is the equivalent of food, the motor the equivalent of muscles, exhaust the counterpart of body waste, and so forth.) We have made frequent use of this device in writing this text—for instance, our military analogy at the beginning of Chapter 4. While authors of content materials often attempt to build analogies into their own writing, it is advisable to be on the lookout for useful comparisons whenever you deal with your discipline. When you come across one, or produce an original, make a note of it for future use with your students.

> *Analogies prove nothing, that is quite true, but they can make one feel more at home.*
>
> Sigmund Freud

We offer one caution concerning the possible "side effects" of analogies. Spiro (1991) warns that analogies can have such a powerful effect on thinking that some students may find it difficult to learn detailed information in cases where it does not conform to the original analogy suggested by the teacher. His solution is not to avoid analogies but rather to use *more than one* wherever appropriate. Suggesting to students the limitations of an analogy may also be helpful.

Marginalia   Marginal notes, sometimes called glosses, represent a good way of providing additional background information at the precise moment it is needed by students as they read. Marginalia can include definitions, restatements of complex information, additional background notes, synonyms for difficult terms, and so forth. A recent trend has involved the inclusion of such glosses in textbooks as they are written. For other texts, the teacher can supply marginalia. Since the task must be done by hand, it may seem formidable, but we suggest the following guidelines for making it a realistic way of building background:

1. Analyze your text for difficult terminology, unclear statements of important ideas, and points at which added background might be helpful to students.
2. Write appropriate marginalia into your own copy of the text as a master.
3. During your planning days just prior to the start of school, transcribe your glosses into several (but not all) student copies. An aide or student volunteer could assist.
4. When school begins, identify those students most at risk of failing to comprehend assigned reading. Use the techniques described in Chapter 3.
5. Make sure that the glossed copies are distributed to these students.
6. Take them aside, privately, and explain that you were the person responsible for the notes. Explain their purpose and convey the expectation that the students will read the notes in the course of reading each assignment.

An alternative to writing directly onto the pages of the book is to prepare gloss sheets (Richgels & Hansen, 1984). The results might be called portable footnotes. These offer the advantage of easy availability to all students but at the same time require a conscious effort to use. We suspect notes written on the actual pages of a book are more likely to be read.

Props   Physical objects can occasionally provide a visual referent that will enhance comprehension enormously. Such props might include the following:

- a three-dimensional model of a DNA molecule
- a terrarium or aquarium
- conic sections used in geometry
- a miniature representation of a theater stage
- a Native American artifact
- a map, diagram, painting, or photograph not reproduced in the text

- a box of black and white marbles used to teach probability
- audio or video tapes, films, filmstrips, records, CDs
- naturally occurring objects (wood, rocks, plants, animals, etc.)
- scientific equipment (telescope, barometer, etc.)

The list is endless. These examples illustrate the variety of ways in which props can be used to introduce written material. As in the case of anecdotes, their use can be attention getting but requires that teachers draw on personal knowledge of the discipline.

SUMMARY

Prior knowledge of a subject is always needed in some degree if we are to comprehend what we read. This is true because new knowledge must be stored in connection with existing memory structures. Authors inevitably make certain assumptions about the prior knowledge of their readers. When too much is assumed, comprehension suffers. Authors who are sensitive to the possible background limitations of their readers produce what has come to be called considerate writing, but even these authors cannot completely anticipate the prior knowledge needs of individual readers.

It is therefore important for teachers to consider the assumptions an author has made in writing a selection—to assess what the author assumes. In particular, references to previous material should be noted, new vocabulary should be inspected in terms of links with previously introduced words, and important references not fully explained should be identified.

It is equally important for teachers to gain a clear idea of how much students actually know about the topics contained in a selection. Many techniques are available for making assessments of this kind, including asking students to use free recall to tell what they know about a topic, providing word associations, asking structured questions that grow successively more specific, posing written multiple-choice questions that may help to identify misconceptions, conducting unstructured discussions whereby students can relate their previous experiences, and presenting writing tasks that require students to recall and apply their prior knowledge.

Because new content is learned in association with existing knowledge, it is important for the teacher to activate, or "switch on," relevant prior knowledge. A traditional way of doing so is to conduct a brief review of material if the selection to be read is a continuation of a topic already being studied. A second method is Langer's PreReading Plan (PReP). Step one involves conducting a brief discussion, in which students begin to organize their prior knowledge; associations with key concepts are generated; the associations are carefully inspected and reformulated if need be. In the second step the teacher analyzes what students have contributed to the discussion and judges just how thorough their knowledge is. A third technique is to present students with structured writing tasks calling on them to recall and apply their prior knowledge. Writing can serve both to assess *and* activate prior knowledge.

It is also important for teachers to add knowledge assumed by the writer but not available to the reader. Numerous effective methods of enchancing prior knowledge have been developed. In organizational walk-throughs, the teacher may discuss the formats an author has used to structure the writing. The Visual Reading Guide (VRG) is an alternative that focuses on the visual aids incorporated into the selection. An overall approach, including both organizational patterns and visual aids, has been suggested by Aukerman (1972). Other methods of building background prior to reading include using advance organizers; introducing facts assumed but not provided by the author; telling anecdotes that may personalize, clarify, and enliven the topic; offering analogies by which abstract new concepts can be related to concrete familiar concepts; using marginalia to fortify a textbook for those students whose prior knowledge is apt to be weak; and presenting props, including physical models, artifacts, audio-visual materials, and so forth.

G E T T I N G   I N V O L V E D

1. Choose a reading selection you plan to use with your students at some point in the future. (You may have done so through the Getting Involved section of Chapter 4.) If you are not now teaching, select an article or work of literature you might be likely to assign. Analyze the selection in terms of (1) references to other materials, (2) new terms introduced, and (3) references not fully explained. Develop methods of preparing your students for these potential problem areas by using the suggestions made in this chapter.

2. Using the same selection, develop a set of structured questions designed to assess students' prior knowledge of the content. Remember that the first question is quite general and that each succeeding question is more specific and requires more extensive background. The questions should be logically linked so that each one is related in some way to the one before.

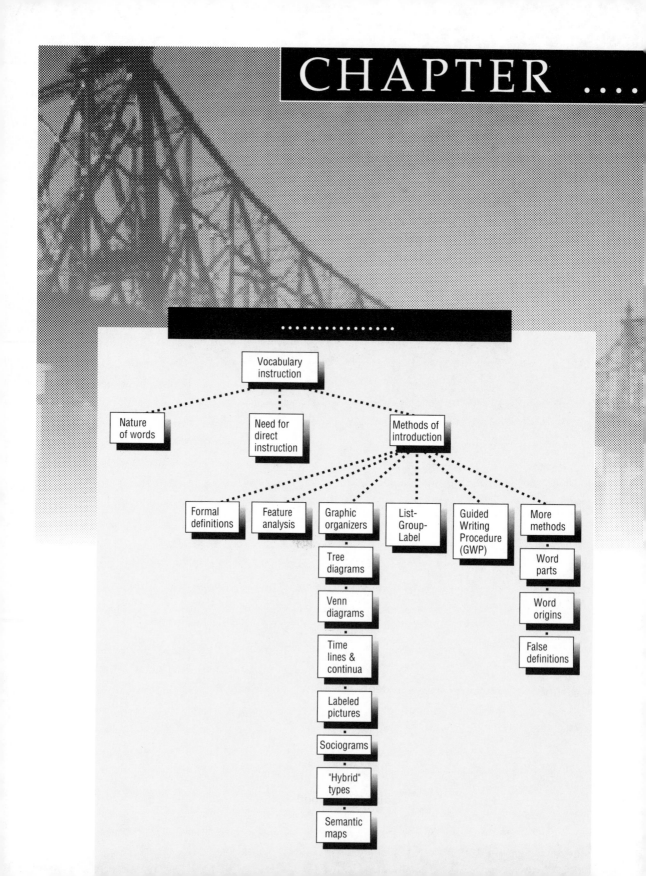

Vocabulary
instruction

Nature
of words

Need for
direct
instruction

Methods of
introduction

Formal
definitions

Feature
analysis

Graphic
organizers

List-
Group-
Label

Guided
Writing
Procedure
(GWP)

More
methods

Tree
diagrams

Word
parts

Venn
diagrams

Word
origins

Time
lines &
continua

False
definitions

Labeled
pictures

Sociograms

"Hybrid"
types

Semantic
maps

SIX

Introducing Technical
Vocabulary

"When I use a word," Humpty Dumpty said in a rather scornful tone, "it means just what I choose it to mean—neither more nor less."
Lewis Carroll, Through the Looking Glass

One of the more painful memories many people have of their early school experiences is the vocabulary lesson. You may recall being faced with a list of words and their definitions and being asked by your teacher to associate one with the other. The words may have had little relationship to one another or, if they did, such relationships were lost because the words were presented randomly, in list form. We suggest that the memories of such experiences may be painful because this approach to vocabulary instruction tends to be inefficient and tedious. Research indicates that the most effective methods of introducing new words involve introducing them in groups that share some characteristic or relationship (Nagy & Anderson, 1984).

Research has also confirmed the need to introduce terminology *before* students read, as a means of removing roadblocks to comprehension. No matter which of the global lesson designs you select, there is a place for the introduction of new key words prior to reading.

Let us consider two teachers who are preparing to introduce such terms. One is a language arts teacher who will ask the students to read "The Gold Bug," a short story by Edgar Allan Poe. The teacher carefully lists all the words likely to be unfamiliar to the students—words like *mortification, consequent, palmetto,* and *horticulturists* (all from the first page!). The teacher writes out a brief definition or common synonym for each of these terms and makes a transparency to introduce them to the students. The second teacher is a biology instructor about to assign a chapter devoted to insects. This teacher also looks through the material and lists terms that might be troublesome: *thorax, pupa, antennae,* and so forth.

While their actions were similar, there is a crucial difference in the lists of words produced by these two teachers. The biology teacher has concentrated on *key* terms—that is, the important new concepts introduced in the chapter. Many of the terms have natural relationships to one another, a feature making them easier to introduce, as we will see. The language arts teacher has listed words that, while useful to know, are not central to understanding the story. Moreover, they will prove very difficult to introduce (many transparencies will be needed!) because they lack logical relationships that link them together.

It is impossible to dissociate language from science or science from language, . . . To call forth a concept, a word is needed; to portray a phenomenon, a concept is needed. All three mirror one and the same reality.

Antoine Lavoisier

Of course, there is another difference in the assignments about to be made by these two teachers. One is nonfiction, a textbook chapter designed for the specific purpose of introducing important new terms that are linked in meaningful ways. The other is fiction, and its primary purpose is not to instruct. Even in the example of the short story, however, we suggest that there *are* key terms, concepts so central to understanding the story that they warrant brief discussion by the teacher prior to reading. Such terms would include the names of characters and places as well as any critical words not adequately defined in context.

Our point in contrasting these two teachers is that introducing key terminology during the prereading phase is important for any reading assignment. It is up to the teacher to decide *which* words to present and *how* to present them.

OBJECTIVES

Your reading of this chapter should improve your ability to make these kinds of decisions. Specifically, when you have finished, you should be able to

1. describe the nature and function of words and their relationship to human experience;

2. identify the two elements of a classical definition;

3. incorporate feature analysis into prereading discussions;

4. construct and use graphic organizers of various kinds; and

5. describe the Guided Writing Procedure, List-Group-Label and other techniques.

THE NATURE OF WORDS

Words are symbols for concepts. As we noted in Chapter 2, a schema is all the information and experiences that an individual has learned in association with a given concept. Your schema for "book" includes all your many experiences with having read and used books. It may include a formal definition and it probably involves emotional associations you tend to make with the notion of "books." Such a process, which depends heavily on personal experiences, obviously leads to differing conceptualizations of just what is meant by the word *book.* The written symbol itself does not "carry" meaning; rather, the reader *brings* meaning *to* the symbol (Smith, 1988).

Words therefore come to have many associations for us. Those associations concerned with the word's general meaning and which are likely to be shared by most users of the word are said to be *denotative.* The word's dictionary definition is sometimes called its denotation. Associations that are not directly connected to a word's denotative meaning are described as *connotative.* Such associations vary with individuals because their experiences vary. To some, the word *golf* might connote doctors, presidents, and country clubs. To others it might connote frustration, fatigue, and wasted hours. These diverse sets of connotations are not directly connected with what the word *golf* denotes. Both denotations and connotations are very much a part of a student's schema for a given word.

As students mature, their schemata for various concepts develop more fully and new concepts are continually added, each represented by a word. Research into vocabulary knowledge has suggested these rather startling facts:

> There is good reason to believe that the average high school senior's vocabulary is in the neighborhood of 40,000 words. Such vocabulary size estimates imply a tremendous volume of word learning, around 3,000 words per year during the school years. This astounding rate of vocabulary growth by average children sets a mark against which the contribution of any program of vocabulary instruction must be measured. (Nagy & Herman, 1984, p. 6)

If each of these newly acquired concepts were associated with only one visual symbol (word), vocabulary learning would be difficult enough. It is complicated, however, by the fact that many concepts may share the same visual word. Vocabulary users must be able to distinguish which of several meanings is the intended one, and problems can result when a reader's knowledge and experiences are limited to definitions not intended by a writer. As an extreme case, consider the following:

> When they took their sixth wicket in the 30th over, there appeared to be some hope for Surrey. But when the fly slip couldn't stop Allan Warner's drive from becoming a four, Derbyshire looked in good nick, and Geoffrey Miller's 4-bye in 38 was sufficient to make sure Surrey was pipped at the post. (Margolis, 1990, p. 3)

Unless you happen to be familiar with the game of cricket, this paragraph has little if any meaning for you. The difficulty in understanding the example is not entirely because the vocabulary is unusual; for most readers it does not bring to mind any previous experiences with the topic being discussed.

Many of the technical terms likely to be introduced in content areas have everyday meanings that can distract and confuse students. Such words as *set, field,* and *ring,* for example, have highly specific applications in mathematics, meanings that have little or no relationship to their more common ones.

Introducing vocabulary must therefore account for, and build on, the past experiences of students (Duffelmeyer, 1985). Techniques must be sought that relate new vocabulary to old and that stress the interrelationships among words. We shall discuss several major techniques for accomplishing this aim, but first it is necessary to dispel a myth that frequently surrounds vocabulary acquisition.

THE MYTH THAT WORDS TEACH THEMSELVES

Many adults, including a great many teachers, are convinced that deliberate teaching of new terms is largely unnecessary. This belief may in part be the result of ineffective teaching episodes recalled from past experiences, episodes based on the teaching of words one by one, in relative isolation. They account for knowing so many words by having met each word in their vocabulary countless times in a variety of contexts. They believe that, over a long period, these repeated exposures allow an individual to internalize word meanings.

The difficulty with this notion is that it is partly true. We suggest, for example, that no one directly taught you the word *book,* certainly not by stating its formal definition for you to remember. Instead, you learned what a book is by encountering numerous examples, both physical (that is, books you came across in the real world and that others referred to as "books") and linguistic (uses of the word *book* to describe books that were not actually present). By exposure to so many examples of books, you were able to arrive at certain generalizations about what makes a book a book. Your conceptualization became more fully developed with each new example you encountered. This is an *inductive* approach to vocabulary acquisition, in which general rules or characteristics are inferred from numerous examples.

The meanings of many common words are acquired inductively. It may therefore be natural to suppose that such a method is adequate for introducing virtually all new words. That is, it is easy to assume that by providing students with enough contexts (both physical and linguistic) in which a word is encountered, a teacher can assure conceptualization. This assumption has three major difficulties.

First, research has revealed that context is often not very useful at helping students infer new word meanings (Schatz & Baldwin, 1986). Context is always helpful at narrowing the range of possible meanings a word might have, but it is seldom sufficient to allow a reader (or listener) to conceptualize the meaning of a word not previously encountered.

But in an inductive approach, one can argue, the student is confronted by so many instances that the deficiencies of any particular occasion will be offset by others. The result would be adequate conceptualization. This reasoning leads to the second difficulty: Such conceptualizations are often inadequate, even after innumerable encounters with a word in context. The notion of a "book," which we have used as a familiar, thoroughly internalized concept, is probably not rigorously conceptualized at all. You would have no difficulty classifying a hard-bound volume like this one as a book, but there are less clear examples that would challenge how precise your idea is. If the cover were removed, would it still be a book? What if the spine were severed so that it became a stack of unattached pages? What about its word-processed form on $3^1/_2$-inch diskettes? The content is, after all, the same, but is it a "book" in that form? Despite your many encounters with the word, the notion of a book remains a bit murky. This circumstance may be acceptable in a case like *book,* but with technical terms possessing precise definitions and important features distinguishing them from related terms, this lack of precision is unacceptable.

The last difficulty with the inductive approach is that many technical terms are not encountered frequently enough to expose students to an adequate number of examples. For instance, the following terms, associated with the content of science and art, were estimated by Nagy and Anderson (1984) to occur less than three times in a billion words of text:

ammeter
cyanide
anneal
template
fresco
ventilate

To argue that the student will encounter such words with far greater frequency while studying them in a given course is true, but the number of repetitions needed for induction to occur may still not be reached. Nor do the authors of textbooks used in these courses rely on the inductive approach. Rather, they tend to introduce new terms along with formal definitions, an approach we consider in the following section.

FORMAL DEFINITIONS

When a teacher (or text) introduces a new word by stating its definition and then offering examples that may or may not conform to the definition, the approach is *deductive.* In deductive instruction, learners progress from a general rule (in this case, a definition) to the consideration of individual examples (here, encounters with the word in contextual settings).

Aristotle suggested that the formal definition of a noun should contain two elements: (1) the class, or category, to which the concept belongs and (2) specific features that allow us to distinguish examples of the concept from any other member of the category. Consider the following definition of the word *hammer:*

a tool for driving nails

We see that any hammer is a member of the larger category, tools, and that we can distinguish a hammer from other tools by its primary function, driving nails. If other tools were used to drive nails, it would be necessary to add more specific features. Plato, half in jest, once defined a man as simply "a two-legged animal." When a friend good-naturedly pointed out that this definition would not enable him to distinguish a man from a chicken, Plato modified his definition: "a two-legged animal without feathers."

Knowing the nature of formal, or classical, definitions can assist teachers in a number of ways. First, the class and distinguishing features can be identified for the students as the definition is presented. Schwartz (1988) has suggested that content teachers take the few moments required to acquaint students with the two elements of classical definitions (see also Schwartz & Raphael, 1985). Second, students can be asked to *construct* formal definitions once they know the two required components. They begin by selecting the category to which a concept belongs and then proceed to add features that would allow it to be distinguished from other category members. They can then compare their definitions with those of a dictionary or glossary. Finally, knowledge of the classical components of a definition makes possible a number of recent techniques that have proved highly effective in the introduction and reinforcement of vocabulary. We now examine these approaches.

FEATURE ANALYSIS

When introducing a group of concepts all of which are members of the same category, a teacher can employ an efficient approach called feature analysis. This technique makes use of a simple chart, like that in Figure 6.1. In the upper left-hand corner of the chart, the name of the category is written. The category members are written in the first column. Across the top of the chart, the column headings are various features that each concept might or might not possess. The chart is completed by placing a "+" in a particular position if the concept on that row has the feature for that column. If not, a "0" is indicated. Some teachers find the letter "s" helpful if the concept *sometimes* has that feature.

The feature analysis chart permits comparisons of any pair of concepts by noting features shared, features possessed by only one of the concepts, and features possessed by neither concept. The chart also facilitates the analysis of each feature by considering which concepts possess it.

The relationship of feature analysis to formal definitions is obvious. Both are ways of considering a concept in relation to its category membership and its key features. From a completed feature analysis chart, definitions of the concepts could actually be written. From Figure 6.1, the following definition of the word *hacksaw* can be composed:

> a tool used for cutting metal and consisting of a thin blade attached to a C-shaped frame

This is close to the dictionary definition, though some of the definitions composed from a feature analysis chart tend to be longer and more awkward. Nevertheless, the two required elements are present: the category and distinguishing features. Definition construction is an excellent writing activity that can be used to follow up a reading assignment that has been introduced by means of feature analysis.

The link between feature analysis and formal definitions has an important implication for determining which features to include in a chart. If any two concepts have the same set of codings ("+," "0," and "s"), the chart is incomplete. Note that in Figure 6.1 there is no way to distinguish a Phillips-head screwdriver from a traditional flathead screwdriver. The codings

FIGURE 6.1

Class: Tools	For driving nails	For inserting screws into wood	For gripping with leverage	For cutting metal	Has c-shaped frame	No movable parts
Hammer	+	0	s	0	0	+
Phillips-head screwdriver	0	+	0	0	0	+
Flathead screwdriver	0	+	0	0	0	+
Hacksaw	0	0	0	+	+	+
Pliers	0	0	+	0	0	0
. . .						

Note: A plus indicates the tool has the feature; a zero indicates it does not; "s" indicates it sometimes has the feature.

Feature analysis chart based on tools

are identical. The chart must be expanded by adding one more feature concerned with the tips of these tools—for example, "has a flat, blade-like end." The coding would then differ for the two concepts.

Feature analysis is not limited to a particular subject or even to technical terminology in the usual sense. For example, a useful chart involving characters from a short story or novel, analyzed by character traits, is quite possible. Such charts are so useful and versatile that we offer a black-line master in Figure 6.2 that can be duplicated as needed.

GRAPHIC ORGANIZERS

In Chapter 2, we used graphic organizers to depict how a student's schemata for concepts might be represented. Since memory is structured this way, doesn't it make sense to use an instructional technique that builds on that structure?

A graphic organizer is a diagram showing how key concepts are related. While diagrams of this sort have existed for years, Barron (1969) first suggested their use for introducing related clusters of new terms. He viewed the graphic organizer as a streamlined version of the advance organizer, a technique pioneered by Ausubel (1960) and consisting of a prose introduction to a reading assignment. Research has demonstrated that graphic organizers tend to be more effective in presenting new terms than was Ausubel's technique (Moore & Readence, 1980). Crawley (1988) has suggested that one reason for their effectiveness is that they help us visualize abstract concepts. When we read narratives, we usually have no difficulty envisioning the events. Expository writing is a different matter, however, and students often need an assist. It should not be surprising that Bos and Anders (1989a, 1989b) found in a series of studies that semantic maps (a special kind of graphic organizer we'll discuss presently) were significantly more effective with learning-disabled students than direct instruction in definitions alone. Visualizing the interconnectedness of new concepts is likely to aid any population of students.

Types of Graphic Organizers

Barron's original notion of graphic organizers (1969) entailed only one type, the tree diagram. Fry (1981), however, has demonstrated the great variety of diagrammatic forms available. We will consider a few of the most broadly useful types.

Tree Diagrams   When some of the concepts to be taught represent subdivisions of other, broader concepts, the relationship can be depicted by means of a branching arrangement known as a tree diagram. The branching usually runs downward so that one encounters smaller and smaller subdivisions as one moves down the page. (These "trees" grow upside-down!) Figure 6.3 (p. 110) depicts how a large concept, musical instruments, could be delineated into subconcepts. (Broken lines indicate undeveloped portions of the diagram.)

FIGURE 6.2

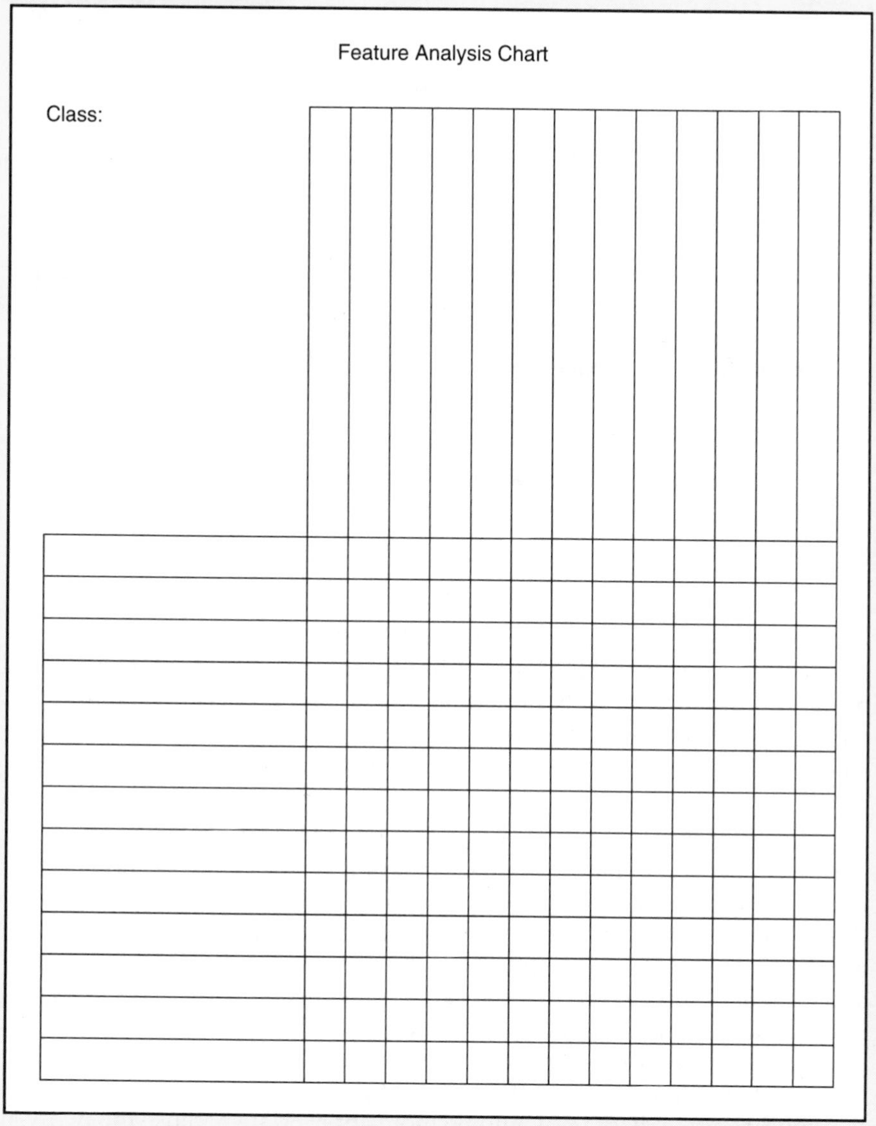

Feature Analysis Chart

Class:

Master feature analysis chart for duplication

Because so many concepts bear this sort of relationship, it was perhaps natural for tree diagrams to be developed first, as a principal type of organizer. Some have argued that much of human knowledge is organized in this hierarchical fashion, and Figure 6.4 (p. 111) illustrates how biologists systematize the classification of organisms. It is reasonably clear that semantic memory (our personal store of concepts) is organized as a network of

FIGURE 6.3

Graphic organizer:
Tree diagram for
musical instruments

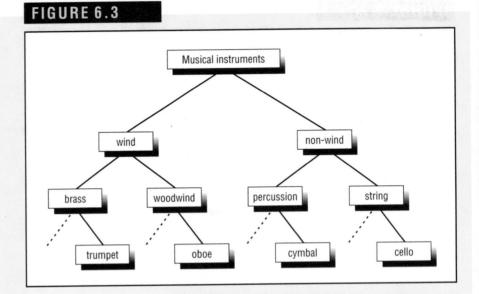

associations that can be diagrammed in this way. The biology teacher who constructs a portion of Figure 6.4 on the chalkboard as a new plant or animal is being introduced is actually providing instruction that is consistent with the nature of memory. Imagine how useful such a framework might be to the student struggling to relate species after species encountered in class.

Venn Diagrams   When concepts cannot be broken down cleanly into narrower concepts—that is, when overlapping is possible—a Venn diagram may be helpful in depicting the relationships. This device is borrowed from mathematical set theory and employs overlapping circles to represent related concepts. Figure 6.5 illustrates the relationship between "liberals" and "Republicans." An individual can be classified in three ways: (1) as a non-Republican liberal (the left-hand crescent), (2) as a nonliberal Republican (the right-hand crescent), or (3) as a liberal Republican (the overlapping, football-shaped intersection). If it were not possible to be both a liberal and a Republican, a tree diagram would be more appropriate because the two Venn circles would not overlap.

To illustrate this difference, consider a science textbook chapter on birds. Assume that the author has employed a very simple organizational pattern in which each species is discussed in succession. If we choose two of the concepts (say, turkeys and robins), we might depict the relationship by means of the simple tree diagram in Figure 6.6 (p. 112). The division is clear-cut in that it is impossible for a bird to be both a turkey and a robin. If we used a Venn diagram, the result would be Figure 6.7, showing lack of overlap.

FIGURE 6.4

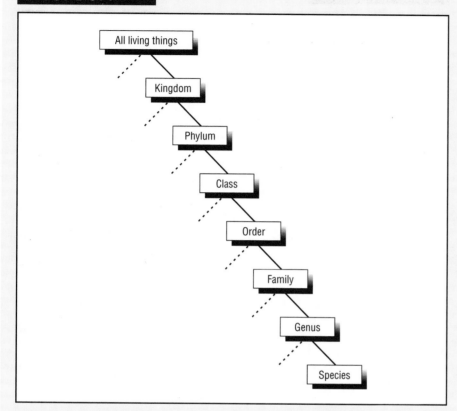

Graphic organizer: Tree diagram for biological classification system

FIGURE 6.5

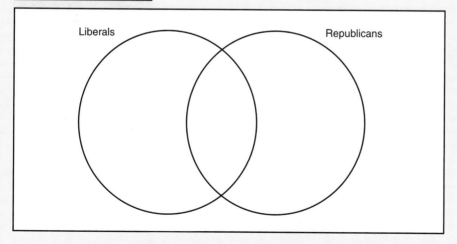

Graphic organizer: Venn diagram for liberals and Republicans.

FIGURE 6.6

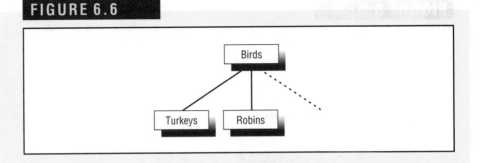

Graphic organizer:
Bird example with a
tree diagram approach

A special kind of Venn diagram is useful in depicting concepts that are contained (or "nested") within other concepts. Figure 6.8 illustrates the nested nature of number systems, for example. It is true that we could have used this arrangement in our bird example, as in Figure 6.9 (p.114), but the nested Venn diagram is useful primarily in cases of *successively* nested concepts, as in the case of number systems.

Time Lines and Other Continua.   When concepts are related along some linear dimension, they can be effectively presented by means of a very simple organizer. Time lines, such as the one depicted in Figure 6.10, are appropriate whenever the terms are related by chronology. When specific dates are known, the line can be marked off accordingly. When they are not, as in a novel, a time line can still be used to sequence the key events (Figure 6.11, p. 115).

FIGURE 6.7

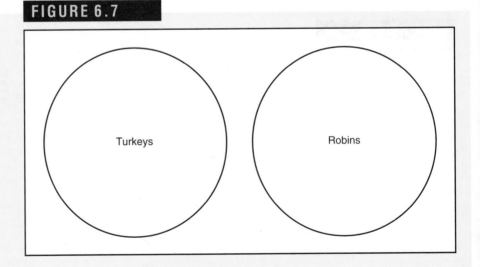

Graphic organizer:
Bird example with a
Venn diagram approach

FIGURE 6.8

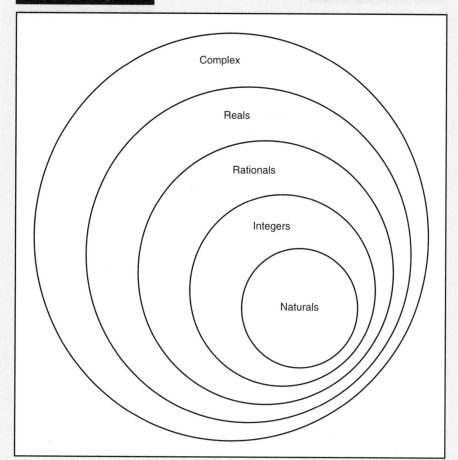

Graphic organizer:
Nested Venn diagram
for number systems

Variations of time lines depart from the traditional left-to-right straight-line arrangement. Figure 6.12 (p. 115) illustrates how the biology teacher we described at the beginning of the chapter might have presented one cluster of closely related terms. Figure 6.13 (p. 116) exemplifies a variation of the time line developed by computer scientists: the flowchart. Flowcharts are useful whenever decision points are encountered in a repeatable process.

Straight lines (surely the simplest type of diagram!) can be used to represent nearly any continuum and are not limited to time. Figure 6.14 is sometimes used by social studies teachers to introduce the concepts associated with political philosophies. Well-known politicians might be added to the scale at points determined by the students to be appropriate. A music teacher

FIGURE 6.9

Graphic organizer:
Bird example with a
nested Venn diagram

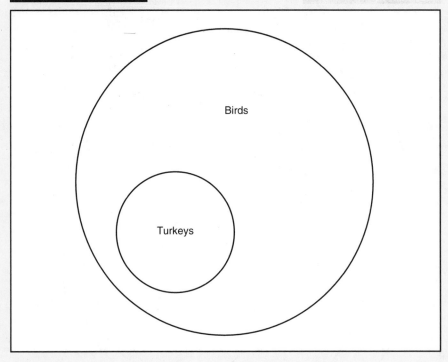

Birds

Turkeys

FIGURE 6.10

Graphic organizer: Time
line over World War II

1930	1940	1950

FDR

WW II

FIGURE 6.11

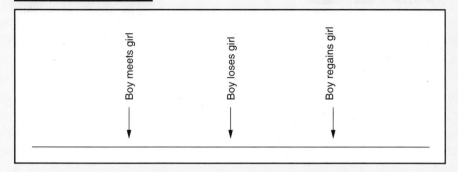

Graphic organizer: Time line without specific dates

FIGURE 6.12

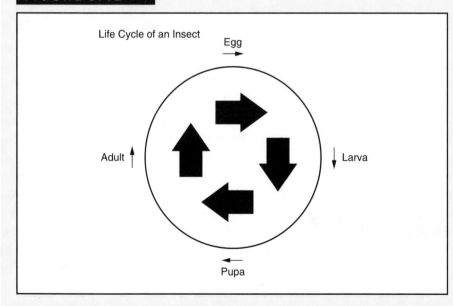

Graphic organizer: Variation of a time line

FIGURE 6.13

Graphic organizer:
Flowchart for a
mathematical process

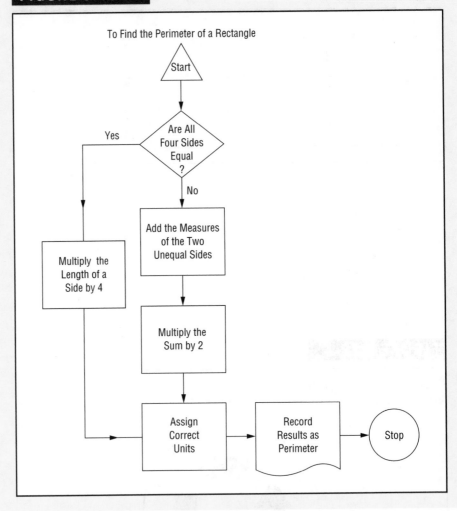

To Find the Perimeter of a Rectangle

FIGURE 6.14

Graphic organizer:
Continuum showing
political orientations

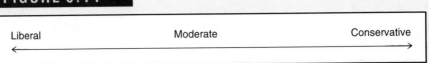

FIGURE 6.15

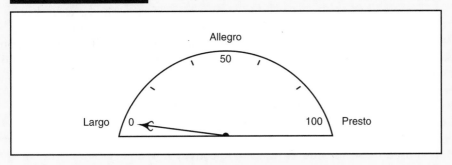

Graphic organizer: A musical "speedometer" (some elements omitted)

developed the "speedometer" depicted in Figure 6.15 to demonstrate the distinctions among the Italian terms used by composers to indicate the pace at which a piece is to be played. The diagram was posted as a reference chart on the band-room wall behind the podium.

Labeled Pictures   When a cluster of terms is related chiefly by the *location* of the things to which they refer, a picture with the terms as labels can be highly effective. Consider again the biology teacher about to assign a chapter on insects. Some of the terms to be introduced may represent the main body parts of any insect. The labeled picture in Figure 6.16 presents these terms in an extremely efficient way.

FIGURE 6.16

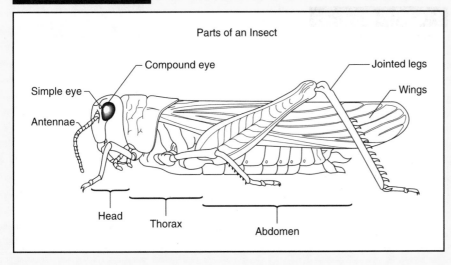

Graphic organizer: Labeled picture of insect parts

We suspect that the oldest form of graphic organizer is a map. Note that maps serve the function of graphic organizers perfectly: They present key terms (the names of places) in a diagram depicting their most important interrelationships (location). Imagine the task of converting all the information contained in an ordinary highway map into the form of prose. Volumes would be required!

Sociograms   When the terms to be introduced represent people or groups of people linked by social relationships, a sociogram can be used to depict these relationships diagrammatically. Figure 6.17 contains an organizer often used by social studies teachers to convey how the system of checks and balances operates among the three branches of government. The arrows represent methods of exercising power or influence. Sociograms vary widely in nature but are always designed to depict some form of social relationship. The organizer used in Figure 2.1 depicts a very specific relationship linking a reader and a writer in the social process of written communication.

"Hybrid" Types   Some graphic organizers combine the characteristics of more than one basic type. The family tree in Figure 6.18 (pp. 120–121), for example, was provided at the beginning of Vladimir Nabokov's lengthy novel *Ada*. (Note that the key terms in fiction tend to be names of characters.) The organizer has the appearance of a tree diagram (it is a *family* tree, after all), but it differs from most in that large concepts are not delineated into narrower components. It is, in some respects, a time line since the generations progress in time from top to bottom, but it is also a sociogram in that it portrays familial

FIGURE 6.17

Graphic organizer:
Sociogram for checks and
balances among the three
branches of government

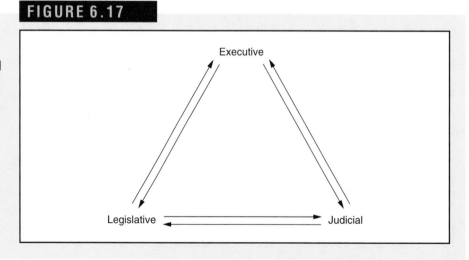

relationships. In constructing a graphic organizer, it is less important to stick with one of the conventional types described here than to produce a diagram that effectively communicates the relationships that link concepts.

Semantic Maps   A more open-ended approach to graphic organizers is the semantic map (e.g., see Johnson & Pearson, 1984). Open-endedness means that students contribute to the map as it is being constructed by the teacher on a chalkboard, overhead, or wall chart. Stahl and Vancil (1986) offer a description of how semantic maps are used (see Figure 6.19, p. 122):

> In semantic mapping, a teacher chooses a key word and other target words from material that the students will read. The key word is listed on the board and students are asked to suggest terms associated with the key word. The teacher writes the suggested words in a list on the board as the students suggest them.
>
> From this list, a map is constructed. The relationships between the key word and the target words are discussed thoroughly. Students are then asked to try to categorize each section of the map.
>
> A copy of an incomplete semantic map is next handed out to the students. They are asked to fill in the words from the map on the board and any other additional categories or words they can add. . . .
>
> The reading is assigned, with instructions for students to work on their maps during reading. After reading, the maps are discussed once more and new terms and categories are added.
>
> In the map shown, the categories and boldfaced words were provided.
>
> The other words listed were student contributions and their relation to the categories and the boldfaced words were discussed in class. The blank category was filled in by a number of students after reading. (pp. 62, 64)

Semantic mapping offers an interesting alternative to the use of preplanned, conventional graphic organizers. It has the advantage of encouraging student involvement during the introduction of words and of helping students discern relationships between new terms and those previously encountered. Not surprisingly, the research base underlying semantic mapping supports its effectiveness (e.g., Johnson, Toms-Bronowski, & Pittelman, 1982; Johnson, Pittelman, Toms-Bronowski, & Levin, 1984; Margosein, Pascarella, & Pflaum, 1982; Pittelman, Levin & Johnson, 1985; Stahl & Vancil, 1986).

FIGURE 6.18

Graphic organizer based
on Nabokov's *Ada*

SOURCE: From *Ada or
Ardor: A Family Chronicle*
(pp. viii–ix) by Vladimir
Nabokov. Copyright
©1967 by McGraw-Hill
International. Reprinted by
permission of the Estate
of Vladimir Nabokov.

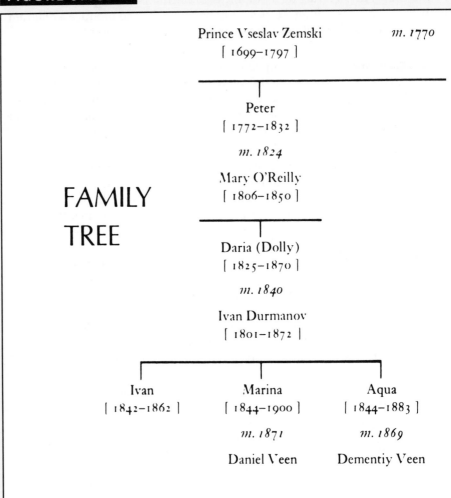

FAMILY
TREE

Prince Vseslav Zemski   *m. 1770*
[1699–1797]

Peter
[1772–1832]

m. 1824

Mary O'Reilly
[1806–1850]

Daria (Dolly)
[1825–1870]

m. 1840

Ivan Durmanov
[1801–1872]

Ivan	Marina	Aqua
[1842–1862]	[1844–1900]	[1844–1883]
	m. 1871	*m. 1869*
	Daniel Veen	Dementiy Veen

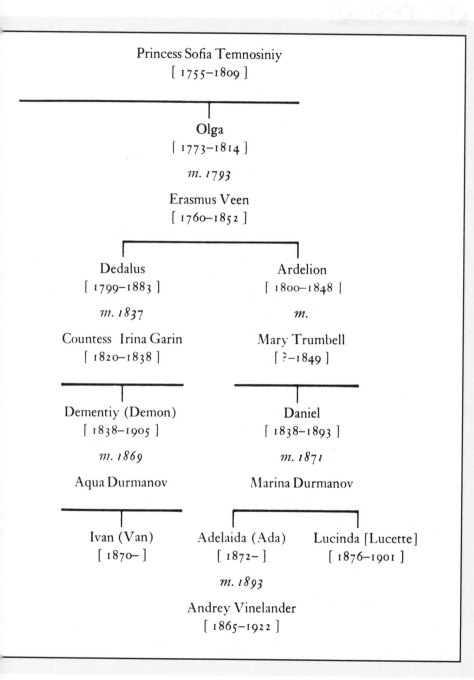

Princess Sofia Temnosiniy
[1755–1809]

Olga
[1773–1814]

m. 1793

Erasmus Veen
[1760–1852]

Dedalus
[1799–1883]

m. 1837

Countess Irina Garin
[1820–1838]

Ardelion
[1800–1848]

m.

Mary Trumbell
[?–1849]

Dementiy (Demon)
[1838–1905]

m. 1869

Aqua Durmanov

Daniel
[1838–1893]

m. 1871

Marina Durmanov

Ivan (Van)
[1870–]

Adelaida (Ada)
[1872–]

Lucinda [Lucette]
[1876–1901]

m. 1893

Andrey Vinelander
[1865–1922]

FIGURE 6.19

Graphic organizer:
Semantic map
over meteorology

SOURCE: From
"Discussion Is What
Makes Semantic Maps
Work in Vocabulary
Instruction" by Steven
Stahl and Sandra Vancil,
October 1986, *The
Reading Teacher, 40,* p.
63. Copyright 1986 by
the International Reading
Association. Reprinted
by permission of Steven
Stahl and the International
Reading Association.

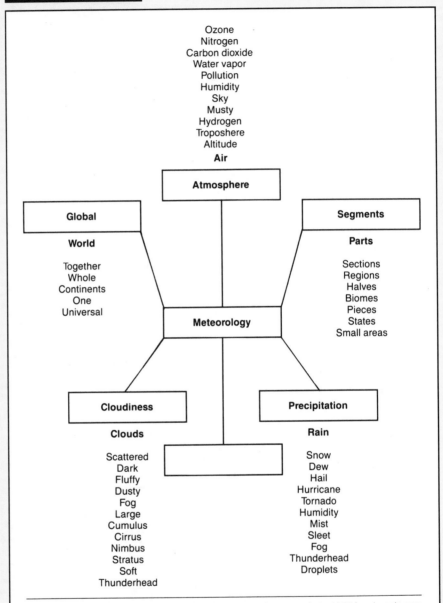

Ozone
Nitrogen
Carbon dioxide
Water vapor
Pollution
Humidity
Sky
Musty
Hydrogen
Troposhere
Altitude
Air

Atmosphere

Global

World

Together
Whole
Continents
One
Universal

Segments

Parts

Sections
Regions
Halves
Biomes
Pieces
States
Small areas

Meteorology

Cloudiness

Clouds

Scattered
Dark
Fluffy
Dusty
Fog
Large
Cumulus
Cirrus
Nimbus
Stratus
Soft
Thunderhead

Precipitation

Rain

Snow
Dew
Hail
Hurricane
Tornado
Humidity
Mist
Sleet
Fog
Thunderhead
Droplets

Words in boxes were taught directly. Bold faced words were given to students. Light faced words were contributed by students during discussion in the full map treatment; some had been taught in the preceding lesson on Clouds (*cumulus, cirrus, nimbus, stratus, water vapor, humidity*). The blank box was for students to fill in a new category during their reading.

The freewheeling nature of semantic maps offers a unique advantage as well. In addition to the vital links between the target word and its category membership, other associations can be attached as offshoots of the diagram. A word's connotations, for example, as supplied by students, can be added. The result, admittedly, can be a cluttered, weblike maze (semantic maps are often called webs), but they act in much the same way that a spider's web traps insects: The more strands the insect touches, the less likely it is to escape. Similarly, the more associations a teacher can provide for a new word, the more likely it is to remain in the student's memory.

Constructing Graphic Organizers

Many textbook authors have begun incorporating graphic organizers and other aids into prose material. In these cases it is merely a matter of discussing the diagram with students before they read. Where no organizer exists, one or more can be developed easily, and we offer the following steps.

1. *Make a list of key terms.* Such a list may have been produced by the textbook author/s, but it may be necessary to construct one. Do not be concerned with how long the list becomes. In fact, it is a good idea to include terms introduced in previous lessons that bear directly on the new content. Our biology teacher might have produced the following rough list.

pupa
thorax
abdomen
larva
egg
wings
head
adult
compound eye
simple eye
jointed legs

2. *Identify clusters of highly related terms.* Go through the list and mark terms that are highly related to one another. You may have several clusters in the overall list you constructed in step one. The idea is to construct a graphic organizer for each cluster (or for those clusters that organizers might in your judgment help to teach). Attempting to construct a single organizer incorporating all of the terms from the master list is nearly always a mistake because the interrelationships are too varied and complex. Simple diagrams are almost always more effective than complicated diagrams. The biology list would have been earmarked into clusters as shown.

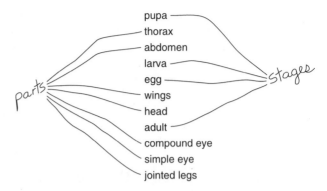

3. Choose a diagram type that reflects how the clustered terms are related. Study each word cluster. Ask yourself what the chief relationship is that links the terms together. The answer to this question will suggest the type of diagram that will be most useful in communicating this relationship. If the terms are related chronologically (steps in a process, phases, events), a time line is called for. This is true for one of our biology clusters and the result was Figure 6.12. If the terms represent people, groups, or institutions, a sociogram may be best. If the terms are hierarchically related, so that some are components, aspects, or examples of others, a tree diagram is suggested. When the terms are spatially related, a labeled picture (such as the one in Figure 6.16) is called for. This brief analysis is essential to the construction of a straightforward organizer that efficiently conveys the most important relationships.

Presenting Graphic Organizers

A sizable body of research has determined that graphic organizers are highly effective tools for helping students understand the important relationships that exist among technical concepts (Alvermann & Swafford, 1989). Researchers have therefore often looked at how best to use organizers. (The question of *whether* to use them has been answered affirmatively.)

Moore and Readence (1980) observed that while graphic organizers are effective devices for introducing vocabulary prior to reading, they may be even more effective when used *after* reading; accordingly, we reconsider their use in Chapter 10. Of course, these uses do not preclude one another: An organizer used to introduce terminology could be revisited following reading.

Darch, Carnine, and Kameenui (1986) contrasted the use of graphic organizers with groups of students and with individuals. They observed that group settings produce the best results, perhaps because of the contributions students might make to the discussion. Stahl and Vancil (1986) found indeed that *discussion* is a critical component during the introductory process. Students must become involved with the organizer—cognitively engaged in considering what it conveys—in order for learning to be maximized (Dinnel & Glover, 1985).

Reinking (1986) has indicated the need on the part of some students to learn exactly what graphic aids are for. Teachers should not take for granted that an organizer, perfectly comprehensible to them, will be equally meaningful to their students. A few moments spent in explaining how an organizer "works" and what its purpose is will be time well spent.

In summary, we offer the following tips regarding the most effective uses of graphic organizers:

1. Keep them simple.
2. Discuss them thoroughly while you present them.
3. Include previously encountered terms where appropriate.
4. Be flexible in using them before or after reading—or both.
5. Make use of organizers developed by others.

A final note with regard to the fifth point: Textbook authors are not the only source of existing graphic organizers. Consult other references within your field for ideas. These might include other texts, encyclopedias, technical dictionaries, and articles. An excellent general source of graphic organizers is Corbeil's *Visual Dictionary* (1986), an extensive volume devoted to a wide range of content areas from science to recreation.

LIST-GROUP-LABEL

Taba (1967) introduced a vocabulary method that may have its greatest utility in reviewing and activating word knowledge. For this reason, the technique is useful *after* new reading has been completed, as a means of refining and extending knowledge. It is useful *prior* to reading as a way of "switching on" words that are already familiar to the student and that will be linked to new terms in the assigned reading.

The teacher begins by suggesting to the class a major topic they have been studying. In the "list" stage, the teacher asks the students to brainstorm all the words they have learned in association with the topic. The teacher records these words on the board or transparency until 25 or 30 have been accumulated. In the "group" stage, the students work together to rearrange the words into categories. Finally, they "label" each category of words with an appropriate designation. Occasionally, some of the words may be left over without clear-cut category membership. The teacher should encourage students not to worry about these cases but to suggest instead category labels for each leftover term.

List-Group-Label has several notable strengths. It stresses the inter-relationships that exist among technical vocabulary words. It provides an environment for actively engaging students with the content (and is especially well suited to collaborative activities). It provides a good method of linking the new with the familiar.

GUIDED WRITING PROCEDURE (GWP)

Smith and Bean (1980) introduced a notable method of linking writing tasks with the study of vocabulary, the guided writing procedure (GWP). Moore, Readence, and Rickelman (1989) have suggested the following modification*:

● ●

Day One

1. Have students brainstorm what they know about an upcoming topic of study (volcanoes) and record their responses on a chalkboard or overhead transparency. A possible list follows.

Volcanoes

lava	Mt. St. Helens
destruction	eruption
ashes	crater
hot	dangerous
steam	fiery

2. Identify categories that encompass the brainstormed terms (physical qualities, descriptions, examples) and list details that support the category titles.

3. Represent the category titles and their details in forms such as an outline, web, or graphic organizer.

   I. Physical Qualities

      A. Crater

      B. Eruption

         1. lava

         2. ashes

         3. steam

*David Moore, John Readence, and Robert Rickelman, Prereading Activities for Content Area Reading and Learning, 1988, International Reading Association, pp. 67–68. Reprinted by permission of David Moore and the International Reading Association.

II. Description
    A. Fiery
        1. hot
    B. Dangerous
        1. destruction
III. Example
    A. Mt. St. Helens

4. Have students write about the topic, using the graphically presented information.

5. Have students read a passage related to the topic of study to determine how their papers could be expanded or modified. For example, students might search for additional information about the physical qualities of volcanoes.

Day Two

1. Display a few students' papers with an overhead projector. Examples of good and poor writing should be demonstrated; they might be selected from students not currently in class in order to avoid embarrassing anyone. Revise the papers according to content as well as two or three writing criteria.

Possible Writing Criteria

	High			Low
Passage Organization				
Informational Writing Major and minor points are distinguishable; topic sentence(s) are stated and supported with relevant details.	4	3	2	1
Narrative Stories Story plot has identifiable beginning, middle, and end with characters introduced, a problem, and a believable or logical solution.	4	3	2	1
Engagement The paper grasps the reader's attention by presenting vivid language in imaginative, effective ways; words are included that sharply and clearly define ideas.	4	3	2	1

	High		Low	
Sentence Structure				
Sentences are well-formed, complete thoughts with no run-ons.	4	3	2	1
Spelling				
All familiar words are spelled correctly; any misspellings of unfamiliar words are quite close to the correct form.	4	3	2	1

2. Have students revise their papers according to the content and writing criteria just demonstrated. Teachers frequently have students evaluate a partner's composition before having them rewrite. (Moore, Readence, & Rickelman, 1989, pp. 67–68)

• •

This modified form of GWP has the advantage of linking the power of writing with two of the effective vocabulary methods already discussed in this chapter: List-Group-Label and graphic organizers. Research on the effectiveness of GWP has been encouraging (Konopak, Martin, & Martin, 1987; Martin & Konopak, 1987; Martin, Konopak, & Martin, 1986), but Moore and colleagues (1989) have pointed out that the technique has yet to be applied to a wide variety of content.

ADDITIONAL METHODS

The techniques we have presented thus far are nearly always useful, regardless of the nature of the material to be read. We now offer some approaches that will occasionally be appropriate, depending on the specific vocabulary to be introduced.

Word Parts

Many words, especially technical terms, were originally coined by combining familiar word elements from Greek and Latin. In mathematics, for example, the family of polygons is made up of words containing clues to the number of sides: *triangle, quadrilateral, pentagon, hexagon,* and so on. The terminology of the entire metric system was similarly constructed from these and other word elements.

When a teacher takes a few seconds to discuss a word's structure, the connection between the word and its meaning is strengthened. The language arts teacher who writes the word *autobiography* in parts on the chalkboard, and then discusses its meaning in terms of these parts, has given students an added tool for remembering and understanding. Of course, not all words lend themselves to this sort of structural analysis, but you should stay alert for those that do.

Word Origins

Most words have historical sources in languages no longer spoken. Tracing their origins through linguistic antiquity has little to recommend it as a means of sparking the interest of students, but some words are different. These have engrossing, sometimes fascinating stories that can assist students in learning the word meanings.

Some words are based on the names of people (e.g., *chauvinist, Einsteinium, pasteurize, decibel, hertz, diesel,* and *sideburns*) while others are based on the names of places (*Francium, tuxedo, bayonet, hamburger, limerick*).

Some words—called portmanteaus, or blends—are combinations of other words:

- -

$$smog = smoke + fog$$
$$lox = liquid\ oxygen$$
$$bit = binary\ unit$$
$$brunch = breakfast + lunch$$
$$motel = motor\ hotel$$

- -

Portmanteaus have an important significance for teachers in content areas because a surprisingly large number of new technical terms are deliberately coined in this manner (Simonini, 1966). For a discussion of these interesting words, see McKenna (1978).

A few words have unusual stories associated with their origins. When a new type of heavily armored vehicle was shipped from England to the continent in World War I, these vehicles were packed in huge wooden crates commonly used for shipping benzene tanks. For security reasons, the word *tank* was painted on the side of each crate. The name stuck.

Discussing word origins does more than increase student interest and engagement. It adds connotative associations to the denotative values of words. The web of meanings for the new word becomes stickier! Locating words with unusual beginnings is easy. While books on word origins are available, there is a simpler way. All standard dictionaries include an etymology as part of the entry for each word. The etymology, or history of the word, is usually in brackets. While most etymologies recount the evolution of words from dead languages, brief anecdotes are also included when the origin is more colorful.

False Definitions

Common words are occasionally "redefined" by skillful writers in ways that are thought provoking and often humorous. Consider a few of these false definitions drawn from a variety of content areas. (In the case of *hammer*, contrast its real definition, given on p. 106!)

- -

hammer	an instrument for smashing the human thumb (Ambrose Bierce)
government	the worst thing in this world, next to anarchy (Henry Ward Beecher)
football	committee meetings, called huddles, separated by outbursts of violence (George Will)
esophagus	that portion of the alimentary canal that lies between pleasure and business (Ambrose Bierce)
engineering	the art of doing that well with one dollar which any bungler can do with two after a fashion (Arthur M. Wellington)
literature	news that STAYS news (Ezra Pound)
mathematics	the science that draws necessary conclusions (Benjamin Pierce)
science	an exchange of ignorance for that/which is another kind of ignorance (Lord Byron)
circle	the highest emblem in the cipher of the world (Ralph Waldo Emerson)
G.O.P.	Grand Old Platitudes (Harry Truman)
grammar	that which knows how to lord it over kings and with high hands makes them obey its laws (Moliere)
education	what survives when what has been learnt has been forgotten (B. F. Skinner)

- -

False definitions have the form of real definitions and are therefore useful in making contrasts with their dictionary counterparts. As in the case of word origins, they are peripheral to teaching denotative meanings but add additional associations that may help a word to be retained. Any book of quotations can be scoured for quips that have the form of classical definitions; also, McKenna (1983) has compiled an entire volume devoted exclusively to false definitions.

SUMMARY

An important part of teaching in content areas is the introduction of new concepts, represented by words. Vocabulary instruction is complicated by the fact that the same visual word can represent numerous concepts and that what a word formally signifies (what it denotes) is only one of many associations a reader may have for the same word, including what the reader may have experienced in regard to that concept (what the word connotes). Many teachers assume that as students are exposed again and again to a given word the word's meaning will be acquired inductively. However, while this process may occur to a degree, the precise meanings of key terminology often need to be explicitly taught through a more deductive approach.

Numerous methods have been developed for the introduction of new words. Taba's List-Group-Label approach is a three-step technique in which students are encouraged to brainstorm all the terms they can generate in association with a given subject, then to group the terms by categories, and finally to label the categories. This method is actually a means of activating and organizing prior knowledge of words related to a topic so that new terms can be more easily integrated into existing word knowledge. Once this integration is accomplished, other techniques can be employed to introduce the new terms. The most traditional of these is to present students with formal definitions, including (1) the class to which a concept belongs and (2) those features that enable one to differentiate the concept from other members of the same class. A more recent technique, feature analysis, involves construction of a chart in which category members are listed in the left-hand column and additional columns represent various features either possessed or lacked by the members.

One of the most important advances in our ability to introduce new words is the graphic organizer, a diagram that depicts relationships among key terms. Major types of organizers include tree diagrams, Venn diagrams, time lines, labeled pictures, and sociograms, although many others are possible, including combination (hybrid) types. Semantic maps are a modified form of graphic organizer with a more freewheeling structure conducive to student input. To construct a graphic organizer, students first list all key terms in a selection, then identify clusters of closely related terms, and finally construct a diagram for each cluster that best represents the relationship among the terms.

Numerous other techniques have been used successfully to introduce new terminology, either alone or in association with the techniques previously mentioned. One approach is to analyze words on the basis of meaningful word elements (prefixes, suffixes, root words, etc.). Another approach is to explore the historical origins of words whenever the origin offers insights into a word's meaning or provides an additional colorful association that may create an interest in the word *and* improve the chances that students will retain it. False definitions are quotations from writers who have offered their own renditions of what certain widely used words mean. These "definitions" can provide the basis of useful contrasts with the word's denotation.

GETTING INVOLVED

1. Figure 6.20 provides a brief paragraph followed by four graphic organizers based on its content. We suggest that none of the organizers is perfect. However, it is possible to decide which ones may be more or less effective than others. Can you make a case for one of the diagrams over the others? Would improvements in that diagram make it even more effective? Could you offer a fifth, altogether different organizer that would be superior to the four that are presented?

2. Figure 6.21 (p. 134) provides an incomplete feature analysis chart based on the instructional techniques described in this chapter. Use the codings "+," "0," and "s" to complete it based on your knowledge of the techniques.

3. The following words are drawn from a variety of subject areas. Each has an interesting origin that is provided in the etymology section of a standard dictionary entry. Choose the words associated with your own area and look up their histories in a dictionary. Don't be surprised if you find yourself looking up *all* the words!

sandwich	gorilla	transistor	saxophone
teflon	quark	boycott	crowbar
nylon	googol	agnostic	Dixie
scuba	Pacific	bazooka	forsythia
quasar	magenta	braille	poinsettia
shrapnel	silhouette	radar	laser
bikini	badminton	calico	damask
marathon	plutonium	uranium	bloomer
derringer	gardenia	sousaphone	volt
watt	zinnia	good-bye	gas
blurb	bleachers	boondocks	cowlick
dynamite	goatee	hydrogen	iron curtain
jack rabbit	jeep	serendipity	spoof
teetotaler	zilch	yippie	jumbo

For additional reading on the educational uses of word origins, see McKenna (1977b).

FIGURE 6.20

1. The shortest method of traveling from London to Paris is, of course, by air. A less expensive though more time-consuming method is to take a train from London's Charing Cross Station and travel southeast to Dover on the English Channel. At that point, a Hovercraft can be taken across the Channel either to Calais or to Boulogne, the latter being the further and less popular of the two ports. In either case, the two rail connections from the French coast to Paris are simple and direct, rejoining one another in Amiens.

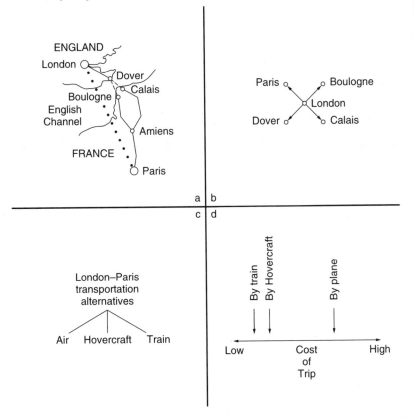

Passage and Four Potential Graphic Organizers

4. When you read in this chapter about feature analysis charts, the technique may have seemed familiar. In Figure 4.4, we presented such a chart and invited you to complete it. Take another look and note whether all the characteristics suggested in this chapter are incorporated. Would you have set up the chart any differently?

FIGURE 6.21

Class: Vocabulary introduction devices	Type of graphic organizer	Used only with highly related terms	Developed by Aristotle	Most open-ended of organizers	Helps categorize terms by class and characteristics
Time line Feature analysis chart Formal definition Semantic map Venn diagram Tree diagram					

Feature analysis chart for selected chapter terms

SECTION.................... three

Strategies for
Guided Reading

In Chapter 2, we examined the roles played by prior knowledge of content and purpose for reading in the process of learning through text. We suggested that content area teachers are perfectly positioned to influence these factors as students undertake assigned reading. We now turn to the second factor: the purposes for which students read.

Chapter 7 presents a variety of techniques for making reading purposeful in a specific sense. The use of questions as a purpose-setting device is discussed in detail. While questions are a mainstay, other methods are also examined. These include reading to confirm a hypothesis or prediction, reading to satisfy a stated objective or outcome, reading to construct (or complete) a graphic organizer or chart, reading to solve a specific problem, reading for the purpose of writing a summary, and reading in order to prepare an outline of the written material.

Chapter 8 presents a method of incorporating the basic purpose-setting devices described in Chapter 7 into a content literacy guide. These guides are designed to be completed by students as they read. The chapter begins with a discussion of the advantages of written guides and when to use them. Numerous guide formats are introduced. This chapter also offers advice in how to construct and use such guides.

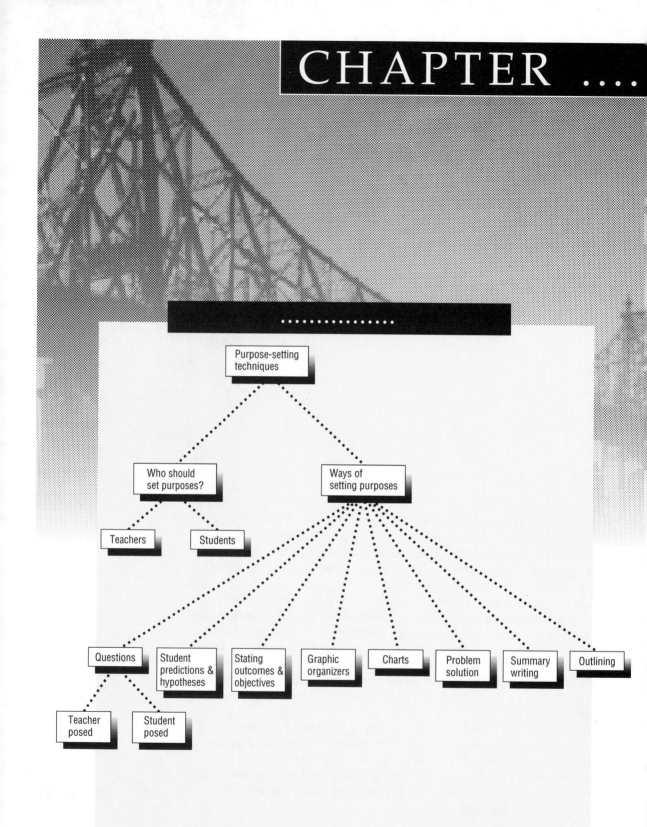

CHAPTER .....

SEVEN

Making Reading Purposeful

The secret of success is constancy to purpose.

Benjamin Disraeli

Dr. Samuel Johnson, whose comments about reading and writing we have quoted liberally in this text, enjoyed a reputation as one of the world's foremost authorities on these subjects during the eighteenth century. The Scottish economist Adam Smith once remarked that Johnson "knew more books" than anyone in the world. The question of how Johnson was able to read so extensively on such a wide variety of subjects was a frequent topic of discussion. An acquaintance once asked him if, when he read a book, he proceeded through it line by line from cover to cover, reading every word as he went. Johnson's reply astonished his friend. He said that he rarely if ever read a book in that manner, for few books were worthy of that sort of reading. Instead, he read selectively to accomplish his own purposes for reading. Johnson's interviewer was surprised because he, like many of us, believed that to do anything less than read every word is not reading at all. In our print-oriented society, however, in which the demands of reading are apt to be extensive, skillful readers tend to adopt strategies like Johnson's and read to accomplish their own purposes. The need to *have* clear purposes is obviously great, especially when materials are challenging and prior knowledge is limited.

Reading without a clear idea of purpose can lead to frustration for students, who may not achieve the results their teachers expect, and to exasperation for teachers, who often fail to understand how their students' comprehension can be so inadequate. For many students, however, it is not enough to read a textbook for the broad purpose of "getting all the facts" or a narrative with the aim of "finding out what happens." They often need specific direction in determining what is important in the midst of what may seem an avalanche of print.

Consider your own experience with this text. Have you caught yourself wondering, or perhaps even inquiring, about what you will need to know for testing purposes? There is nothing wrong with such a question, for it reflects the thinking of a strategic reader—one who reads purposefully, using whatever strategies may help to achieve specific goals. When, as in many

He has only half learned the art of reading who has not added to it the even more refined accomplishments of skipping and skimming.

Arthur, Lord Balfour

classroom situations, the purposes are determined by the teacher, it makes sense to discover them by asking.

Teachers who are not forthcoming about what they expect their students to derive from reading are inviting poor comprehension. Some teachers defend this policy, however, by suggesting that any effort on their part to limit the scope of reading assignments will result in their students' reading *only* for the prestated purposes. This response acknowledges how powerful purpose setting can be! The object is to set the *right* purposes—those that go beyond literally stated facts and get at their significance. Teachers who establish purposes in this manner can have the confidence to permit, and even encourage, students to read strategically. Whenever purposes for reading encompass the curricular goals envisioned by a teacher, the goal of reading should be to achieve those purposes and not simply to reach the last page of an assignment. Students are then free to model themselves after Dr. Johnson and read for what they need.

OBJECTIVES

This chapter will acquaint you with ways of making your students' reading more purposeful. When you have completed it, you should be able to

1. describe the reasons for setting purposes prior to reading;

2. pose questions at the literal, inferential, and critical levels;

3. explain how student-posed questions might best serve certain reading assignments;

4. describe and use alternative methods of purpose setting, including hypothesizing, stating objectives, completing graphic organizers and charts, solving problems, writing summaries, and outlining;

5. identify the strengths and limitations of these techniques that may make them more suitable to some global plans than others; and

6. vary and combine purpose-setting techniques.

WHO SHOULD SET PURPOSES FOR READING?

You will recall that three of the global lesson plans presented in Chapter 4—DRA, DR–TA, and KWL—center around a specific reading assignment. An important feature distinguishing the Directed Reading Activity from both the DR–TA and KWL is the teacher's role in setting purposes for that assignment. In the DRA, the teacher sets purposes unilaterally based on curricular judgments made in advance. In the other two plans, the teacher involves students in the process of establishing purposes for reading, serving more as one who guides than one who prescribes. This diversity of roles not only affords teachers a choice of lesson designs that will suit their needs and philosophies but also indicates a widespread division of opinion as to whether students or teachers are ultimately responsible for deciding what is learned.

Few would dispute that an important goal of schooling is to produce strategic readers capable of setting their own purposes and of reading flexibly to achieve those purposes. Our recommendation, however, is that content teachers be somewhat directive in the process of setting purposes. There are three good reasons behind this suggestion. To begin with, the teacher's prior knowledge of the subject is apt to exceed that of students to such an extent that the teacher is better able to establish reasonable goals for reading. In addition, many students have limited experience in setting purposes *regardless* of their knowledge of content. Finally, we would argue that the ability to read strategically in order to achieve purposes set by others will eventually be at least as important to students (when they reach the workplace) as reading to satisfy their own purposes.

We are not suggesting that teachers use the DRA to the exclusion of DR–TA and KWL. We do recommend that, while guiding the process of purpose setting in these techniques, they continue to realize that student-generated purposes may be unsophisticated, vague, and incomplete. In these cases, teachers may be wise to encourage students to modify their purposes in accordance with teacher suggestions. Tact is important in order not to dampen student initiative and thought.

WAYS OF SETTING PURPOSES

The goal of purpose setting is to "direct student attention to the most important information" (Marshall, 1989, p. 64). There are several methods for accomplishing this goal. No one method is best for all reading assignments and familiarity with several techniques will give you the power to select one that is well suited to a given occasion. In the next chapter, we take the additional step of incorporating these methods, often in combination, into reading guides used to focus the efforts of students as they read.

Questions Posed by the Teacher

A traditional means of focusing students' attention is by posing prereading questions. This practice, more than most, is likely to occasion the complaint we mentioned earlier—that if students are told what to read for, told in advance which questions they'll be called on to answer, they will read for this purpose alone. An excellent response to this objection is this: If teachers ask the *right* questions, they need not worry about students' limiting their focus to these ends.

Types of Questions   Knowing the right questions requires knowing something about the types of questions one might ask. In the past, reading researchers have examined detailed lists, or taxonomies, of comprehension skills (e.g., Barrett, 1972; Pearson & Johnson, 1978). The skills contained in these taxonomies, such as inferring cause-and-effect relationships or predicting outcomes, can be used to define types of comprehension questions. This highly detailed approach to question formulation is not really necessary for most purposes, however. Instead, we recommend a simpler approach based on three widely acknowledged *levels* of comprehension. These levels, along with the kinds of questions they suggest, are depicted in Figure 7.1.

At the lowest level, the literal, questions call for students to recognize explicitly stated information. Some years ago, an eighth-grade student of the first author described them as "Christopher Columbus" questions because "you search for the answer until you land on it." It is no doubt the literal question that causes some teachers to have reservations about the notion of posing prereading questions at all.

FIGURE 7.1

Three levels of questions

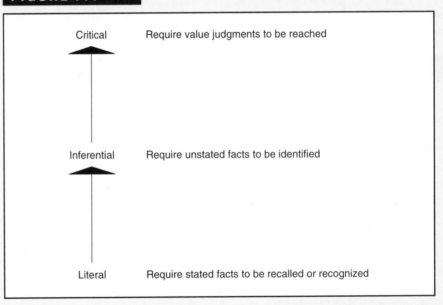

Critical	Require value judgments to be reached
Inferential	Require unstated facts to be identified
Literal	Require stated facts to be recalled or recognized

Students can look up answers to such questions without giving much thoughtful attention to an answer's context and implications. It is for this reason that literal questions should seldom form the sole basis of a reader's purpose. There are exceptions to this rule, as when we look up a population figure in an almanac or a pronunciation in a dictionary. But the reading of longer selections with the goal of fully comprehending their content requires more than the acquisition of individual facts. The student must integrate facts, both with one another and with prior knowledge, in order to make sense of them, to apply them, and, in Aquinas's words, to realize their significance. Purposes of this sort call for questions of a different kind. While literal questions have their uses in helping students acquire the facts they need, they should not be an end in themselves.

> *Truth is not facts. Truth is the significance of facts.*
>
> Thomas Aquinas

Inferential questions require students to use explicit facts in order to reach unstated, or implicit, conclusions. Teachers should encourage students to draw on prior knowledge in this process as well. The result is the identification of new (that is, unstated) facts or *suspected* facts. Some inferences are clearly and indisputably correct. When we read that a painter mixes equal portions of blue and yellow paint, we can safely infer that the result is green even though this fact may not be stated. (Note that we used prior knowledge along with information provided through reading in order to reach this particular conclusion.) On the other hand, some inferences are less than certain. Consider the social studies teacher who assigns a series of newspaper and magazine articles about a coming election and then asks students who they think will win. Even though the students cannot be sure of their answer, the reasoning process is nevertheless inferential. This is because known facts are being used to determine unstated ones. Noted linguist S. I. Hayakawa once defined an inference as "a statement about the unknown made on the basis of the known" (1939, p. 41). It is less important that a student's "statement" about the election's outcome eventually be proved correct than that it be based on presently known facts.

At the critical level, questions call on students to judge what they read. These judgments can serve a variety of purposes:

- synthesizing information from a variety of sources
- selecting facts that support a particular viewpoint
- identifying biased writing
- recognizing inadequacies in an author's treatment of a topic
- evaluating the literary merits of writing
- interpreting information in order to apply it to a new situation
- deciding how to read a given assignment selectively in order to accomplish one's purposes

- comparing one reading selection with others
- choosing the most efficient method of solving a problem in mathematics or science

Critical questions do not have factual answers. Reasonable, comprehending readers may differ in their responses to such questions because the answers depend on personal values, experiences, desires, and tastes. As in the case of inferential questions, the important aspect of a critical response is not the response itself but the reasoning behind it. Answers to critical questions are not correct or incorrect; they are more or less *defensible* depending on their basis in fact.

To illustrate the difference among literal, inferential, and critical questions, consider the passage presented in Figure 7.2 about the planet Pluto. This objectively written, highly factual, expository selection invites many sorts of questions, and we offer one at each level of comprehension:

1. What is the temperature range on Pluto?

This question has a factual answer that is clearly stated in the selection. It is a clear-cut, "Christopher Columbus" example. Contrast it with this one:

2. Is there life on Pluto?

This question has a factual answer (there either is or is not life on Pluto), but you will find no mention of life in the selection. The question is therefore not literal but inferential. Because it is not a certain inference, some teachers might categorize it as critical, but the answer is factual, like our earlier example of predicting the results of an election. The third example is undeniably critical. Contrast it with the second in terms of the sort of answer it calls for:

3. Should the United States send a space probe to explore Pluto?

Here, the answer is not a fact but a judgment—one that may well vary from one reader to the next despite how well those readers have understood the selection. The usual confusion between critical questions and questions calling for probable (less than certain) inferences is that each asks the reader for an *opinion.* However, the inferential question asks for an opinion based on facts while the critical question calls on the reader to examine values and desires.

We emphasize that these three levels are not entirely distinct. There is a "gray" area between the literal and inferential levels, where some questions appear to fall, and another between the inferential and critical levels. This is of little concern to us, however, since the three-level system is designed as a tool

FIGURE 7.2

Portion of an encyclopedia entry for "Pluto"

Pluto

Pluto, symbol P in astronomy, is the ninth and most distant of the known planets in the solar system. The principal orbital and physical data of Pluto and its satellite, Charon, are shown in Table 24.

DISCOVERY OF PLUTO AND CHARON

Before Pluto's discovery in 1930, several astronomers had interpreted the motions of Uranus and Neptune as revealing gravitational perturbations beyond those accountable for by all of the planets known at that time. Their calculations were similar to those that led John Couch Adams and Urbain-Jean-Joseph LeVerrier in the 1840s to predict correctly the position of Neptune. Also among those who thus predicted a planet beyond Neptune was Percival Lowell, to whom credit for a successful prediction was generally given. Not only were his predicted orbital elements close to those of Pluto but he also initiated the effort that led ultimately to its discovery by his successors at the Lowell Observatory in Flagstaff, Arizona. Although Lowell's *Memoir on a Trans-Neptunian Planet (Memoirs of the Lowell Observatory*, vol. 1) was not published until 1915, the year before his death, he and his colleagues carried out intermittent searches between 1905 and 1916 with a variety of telescopes of limited capability. On the basis of experience gained while conducting these early efforts, a fast wide-field telescope was designed specifically for the trans-Neptunian planet search.

Percival Lowell's contributions

After the telescope was completed in 1929, the project was placed in the hands of Clyde Williams Tombaugh. He painstakingly compared pairs of photographic plates of selected sky regions, taken several days apart, looking for images of moving objects. The project was carefully planned so that, among the millions of stellar and starlike images, other moving bodies such as the numerous asteroids could be easily recognized and not be incorrectly identified as the sought-for planet. On February 18, 1930, Tombaugh discovered the trans-Neptunian planet on plates that he had taken on January 21, 23, and 29, 1930. Announcement of the successful discovery was not made until March 13, 1930, the anniversary of Lowell's birth, but in the interval the Lowell Observatory astronomers were able to assemble further supporting evidence to confirm the discovery. After a long deliberation over many suggested names for the new planet, the name Pluto was chosen because it could be represented by the symbol P made up of Percival Lowell's initials.

Even while the announcement of this significant discovery was drawing the attention of the entire astronomical world to the new planet, certain grave doubts were being expressed as to whether it indeed was Lowell's trans-Neptunian planet. The difficulty was that Pluto was much fainter—about one-tenth as bright—than had been expected, and its telescopic image had no measurable diameter. It was therefore difficult to resist the conclusion that Pluto was altogether too small and, hence, of insufficient mass to have caused the large perturbations in Uranus' and Neptune's motions that had led Lowell and others to predict its existence and orbital motion. Soon after Pluto's discovery, Ernest William Brown demonstrated mathematically that Lowell's prediction was, in fact, dynamically invalid. Then, while he was associated with the Lick Observatory, Mt. Hamilton, California (1932–36), E.C. Bower, among others, convincingly demonstrated that Pluto's mass was probably less than one-half that of the Earth and that the resulting perturbations to the motions of Uranus and Neptune must have been significantly smaller than the probable errors of the earliest observations of these bodies. Modern data have since confirmed this conclusion. Thus Pluto, at first considered as the second planet, after Neptune, to have been discovered through prediction, is actually the second planet, after Uranus, to have been discovered by accident. Or perhaps more properly, it is the first planet to have been discovered through a systematic, comprehensive search.

In 1978, the existence of a satellite of Pluto was established by James W. Christy and Robert S. Harrington of the U.S. Naval Observatory, who discovered that photographic images of Pluto periodically appeared slightly elongated. Even with the best telescope under the most favourable conditions, the satellite's image had not been resolved from that of Pluto by 1981. There is sufficient evidence, however, to show that the satellite orbits the planet with a period of 6.39 days, in synchronism with the known period of variation in Pluto's brightness. The satellite's orbit is probably circular, with a radius of about 20,000 kilometres. Pluto's satellite has been designated 1978 Pl and is tentatively named Charon.

BASIC ASTRONOMICAL DATA

Pluto's orbit. Pluto moves in a markedly eccentric orbit about the Sun with a period of about 248 years. The orbit is more eccentric than that of any other planet and has a very high inclination, about 17°, to the mean plane of the solar system. Because of the high eccentricity of the orbit, Pluto is closer to the Sun than is Neptune at times around perihelion as, for example, in the interval 1979–99.

The near commensurability of the periods of revolution of the three outermost planets brings the planets into successive conjunctions at about the same places in space. At intervals of approximately 500 years, during which Pluto makes two revolutions and Neptune three, these two planets come closest to each other and are then separated by only 18 astronomical units; this phenomenon last occurred in 1891 and will occur again in 2391. Similarly, Pluto and Uranus have close conjunctions, although in two series. For example, in the years 1854, 2107, and 2360, Pluto and Uranus are approximately 29 a.u. apart, and in the years 1713, 1966, and 2220 they are only 14 a.u. apart.

Conjunctions with Neptune and Uranus

Mass, diameter, and density. The difficult problem of determining the mass of Pluto was resolved with the discovery of Pluto's satellite and the determination of its orbital period around, and its mean distance from, the planet. Before the discovery of Charon, estimates of Pluto's mass ranged from about 1/5 that of Earth to about seven times that of Earth, with indeterminate uncertainties. The combined mass of Pluto and Charon is now believed to be about 1/400 that of the Earth, with an uncertainty of about 20 percent. While these later figures are subject to improvement as refined studies progress, there is no doubt that they are more trustworthy than those made before the discovery of Charon. The discrepancies among the various mass determinations reflect the virtual indeterminacy encountered in the case of a small planet with no known satellite, located far away from its nearest, massive neighbours.

In the early 1980s, the individual masses of Pluto and Charon could only be estimations based on their different brightnesses and the reasonable assumption of similarity in composition, density, and surface reflection properties. The scant evidence available suggests (see table) that Pluto is about five times as bright as Charon and is, accordingly, about twice as large in

Table 24: Orbital and Physical Data for Pluto	
Mean distance from Sun	39.53 a.u.
Least distance from the Sun	29.81 a.u.
Greatest distance from the Sun	49.26 a.u.
Eccentricity	0.246
Inclination to ecliptic	17.123°
Period of revolution	248.5 years
Time of perihelion	1989.8
Visual magnitude at mean opposition	15.0
Period of axial rotation	6.3867 days
Satellites	one known: 1978 P1 (Charon)
Diameter (estimated)	Pluto: about 3,500 kilometres
	Charon: about 1,800 kilometres
Mass	Pluto and Charon together: 0.0025 terrestrial mass
	Pluto probably about 10 times as massive as Charon
Density	probably between 0.4 and 0.9 gram per cubic centimetre
Composition	uncertain; may consist of a large proportion of frozen methane
Inclination of Charon's orbital plane with respect to Pluto's orbital plane around the Sun	111°

diameter and about 10 times as massive as its satellite.

Following upon the determination of the combined mass of Pluto and Charon, the chief problem is the measurement of their diameters. This is not to say that other unknowns — such as their chemical compositions, the physical nature of their surfaces, or their origins — are less interesting or important. It is simply an acknowledgement that, without reliable determinations of Pluto's and Charon's diameters and mean densities, many of these other problems will remain obscured and their answers speculative.

Pluto's diameter   The diameter of Pluto has been the subject of several investigations, but it had not been determined with confidence by 1980. Efforts involving a sophisticated technique known as speckle interferometry indicate a diameter in the range of 3,000 to 4,000 kilometres. Complicating the problem is the fact that telescopic images of Pluto are actually composite images of Pluto and Charon.

A secure measurement of the diameters of celestial bodies can be made if the bodies occult a star in the course of their apparent motion across the sky and if the occultation is observed from two observatories located at different latitudes on the Earth. In 1980, such an occultation occurred in the Pluto-Charon system, but it was evidently observed only at the South African Astronomical Observatory. The occulting body apparently was Charon, and the results show that Charon is at least 1,200 kilometres in diameter. In 1965, numerous North American observatories had been alerted to a possible occultation by Pluto-Charon, but no

such occultation was observed. Nevertheless, the results of the attempted observation demonstrated that Pluto was no larger than 6,000 kilometres in diameter.

On the basis of the data given above for current estimates of the masses and diameters of Pluto and Charon, it appears that the mean density of Pluto and Charon lies between 0.4 and 0.9 grams per cubic centimetre. This low value of density has led some investigators to propose that these bodies may be made up of a large proportion of solid methane, instead of the denser, rocky materials found in the terrestrial planets.

THE SURFACES OF THE PLANET AND ITS SATELLITE

Because the telescopic image of Pluto is generally indistin-guishable from that of a faint star, all efforts made by the early 1980s to detect surface features by conventional methods were unsuccessful. That the surface is not uniform has been known since 1955, when M.F. Walker and R.H. Hardie at the Lowell Obsevatory found that the brightness of the planet varied regularly by about 12 percent within a period of 6.39 days. The variation in apparent brightness is now interpreted as due to the combined effects of irregular surface reflection properties and an axial rotation of the planet with a period of 6.39 days. Studies since 1955 have shown that the range of brightness variation has gradually increased; analysis of this increase has in turn allowed for an estimation of the orientation of Pluto's spin axis in space. The character of variation in brightness observed through 1980 did not admit of an interpretation of mutual eclipses of the satellite by Pluto or of Pluto by the satellite. During the 1980s, however, such eclipses and their attendant additional variations in brightness appear to be distinctly possible and, if realized, they will provide much new data about the system. *Varia-tions in apparent bright-ness*

While the detailed nature of the surfaces of both Pluto and Charon remains unknown, the best spectroscopic and infrared evidence points to surfaces composed largely of methane frost and ice, having a reflectivity between 20 and 50 percent in the visual wavelengths. As noted above, it is estimated that Pluto is about five times brighter than Charon.

POSSIBLE ATMOSPHERE

Whether Pluto has an atmosphere is not known with any degree of assurance, but certain conditions relating to a possible atmosphere can be stated in general terms. It can be estimated that the average surface temperature on the sunlit portion of Pluto's surface is about 60 K when the planet is at perihelion and 47 K at aphelion. The dark side of the planet probably has a temperature of about 20 K. At such temperatures, virtually all materials are frozen, or at least liquefied, except for a few gases such as hydrogen and helium. These gases are so light in molecular weight, and Pluto's gravity is so low, that it is unlikely that they could be retained in free form. There is some possibility, however, that frozen methane might sublimate slightly on the sunlit side of Pluto to produce an atmosphere of low density. Definitive evidence for the presence or absence of methane gas had not been acquired by 1980. A clearer picture of the atmospheric and surface conditions of Pluto awaits improvements in the resolution of spectrophotometric techniques and further exploration by spacecraft.

SOURCE: From "Solar System," *Encyclopaedia Britannica*, 15th ed. (Vol. 27, pp. 574–576) 1987. Reprinted by permission of Encyclopaedia Britannica.

FIGURE 7.3

Critical Questions

- Always open-ended; never have a single answer
- Have answers that are not facts but that reflect values
- Often contain the word *should*

Inferential Questions

- Have factual answers even though the answer may not be certain
- Require two or more facts to be considered together in order to produce an unstated fact (or suspected fact)
- May rely on facts in the reader's prior knowledge as well as facts stated in the reading selection

Literal Questions

- Have answers that can be located in the reading selection
- Require minimal use of prior knowledge to answer

Characteristics of questions

for formulating new questions, not classifying existing ones. In Figure 7.3, we offer a few tips for using the three-level approach more effectively in setting purposes.

Teacher-posed questions fit naturally into the second step of the Directed Reading Activity, discussed in Chapter 4. They also have an obvious influence on the postreading discussion since the teacher's blueprint for discussing the material is in fact the questions posed in advance. Other questions are asked as well, as we describe in Chapter 9, but the framework of the discussion is planned before the reading assignment is ever made.

The value of suggesting questions to students has not been lost on textbook writers; they have largely abandoned the age-old practice of placing "review" questions at the ends of chapters and now position them at the beginning or embed them at strategic points within. These questions can provide valuable assistance to the content teacher who used them in planning. Figure 7.4 provides an example of embedded questions.

Questions Posed by Students

In the DR–TA and KWL global plans, students play an integral part in establishing the questions that will be used to focus reading. A teacher's understanding of a three-level approach to questioning can assist this process. Even though students actually generate the questions, the teacher is expected to guide the process and can use this role to encourage higher-level reading objectives. Moreover, some have argued (e.g., Dennis, McKenna, & Miller, 1989) that teachers should take a few moments to explain the three-tier rationale so that they can more readily elicit responses from a student whose very notion of comprehension has been deliberately expanded.

FIGURE 7.4

Examples of embedded
questions in a textbook

SOURCE: From *Land of Promise: A History of the United States* (2nd ed.), by C. Berkin and L. Wood, 1987, Glenview, IL: Scott, Foresman. Copyright 1987 by Scott, Foresman. Reprinted by permission of Scott, Foresman.

Question embedded
at a key point
in the prose itself

Questions embedded
between sections

---

system because it would end the spoils system as the source of their political power. Others opposed the new system because they feared it would create a permanent elite class of officeholders. The uneducated and poor would be driven from their jobs. Like the Jacksonians of the 1820s, these senators insisted that the common sense of the "common man" was as good a basis for office as a formal education.

Despite this coalition of selfish and unselfish opposition, the Pendleton bill passed in 1883. To the surprise of everyone who knew him from his Customs House days, President Arthur came out strongly in favor of the bill. The shock of Garfield's assassination seemed to have changed the old spoilsman's outlook, much to the sorrow of the Republican bosses.

How did the new system work? Under the **Pendleton Act**, the civil service law, the President appointed a Civil Service Commission of three people from both parties. The commission made a list of "classified jobs" that would be filled on the basis of competitive examinations. The number of classified jobs was small at first, only about 14,000 out of some 117,000 appointive positions. But the law allowed Presidents to add to the classified list. Each President took advantage of this provision by extending "classified" status to jobs held by his own appointees. In this way he prevented his successors from replacing them with their own favorites. So the number of gov-

ernment jobs under the merit system tended to increase with each new administration. By 1900 almost 100,000 positions were classified. The Pendleton Act also forbade the collection of campaign contributions from federal employees.

Despite the civil service law, politicians found ways to keep the spoils system alive. The Civil Service Commission usually accepted several candidates for each classified position and then left the final appointment to department heads. This allowed them to choose candidates from their own faction or party. Also, most high-paying jobs remained under the spoils system for several decades. In spite of its early weaknesses, however, the Pendleton Act became the foundation on which American Presidents were able to build the modern civil service system.

There was one unexpected consequence of the Pendleton Act of 1883. Under the old spoils system, office seekers and government employees had financed the campaigns of their political patrons. The rise of the merit system meant a sharp decline in these campaign funds. Politicians, seeking money for re-election or election, were forced to tap other sources. They came to rely even more than before on business leaders and industrialists, whose contributions depended on getting political favors in return. Business influence on legislation thus increased dramatically after 1883.

SECTION 2 REVIEW

 Key Terms and People: civil service, Chester A. Arthur, James A. Garfield, Pendleton Act

Main Ideas

1. How did Grant try to reform the civil service? What were the results of his efforts?
2. List one accomplishment and one failure of Rutherford B. Hayes' attempt to reform the civil service.
3. What effect did the Garfield assassination have on civil service reform?
4. Why did some political leaders oppose the Pendleton Act? Describe its effects on officeholding and elections.

Chester A. Arthur (1830–1886)

IN OFFICE: 1881–1885

Republican from New York. Although a powerful supporter of the spoils system before becoming President, Arthur reversed his position after Garfield's assassination. During his administration, Congress passed the first civil service act, the Pendleton Act (1883), which set up a merit system for the employment of federal workers.

456

As an experiment, we described the Pluto selection (Figure 7.2) to a group of eighth graders without allowing them to see the selection. We told them the source was a basic encyclopedia entry and asked them what they would expect to be able to learn from reading the selection. Here is a sample of what they suggested:

- how cold it is on Pluto
- how far Pluto is from Earth
- what Pluto looks like
- what might live on Pluto
- what kinds of rocks might be on Pluto
- how big Pluto is
- whether Pluto has any moons
- where you might look for Pluto in the sky

In effect, we took the students through the second step of KWL—establishing what they wanted to learn. Because of how we posed our question (asking what they would expect to find in an encyclopedia entry), we assumed the students would also include a few of the facts they already knew and that would have come to light during the initial "K" step.

Examining the list might give confidence to teachers who are skeptical that students are capable of setting prudent, defensible purposes for reading when encouraged to do so. Note that the items in our list are in the form of indirect questions because of how we had asked our question. Note, too, that these questions are either literal or inferential, depending on how the encyclopedia author treated the topic. The students had no way of knowing whether they might actually find the information literally stated in the selection. In cases where the information was not explicit (such as "what might live on Pluto"), the students' purpose would be to identify facts supporting an eventual inference (such as the extremely low temperatures, the near-absence of life, and the hostile atmosphere). Finally, note that critical questions are not present. This may well have been because the students did not expect such issues to be addressed in an encyclopedia. It may also have been the result of their limited experiences with critical thinking and reading. Teachers interested in encouraging these processes may find it necessary to nudge students in this direction during the prereading discussion.

Question–Answer Relationships (QARs)   Raphael (1984) has suggested a straightforward method of teaching students about the levels of questions. Rather than use technical terms like *literal, inferential,* and *critical,* she recommends the following easy-to-understand category labels:

1. *Right There.* Words used to create the question and words used for the answer are in the same sentence.

2. *Think and Search.* The answer is in the text, but words used to create the question and those used for an appropriate answer would not be in the same sentence.
3. *On My Own.* The answer is not found in the text. (pp. 304–305)

Raphael intended the third category to include inferences requiring the reader to use a combination of prior knowledge and printed information. Her system actually recognizes two kinds of inferences: those based entirely on a selection and those requiring information not provided by the selection. Her success in teaching these distinctions using three simple labels is encouraging. We suggest modifying the system slightly, however, by allowing the third category to include critical judgments. This expansion is already implied by Raphael's definition that answers to this type of question are "not found in the text." Moreover, the phase "on my own" certainly suggests evaluative questions as well as inferences. By broadening the third category in this manner, a teacher can incorporate the three traditional levels of questions into Raphael's system.

Student Predictions and Hypotheses

The Directed Reading–Thinking Activity emphasizes the formation of predictions by students, who then read to test their predictions. In Chapter 4, we noted that a traditional limitation of the DR–TA is that it seems better suited to narrative than expository materials. It was, after all, originally designed for use with basal reader stories. We also indicated, however, that prediction can be an important tool in content areas when the topic to be studied involves processes, discoveries, or the description of historical events.

What if we had taken our middle-grade students in the direction of a DR–TA rather than KWL? We might have examined what they already knew about Pluto in order to form hypotheses about what they did not yet know. Instead of indicating what they wanted to know, as in KWL, they would have suggested what they expected to be true. We would have encouraged the prediction of actual temperature ranges, for example, along with the reasons for the prediction.

In a sense, the DR–TA is the scientific method in microcosm. In each, we begin with facts and principles and use these to predict new facts. Correct predictions lend further support to the principles while incorrect predictions cause us to reexamine them. The DR–TA has a major advantage over the scientific method in terms of instruction, however. In science, hypotheses are tested through experiments, which are often time-consuming and expensive. In the DR–TA, they are tested through reading, where the immediacy of having one's prediction confirmed or refuted can be a powerful tool for learning.

Stating Objectives and Outcomes

One of the most directive ways to set purposes is to make clear to students precisely what they should know or be able to do once they have completed a selection. Consider the teacher about to assign the Pluto article, who says to students:

> After you've read, you should be able to state the temperature range on Pluto, describe its atmosphere, and so on.

You may recall that an important part of the explicit teaching model is communicating to students what they will learn. Specifying the desirable outcomes of reading, as in this example, is therefore well aligned with this global plan whenever a reading selection is to play a central role. It is also well suited to the DRA as an alternative to posing questions. Naturally, the outcomes or objectives of reading can always be cast in question form and vice versa. Questions have the advantage of merging rather naturally into a postreading discussion. On the other hand, they are often wordier than the succinct phrases needed to specify what students should learn.

Providing students with specific objectives for which to read is obviously not desirable with the DR–TA or with KWL, both of which invite student-generated purposes. This disparity in methods suggests the need for teachers to choose a global design first and only then to consider what devices to use within it. Another consideration is whether a textbook assignment contains built-in objective statements, like those in Figure 7.5.

> You've undoubtedly noticed our use of objectives as embedded purpose-setting devices in all the chapters you've read. How effective have they been for you? (Have you taken the time to read them?) Would secondary or middle-grade students be likely to read them? What if a teacher deliberately discussed such objectives before the students read? Would you predict that their comprehension would improve?

Graphic Organizers

In Chapter 6, we discussed how presenting new technical terms by means of graphic organizers can be an effective method of building prior knowledge. Graphic organizers also provide a means of setting purposes for reading. Students who are familiar with the nature of organizers from exposure to them in textbooks and discussions are in a position to produce organizers of their own. A purpose for reading can be to complete, or in some cases to construct, a graphic organizer. This approach can be very effective when several guidelines are observed:

- -

1. Familiarize students with the nature of graphic organizers by introducing organizers frequently in your discussion of course material and by calling attention to the different types of organizers and their characteristics.

2. Suggest the three-step process for construction of a graphic organizer presented in Chapter 6. You will recall that these steps include (a) listing key terms, (b) identifying within the list clusters of closely related terms,

FIGURE 7.5

Textbook example
of purpose setting
by objectives

SOURCE: From *Life
Science* (p. 294) by
L. Balzer, L. A. Berne,
P. L. Goodson, L. Lauer,
and I. L. Slesnick, 1990,
Glenview, IL: Scott,
Foresman. Copyright
1990 by Scott, Foresman.
Reprinted by permission
of Scott, Foresman.

Objectives

After completing this section you
will be able to
A. Describe the special structures
of mollusks.
B. State how mollusks get food.

Figure 14-1 All mollusks have a
similar body structure.

14-1 Mollusks

Mollusks Have Mantles

Perhaps you have ordered a plate of mollusks in a restaurant. Many people enjoy eating these soft-bodied invertebrates. **Mollusks** (mol'əsks) have soft bodies, generally covered by a hard shell. This phylum includes clams, oysters, scallops, octopi, slugs, snails, and squid. Some mollusks, such as snails, are small and live inside tiny shells. Other mollusks, such as giant clams, grow quite large, and have massive shells. The cuttlefish is a mollusk with only a small remnant of a shell inside its body. Other species, such as squid, have no shells at all. The North Atlantic squid grows over 18 meters long!

Even though the mollusks in *Figure 14-1* do not look alike, they do have the same basic body structure. All mollusks have a soft body and a special fold of tissue called the **mantle** (man'tl). Look for the mantle in each of the mollusks in *Figure 14-1*. As you can see, the digestive system is found under the mantle. In addition, all mollusks have a muscular foot. The foot helps the mollusk move and capture prey.

The mantle of most mollusks secretes a hard, protective shell. Find the scallop in *Figure 14-1*. It is a **bivalve** (bī'valv), because it has two shells hinged at the base. The marine snail in *Figure 14-1* is a **univalve** (yu'nə valv). It has only one shell. Bivalves and univalves move by gliding, digging, or swimming with the aid of their strong muscular feet.

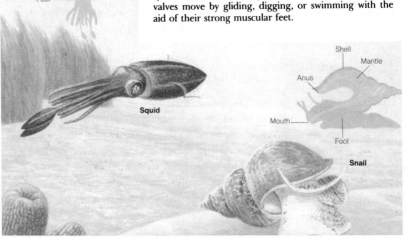

150

and (c) designing a diagram that best predicts the relationship among the terms in a given cluster.

3. Do not begin by requiring students to follow this three-step process in its entirety. Instead provide them with the opportunity to *complete* graphic organizers by inserting terms at appropriate positions. As students acquire experience in completing the diagrams, present them with progressively more demanding tasks. Such a progression might proceed as follows:

   a. *From a list,* students select terms and write them into the appropriate positions within a partially drawn organizer.

   b. *Without a list,* students write terms into a partially drawn organizer, selecting them from the reading material in general.

   c. Students construct an organizer given *only* a cluster of terms, but no diagram.

   d. Students produce a viable organizer without the teacher's having specified which terms or the type of organizer.

   The first three steps in this progression are illustrated in Figure 7.6, which is again based on our reading selection about the planet Pluto.

• •

FIGURE 7.6

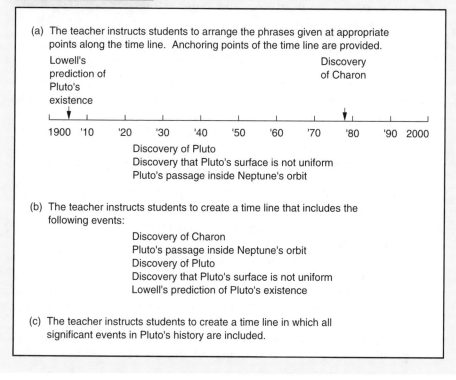

(a) The teacher instructs students to arrange the phrases given at appropriate points along the time line. Anchoring points of the time line are provided.

Lowell's prediction of Pluto's existence

Discovery of Charon

1900 '10   '20   '30   '40   '50   '60   '70   '80   '90 2000

Discovery of Pluto
Discovery that Pluto's surface is not uniform
Pluto's passage inside Neptune's orbit

(b) The teacher instructs students to create a time line that includes the following events:

Discovery of Charon
Pluto's passage inside Neptune's orbit
Discovery of Pluto
Discovery that Pluto's surface is not uniform
Lowell's prediction of Pluto's existence

(c) The teacher instructs students to create a time line in which all significant events in Pluto's history are included.

Three progressive graphic organizers based on "Pluto"

Producing graphic organizers is a relatively structured process that lends itself to the more highly structured of our global plans—namely, the DRA and the Explicit Teaching Model. The technique also seems suitable to the Directed Reading–Thinking Activity, for the teacher could encourage student predictions about how a given organizer should be correctly completed. During a prereading discussion, the teacher might also elicit competing graphic organizers from students with the idea that they would then read to decide which organizer best reflected the content. Producing graphic organizers is perhaps least suited to KWL and to the rather open-ended discussions this plan invites prior to reading.

ConStruct   Vaughan (1982) has suggested a technique in which students with some familiarity with organizers read for the purpose of constructing a single, comprehensive organizer. In this process of *concept structuring*, the students initially read rapidly, striving only to produce a sketchy, skeletal diagram involving the main topic and major subtopics. The students read a second time (more carefully) with the goal of elaborating on this scant beginning. A much more detailed organizer results. After studying this diagram, the students read for a third time to clear up any remaining points of confusion. The ConStruct approach clearly requires that students be familiar with graphic organizers in advance and Vaughan suggests modeling them before using ConStruct itself.

Charts

A good approach to many factually rich reading selections is to provide students with a chart requiring them to categorize information they encounter while reading. The teacher provides students with the structure of the chart, including column headings and in some cases the entire *first* column. The feature analysis chart can serve as a purpose-setting device as well as a means, discussed in Chapter 6, of presenting the terms in a prereading discussion. Figure 7.7 depicts how such a chart might be used to guide students through the Pluto selection. Note that the column headings are completely provided and, in addition, the first column has been completed to further limit the students' focus as they read. Completing an example or two while explaining the chart to students can be helpful.

As in the case of graphic organizers, students will become accustomed to the nature of feature analysis charts when teachers make frequent use of them during the introduction of technical vocabulary. They should come to consider completing such charts while they read as a natural application of charting activities.

A wide variety of charts is available, and feature analysis is only one of many possibilities. To illustrate the range of types, we have included a very

FIGURE 7.7

The following chart allows students to integrate information about Pluto with information previously learned about other planets.

Planets	Mainly gaseous	Larger than Earth	Has at least one moon	Has an atmosphere	Has rings	Nearer sun than Earth
Mercury						
Venus						
Earth						
Mars						
Jupiter						
Saturn						
Uranus						
Neptune						
Pluto						

A feature analysis chart over "Pluto"

simple "T"-chart in Figure 7.8, also based on the Pluto passage. Like the feature analysis chart, it requires higher-level thinking (inferential and critical). As with the construction of graphic organizers, the completion of charts helps to make reading an active process, one that engages students as they read.

When teachers specify the structure of a chart, indicating what information it will contain and how that information will be arranged, the approach is compatible with the more directive global plans, such as the DRA and the Explicit Teaching Model. We believe charting is more broadly viable, however. For example, a teacher might propose the chart in Figure 7.8 as a way of helping students test their DR–TA predictions about the existence of life on Pluto. In addition, charts can help organize the information supplied by students during the "K" step of KWL. These same charts could then help them decide what they wish to learn during the "W" step.

Problem Solution

Providing students with the opportunity to apply what has been learned to the solution of a problem is a good way to direct comprehension toward a higher-level purpose. Dahlberg (1990) argues that students are already

FIGURE 7.8

A "T"-chart over "Pluto"

The teacher instructs students to read in order to complete the chart below.

Evidence that argues *against* the existence of life on Pluto	Evidence that argues *for* the existence of life on Pluto

experienced problem solvers in out-of-school contexts and that teachers can and should tap their ability. Let's begin by differentiating between two types of problems useful for setting purposes.

One involves mathematics and science content designed to develop students' abilities to solve a particular kind of problem (for example, solving a second-degree equation using the quadratic formula or computing force vectors in beginning physics). This type of problem solving differs very little from the technique of merely making the objectives of a reading assignment clear in advance. That is, learning to solve problems of a particular kind is one type of objective that a teacher might specify prior to reading. Naturally, the material to be read focuses on problems of precisely this sort.

The second kind of problem-solving purpose is considerably different. It involves presenting students with a single, overarching problem that can be approached using the information acquired through reading. The selection to be read, however, may not directly focus on such problems. For example, the social studies teacher might assign students the task of creating a plan to contend with their community's air pollution problem. This teacher instructs the students to consider carefully the information acquired by reading a specific selection on air pollution together with information presented through class discussion and lecture. A math teacher might begin a trigonometry unit by providing students with a diagram of their school grounds complete with precise measurements and angles, suggesting to them the need for determining specific missing measurements. Their study of the trigonometry materials should eventually permit them to solve the myriad of problems such a framework might provide. These are examples of what Dahlberg calls "real life problems" (1990, p. 14), the sort most likely to motivate students by demonstrating how content relates to their lives.

As a third example, consider again our Pluto selection. A science teacher might provide the following task to students prior to reading:

> Imagine that you are assigned the task of designing a spacesuit for use on a mission to Pluto. Begin your assignment by reading the selection to discover what conditions are like there. Then describe the special characteristics your suit might need to possess.

Problem solving is teacher directive, making it highly suitable to the DRA and Explicit Teaching Model. However, after providing students with teacher-generated problems of this sort, instructors might be able to use a problem format as a way of encouraging predictions during the Directed Reading–Thinking Activity. In other words, a teacher might propose a problem and request that students formulate specific predictions with respect to solving it. They would then read to test their predictions and thereafter to reexamine the problem.

Summary Writing

Reading for the purpose of later composing a summary of what is read has a number of distinct advantages. It stresses the interconnectedness of reading and writing. It gives students the opportunity to reconsider content and

It is my ambition to say in ten sentences what everyone else says in a whole book.
Friedrich Nietzsche

to reorder it within their own thinking. It also compels students to identify the most important ideas contained in a reading selection. In fact, the most important comprehension skill underlying the ability to summarize is the capacity to distinguish more important from less important information. Finally, summarization is suitable for use with any kind of prose material, expository or narrative. It is perhaps an especially useful device with (1) selections containing a large amount of detailed, though not always highly pertinent, information and (2) narrative selections involving extremely complex sequences of events.

Writing good summaries is usually an acquired skill, however, and some direct instruction may be needed. Two recommendations for guiding students in writing summaries have been examined in recent years. Both have proved effective.

Hill (1991) has suggested that students often find it more difficult to write summaries of expository material (such as textbook chapters) than of narrative selections. Teachers might be wise to begin summary writing with material organized chronologically (e.g., historical accounts and descriptions of processes). In Chapter 10, we specifically describe a writing activity aimed at summarizing the steps of a process.

In one approach to expository summaries, the teacher suggests that students write a single summarizing sentence for each section of the assigned reading selection. For example, for a textbook chapter that is divided by a number of subheadings, the students might compose one sentence per subsection. The resulting summary is the chaining together of these summarizing sentences. Miller and McKenna (1989) have suggested the additional step of segmenting the resulting summary into paragraphs based on major chapter sections. Students would need to write a topic sentence for each of these paragraphs. Cunningham (1982) conducted a study in which he found that this technique significantly enchanced the comprehension of fourth graders.

The second approach to teaching students how to summarize involves providing them with general guidelines. Bean and Steenwyk (1984) found that instruction based on the following six rules (originally suggested by Kintsch and van Dijk, 1978) resulted in significantly better products than those produced by students who had not been taught the rules:

1. Delete unnecessary and trivial material.
2. Delete material that is important but redundant.
3. Substitute a higher-order term for a list of terms.
4. Substitute a higher-order term for components of an action or process.
5. Select and incorporate topic sentences.
6. Where there are no topic sentences, write them.

One caution about the use of summary writing as a purpose-setting technique is that it tends to focus the attention of students on the *most* important information they encounter. Not surprisingly, Rinehart, Stahl, and Erickson (1986) found that comprehension of details was not enhanced through summary writing. Whenever a selection presents a large amount of factual information, teachers might consider using summarization as a postreading activity and relying on other techniques to ensure that comprehension is adequately detailed. For this reason, we return to the subject of summary writing in Chapter 10. A further limitation is that summary writing is teacher directed despite its apparent open-endedness. The task itself is clear-cut and does not lend itself to the predictions generated through the Directed Reading–Thinking Activity or to the goals set by students during the "W" step of KWL.

Outlining

When students read for the purpose of outlining a selection, two important benefits can result. One is that the *product* they produce—the outline itself—can have later usefulness as a review guide. The other is that the *process* of outlining as they read encourages them to see important relationships that exist among ideas. Disadvantages of outlining are that it can be highly tedious and that many materials are not amenable to outlining (such as narratives and loosely structured nonfiction).

Like summarizing, outlining may require some direct attention from teachers if students are to engage in it successfully. Because one of the most important skills underlying successful outlining is the classification of concepts into categories and subcategories, it is advisable to precede any use of outlining with practice in such vocabulary techniques as List-Group-Label (discussed in Chapter 6) and nested categorizing (presented in Chapter 10). These techniques should adequately familiarize students with the logical skills needed in outlining. Once students are familiar with the notion of subcategorizing ideas, the teacher can provide sample outlines. These are complete, model outlines that represent the content of a given selection. For example, after students have completed a textbook chapter, the teacher might distribute an outline of its content, pointing out key characteristics of the outline and advising students to keep it as a review aid. The teacher should then progress toward providing students with incomplete outlines prior to reading—outlines with the innermost entries deleted and marked only with appropriate letters or numbers. These "shells" have most of the entries intact but omit certain details that the students must identify and insert. Figure 7.9 provides an example based on the Pluto selection we saw in Figure 7.2.

Some authorities argue that the final goal of using outlining as a purpose-setting technique is for the student to be able to outline a selection without the assistance of a shell. Our opinion is that this goal may be unrealistic

Portion of a shell outline for "Pluto"

FIGURE 7.9

I. Basic Astronomical Data
   A. Orbit
       1. Duration:

       2. Angle:

       3. Comparison with Neptune and Uranus:

Note that in this example colons indicate points at which students should enter information. The space provided should correspond to what the teacher expects students to record. Note too that outlining is less appropriate to the initial subsection, which is narrative rather than expository.

---

for many students and is certainly problematic with respect to many of the reading materials they are apt to encounter. We believe it is nearly always better to provide a partially completed shell outline. This practice affords students a degree of structure, content, and focus as they read. Such a technique is similar to providing students with a chart or incomplete graphic organizer for purpose setting. It is also similar to Lazarus's idea of *guided notes,* which we examine in Chapter 12, and to the notion of *content literacy guides,* explored in Chapter 8.

Requiring students to outline a selection is clearly teacher directive and is therefore more suitable to Explicit Teaching and the DRA than to KWL or the DR–TA. As we suggested, outlining may also possess an attitudinal limitation as well. Bromley (1985) found that middle-grade students clearly preferred summary writing to outlining, for example. She also observed, however, that these same students believed outlining placed them in a position to perform better on tests.

VARYING AND COMBINING TECHNIQUES

Being able to use a variety of purpose-setting techniques provides four powerful advantages. First, it allows teachers to introduce elements of novelty and variety that are now well recognized as ingredients of effective instruction. Second, teachers can match the type of technique to the nature of the material to be read. Third, they can combine two or more techniques for use with the same reading assignment. Finally, from exposure to a variety of techniques, students not only learn that reading should be purposeful but they also acquire an array of methods for making it so. Eventually, they can use these methods independently.

In the next chapter we examine ways in which purpose-setting techniques can be varied and combined to produce content literacy guides. These devices focus students' attention on the most important aspects of content, make reading an active rather than a passive process, integrate writing and reading, lead to the production of a useful review guide, and provide students with a resource to assist them in responding during class discussions. Such guides are based entirely on the various approaches to purpose-setting described in this chapter.

SUMMARY

The most effective reading is purposeful. Good readers have relatively clear notions of what they hope to accomplish through reading. Good teachers, therefore, either provide students with specific purposes prior to an assignment or help them to establish their own purposes. A variety of techniques is available for purpose setting, and in some the teacher plays a more directive role than in others. The degree to which the teacher directs student purposes depends both on the nature of the material and on the philosophy of the teacher.

Prereading questions are among the most versatile devices for setting purposes. They are well suited to developing multiple levels of comprehension (literal, inferential, and critical). They are useful with virtually any reading selection. They are often embedded by textbook authors. And they can be posed by students as well as teachers.

Numerous alternatives to prereading questions are available. Teachers can lead students to form predictions, or hypotheses, that they will then "test" by reading. This approach is less teacher centered than many but is not equally useful with all assignments. In contrast, teachers can simply specify in advance the objectives, or outcomes, of reading. This approach is highly directive and obviously well geared to Explicit Teaching.

Graphic organizers and charts provide students with the task of interpreting, classifying, and recording information as they read. In the former, they complete or construct a diagram; in the latter, they organize information in tabular form, given the headings of columns and the nature of rows. These techniques can be more or less teacher directed as desired.

Three relatively teacher centered approaches have been used successfully in recent years. Providing students with problems to be solved is a traditional mainstay of math and science instruction but can be extended to many disciplines with a little creativity. Summary writing encourages students to integrate content and identify its most important components. Outlining has the advantage of giving students a useful review guide. It works best when the teacher provides an unfinished, or "shell," outline to be completed by students during reading.

This wide variety of techniques allows teachers to match method with materials and to combine approaches for use with the same reading selection Exposure to a range of purpose-setting techniques also serves to model for students how they can make reading more deliberately purposeful as they work independently.

G E T T I N G   I N V O L V E D

In this chapter, we have described a number of methods useful in setting purposes. We have attempted to indicate how each method might be incorporated into the global plans introduced in Chapter 4. To summarize these connections, complete the chart presented in Figure 7.10. Each technique is listed in the first column while the four global plans head the remaining columns. Complete the chart by using the following coding system:

+ – Always or nearly always useful
s – Sometimes useful, perhaps with modifications
0 – Rarely useful; other methods preferable

FIGURE 7.10

Judge each of the purpose-setting techniques described in this chapter as suitable (+), unsuitable (0), or as sometimes suitable (s) in each of the global plans.

Purpose-setting Technique	DRA	DR–TA	KWL	Explicit Teaching Model
Teacher questions				
Student questions				
Predictions/hypotheses				
Objectives/outcomes				
Graphic organizers				
Charts				
Problem solution				
Summary writing				
Outlining				

Purpose setting in global lesson contexts

Be warned that while we have addressed these questions explicitly in a number of cases, you will be operating at the inferential and critical levels much of the time. Your answers may therefore differ from those of your classmates. This variation should not concern you as long as (1) you are able to indicate the facts underlying your inferences and critical judgments and (2) you remain open to changing your mind when you hear the explanations of others.

EIGHT

Content Literacy Guides

The whole art of teaching is only the art of awakening the natural curiosity of young minds for the purpose of satisfying it afterwards.

Anatole France

Imagine that you have arranged a field trip to a large national museum associated with your content area. Because the trip will afford your students a special opportunity to enhance their understanding of the subject, you want to do everything possible to ensure that their time will be well spent. You might begin by contacting the museum far in advance to acquire information about exhibits, the building's floor plan, and so on. You may then share this information with your students to acquaint them with what they can expect to find once they enter the facility. When the day of the trip arrives and you enter the museum with your class, you discover that for a small fee, tour guides are available to assist with your visit. While you personally prefer to explore museums on your own, you decide that a certain amount of guidance may be in the best interests of your students.

Once the tour begins, you become convinced that you made the correct decision. The guide leads your students along a preplanned route and stops at key points of interest. During each stop, the guide offers additional information about the exhibits and calls the students' attention to interesting and important features. Sometimes the guide raises questions or elicits student reactions in other ways.

Now consider the effect of not hiring a tour guide. Do you think that simply "turning the students loose" in the museum would produce results comparable to a guided situation? It is true that some of your more capable students would, like yourself, fare well in such circumstances. For most, however, the museum experience would likely be a random, structureless walk during which much was missed and much more was misunderstood. We suspect that even your more capable students would not have benefited to the same degree without a guide.

Our museum analogy closely parallels the situation in which a content area reading selection is assigned. Without guidance, students may wander rudderless through a sea of print, unable to distinguish what is important from what is not, comprehending its meaning inadequately.

OBJECTIVES

This chapter introduces methods of guiding your students through assigned reading. When you have completed it, you should be able to

1. list the key advantages of using guides in written form;

2. defend the use of guides for a wide range of reading selections and for students of high reading ability as well as weaker readers;

3. describe the major types of literacy guides and identify their advantages and potential drawbacks;

4. outline the steps of constructing a literacy guide; and

5. indicate how such guides are best employed in the classroom.

ADVANTAGES OF A WRITTEN GUIDE

We concluded the last chapter by suggesting several benefits of providing students with a literacy guide. It's true that some purpose-setting techniques can be used orally, such as posing key questions prior to reading. We argue, however, that the advantages of a written format are so persuasive that written guides should easily be the method of first choice. Let's reexamine the benefits in more detail.

First, guides help students to focus their attention on important aspects of content. A written format ensures that this focusing occurs at the appropriate time in their reading. The teacher who orally poses a number of questions before students read risks their forgetting one or more of these questions when they reach the appropriate portions of the assigned reading selection. If, on the other hand, the teacher provides these same questions in written form, along with page numbers of the material to which they relate, the student is in a position to reference each question at precisely the moment it will do the most good as a purpose-setting device.

Second, guides make the reading process active rather than passive (Herber, 1978). Suddenly, reading is more than turning pages until the last is reached. The immediate goal is to consult the guide and respond to it—in writing. By making reading *physically* active, chances are good that it will become *mentally* active as well. No longer can students engage in silent decoding without giving adequate thought to the ideas they encounter, for this is merely the illusion of reading. The guide prompts such thinking at the moment it is most opportune.

Third, guides help to integrate reading and writing. We have already described how the use of literacy processes complement one another as the student learns from written materials. Reading provides new information;

writing enables students to organize, refine, and extend their understanding of it. Guides permit these processes to work simultaneously, a synthesis that tends to be more productive than postponing all writing activities until after the students finish reading.

Fourth, written guides and students' responses to them produce a useful tool for review. In studying for tests, students with guides will have far more tangible assistance than the text itself, which they may have comprehended poorly to begin with. Moreover, well-constructed literacy guides serve as note-taking models that students may come to emulate when reading on their own.

Fifth, the completed guide provides students with a valuable discussion aid. Few experiences are as disconcerting for teachers as asking questions that students cannot answer. We are not suggesting that literacy guides will completely remedy this problem, but there is no doubt that postreading discussions will generally be smoother, quicker, and far less frustrating for students and teachers alike when students have completed literacy guides. The guide amounts to a blueprint of the ensuing discussion. While postreading talk may occasionally digress, the guide itself serves as the primary source of questions. Regular use of guides will rapidly instill in students an expectation that both discussion and examinations will follow the guides and that they are therefore well worth attending to while reading.

WHEN SHOULD LITERACY GUIDES BE USED?

Vacca, Vacca, and Rycik (1989) have suggested that literacy guides be used only with unusually difficult reading selections. They have argued that adequate comprehension will in most cases result when teachers take the trouble to prepare students orally for a reading selection. We strenuously disagree with this reasoning. It may be true that comprehension will be reasonably good without guides, for most students and most selections. However, there is now ample evidence that comprehension is better for students who make use of guides (Alvermann & Swafford, 1989). Armstrong, Patberg, and Dewitz (1988, 1989) observed not only superior comprehension but better transfer of learned strategies to new material among students who had used literacy guides. These results are hardly surprising since the advantages we have just discussed will always be present regardless of a selection's difficulty.

Another limitation often ascribed to literacy guides is that they are useful primarily for poor readers. It is probably natural for teachers (who tend to be good readers) to infer that because they can comprehend well without guides their better students also don't need them. These teachers tend to forget, however, that even their best students are not likely to be as sophisticated as they are in reading, especially when selections are drawn from the area of the teacher's greatest expertise.

There is now evidence that better students may actually benefit the most from literacy guides. Armstrong and colleagues (1988) found greater comprehension gains for good readers using guides than for poor readers also using guides. This research finding tends to confirm Savage's recommendation (1983) that guides be used with gifted students.

In summary, the two long-prevailing reservations about using literacy guides appear to be myths. One is that they are useful only with difficult selections. The other is that they are helpful only to poorer readers. The evidence suggests that guides are a powerful tool for a wide range of readers and a wide variety of selections. We now look at various types of guides in common use. As you read about them, it is important for you to consider each type in relation to your own content area. Consciously look for those you feel are most suitable to the sorts of material you intend to assign.

TYPES OF GUIDES

Content literacy guides come in an assortment of shapes and sizes. This diversity is natural since written materials vary considerably and the type of assistance students may need will vary also. Some formats are better researched than others and some have a better track record in content classrooms. Below, we examine the most common types together with one or two promising innovations.

Hierarchical Guides

In 1969, Earle suggested a format designed to lead students through three levels of mental processing as they read. His three-level guides consisted first of questions of a literal nature, having factual, explicitly stated answers. Next came a series of inferential questions that required students to arrive at logical conclusions based on stated facts. The final set of questions required students to apply and interpret what they had read. Herber (1978) and later Vacca and Vacca (1989) have subsequently urged content teachers to make use of three-level guides. An example of such a guide, which Armstrong and associates (1988) call a hierarchical guide, appears in Figure 8.1, for use with *The Grapes of Wrath*.

The rationale of the three-level guide is appealing. Presumably, it takes students through the proper process of critical reading—namely, by starting with stated facts, inferring other facts, and arriving last at judgments and applications. The main difficulty with such guides is that efforts to validate them through research have as yet been disappointing (Alvermann & Swafford, 1989). While the reasons for their failure are not entirely understood, one problem may be that students must answer every literal-level question first before answering a single higher-order question. Consequently, to make an inference based on the first subsection of a textbook chapter students must wait

FIGURE 8.1

Hierarchical reading guide for Steinbeck's *The Grapes of Wrath* (pp. 1-16)

Sample hierarchical reading guide

SOURCE: From "Reading Guides—Helping Students Understand" by D. Armstrong, J. Patberg, and P. Dewitz, March 1988, *Journal of Reading, 31*, p. 535. Copyright 1988 by the International Reading Association. Reprinted by permission of Diane Armstrong and the International Reading Association.

Directions: Place a ✓ beside the following statements that are true. You may use your book. The first number in the parentheses ( ) refers to the page where the information can be found; the second number refers to the paragraph(s).

1. _____ The sun flared down on the growing corn day after day. (1,1)
2. _____ By mid-June, the sky was darkened by the dust. (2,2)
3. _____ Everyone wore handkerchiefs and goggles over their nose and eyes whenever they went outside. (3,1)
4. _____ The children, who stood near their parents, were yelled at for playing in the dust. (4,1)
5. _____ The man who sat on the running board of the truck that said "No Riders" was dressed in old and mended clothes. (5, 1 and 2)
6. _____ The trucker wanted to be a good guy, so he let the hitch-hiker ride. (7,6)
7. _____ Tom Joad tells the trucker that he was in McAlester for 4 years for murder. (13)
8. _____ A land turtle tried to climb the highway embankment but failed because it was too high. (15,1)
9. _____ The lady in the sedan swerved her car to avoid hitting the turtle. (16,1)
10. _____ The truck driver hit and killed the turtle. (16,2)

Directions: Write a response to the following items. Be as specific as possible.

11. Chapter 1 presents the essential background information which causes the great migration toward California. *Briefly* explain the events that lead up to this (*and* the Joad family's) migration to California. (Ch. 1)

12. In Chapter 1, Steinbeck states: "And the women came out of the houses to stand beside their men—to feel whether this time the men would break." Explain how the next quote makes the first quote clear. "Women and children knew deep in themselves that no misfortune was too great to bear if their men were whole."

13. Explain what Tom Joad meant when he said: ". . . sometimes a guy'll be a good guy even if some bastard makes him carry a sticker." (7)

14. Often in Steinbeck's writing, there is the suggestion that human beings are victims of a hostile universe and have little or no control over their own destiny. Explain how the turtle in Ch. 3 is also a victim of this hostile universe.

Directions: Attempt to picture yourself in the following situations. Consider and react to each side of the situation. Also, point out the long term effects for each solution or decision.

15. You are driving along a deserted highway and see an injured dog (or cat) lying along the edge of the road. You are on your way to an important meeting and may be severely reprimanded (yelled at) or fined if you are late.

   (a) You stop and help the animal.
   (b) You continue on your way without stopping.

16. You have just moved to a new school district where no one knows you. Before you moved, you were arrested for shoplifting, but you don't want anyone in your new school to find out. Soon after school begins, one of your new friends casually asks you if you've ever "been in trouble."

   (a) You say no.
   (b) You say yes.

until they have completed the entire chapter. In our view, timing is a crucial difficulty with the traditional three-level guide and may in some cases actually hinder higher-level thinking.

Cluster Guides   Dennis and her colleagues (1989) reported remarkable success by modifying the three-level format. They simply arranged the questions in *clusters,* so that one or more literal questions were followed immediately by higher-level questions pertaining only to the literal questions preceding them. Then another cluster was encountered, again with literal questions first, and so forth. In this way higher-level thinking was encouraged at appropriate points in time before the students had progressed to other portions of the reading selections.

Nonhierarchical Guides

Armstrong and colleagues (1988) tested an alternative to the three-level guide, one in which questions at various levels were intermingled. This nonhierarchical guide follows the reading selection from start to finish. The teacher writes questions without concern for their level and arranges them in the order students will encounter the appropriate portions of the selection. Contrast the nonhierarchical guide depicted in Figure 8.2, also for *The Grapes of Wrath,* with the hierarchical approach represented in Figure 8.1.

Nonhierarchical guides have the advantage of positioning questions at the points where they are most answerable. Teachers merely concern themselves with what is important and leave the issue of levels to take care of itself. What these guides lack, however, is assistance in responding to the questions. The questions themselves offer a kind of guidance, of course, but there is little help in how to answer them. For this reason we prefer the cluster approach described in the previous section. Armstrong and her colleagues found that both hierarchical and nonhierarchical guides improved students' comprehension to about the same extent.

Guided Notes

Questions provide an effective format for content literacy guides, but they are not the only format. Lazarus (1988) has developed an approach called guided notes, which consists of an incomplete outline of the material. Originally designed for use with lectures, this technique required teachers to prepare a skeleton outline of the material they wished to present. Enough space was available for students to fill in the outline as the teacher spoke. Lazarus observed remarkable successes using guided notes with learning-disabled students.

While guided notes can be an effective device for use during lectures, modifying the technique for reading selections is a simple matter. Subheadings provide a natural basis for the skeletal framework, but it is probably a

FIGURE 8.2

Nonhierarchical reading guide for *The Grapes of Wrath* (pp. 1-16)

Directions: Complete the following guide. You may use your book. The first number in the parentheses ( ) refers to the page where the information can be found; the second number refers to the paragraph(s).

1. Which of the following statements are true? (Indicate with a T.)

    (a) _____ The sun flared down on the growing corn day after day. (1,1)

    (b) _____ By mid-June, the sky was darkened by the dust. (2,2)

    (c) _____ Everyone wore handkerchiefs and goggles over their nose and eyes whenever they went outside. (3,1)

    (d) _____ The children, who stood near their parents, were yelled at for playing in the dust. (4,1)

2. Chapter 1 presents the essential background information which causes the great migration toward California. *Briefly* explain the events that lead up to this (*and* the Joad family's) migration to California. (Ch. 1)

3. In Chapter 1, Steinbeck states: "And the women came out of the houses to stand beside their men—to feel whether this time the men would break." Explain how the next quote makes the first quote clear. "Women and children knew deep in themselves that no misfortune was too great to bear if their men were whole." (Ch. 1)

4. _____ (T or F) The man who sat on the running board of the truck that said "No Riders" was dressed in old and mended clothes. (5, 1 and 2)

5. _____ (T or F) The trucker wanted to be a good guy, so he let the hitch-hiker ride. (7,6)

6. Explain what Tom Joad meant when he said: ". . . sometimes a guy'll be a good guy even if some rich bastard makes him carry a sticker." (7)

7. _____ (T or F) Tom Joad tells the trucker that he was in McAlester for 4 years for murder. (13)

8. Attempt to picture yourself in the following situation. Consider and react to each possible solution. Also, point out the longterm effects for each.

    You have just moved to a new school district where no one knows you. Before you moved, you were arrested for shoplifting, but you don't want anyone in your new school to find out. Soon after school begins, one of your new friends casually asks you if you've ever "been in trouble."

    (a) You say no.

    (b) You say yes.

9. _____ (T or F) A land turtle tried to climb the highway embankment but failed because it was too high. (15,1)

10. _____ (T or F) The lady in the sedan swerved her car to avoid hitting the turtle. (16,1)

11. _____ (T or F) The truck driver hit and killed the turtle. (16,2)

12. Again, attempt to picture yourself in the following situation. Consider and react to each side of the situation. Also, point out the longterm effects for each solution or decision.

    You are driving along a deserted highway and see an injured dog (or cat) lying along the edge of the road. You are on your way to an important meeting and may be severely reprimanded (yelled at) or fined if you are late.

    (a) You stop and help the animal.

    (b) You continue on your way without stopping.

13. Often in Steinbeck's writing, there is the suggestion that human beings are victims of a hostile universe and have little or no control over their destiny. Explain how the turtle in Ch. 3 is also a victim of this hostile universe.

Sample nonhierarchical reading guide

SOURCE: From "Reading Guides—Helping Students Understand" by D. Armstrong, J. Patberg, and P. Dewitz, March 1988, *Journal of Reading, 31,* p. 536. Copyright 1988 by the International Reading Association. Reprinted by permission of Diane Armstrong and the International Reading Association.

FIGURE 8.3

Portion of a guided
notes guide over "Pluto"

Compare this example with the simpler outline format of Figure 7.9.

Basic Astronomical Data

Orbit

    Length in years: _____

    Angle of tilt: _____

    Planet now furthest from the sun: _____

    Nearest distance between Pluto and Neptune: _____

good idea to go one step further and indicate the sorts of information and conclusions students should derive from *within* each subsection. Even though guided notes are not based on questions, the resulting product is nevertheless a useful tool during postreading discussions. In fact, Lazarus and McKenna (1991) found that a combination of guided notes and subsequent review produced the best results. Figure 8.3 provides an example of guided notes applied to the selection on the planet Pluto presented in Chapter 7 (Figure 7.2). Note how this example differs slightly from the simpler outlining approach (Figure 7.9) by providing additional suggestions about what the student should write. Take a moment to contrast the two examples.

Selective Guides

Cunningham and Shablak (1975) developed a guide that not only focuses attention on elements a teacher feels are important but actually encourages students to skim or skip other portions of a selection. This approach may remind you of Samuel Johnson's remark, quoted in Chapter 7, that he seldom read every word contained in a book. The rationale behind selective guides is the same as Johnson's: All parts of a reading assignment may not deserve equal attention and concentration.

We are too civil to books. For a few golden sentences we will turn over and actually read a volume of four or five hundred pages.

Ralph Waldo Emerson

By means of a selective guide, the teacher makes these decisions for students in advance, and Cunningham and Shablak reasoned that repeated use of such guides would encourage students to become more flexible and selective readers by themselves.

Selective guides address two of the recurrent problems of textbook reading assignments. One is that readability tends to fluctuate among chapters and even among sections of the same chapter. The other is that the writing is often dense with facts, not all of which are vital to an understanding of the content. Selective guides aid students in selecting the wheat and ignoring the chaff. Teachers must begin by closely examining the selection to be assigned. They must first decide what students should *know* after completing the assignment by identifying important ideas, concepts, and supporting details. They must then decide what students can be expected to *do* as well, and to identify the information needed to do it. The result is a blend of questions, comments, and suggestions. Tierney and associates (1990, pp. 240–241) offered these examples of the kinds of remarks a teacher might include in a selective guide:

- P. 93, paragraphs 3–6. Pay special attention to this section. Why do you think Hunter acted in this manner? We will discuss your ideas later in class.
- P. 94, subtopic in boldface print at top of page. See if you can rewrite the topic to form a question. Now read the information under the subtopic just to answer the question. You should pick up the five ideas very quickly. Jot down your answers in the space provided below.
- P. 94, picture. What appears to be the reaction of the crowd? Now read the fifth paragraph on this page to find out why they are reacting as they are.
- P. 95, paragraphs 5–8. Read this section very carefully. The order of the events is very important and you will want to remember this information for our quiz.
- P. 179, all of column 1. The author has provided us with some interesting information here, but it is not important for us to remember. You may want to skim over it and move on to the second column.
- Pp. 180–181. These pages describe a fictitious family who lived during the Civil War. You may skip this section because we will learn about the life-styles of the time through films, other readings, and class discussions.
- Pp. 221–222. Recent discoveries in science have improved the information contained on these pages. I will discuss this information with you in class. Now move on to page 223.

Note how the last three examples encourage students to skip and skim particular sections of the assignment.

Tierney and his associates (1990) have suggested that content teachers gradually wean students away from selective guides. Our belief is that there is little reason to do so. Molding students into independent readers is not likely to result from gradually reducing the support that guides offer for a single textbook. A sizable advantage in prior knowledge of content will always place the teacher in the better position to judge what should be skimmed and what should be read with deliberate care.

Point-of-View Guides

Wood (1988) introduced a new type of guide designed to assist middle-level students with textbook assignments. Her point-of-view guide uses questions in an interview format "to allow students to experience events from alternative perspectives" (p. 913). A variety of interview questions pushes the student to comprehend at more than one level of thought. The teacher begins by choosing an appropriate perspective on the material the students will read. In Wood's own example (see Figure 8.4), students will respond to a guide covering materials on the War of 1812 by assuming the role of a U.S. inhabitant during the period. The viewpoint the teacher selects, however, might just as well as be a specific person, such as a leader, scientist, or writer.

FIGURE 8.4

Example of a point-of-view guide

SOURCE: From "*Guiding Students through Informational Text*" by K. Wood, 1988. *The Reading Teacher, 41*, p. 914. Copyright 1988 by the International Reading Association. Reprinted by permission of Karen Wood and the International Reading Association.

Chapter 11: The War of 1812

You are about to be interviewed as if you were a person living in the United States in the early 1800s. Describe your reactions to each of the events discussed next.

Planting the Seeds of War (p. 285)
1. As a merchant in a coastal town, tell why your business is doing poorly.

The War Debate (p. 285-7)
2. Explain why you decided to become a war hawk. Who was your leader?
3. Tell why many of your fellow townspeople lowered their flags at half mast. What else did they do?
4. What was the reaction of Great Britain to you and your people at that time?
5. In your opinion, is America ready to fight? Explain why you feel this way.

Perry's Victory (p. 287)
6. In what ways were your predictions either correct or incorrect about Americans' readiness to fight this war?
7. Tell about your experiences under Captain Perry's command.

Death of Tecumseh (p. 288)
8. Mr. Harrison, describe what really happened near the Thames River in Canada.
9. What was Richard Johnson's role in that battle?
10. Now, what are your future plans?

Death of the Creek Confederacy (p. 288)
11. Explain how your people, the Cherokees, actually helped the United States.
12. Tell about your leader.

British Invasion (p. 288-90)
13. As a British soldier, what happened when you got to Washington, D.C.?
14. You headed to Fort McHenry after D.C.; what was the outcome?
15. General Jackson, it's your turn. Tell about your army and how you defeated the British in New Orleans.

The Treaty of Ghent (p. 290)
16. We will end our interview with some final observations from the merchant questioned earlier. We will give you some names and people. Tell how they fare now that the war is over: the British, the Indians, the United States, Harrison, Jackson.

The point-of-view guide offers several advantages that we feel make it useful, even with students above the middle grades. First, it encourages writing about what is read, sometimes at length. Second, Wood's experiences reveal that students feel less pressure to use "textbook language." They feel freer to reexpress content in their own words. Third, the point-of-view guide seems applicable to a variety of content subjects. As Wood (1988) observes, "In literature students can assume the role of various characters as they react to events in a story. In science, they can describe the process of photosynthesis from the perspective of a plant or the act of locomotion from the perspective of an amoeba" (p. 915). Fourth, such guides encourage perspective taking—seeing issues from another's viewpoint. Gardner and Smith (1987) observed that this ability is related to inferential comprehension. Point-of-view guides may therefore offer the bonus of enhancing student inferences.

Anticipation Guides

Readence, Bean, and Baldwin (1981) developed a very different kind of guide, especially for use with materials involving controversy or factual misunderstanding. Their anticipation guide consists of a series of statements about the material covered by the selection. Students read the statements prior to the selection and indicate whether they agree or disagree with each. The teacher and the class openly discuss the statements, but the teacher refrains from suggesting responses. The rationale of the anticipation guide is simple: The statements serve to activate appropriate prior knowledge while a student's responses provide hypotheses to be tested through reading. You may see a similarity between anticipation guides and the Directed Reading–Thinking Activity (DR–TA). Both are based on hypothesizing as a purpose-setting technique, and these guides can play a natural role in the DR–TA global format.

Figure 8.5 shows an example of an anticipation guide based on the Pluto passage from Chapter 7. This particular illustration is a modification of the basic idea and is sometimes called an anticipation–reaction guide. Students place a check in the first column when they agree with the statement prior to reading. They place a check in the second column if they *still* agree with the statement after they have finished reading.

In our view, teachers need to be cautious about using anticipation guides. To date, the research on their effectiveness has not been especially encouraging (Alvermann & Swafford, 1989). One reason may be that the statements are not linked clearly to specific portions of the selection (for example, by the indication of subheadings or page numbers). Another reason may be that by focusing on controversial issues for possible points of misunderstanding, the teacher may tend to ignore other important aspects of content. Finally, while emphasizing controversy may have the effect of motivating students (Lunstrum, 1981), it may also interfere with their adequate comprehension of a selection (Lynch & McKenna, 1990). The best advice may be to use anticipation guides with caution, perhaps in conjunction with other types of guide formats.

FIGURE 8.5

Example of an anticipation–reaction guide over "Pluto"

The teacher instructs students to read each statement in advance and to place a check in the first column if they agree with it. After they read, students are to return to the guide and put checks in the second column for each statement with which they still agree.

Before   After

_____   _____   1. Pluto has been observed by astronomers for centuries.

_____   _____   2. Pluto has a moon.

_____   _____   3. Pluto probably has life forms.

_____   _____   4. Pluto is the farthest planet from the sun.

_____   _____   5. Pluto is denser than Earth.

_____   _____   6. Pluto is smaller than Earth.

_____   _____   7. Pluto's day is longer than Earth's.

_____   _____   8. Pluto has an atmosphere.

CONSTRUCTING A LITERACY GUIDE

Our discussion of various formats for content literacy guides should in no way limit your thinking about to how construct them. The reading selection itself should always be the major factor in developing a guide. Rather than using one of these formats you may wish to improvise a unique format. You can use any of the purpose-setting devices discussed in Chapter 7—including questions, charts, graphic organizers, problems, and the like—to develop a guide. These hybrid guides are ideally suited to the reading selections they cover. The key to constructing them is to be familiar with a wide variety of purpose-setting techniques. Figure 8.6 (pp. 176–177) presents such a guide, based on the Pluto section of Figure 7.2.

We offer the following suggestions for constructing a content literacy guide that will effectively focus attention and enhance comprehension as students read. The first four suggestions come from Earle (1969) in an early discussion of study guides.

1. *Analyze the material.*   Read the selection carefully to decide which information to emphasize. Ask yourself what thought processes students will need to use as they read. For example, will they need to classify

information into categories? If so, the completion of a chart may be an effective format for a guide. Will they need to understand the relationships among clusters of concepts? In this case, the completion or construction of a graphic organizer may be warranted. Do they need to be able to recall detailed factual information? Guided notes may be indicated. Do they need to arrive at inferences based on the factual information presented? Here, question clusters proceeding from literal to inferential thinking would be ideal.

2. *Don't overcrowd the print.*   A page teeming with type may overwhelm some students, particularly weaker readers. Effective guides contain plenty of white space, inviting the students to make notes. The best guides are friendly aids, not laborious appendages that simply add to the total reading assignment.

3. *Make the guide interesting.*   There is no reason a guide shouldn't motivate as well as assist. Use clear and considerate wordings. Rely on your own background knowledge to add an occasional (though brief) interesting tidbit or sidelight. From time to time, you might also include a little cheerleading ("We're about to wrap this up," "You're doing great—only two more sections," etc.).

4. *Review your own purposes.*   When you have finished the guide, read over it to ensure that it captures your own instructional objectives. Ask yourself whether students who successfully complete the guide will have the knowledge and skills that the reading and writing activities should give them. Be prepared to modify the guide whenever you are not satisfied.

5. *Use word processing to prepare the guide.*   Like any writing, the best literacy guides are not first drafts. Word processing tends to make revisions relatively painless. Since some of your best ideas for revision will come as a result of actually using the guide with students, it is important to keep your thoughts about a guide as fluid as possible so that changes can easily be made long after the guide is initially printed. Using a word processor helps to keep your thinking flexible.

6. *Include page numbers or subheadings.*   Students must know how each part of a guide relates to the reading selection. You can make this relationship clear by indicating the page numbers or subsections to which questions, charts, and so forth refer. Providing this information helps ensure that students will read and complete each section of a guide as they encounter the corresponding portion of the selection, rather than reading the entire guide in advance.

7. *Label the thinking skills students will need.*   When a guide consists of questions, consider labeling them according to the level of comprehension they require (literal, inferential, and so forth). In other cases, make sure to emphasize the skill in the instructions to the student. You might precede a chart with instructions like these: "In this section, be on the lookout for ways in which igneous, sedimentary, and metamorphic rocks are different. Classify them by putting a check mark in the chart when you find one of the characteristics listed."

FIGURE 8.6

Example of a hybrid
guide over "Pluto"

A hybrid guide, incorporating a number of types, is probably the most appropriate for
this selection because it varies so greatly in organization and readability. Note in
particular the cluster format over the final section and the summary writing task
designed to encourage students to select and reorganize the most important
information.

Discovery of Pluto and Charon

Skim this section rapidly. It gives a history of the planet and major discoveries about it.
Do note these years:

    Discovery of Pluto: ————

    Discovery of Charon: ————

Basic Astronomical Data

Pluto's Orbit

    "Eccentric" means unusual, not like the other planets

    What is the length of a year on Pluto (in Earth years)? ————

    What is the farthest planet from the sun at this time? ————

    The 2nd paragraph merely says that Pluto, Neptune, and Uranus take about the
same time to revolve once around the sun. This means they show up in about the
same places in the sky at periodic times.

Mass, diameter, density

    From the 1st paragraph, what is the current estimate of Pluto's density?

    Based on the 2nd paragraph, compare Pluto and Charon

      in diameter:

      in density:

    Table 24 gives the average distance of Pluto from the sun in astronomical units.
Since 1 a.u. = 93 million miles, compute the distance in miles.

    Skip the remainder of this section. It deals with the masses and diameters of Pluto
and Charon. Simply note these figures in Table 24 and record below:

	Mass	Diameter
Pluto	———	———
Charon	———	———

The Surfaces of the Planet and Its Satellite

Skim the 1st paragraph to see how scientists determined that Pluto's surface is irregular.

Read the 2nd paragraph carefully to answer these questions:

1. What does our best evidence tell us about Pluto's surface?

2. How does Pluto compare with Charon in brightness?

Possible Atmosphere

(Lit.) 1. What does Pluto's temperature tell us about its atmosphere?

(Lit.) 2. Why are hydrogen and helium probably not a part of Pluto's atmosphere?

(Lit.) 3. If Pluto has an atmosphere, the most likely gas within it is _____ .

(Inf.) 4. What do these facts suggest about the possibility of life on Pluto?

Now imagine that *Encyclopaedia Britannica* has assigned you the task of rewriting the Pluto entry for use in a children's version of their series. Plan how you would organize the new entry and decide which facts to include and which to delete. Finally, write your entry as though it will be read by students in the upper elementary grades. Include whatever charts, diagrams, and so on you think would help such readers. Make sure to use subheadings. Aim for a total entry of about two pages.

8. Include comprehension aids. Some of the formats we've discussed, such as the selective reading guide, incorporate help with possible comprehension problems. We suggest that the best guides anticipate possible difficulties. That is, they should do more than set purposes; they should also assist students through potential pitfalls so they can actually accomplish the purposes. This assistance might include the following:

- quick definitions or synonyms for key terms
- bridging comments (for example, "This is like the example we read about in Chapter 2")
- clarifying comments that might paraphrase or summarize difficult passages
- indications of material that is extremely important
- indications of material that may be skipped or skimmed

USING CONTENT LITERACY GUIDES

There is more to using a content guide than simply distributing it—construction is only half the job. Begin with a final check of its adequacy by filling one out yourself. This exercise may alert you to important aspects of a selection that the guide may have ignored. It will also provide you with a convenient reference when conducting the postreading discussion. If you have produced the guide on a word processor you can easily correct those places where too much to too little space is available.

Guides and Inventories

For some students, being given a content literacy guide without further explanation will always be sufficient, but for many this is not enough. When you first begin using guides, it is a good idea to plan a minilesson around their use. Such instruction should make the purpose of the guide clear, and it should feature examples based on materials the students have already read. An excellent way to introduce guides at the beginning of a course is to tie them to a content literacy inventory (see Chapter 3). Recall that such an inventory presents students with questions pertaining to a brief portion of a chapter or other selection. Its open-book format makes the process very similar to completing a content literacy guide. In Chapter 3 we argued that inventories should be based on the initial chapter of a textbook so that the requirements of prior knowledge would be minimized. Another reason for placing them at the beginning of a course is to allow them to serve as models of the literacy guides that will become a regular feature of instruction. While discussing with students the results of their encounter with the inventory, you should make clear that you will be providing similar structure with subsequent reading assignments.

Guides and Comprehension Monitoring

An ample body of research informs us that good readers constantly monitor their own comprehension as they read (Paris, Wasik, & Turner, 1991). When a sentence or paragraph does not make sense, they reread to discover the source of the difficulty. When textual information jars their prior understanding of a topic, they consciously reason the matter through. When their purposes for reading are not being met, they ask why and seek out ways of meeting these purposes.

Content literacy guides facilitate the process of comprehension monitoring. Because they require written responses, students cannot proceed until they have fashioned an acceptable response to each task the guide presents—or at least until they *realize* they have been unable to do so. In this sense, guides model for students the very processes that mature readers use to check their understanding as they read. Teachers must make this fact clear to students. They must inform them that this is the manner in which effective reading should work and that students should endeavor to check their understanding whenever they read.

To the list of basic purpose-setting devices presented in Chapter 7, we can now add another: Assigning students the task of constructing a literacy guide, or of modifying, refining, or critiquing one that you provide. To do so, of course, they would need to be fairly familiar with guides of various types.

Using Guides from Day to Day

Once students become familiar with literacy guides, do not assume that no introduction is necessary. Always take a few moments to walk the students through a new guide. You might undertake this as part of a chapter walk-through, as discussed in Chapter 5. When the time for discussion comes, ask the students to place the completed guide on their desks and to refer to it as necessary when responding. By using the guide as a blueprint for your postreading discussion, you will reinforce for your students the expectation that completing it has benefits. Once the discussion is over, encourage students to keep the guide as an aid to review. You can reinforce this suggestion by basing examinations, in whole or in part, on the content of completed guides. Other ways to encourage students to complete guides include (1) assigning grades occasionally to the guides themselves and (2) administering tests during which the guides may be used (open-note tests).

Finally, be reflective. During class discussions be attentive to possible deficiencies, or "bugs," in your guides. Look on each discussion as a field test of the content literacy guide and be prepared to revise it when you discover problems. Having the guide on a word processor will make this procedure simple.

Guides and Cooperative Learning

Cooperative learning involves placing students in groups that work collaboratively to achieve common goals. An underlying idea is that cooperation is healthier and more productive than the competition that individual work may foster (Johnson & Johnson, 1989). Research on cooperative learning has been encouraging, with respect both to students' achievement and to their growth in social skills and attitudes (Slavin, 1988, 1989–1990). However, content area teachers in the secondary grades are often reluctant to experiment with the approach, perhaps because it differs so markedly from the lecture-oriented instruction they find more familiar.

Content literacy guides provide an excellent way of introducing cooperative learning in a limited, structured way. A good approach for teachers to begin with is Jigsaw (Aronson, Stephan, Sikes, Blaney, & Snapp, 1978). Freely adapted for use with literacy guides, the Jigsaw technique involves these steps:

1. Choose a reading selection that can be divided into relatively independent sections. For example, a biology chapter on mammals might contain sections on physical characteristics, different types of mammals, their geographic distribution, and so on. The idea is that each section could be comprehended adequately without first having read other sections. (This type of reading selection is necessary because each student will read only one section.)

2. Partition your literacy guides into sections corresponding to the sections of the reading assignment.

3. Develop an objective quiz over the entire selection.

4. Assign students to groups of about four. The groups should represent the ability distribution of your class. For a heterogeneous class, one above-average student, one below-average student, and two average students are recommended.

5. Build background for the reading selection in the usual manner, using techniques described in Chapters 5 and 6.

6. Give each student a portion of the literacy guide. Each group will have one person responsible for reading and completing a different portion of the partitioned guide.

7. Give each student an opportunity to teach the other group members the material he or she was assigned.

8. Administer the quiz to all students.

The knowledge that they must eventually pass a test over the material motivates the students to do well on their assigned work. Peer pressure is brought to bear in an unusual way, for students expect other group members to do well since their own grades depend on it.

Tierney and his associates (1990) list several potential problems with Jigsaw, including (1) the effect of student absences when the activity lasts more than one day, (2) the possibility that team members may not get along, and (3) the chance that a predominance of slow learners may prohibit the effectiveness of groups.

These problems are not without solution, however, and our experience is that Jigsaw is well worth the effort. A useful variation of the technique involves letting each team work collaboratively on completing an assigned section of the literacy guide. Each group then teaches their section to the rest of the class.

SUMMARY

Content literacy guides provide students with a variety of writing tasks as they read. They offer teachers and students a number of powerful advantages. Such guides focus the attention of students on important information and ideas as students encounter them in print. Guides make reading an active process during which students are involved in specific thinking tasks. In this way they provide an excellent means of integrating reading and writing. Completed literacy guides serve as review aids and as a prompt during class discussions.

Authorities differ on the subject of when to use content literacy guides and with which students. We discussed evidence suggesting that guides can improve comprehension of virtually any reading selection and that better students may profit from them as much as or more than students experiencing reading difficulties. These are strong arguments for the use of guides at all times.

Numerous types of guides have been developed and researched. Hierarchical guides use questions to move students from the literal to higher levels of comprehension. Three-level hierarchical guides pose all literal questions first, then progress to inferential questions and so forth, while cluster guides repeatedly move from literal to inferential or critical with each new subtopic. Nonhierarchical guides present questions in the order in which the material is organized, without regard to the question levels. Guided notes are composed simply of subheadings, suggestions as to important points students must work for with regard to each, and plenty of blank space in which to write. Selective guides assist students by indicating sections of greater or lesser importance and suggesting appropriate reading speeds. Point-of-view guides present questions in interview form, requiring the students to adopt the role of a specified individual. Anticipation guides survey the prior beliefs and expectations of students in the hope of alerting them to issues on which their thinking may change as they read. All of these types of guides have been the subject of numerous research studies. Some now seem to be more effective than others. In particular, the anticipation guide and the traditional three-level guide are currently somewhat suspect.

While no magic formula can produce perfect guides every time, a few simple suggestions will help. Teachers should begin by analyzing reading selections to determine what they actually expect students to derive from them. The guide itself should be unintimidating, with plenty of white space in which to write and with a format as interesting as possible. Teachers should review their own purposes in an effort to ensure that the guide reflects them. Word processing will make revisions reasonably easy. With lengthier selections, subheadings or page numbers will provide students with landmarks enabling them to correlate the guide with the selection. It is a good idea to label the thinking skills or levels associated with each writing task and to provide comprehension assistance—definitions, synonyms, restatements, and so on—wherever needed.

Prior to actual use, a teacher should complete the finished guide with expected responses, both as a final check for "bugs" and as a means of providing a discussion aid. A teacher should walk students through the guide rather than simply handing it out. It is important to familiarize students with the nature of literacy guides early on. Describing the content literacy inventory as the first in a series of guides can be highly effective. Also, presenting guides to cooperative learning groups can be an effective way to engage students in completing them. Teachers must use content literacy guides reflectively, remaining alert to problems and willing to revise whenever deficiencies become evident.

GETTING INVOLVED

1. Figures 8.3 and 8.5 present two possible guides for the same reading selection. Which of these formats, if either, would be suitable for the entire Pluto selection? Do you agree that a combined format, such as that of Figure 8.6, is preferable?

2. What part can literacy guides play in such global lesson plans as KWL and DR–TA? These plans compel students to develop their own purposes for reading. Would some types of literacy guides nevertheless be helpful in such lessons? On the other hand, could teachers effectively work with students to *produce* literacy guides as a group consensus activity before reading begins?

3. If you are currently teaching, prepare a content literacy guide for a selection you will assign in the near future. When the time comes, try an action research experiment in which you compare the discussion following use of the guide with the discussion of a comparable reading selection for which no guide was developed. Do the results convince you?

4. If you are not currently teaching, develop a literacy guide for a stand-alone selection that you may assign regardless of the official text or curriculum from which you may eventually teach. (We hope you have

chosen such a selection already, as part of Getting Involved activities in previous chapters.) It could be a magazine article, short story, essay, or poem. Follow the construction guidelines provided in this chapter as closely as you can. If you lack students with whom to field test your guide, exchange guides with a colleague in the same subject area and provide one another with feedback.

SECTION.............................four

Postreading Strategies

For at least three reasons content area teachers must follow up the reading material they assign before going on to other topics. One is the need to monitor how well students have comprehended. Another is to give them opportunities to practice applying the knowledge they have gained. A third is to extend that knowledge beyond what the text has provided. The two chapters in this section offer techniques for accomplishing these aims.

Chapter 9 discusses postreading questioning techniques. We suggest a distinction between true discussion and mere recitation and recommend a compromise position. We provide advice on how to plan, and we discuss such issues as deciding which students to call on, using time prudently, responding to unacceptable answers, and responding to acceptable ones. Chapter 9 also addresses alternatives to traditional teacher-led discussions, such as techniques that link questioning and writing.

Chapter 10 looks beyond postreading discussion to examine methods of reinforcing and extending students' knowledge of what they have read. We revisit some of the techniques for introducing vocabulary (see Chapter 6), this time as postreading reinforcement activities. We consider more extensive writing projects to further develop student understanding. We also describe activities with game formats. Last, we describe how previous content can be reinforced while new content is introduced by using such techniques as review and bridging.

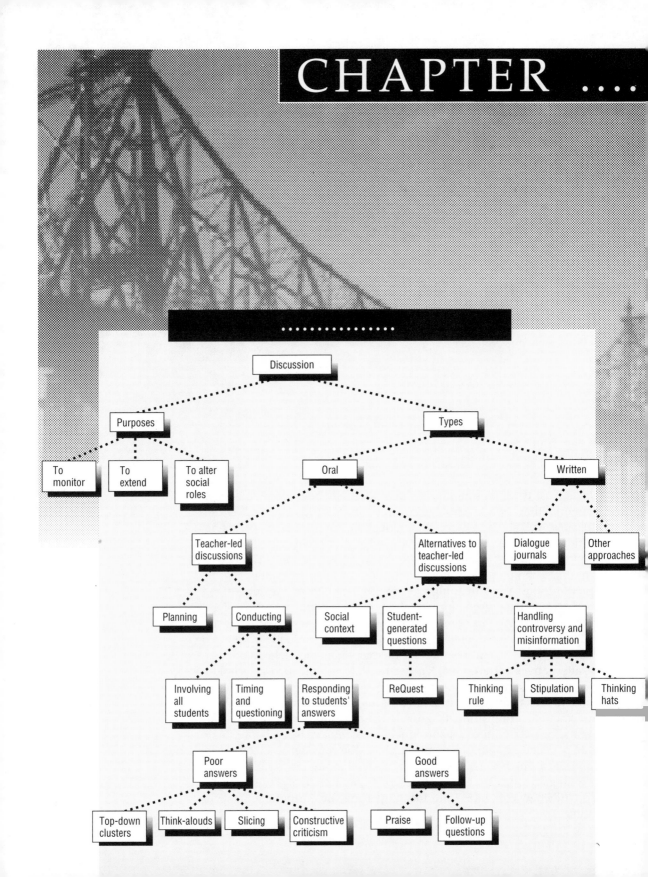

NINE

Effective Questioning

The first key to wisdom is this—constant and frequent questions . . . for by doubting we are led to arrive at the truth.

Pierre Abelard, c. 1120

Think back to the last classroom discussion in which you participated *as a student*. Did the experience focus on literal-level questions posed by the teacher, questions that required the recitation of clipped, parroted facts from the material covered? Now consider the last time you worked with friends in a study group or joined in an after-class conversation about the content of the presentation. Was the experience something more than a mere bandying of facts? Was it conducive to inferences and judgments? Was it dependent for direction on all the participants rather than a single individual?

This contrast is somewhat exaggerated and represents extreme positions concerning the proper purpose of questioning and discussion. Your own views of these purposes will do much to determine the kind of questioner, and the kind of discussion leader, you become. It is important for you to think through the issues involved and to develop a coherent philosophy of how questioning can best serve your students.

OBJECTIVES

When you have read this chapter on questioning, you should be able to

1. plan an effective discussion based on your instructional purpose or objectives;

2. identify the principles of effective questioning documented by research;

3. explain and apply such techniques as question clusters and think-alouds;

4. describe the importance of student-generated questions and explain methods for encouraging such questioning;

5. describe how the social context of a discussion influences how students participate;

6. suggest methods of taking the social context into account in encouraging student participation;

7. link discussion to the literacy processes of writing and reading; and

8. suggest classroom methods of encouraging students to formulate questions.

THE PURPOSES OF DISCUSSION

While we discuss questioning in the context of a postreading activity, geared to the content of the material read, most of the points to be made in this chapter apply to *any* instructional discussion, whether or not it is related to reading. Broadly considered, discussion can serve a variety of purposes, three of which are especially useful in classroom settings. Discussion allows teachers to monitor the extent to which students understand content. Moreover, it provides a means of developing their understanding further, especially when inadequacies are discovered. Finally, it serves as a vehicle for social interaction among teacher and students, who extend their learning and modify their perspectives by using language to share knowledge and ideas. Some authorities (e.g., Alvermann, Dillon, & O'Brien, 1987) prefer the term *recitation* to *discussion* whenever the activity is limited to the first of these purposes. Because we believe all three purposes can be served during the same activity, we use the more general term *discussion* in the remainder of the chapter.

Questioning used to monitor the extent of student understanding is the most common application. Research on effective teaching certainly confirms the need to keep abreast of how well students have comprehended new material, whether introduced by reading or other means (e.g., Rosenshine, 1986). And yet a discussion that consists entirely of low-level monitoring questions (the first type of experience we asked you to recall in the opening paragraph) seems overly tedious and not very likely to enhance students' interest or deepen their understanding. Nevertheless, such questioning has its place, as in the course of short, intensive review sessions. Literal questions can also serve the goal of monitoring effectively when embedded in the context of broader, meaning-extended questioning. This is the sort of discussion we argue for.

Questioning used to develop understanding further, to push students beyond facts toward an appreciation of their significance, is an equally worthwhile goal of discussion. A classic example of questioning used for this purpose is Socrates helping a student reach a mathematical inference. Note, however, that several of Socrates's questions called for everyday factual information. He asked these questions both to bring out the facts his student needed to arrive at the inference about the square root of 2 (the real point of the discussion), and to assure himself that the boy was actually in possession of these facts. If he hadn't been, Socrates could have helped him acquire the necessary information before continuing on toward the objective. The same process can guide students to the formation of defensible critical judgments. As with inferences, the formula is the same: *facts first, conclusions afterward.*

Vintage Questioning: Socrates and Meno's Boy

Soc.   Tell me, boy, do you know that a figure like this is a square?

Boy.   I do.

Soc.   And do you know that a square figure has these four lines equal?

Boy.   Certainly.

Soc.   And these lines which I have drawn through the middle of the square are also equal?

Boy.   Yes.

Soc.   A square may be of any size?

Boy.   Certainly.

Soc.   And if one side of the figure be of two feet, and the other side be of two feet, how much will the whole be? Let me explain: if in one direction the space was of two feet, and in the other direction of one foot, the whole would be of two feet taken once?

Boy.   Yes.

Soc.   But since this side is also of two feet, there are twice two feet?

Boy.   There are.

Soc.   Then the square is of twice two feet?

Boy.   Yes.

Soc.   And how many are twice two feet? Count and tell me.

Boy.   Four, Socrates.

Soc.   And might there not be another square twice as large as this, and having like this the lines equal?

Boy.   Yes.

Soc.   And of how many feet will that be?

Boy.   Of eight feet.

Soc.   And now try and tell me the length of the line which forms the side of that double square: this is two feet—what will that be?

Boy.   Clearly, Socrates, it will be double.

Soc.   Do you observe, Meno, that I am not teaching the boy anything, but only asking him questions; and now he fancies that he knows how long a line is necessary in order to produce a figure of eight square feet; does he not?

Men.   Yes.

Soc.   And does he really know?

Men.   Certainly not.

Soc.   He only guesses that because the square is double, the line is double.

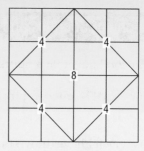

SOURCE: *From* Dialogues of Plato *(pp. 41–42) trans. by B. Jewett, 1892, New York: Macmillan.*

Questioning used to take advantage of social dimensions inherent in the classroom structure is just beginning to be understood. We do know that students and teacher alike adopt social roles as they discuss content and that these roles have important implications for the nature and extent of the thinking students do. A teacher cannot afford to pursue the first two purposes we have mentioned while ignoring the third, for social factors can reduce the effectiveness of a discussion if they are not considered.

Discussion as a Language Process

You may have noted that when discussion is used for the second of these purposes—extending and clarifying understanding—its role is similar to that of the literacy processes of reading and writing. Indeed, discussion involves the oral counterparts of these processes: listening and speaking. We have already seen that writing and reading are *constructive* activities, for through them students build an internal, mental representation of content. In this respect, speaking and listening are no different. In asking a question, the teacher places the student in the position of thinking through what he or she knows in order to *construct* a response. This construction does not simply evaporate once the response has been given. The act of having thought through the response affects the student's conceptualization of the topic. There are thus knowledge-building forces at work in a good classroom discussion—the same forces that lead to knowledge acquisition in reading and writing. Even when the teacher has posed key questions in advance (by means of a literacy guide, for example), so that students have thought through their responses before the discussion begins, the prudent teacher pushes, nudges, suggests, and encourages. Follow-up questions, not previously posed, extend the student's understanding as do the input of peers and the commentary of the teacher.

The Rarity of True Discussion

Classroom observational research, most notably by Dillon (1984) and Good and Brophy (1991), has shown that the actual use of discussion by teachers is rare. What is frequently referred to as discussion is in reality student recitation under the direct control and authority of the teacher. Student responses consist almost entirely of repeating information encountered in text or presented by the teacher through lecture. True discussion, during which there is a sharing of opinions and ideas by both teacher and students in an atmosphere of mutual trust and respect, simply does not happen in many content classes.

> *The only interesting answers are those which destroy the questions.*
> Susan Sontag

Alvermann, Dillon, and O'Brien (1987) have suggested three criteria for a true discussion:

1. the discussants must present multiple points of view and then be ready to change their minds after hearing convincing counterarguments;
2. the students must interact with one another as well as with the teacher; and
3. a majority of the verbal interactions, especially those resulting from questions that solicit student opinion, must be longer than the typical two or three word phrases found in recitations. (p. 3)

Note that these criteria do not preclude incorporating lower-level questions, used to monitor and reinforce. Figures 9.1 and 9.2 are examples offered by Alvermann and associates (1987) to aid in distinguishing recitation from discussion. They may be best seen as extremes on a continuum, however. Our view is that intermediate approaches are possible in which monitoring coexists with the open exchange of ideas. As noted earlier, we use the word *discussion* to refer to such approaches.

As you continue in this chapter, consider carefully the following points in the development and the encouragement of effective discussion in your own content classes:

1. What do you perceive to be the proper role of the teacher in classroom discussion?

FIGURE 9.1

An example of recitation

SOURCE: From *Using Discussion to Promote Reading Comprehension* (pp. 2–3) by D. E. Alvermann, D. R. Dillon, and D. G. O'Brien, 1987, Newark, DE: International Reading Association. Copyright 1987 by the International Reading Association. Reprinted by permission of Donna Alvermann and the International Reading Association.

Setting *Students in an eighth grade health class read a portion of the chapter on poison control the day before the videotaping. In the beginning segment of the transcript, which was typical of the entire lesson, Ms. Sneed quizzed the class on their assigned reading.*

Sneed
　All right, Vinny. Would you try to identify the poison for all victims or only the ones that are conscious?

Vinny
　All victims.

Sneed
　All victims. Good. Roger? Would you call the poison center for all victims or only the ones that are conscious?

Roger
　All of them.

Sneed
　All of them. Good. Lee? Would you treat for shock only those victims who are conscious or all victims?

Lee
　All victims.

Sneed
　All victims. Good. Would you watch to be sure that all victims keep breathing, Jeri, or only the conscious ones?

Jeri
　All.

2. Will you allow students to contribute new information and ideas to the class discussion?

3. What are your chief purposes for conducting discussions?

4. Do your students know how to participate in a discussion?

5. Are you willing to allow students to address one another during the discussion, or do you believe all student input must be directed at the teacher?

PLANNING A DISCUSSION

　　Good discussions don't just happen. They are the result of teachers' first deciding what they wish to accomplish and then planning to bring it about. We have described three general purposes for discussion, but more specific objectives are needed when a discussion is actually planned.

　　In the case of postreading discussions, the literacy guide provides a blueprint of the key points to be covered. In effect, the teacher plans the dis-

FIGURE 9.2

Setting *Students in Mr. McKay's all male eighth grade human development class had been assigned to read a chapter on sexist beliefs and behaviors. As this segment of the dialogue opens, McKay is attempting to get Manny to elaborate on an earlier response and, in so doing, to change his opinion.*

McKay
All right, Manny, what form of prejudice do you have toward females? Give me an example. (long pause; Manny looks up at the ceiling) Do you think it's all right for a female to play on the football team?

Manny (hesitantly)
No, because they aren't as strong as...I mean they have a different body structure than men.

Sam
But suppose you have a female who is as strong as the strongest male player on the football team?

Manny
I think she'd do the same or maybe better. (pause) What's your opinion, Reginald?

Reginald
I think they can be equal in jobs and stuff, but I don't think they should play, you know. I can undersand them playing baseball and soccer and maybe basketball. But I don't think they should play football. I wouldn't like it if they brought a woman into football.

McKay
A school in a neighboring county has a girl in football and she's strong.

Students (in unison)
In *football?*

McKay
Yes, she plays safety.

An example of discussion

SOURCE: From *Using Discussion to Promote Reading Comprehension* (pp. 3–4) by D. E. Alvermann, D. R. Dillon, and D. G. O'Brien, 1987, Newark, DE: International Reading Association. Copyright 1987 by the International Reading Association. Reprinted by permission of Donna Alvermann and the International Reading Association.

cussion before the reading assignment is made, while constructing the guide. Using the guide to determine the general course of the discussion is a major help, and it develops in students an expectation that discussions will be organized around guides. There is more to do, however. We offer a few suggestions for thinking through a discussion from start to finish, though we will see in the next section that not everything can be anticipated in advance.

1. Decide how to introduce the discussion. Like all instructional activities, discussions must be introduced in such a way that students are prepared for what is to come. Just as you now know to activate prior knowledge and set purposes before a reading assignment, you should plan similar measures for the beginning of a discussion. Reminding students of the key topics and telling them succinctly what you hope to accomplish are ways to start. You may occasionally vary this approach by asking a rhetorical question, offering a provocative quotation, or employing some other attention-getting device.

2. Decide where to depart from the guide. A discussion that merely "covers" the guide risks becoming as tedious as a discussion comprising only literal-level questions. Even if the guide contains higher-order questions, you have asked the students to think through them in advance so that sticking rigidly to the guide may have a deadening effect. Examine the guide for points where you wish to extend the knowledge and understanding of the topics a little further than the text. Think about how an effective departure question might be framed or what additional facts or examples you might wish to add. Students should come to expect these departures and may, with numerous chances, begin to anticipate them.

3. Decide whom to ask. In the next section we describe the importance of involving every student in every discussion. This does not mean that certain students should not be matched with specific questions. If you are trying to develop certain insights or comprehension skills in a particular student, then you might wish to earmark key questions. If you do not want a smoothly progressing discussion to bog down at a critical point, you might select in advance a capable student to handle an especially difficult question at that juncture.

4. Decide on an effective closure. Good discussions don't simply trickle away with the last question. They end, like all well-planned instructional episodes, with a summing up, an effective closure, in which important facts and conclusions are summarized in brief review. Students should develop an expectation that discussions will routinely end in this manner. You may involve them in this process by calling on them to offer key summary statements themselves. This is an excellent exercise in deciding which ideas and concepts are the most important.

CONDUCTING A DISCUSSION

Even though you have planned your discussion, conducting it is more than a matter of simply proceeding through your plan step by step. Unforeseen situations will inevitably arise. Being able to think on your feet and apply what is now known about effective questioning is the mark of the expert teacher. The guidelines we present in this section are powerful techniques that should become second nature.

Assuring Student Involvement

Not long ago, the first author observed a middle school teacher as she videotaped a class discussion. Her class consisted of equal numbers of boys and girls and an equal proportion of blacks and whites. During the discussion, the teacher addressed 90 percent of her questions to white females. When asked afterward why this had been her practice, she denied that she had done it. It was not until she reviewed the videotape that she became convinced of the fact! Her case is similar to that of many teachers who *think* they are distributing questions equitably but instead tend to direct them to a small subset of the class, usually abler students, who are most likely to respond appropriately.

Asking questions of students who can answer them creates the illusion of effective teaching. It may soothe our egos and deceive us into believing that widespread learning is occurring, but we are in fact denying ourselves the opportunity to monitor all students and to remediate difficulties when, through such monitoring, we discover them.

Effective questioners are systematic. They ensure broad student involvement by keeping track of which students have participated and which have not. Some studies have shown that even an obvious system can be effective, such as proceeding up one row, down the next, and so on. A difficulty with this approach is that it is predictable and may lose some students once their turn has passed. In addition, it does not mesh well with our advice about earmarking key questions in advance for certain students. A system that ensures involvement of students, while preserving some spontaneity and flexibility, is that of placing checks next to students' names once they have responded. You can tell at a glance who has yet to participate. (See Figure 9.3.) Two suggestions may make this approach especially effective. One is to use a plus (+) or minus (−) instead of a check to denote whether a question was successfully answered. You can then return to unsuccessful students in order to give them additional opportunities. The second suggestion is to make it a point to call on some students more than once even before everyone has had a chance. This policy prevents the notion that it is safe to drift off as soon as an answer is given (a problem with the up-one-row-down-the-next approach). In short, you can keep attentiveness relatively high by not being too predictable.

FIGURE 9.3

Student	Oct. 3
Adams, Bill	‿ − +
Cane, Brenda	+
Douglas, Rich	−
Elkins, Maxine	

. . .

Note: A plus indicates a correct or defensible response. A minus indicates a wrong answer or one that lacks a reasonable basis in fact.

The class roll can be used to chart student responses

Timing and Questioning

How questions are timed is an issue of great interest to classroom researchers. Four recurrent findings are noteworthy.

First, student attentiveness tends to increase when the teacher occasionally poses the question prior to naming a particular student to answer it. A teacher might say, for example, "In a moment, I'm going to ask someone to define *photosynthesis.*" This approach should not be the primary one used but should serve instead as a way of introducing variety and enhancing interest.

Second, it is a good idea to wait a few seconds following an incorrect answer or a failure to respond at all. This "wait time" provides the student a chance to think further, which is especially important in the case of higher-level questions. When a response is incomplete, incorrect, or otherwise inappropriate, wait time subtly conveys the message that more is expected. If you have never practiced wait time before, do not be surprised if it seems a little uncomfortable at first. Society conditions us to avoid "dead air"—periods of silence during conversation—but these are vital if thinking and talking are to occur together. (They don't always, as you know!)

Third, a subtle device useful on occasion (though not frequently) is to wait a few seconds after an appropriate response to an inferential or critical question. The wordless message that you expect more will often prompt students to elaborate on what they have already said.

Fourth, regardless of whether an answer is correct or incorrect, appropriate or inappropriate, the student needs feedback quickly. This knowledge may come from the teacher, from another student, or from printed materials referenced during the discussion, but it must come quickly. A recent comprehensive review of research on the timing of feedback can be summarized in four words: the sooner the better (Kulik & Kulik, 1988).

Responding to Incorrect or Inadequate Answers

We have been making a distinction between answers that are plainly wrong and those that are somehow inappropriate or inadequate. Our distinction concerns the *level* of the question. Literal questions, with clear-cut, "Christopher Columbus" answers, can be answered incorrectly. But when questions require students to arrive at inferences or critical judgments, the situation is more complex. With every critical judgment and many inferences, the issue is not correctness but defensibility, as in the example of Mr. Williams and his student, Harold. Has the student reasoned appropriately on a foundation of fact? This distinction—between questions with clear, factual answers and questions that require reasoning and judgment—is important in deciding how to react when a student has responded unacceptably.

Vintage Questioning: Mr. Williams and Harold

Not long ago, the first author observed the following interaction between an eleventh-grade student, Harold, and Mr. Williams, an American history teacher. The class had just finished reading a textbook chapter on the American Revolution and were about to begin a discussion. Mr. Williams led off with what he apparently thought was a rhetorical question.

"The Revolution," he said, "is the best thing that ever happened to this country. I think you'd all agree with that, wouldn't you?"

Toward the back of the room, one student raised his hand. Mr. Williams' expression wilted, just a little, as though he was afraid of what was to come.

"Harold?" he said.

The boy lowered his hand. "I'm afraid I disagree," he said. "I know most people don't think so, but I think the Revolution was the worst thing that ever happened, not the best."

Mr. Williams at that moment faced a classic dilemma. He had asked a critical-level question and was met with a response that he felt was inconsistent with the facts. His decision was to drop to the literal level, challenging Harold to back up his judgment.

"That's a pretty radical view," he said. "How did you arrive at it? Give us a few facts."

"Well," Harold began, "in the first place, we'd have avoided a lot of casualties on both sides. Surely that's worth something." He paused briefly and half smiled at Mr. Williams. "Plus, I've read ahead a little," he went on. "I learned that all the other colonies in Britain's empire were simply given their independence without a war. If we'd bided our time, that would probably have happened to us. We might have had a parliament instead of a congress, and a prime minister instead of a president, but so what?"

Mr. Williams looked thoughtful. "Anything else?"

"There's one thing," said Harold. "Britain abolished slavery in the 1820's. This affected all its colonies. But of course we were no longer in the empire so it didn't affect us. If we had been, we'd have been spared 40 years of slavery and probably the Civil War too."

"The Civil War?" someone asked.

"Sure. The South couldn't have fought the North plus Britain in the 1820's. They'd have had to give in."

By now even I was nodding my head. Harold had brought some "extra" facts into the discussion in order to defend an unpopular position in a novel way. To his credit, Mr. Williams acknowledged Harold's resourcefulness (though a little grudgingly, it seemed to me). When we ask critical questions, the results can sometimes challenge even our firmest judgments. So be prepared to model what you expect of your students!

Prompting   For literal questions, a useful technique is prompting. This is the process of providing the student with additional information, hints, and clues that might elicit a correct response. Good prompts progress from subtle nudges to heavy-handed pushes in the right direction. In the case of James Thurber's classmate, we see a student unable at first to recall a specific fact but compelled by stronger and stronger prompts to arrive at last at the answer. Prompting isn't always successful, to be sure (as Thurber's example shows!), but it is a skill worth developing and applying.

Vintage Questioning: James Thurber

Another course that I didn't like, but somehow managed to pass, was economics. I went to that class straight from the botany class, which didn't help me any in understanding either subject. I used to get them mixed up. But not as mixed up as another student in my economics class who came there direct from a physics laboratory. He was a tackle on the football team, named Bolenciecwcz. At that time Ohio State University had one of the best football teams in the country, and Bolenciecwcz was one of its outstanding stars. In order to be eligible to play it was necessary for him to keep up in his studies, a very difficult matter, for while he was not dumber than an ox he was not any smarter. Most of his professors were lenient and helped him along. None gave him more hints, in answering questions, or asked him simpler ones than the economics professor, a thin, timid man named Bassum. One day when we were on the subject of transportation and distribution, it came Bolenciecwcz's turn to answer a question. "Name one means of transportation," the professor said to him. No light came into the big tackle's eyes. "Just any means of transportation," said the professor. Bolenciecwcz sat staring at him. "That is," pursued the professor, "any medium, agency, or method of going from one place to another." Bolenciecwcz had the look of a man who is being led into a trap. "You may choose among steam, horse-drawn, or electrically propelled vehicles," said the instructor. "I might suggest the one which we commonly take in making long journeys across land." There was a profound silence in which everybody stirred uneasily, including Bolenciecwcz and Mr. Bassum. Mr. Bassum abruptly broke this silence in an amazing manner. "Choo-choo-choo," he said, in a low voice, and turned instantly scarlet. He glanced appealingly around the room. All of us, of course, shared Mr. Bassum's desire that Bolenciecwcz should stay abreast of the class in economics, for the Illinois game, one of the hardest and most important of the season, was only a week off. "Toot, toot, too-tooooooot!" some student with a deep voice moaned, and we all looked encouragingly at Bolenciecwcz. Somebody else gave a fine imitation of a locomotive letting off steam. Mr. Bassum himself rounded off the little show. "Ding, dong, ding, dong," he said, hopefully. Bolenciecwcz was staring at the floor now, trying to think, his great brow furrowed, his huge hands rubbing together, his face red.

"How did you come to college this year, Mr. Bolenciecwcz?" asked the professor. "*Chuf*fa chuffa, *chuf*fa chuffa."

"M'father sent me," said the football player.

"What on?" asked Bassum.

"I git an 'lowance," said the tackle, in a low, husky voice, obviously embarrassed.

"No, no," said Bassum. "Name a means of transportation. What did you *ride* here on?"

"Train," said Bolenciecwcz.

"Quite right," said the professor. "Now, Mr. Nugent, will you tell us —"

SOURCE: *James Thurber, "College Days" in* My Life and Hard Times.

Top-Down Question Clusters   For higher-level questions, prompting is less appropriate. Because such questions call for students to reason on the basis of facts, the problem is more often a matter of selecting and using facts than of recalling them. A useful strategy in these instances is the top-down question cluster. You will recall from Chapter 8 that cluster guides endeavor to lead students to appropriate inferences and judgments by taking them first through a series of relevant literal questions. This bottom-up approach can be reversed whenever a student stumbles on a higher-level question. A *top-down cluster* begins with an inferential or critical question that a student answers inappropriately. It then proceeds to one or more literal questions, the answers to which should provide the basis of the reasoning required by the initial question. The teacher therefore drops to the literal level until the relevant facts are introduced into the discussion. The focus then returns to the original question. The example of Socrates and Meno might have involved a top-down cluster if Socrates had begun by asking the boy to infer whether the square root of 2 is a real number. You can see that the top-down cluster is akin to prompting because the teacher is not content to give up on the student but wishes to urge her or him to reason out an appropriate response. Top-down clusters are not possible, of course, when the initial question is itself at the literal level: You are already at the level of explicitly stated factual information.

Think-Alouds   An excellent method of demonstrating how thinking ought to occur in responding to higher-level questions is the think-aloud. The teacher "makes thinking public" by talking through the process of arriving at an inference or critical judgment. Davey (1983) suggested ways in which teachers might use think-alouds to gradually build comprehension ability (see also Duffy & Roehler, 1987). However, think-alouds are also useful in content classrooms when students experience difficulty with higher-level thinking. That is, it is not necessary to make thinking skills a specific focus of your teaching in order to employ think-alouds. They are quite helpful as a troubleshooting device, one in which the teacher briefly models proper thinking (without making an issue of it) and then moves on to other matters. Consider the following exchange, based on "The Worst Bank Robbers":

Teacher:	Maria, do you think the bank robbers might have been better off to abandon their plan after they left the first time?
Maria:	Considering how it all turned out, yes.
Teacher:	But what about before they made the second attempt. Did they have good reason to just give up and go home?
Maria:	I'm not sure I know what you mean.
Teacher:	Well, let's think about that first episode. You'll recall they got caught in the revolving doors.
Maria:	Yes.
Teacher:	The staff had to help them out. Now I don't suppose people got stuck in the doors very often, so it was all quite a spectacle. Think about it: Three grown men caught in those doors. Everyone's attention was drawn to them, people who might later be witnesses who could identify them. And, of course, they would need to pass through those very doors again to get away with the money. I'm not sure I'd trust myself to do that if I'd had trouble the first time. Would you?
Maria:	No. If they'd really thought about it, they might have considered a different bank.
Teacher:	Yes, or a different line of work!

Think-alouds offer several powerful advantages. They provide an effective means of modeling a complex process. They tend to be quick and are therefore

---

The Worst Bank Robbers

In August 1975 three men were on their way in to rob the Royal Bank of Scotland at Rothesay, when they got stuck in the revolving doors. They had to be helped free by the staff and, after thanking everyone, sheepishly left the building.

A few minutes later they returned and announced their intention of robbing the bank, but none of the staff believed them. When, at first, they demanded £5,000, the head cashier laughed at them, convinced that it was a practical joke.

Considerably disheartened by this, the gang leader reduced his demand first to £500, then to £50 and ultimately to 50 pence. By this stage the cashier could barely control herself for laughter.

Then one of the men jumped over the counter and fell awkwardly on the floor, clutching at his ankle. The other two made their getaway, but got trapped in the revolving doors for a second time, desperately pushing the wrong way.

SOURCE: *Stephen J. Pyle,* The Book of Failures.

---

useful when available time is short or when a discussion is proceeding smoothly and you do not wish it to bog down. Moreover, there is now good research evidence that think-alouds do work as a method of improving comprehension (e.g., Duffy et al., 1987). Wade (1990) has suggested an interesting twist: asking students to share their own think-alouds. The teacher can then assess the thought processes a particular student is employing.

Slicing   A second device sometimes useful when students balk at a higher-order question is slicing (Pearson & Johnson, 1978). *Slicing* involves reducing the scope of a question without altering what it essentially asks. Consider a social studies teacher who asks a student to project the possible consequences of a given piece of legislation. When the student selected does not respond, the teacher might "slice" the question: "Can you suggest just one possible result?"

Slicing is also useful with literal questions whenever they ask students to recall a large amount of information. A history teacher might be frustrated when students cannot recite the three principal causes of the Civil War, even though they were clearly delineated in the text. A science teacher may throw up her hands when a top student cannot recall the steps of the scientific method—steps that were plainly enumerated in a key figure. These questions call for an extensive response, however, and even good students might be reluctant to begin something they may not be able to finish with success. One solution is to slice the question. "All right," the history teacher might continue, "who can remember *one* of the causes?" Likewise, the science teacher might proceed by paring the question down to size: "Let's start with the *first* step. Do you recall that?"

Constructive Criticism   The techniques we have been describing—top-down clustering, slicing, and prompting—have the effect not only of facilitating good comprehension but of positively reinforcing self-esteem as well. Because such techniques leave the student with a feeling of success, they have a face-saving impact that is important in promoting productive attitudes toward learning. Any technique useful in providing negative feedback (that is, in telling a student an answer is inaccurate or inappropriate) is a means of constructive criticism. The message is not pleasant, to be sure, but it must be conveyed if learning is to continue. However, there is no reason for the message to be punitive, sarcastic, or perceived as an attack on the student's self-worth.

In addition to the devices already introduced, we suggest the following guidelines for becoming a constructive critic.

1. Never equate the student with the response.   Through your comments, try to make clear that it is the answer that is incorrect, inadequate, or unacceptable—not the student. This may seem like a trivial distinction, but it can speak volumes to the pupil who lacks self-assurance and breadth of knowledge.

2. Find something positive to stress.   Accentuating some positive aspect of a wrong answer can be reassuring and encouraging. It is a technique you should probably reserve for occasions when the need for such encouragement seems substantial, however. Making positive comments about every unacceptable response may convey an undesirable message to students. When circumstances warrant, however, several approaches are useful. One involves identifying some portion of the answer that is acceptable. When a student responds correctly to half of a two-part question, you should acknowledge the correct portion. Likewise, when the response is in some way near the mark, the teacher should underscore the closeness. Consider:

Teacher: John, can you name a nineteenth-century president?
John: Franklin Roosevelt.
Teacher: Well, he was *born* in the nineteenth century.

> A *word is dead*
> *When it is said*
> *Some say.*
>
> *I say it just*
> *Begins to live*
> *That day.*
>
> *Emily Dickinson*

Another method of responding to an incorrect answer made in good faith is to suggest a question that would fit the answer. For example:

Teacher: Mary, what's the chemical symbol for carbon?
Mary: Ca?
Teacher: Close. If I'd said calcium, you'd be right on!

This approach can be overdone but occasionally provides an alternative means of accentuating some positive aspect of an incorrect response.

3. *Try focusing on the thinking process.*   When the product (the answer itself) is wrong, there may be something praiseworthy in the process (the thinking that led to the answer). Asking a student to recount how he or she arrived at an answer can be an effective way to lay the thought process bare and find something positive to say, something like "You were on the right track to this point."

Responding to Correct and Appropriate Answers

What happens when there is no discernible problem with an answer? In some respects, this question may seem too simple to take seriously. After all, if there's no problem for the student, there's none for the teacher, right? Actually, there are decisions to make even when all goes well.

Praise   One issue is whether to praise the response. By "praise" we do not mean feedback that the answer is correct or acceptable. Such feedback is a necessary part of any exchange. By praise we mean verbal reinforcers that go beyond mere feedback and communicate that the response was exemplary in nature. It might seem natural to suggest that there can never be enough praise, that if some is good, more is better. Research suggests otherwise, however. Effective teachers tend to be stingy with praise, applying it to as few as 10 percent of the correct answers that occur in discussions (e.g., Brophy, 1986). Praise, it would appear, is like money—the more of it there is in circulation, the less any of it is worth.

To be most effective, praise must be more than sparing. It must be *specific.* Students must know what it is that makes a response praiseworthy if they are to be able to produce similar responses in the future (which is the point of praise). Rather than saying, "That's a good answer," it is more effective to say, "That's a good answer because..." Praise must also be *varied.* For students who hear the same congratulatory word or phrase repeatedly, the expression soon rings hollow. For teachers who concentrate on making their praise specific, however, variety ordinarily takes care of itself.

Follow-Up Questions   Another decision is whether to follow a correct or appropriate answer with additional questions. There are at least three reasons for doing so. One involves inferences and critical judgments that may be difficult for some class members. By asking the student how an appropriate conclusion was reached, the thought process is revealed for all to hear. Another reason is to extend the student's thinking a bit. Even though the answer was appropriate, a teacher might press for additional development of a line of thought. Finally, a student may need to clarify some aspect of a response. For example, a word or expression that is familiar to the teacher may require explanation for some students.

ALTERNATIVES TO TEACHER-LED DISCUSSIONS

Traditional instruction gives the teacher a central role in planning and conducting a discussion. More recent thinking urges a reduced role, at least at times, in an effort to develop within students the capacity to formulate their own questions and to see material from more than a single perspective en route to becoming independent learners. Traditionalists often view this notion skeptically, but it is easy enough to take a few short steps in the direction of student-led discussions. Getting one's feet wet by encouraging students to produce their own questions and to don various roles during a discussion may convince you of the utility of instructional options in which the normal roles of teacher and student are occasionally reversed.

The Social Context of Discussion

Because discussion requires two or more people, we must also consider its social aspects. The discussants assume certain roles with respect to one another, and these roles affect both how the experience proceeds and what is gained from it. In the teacher-directed discussions we have been describing, the teacher can assume a variety of roles, from recorder to coach to critic. The student's role is generally the traditional one of an inferior progressing toward equality with the teacher in content understanding. Both teacher and student assume, without ever saying so, that such equality will not occur, at least not during the course of instruction. The relationship is similar to that between master and apprentice. The former, through discussion, monitors, corrects, and extends the performance of the latter. Not surprisingly, this difference in status leads to observable differences in the way both students and teachers take part in discussions. In his review of research, Carlsen (1991) noted findings that students react differently to teacher questions than to questions posed by their peers (usually giving shorter, more declarative answers to teachers) and that teachers tend to wrest control of the discussion away from students who ask questions, often by responding with another question.

Social relationships also exist among students. Some of those relationships involve inevitable comparisons in terms of content mastery. The roles of "brain" and "failure," with various degrees in between, are inescapably clear to students. Other social relationships exist, many of which may be invisible to the teacher. These may involve friendship, role modeling, romance, rivalry, or antagonism. They involve perceptions of broad socioeconomic class membership and ethnic identity as well as membership in school circles and cliques. Whenever a teacher calls on a student to answer a question (or participate in any other activity), the response depends in part on the impact the student believes it will have on others.

Most important, each student is involved in social relationships that extend outside the classroom, to parents, peers, and siblings. These relationships exert powerful influences on the thoughts and attitudes of students and cause school (and any course taught in school) to be viewed in the context of these forces. For some students the forces are quite positive and compel them to become active learners; for many, they are negative and inhibit participation to the extent a teacher may desire.

One way of breaking the hold of negative social forces on classroom learning is to deliberately alter the roles played by teachers and students. The result can be students who, caught temporarily off balance, must think in new ways from novel perspectives. We now look at several methods of altering social roles for this purpose.

Student-generated Questions

Placing students in the role of questioner upsets the normal order of a classroom, and the results can be productive. Researchers have looked rather closely at student questioning over the past two decades and the results are encouraging. Gillespie (1990–1991), in her comprehensive review of research, came to these conclusions:

- All students can be taught to generate questions but some direct instruction in how to do so is usually necessary.
- A good place to begin is by teaching the types of questions possible.
- The poorest readers tend to benefit the most from producing questions.
- Asking questions tends to improve both comprehension and motivation to read.
- Student-produced questions probably work because they focus attention during reading and compel the student to seek to understand before a good question can be formulated.

The findings are encouraging but also make it clear that some preparation will be necessary. Students should know before reading that questions will be required so that this expectation can become an added purpose for reading. They must also understand basic question types (literal, inferential, and critical in particular) if the questions they produce are to comprise anything beyond the literal. You will recall that we have already recommended direct instruction in these types while familiarizing students with content literacy guides. Student-generated questions are therefore not an unreachable goal requiring prohibitive preparation. We now look at one of the best-known approaches to making them work.

ReQuest

Reciprocal Questioning (ReQuest) is a technique developed by Manzo (1968, 1969) for giving students the dual roles of questioner and respondent in the same discussion. A belief underlying ReQuest is that the task of formulating a question requires a student to think actively about the content of the material.

Manzo originally viewed the technique as a global plan in which the teacher begins by introducing the reading selection, as in the DRA and DR–TA. Teacher and student then read a portion of the selection silently. When they finish, the student asks questions of the teacher. The teacher responds with book closed and may reinforce good questioning technique on the part of the student. The student is free to ask as many questions as he or she desires. The roles are then reversed, and the teacher attempts to move the discussion to a point at which the student can make reasonable predictions about what is to come. After completing the selection, the two reconsider the student's prediction and may also engage in other follow-up activities.

A limitation of ReQuest as a global plan is that it assumes a tutorial situation (one student only), or at most the presence of only a small group. It also has many of the features of a DRA or DR–TA. Not surprisingly, many teachers have modified the technique to make it work in larger groups and in the context of other global lesson designs. One modification, called *reciprocal teaching*, places students altogether in the role of teacher, requiring them to conduct short lessons over the material in addition to questioning (Palincsar & Brown, 1984).

Another modification, suggested by Tierney, Readence, and Dishner (1990), involves an exchange of roles after each question. This format allows for any number of students to become involved in the discussion as questioners. It also works well as a postreading device. That is, the teacher can delay reciprocal questioning until the students have finished the selection. While ReQuest can work as an "unannounced" alternative to a traditional discussion, a teacher can also prepare students for the experience. Asking students to read with the idea of forming good questions to be used later in a give-and-take round of questioning is an excellent way of setting purposes. You should add it to those introduced in Chapter 7. However, this particular approach to purpose setting does not mean that content literacy guides cannot be used. In fact, question formation can be built deliberately into various portions of a guide.

Cooperative Learning Revisited

You will recall that the Jigsaw technique, described in Chapter 8, also involved students in the act of teaching. Each student was made responsible for a section of the reading material and used a corresponding content literacy guide to plan and deliver a lesson to other group members. Jigsaw provides one means of encouraging student-generated questions by placing students in the role of teachers. Our experience, however, has been that most students need to be reminded that questioning should be a part of instruction. Otherwise, there is an alarmingly strong tendency to resort to a questionless lecture approach to teaching.

Strategies for Controversy and Misinformation

You may suspect that controversial issues enliven discussion and promote the kind of active engagement that enhances learning. The actual result can be quite different, however. When students encounter material that conflicts with their existing beliefs and values, learning and retention often suffer.

Two situations are important to consider. In one, the new material is in conflict with a student's values and past critical judgments. In the other, new information is at odds with "facts" the student had previously believed to be true and that may prove difficult to supplant (Dole & Niederhauser, 1990). In both cases, the introduction of the new material creates what Festinger (1957) called "cognitive dissonance." The student can, on the one hand, reject or somehow discount the new information. ("That can't be true," "I don't believe it," "That's not always the case," the student may respond.) On the other hand, the student can accept the new information, but only at the cost of modifying prior notions. You will recall from Chapter 2 that Piaget described this process as accommodation. It is not always easy and may involve discomfort, soul searching, and self-criticism. As Lynch and McKenna (1990) recently put it:

> Changing schemata may be difficult because doing so requires that students recognize why their prior notions were incorrect or indefensible. If the controversial topic engages their emotions, it is often more comfortable for the students to reject the teacher or the text rather than reexamine their erroneous beliefs. (Teachers who deal with controversial issues often notice that students take challenges of their ideas as a personal attack on their self-worth and react defensively.) (p. 317)

Student-generated questions can be an effective way of setting purposes for reading. To the methods listed in Chapter 7, we can now add the technique of asking students to read in order to construct good discussion questions! This device can also be built into content literacy guides (Chapter 8).

Misinformation and controversy are frequent factors in classroom discussions and deserve conscious attention from teachers. You should begin by realizing that they can inhibit learning even while they arouse your students. Beyond this realization, the following strategies may be useful.

The Thinking Rule   A teacher must make clear the guidelines for discussing sensitive issues. When, on occasion, some students become abusive, Berman (1987) has suggested the *thinking rule*. When enacted by the teacher, the rule requires that the next five minutes of discussion be devoted to producing ideas in support of the person who had just been attacked. The thinking rule causes students to view matters from perspectives very different from those they prefer. It subtly conveys the message that other perspectives are possible.

Stipulation   Heated discussions can sometimes end abruptly when one student makes a sweeping pronouncement, phrased as a fact, but without documentation. Statements like these can cause a discussion to die prematurely: "With all the cars and factories it's impossible to save the environment, so why talk about it?" Newmann and Oliver (1970) have recommended the use of *stipulation* at such points; this technique involves the temporary invention of facts or assumptions to restart the discussion. Here is an example of a teacher employing the technique to lead a discussion out of a dead end:

Tom:	Hardened criminals should be executed because the prisons aren't making them any better anyway.
Mary:	You don't know that! How many criminals do you know?
Teacher:	Let's stipulate a fact here—let's assume that prisons could be changed from their current form to some other form that did indeed rehabilitate criminals. If that were true, Tom, what would you think of the death penalty? (Lynch & McKenna, 1990, p. 318)

Note that the word *stipulate* does not mean that an actual fact is necessary. The teacher simply imposes a "fact," which the students assume is true *for the sake of argument*.

Thinking Hats   DeBono (1985) has offered a novel suggestion for encouraging students to adopt perspectives different from those they normally would have. The teacher assigns various students to wear one of six color-coded "thinking hats" to designate a range of viewpoints. The colors are suggestive of the perspective they represent and add a definite sense of imagery to the discussion. The colors are these:

White = objective, fact-oriented thinking
Red = emotional, intuitive thinking
Black = critical, fault-finding, judgmental thinking
Yellow = optimistic, positively focused thinking
Green = creative, innovative thinking
Blue = overseeing, managerial thinking

The hats probably do not need to exist in reality, but we believe it is better to acquire six hats and physically distribute them at the beginning of a discussion. The student wearing a particular hat will be more likely to keep in mind the responsibility it entails while other students will have visual reminders of which students have donned each of the roles.

Assignment of the hats should vary from one discussion to the next; you could even have students exchange hats in the midst of a lengthy discussion. You can use knowledge of your students to make assignments that encourage them occasionally to alter their perspectives. A typically argumentative, fault-finding student might profit from wearing the yellow hat on occasion. A student who tends to react emotionally and impulsively to situations requiring critical thinking would do well to don the white hat at times.

DISCUSSION AND RECITATION: A SECOND LOOK

In this chapter we have maintained that recitation, in which a teacher simply monitors content acquisition, and discussion, in which a teacher encourages open exchanges of comments, questions, and reactions, can coexist in the same activity. Now that your background includes some of the issues and research findings that touch on the problem, it is time to reconsider our suggestion.

We now know that social relationships in the classroom, especially those between teacher and student, influence the ways in which students participate. Teacher questions, for example, can have the effect of inhibiting true, invitational discussion by provoking short, factual answers without elaboration (Boggs, 1972; Dillon, 1985; Edwards & Furlong, 1978). How does a teacher balance the need to monitor with the need to stimulate shared thinking?

Several answers are warranted. First, not all classes are alike. You may find that a given group participates fully and freely in teacher-led discussions during which some questions serve a monitoring function. Second, your reliance on inferential and critical questions as mainstays should do much to prevent terse, lower-level responses since they are inappropriate to such questions. Third, building discussions around content literacy guides that both rely on such questions and give students ample opportunity to formulate answers should help still further.

If even these measures fail to foster open and uninhibited discussion, try partitioning the discussion into phases. Herber (1978) recommended laying the literal groundwork first, then the inferential, and finally the critical. As we mentioned in Chapter 8, we believe this approach is a little disjointed since relevant factual information is widely separated from related inferences and judgments. It seems more productive to complete the discussion according to the guide's organization and then to open things up to more freewheeling commentary. This suggestion means a two-stage discussion. During the first, a range of questions issues largely from the teacher, who monitors, while at the same time encouraging and modeling, higher cognition. During the second stage, the teacher relinquishes control and allows students to take the conversation where they will with a minimum of intervention. Alpert (1987) found that students tended to participate actively in such discussions when teachers observed the following guidelines:

1. Ask questions that are personal or critical, not factual. Avoid inferential as well as literal questions.
2. Do not evaluate student responses. Do not pass judgment. Accept and encourage instead.
3. Do not decide who shall speak. That is, do not call on students. Let the discussion take its course.

It is up to you to gauge the need for such measures in your own classes. Techniques for accomplishing a variety of purposes through discussion are now clearly available. You must decide your own purposes, assess whether they are being met, and then select among the techniques accordingly.

DISCUSSION AND WRITING

Imagine a discussion in *written* form, one in which teacher and students exchange comments and questions after writing them out. Most of the advantages of an oral discussion would still apply, such as monitoring students' understanding of content and correcting and extending that understanding. Some of the features would be absent, of course, including the speed, spontaneity, and give-and-take of a productive classroom dialogue. Nor would feedback from the teacher be immediate.

There is no subject so old that something new cannot be said about it.
Fyodor Dostoevsky

On the other hand, there are compensating strengths to make written dialogue well worth considering. It limits the negative impact of social forces exerted by peers. It gives students ample time for considering replies to higher-order questions. It permits the exchange of sensitive comments in private. It can combine replies with other activities. (For example, a teacher might write, "I think this will be clearer when we've finished Chapter 6. Let's come back to it then.") Perhaps most important, written interchanges take full advantage of writing as a learning tool, a function we discussed in Chapters 1 and 2.

In the next section we describe a number of techniques for converting discussion (or parts of discussion, such as question generation) to written form. We do not intend these as alternatives to oral discussion but as supplements that offer additional benefits.

Dialogue Journals

Staton's original intent (1980) in using the term *dialogue journal* was to denote a correspondence focused on students' understanding of and responses to literature. The technique has clear applications to other content areas. Of all the possible writing-based approaches to discussion, it is closest in form to oral discussion because of the progressive nature of the interchange: from teacher to student, back to teacher, and so forth. As we shall see, this alternating form is not necessary to writing adaptations.

Kirby and Liner (1981) have stressed the need for affective considerations in teacher contributions to dialogue journals. These include accentuating positive aspects of what the student has written, responding at the same time with sincerity and meaning, and protecting the feelings of each student. Such guidelines not only make sense but are largely congruent with those associated with oral questioning listed earlier in this chapter.

Dialogue journals have much to offer, but they also have several drawbacks. First, they may not be effective with some students, especially those with poor verbal skills and those whose feelings are not readily expressed. Second, they become tedious if overused or used mechanically or with indifference. Third, they tend to be time-consuming if meaningful teacher input is to be a part of the exchange.

You may have noted a similarity between a dialogue journal and a content literacy guide. A crucial difference is that students respond to all of the guide's tasks before receiving *any* response from the teacher. In the journal, the exchange of comments and questions after each entry means that the "discussion" may assume a direction of its own as entries build on and react to one another.

The ideal place for dialogue journals in content classrooms may well be *after* students have completed literacy guides and *after* oral classroom discussion. Content knowledge of present topics will by then be adequate for the kind of extension, refinement, and individual pursuit that journals afford.

Clearly, journals offer an opportunity for students to pursue lines of thinking with the input and guidance of an expert. Edwards (1991–1992) has suggested that teachers can sometimes involve students in a "dialectical" thinking process—one in which, by raising tactful counterpoints to a student's statements, the teacher encourages an evolution in the student's viewpoint. Applications like these argue against any attempt to correct the mechanics of writing, as attempts to do so would probably dampen student participation. As Strackbein and Tillman noted, "The journal is for a private audience—not a critical public" (1987, p. 29). This no-red-pencil policy not only encourages student involvement but also makes the demands on teachers realistic by focusing on meaning.

> Talking is a hydrant in the yard and writing is a faucet upstairs in the house. Opening the first takes all the pressure off the second.
>
> Robert Frost

Other Approaches to Written Discussion

There are few limits to the variations possible on written interchanges with students. We offer here just a few.

Anonymous Questions   You may have viewed talk shows during which the host responds humorously to questions written in advance by members of the audience. This technique can work in classroom settings. The teacher asks students to submit questions following a class discussion. They can be collected in a "question box" (like a suggestion box). Students who still fail to understand certain aspects of new material even after a discussion may be too embarrassed to continue asking questions in class. The question box approach allows students to ask their questions without being identified.

Questions to Outsiders   Students can involve others besides the teacher in written discussion by writing letters that include questions and observations (see Figure 9.4). Students who share a particular interest might undertake this project as a group. You will need to provide specific suggestions in terms of where they should send their inquiries. The beginnings of such a list might include the following:

- governmental agencies (the Freedom of Information Act means they *have* to respond!)
- organizations associated with a topic
- textbook authors
- nearby university professors in the field being studied
- local individuals with expertise in the area

Student Self-Questioning   Try asking students to compose dialogues in which they both pose and respond to questions. These Socratic "exchanges" will encourage students to form their own questions as they encounter new

FIGURE 9.4

Office of the Mayor
Port Radium
Northwest Territories
CANADA

Dear Sir or Madam:

Our sixth grade class has been studying the geography of North
America. Our teacher often uses a large rolled map that pulls down
like a blind. Several of us noticed your town, located on the shore of
Great Bear Lake. There do not appear to be any cities anywhere near to
you. There also seem to be no roads leading in or out. Some of us think
your town is there because of mining. This would explain its name. It
is so far north, we think it must be snowed in much of the year. Are we
right? What can you tell us about your town? Thank you for any
information you can give us.

                           Sincerely,

                           (Signed by 27 class members)

Handwritten note on the envelope, which was returned unopened:

    Dear Sender —

      Town no longer exists.

          —Postmaster
           Yellowknife
           Northwest Territories
           CANADA

Sample of a class
letter, drafted as a
collaborative project,
and the unexpected
reply it received

material. Your responses to the dialogues should be directed
not only at the accuracy and defensibility of answers but
at the appropriateness and insights of the questions as
well. A specific application requires each student to select
an individual (real or generalized) and then write both sides of an interview
conducted with that individual. This technique takes Wood's point-of-view
(1988) guide (Chapter 8) a step further by asking students to formulate their
own interview questions.

*Writing, when properly managed ... , is
but a different name for conversation.*
                              Laurence Sterne

SUMMARY

Questioning serves many purposes in content classrooms. It enables a teacher to monitor learning. It provides an opportunity to further develop students' understanding. It also takes advantage of social relationships that inevitably exist among teacher and students.

Discussion amounting to more than student recitation of factual material is rare. This is unfortunate because discussion that invites students to share ideas and think aloud in a nonthreatening environment takes advantage of the fact that answering questions is a constructive process. Students refine and clarify knowledge through the process of responding. In this respect, responding is analogous to writing.

Planning a good discussion begins with the content literacy guide, but there is more to it. The teacher must decide how to introduce the discussion, at what points to depart from the guide, which students to call on, and how to close the discussion effectively.

Recent research has enlightened the issue of how to conduct a good discussion. Teachers must ensure that every student is involved. They must attend to the way questions and feedback are timed. They must react to wrong or inappropriate answers in productive ways, such as using prompting, top-down clusters, think-alouds, slicing, and constructive criticism. They must be equally attentive to how they react to acceptable answers. Praise must be sparing, specific, and varied. Follow-up questions should occasionally be used to extend thinking.

Alternatives to teacher-led discussion grow increasingly popular. They involve manipulating the social relationships that exist among teacher and students. An important technique is to place the student in the role of questioner. One approach to doing so is through reciprocal questioning (ReQuest), in which the teacher and students take turns asking and answering questions. Other techniques are useful when topics involve controversy or misunderstanding. The thinking rule compels students to support the victim of verbal attacks. Stipulation involves the teacher's statement of an assumption in order to get past an impasse. DeBono's "thinking hats" technique (1985) allows students to play a variety of predefined roles during the course of a discussion.

Many of the benefits of an oral discussion are available by conducting it in written form. Dialogue journals, which incorporate a written exchange between an individual student and the teacher, are closest in form to an oral discussion. Other techniques use anonymous student questions, questions sent to outsiders, and question-and-answer dialogues composed entirely by students.

GETTING INVOLVED

1. Identify a prominent teacher and ask permission to observe him or her during a discussion. Be sure to obtain in advance a copy of any materials the students will have read. As the discussion proceeds, keep track of the number of literal, inferential, and critical questions the teacher asks. Make notes on specific classroom incidents that involve techniques such as top-down clustering, slicing, constructive criticism, and think-alouds. Afterward, discuss these incidents with the teacher.

2. Practice student-generated questioning by applying it to this course. Compose a few inferential and critical questions over the material to be discussed during your next class meeting. Then attempt to interject them at appropriate points into the discussion. Study the instructor's reaction. Was he or she receptive to such questions? Did certain questions "work" better than others? If so, which ones and why?

3. Using a concept, fact, or principle from your field of expertise, compose your own Socratic dialogue in which you use questions to guide a hypothetical child to a particular conclusion or insight. Write both the teacher's and the student's contributions to the exchange. Where the latter is concerned, try to predict how a typical student might respond. Next, look for an opportunity to try out the dialogue on a real student. Did the student respond as you predicted? If not, were you able to recover and adjust, ultimately reaching the goal of your dialogue?

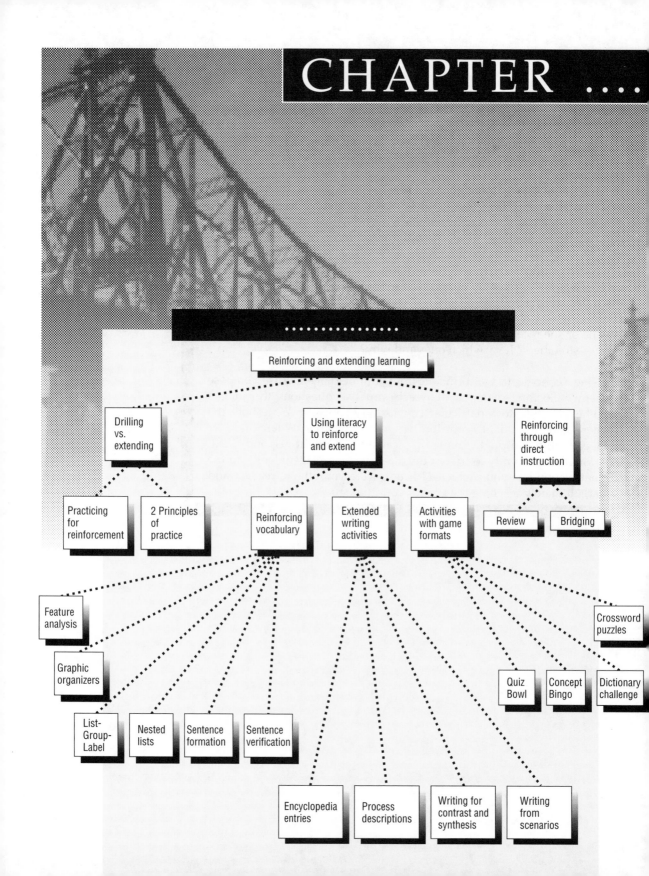

CHAPTER ....

Reinforcing and extending learning

Drilling vs. extending

Using literacy to reinforce and extend

Reinforcing through direct instruction

Practicing for reinforcement

2 Principles of practice

Reinforcing vocabulary

Extended writing activities

Activities with game formats

Review

Bridging

Feature analysis

Graphic organizers

List-Group-Label

Nested lists

Sentence formation

Sentence verification

Encyclopedia entries

Process descriptions

Writing for contrast and synthesis

Writing from scenarios

Crossword puzzles

Quiz Bowl

Concept Bingo

Dictionary challenge

TEN

Reinforcing and Extending Content Knowledge

Practice is the best of all instructors.

Publilius Syrus (1st century B.C.)

Imagine reading about the discovery of a new mineral, borite, useful in the manufacture of rocket fuel. The account you come across is brief and offers few details. Do you think you would be able to remember what borite was a week after reading the account? A month later? A year? If the initial brief announcement were your only stimulus, the chances of your recalling it after any length of time would be remote indeed.

Now imagine that you decided to incorporate *borite* into a self-help program for expanding your personal vocabulary. Assume that your method is to write interesting new words and their definitions onto note cards and then to review the cards periodically. Let's further assume that you review the word *borite* and its meaning each evening for a month, along with the other, unrelated words. Do you think this activity would be likely to increase your long-term retention of the concept?

Finally, imagine that after reading of the discovery of borite you took no deliberate measures to drill yourself on the word and its meaning. Assume instead that the fictitious events recounted in Figure 10.1 actually began to occur over a period of several years. Your encounters with borite would involve a variety of exposures, including articles in newspapers and news magazines, electronic media accounts, critical commentary, the opinions of acquaintances, your own introspection, and so forth. In short, your interactions with the concept of borite would be numerous and varied after your initial introduction to it. They would also occur in meaningful contexts that would serve to associate borite with other information relevant to it. How would you compare this set of experiences with our first two scenarios in terms of the effects on learning?

As you might suspect, similar comparisons have long been a focus of educational research, and we can predict the results of our three scenarios with confidence. The second condition leads to better retention than the first while the third condition is better still. Put differently, rote drill is more effective than no drill, but repeated meaningful involvement is even more effective.

FIGURE 10.1

Scenario for learning about "borite"

SOURCE: From "Concurrent Validity of Cloze as a Measure of Intersentential Comprehension" by M. C. McKenna and K. Layton, 1990, *Journal of Educational Psychology*, *82*, pp. 372–379. Copyright 1990 by the Journal of Educational Psychology. Reprinted by permission of M. C. McKenna and the American Psychological Association, Inc.

THE SEARCH FOR BORITE

Borite is a very valuable mineral. Because it burns so quickly, it is used to make rocket fuel. Its bright red color makes borite easy to see, but unfortunately there is very little of it on earth. It is mined only in the eastern United States, where the largest mine is near a town called Midville. This single mine produces over half of all the world's borite!

To reduce the danger, the miners pack the walls of the mine with ice before cutting into the borite, so that the mineral is frozen for a short time. Because of the risk they take, the miners are paid high wages to bring borite out of the ground. The miners in a town called Borite City are so wealthy they built the town a brand new park. To show what their job is, the miners wear clothes the same color as borite.

Scientists have begun to look hard for new sources of borite. A yellow asteroid was discovered in 1980 between Mars and Jupiter. (Yellow is the color borite becomes in cold temperatures.) The asteroid might be made of pure borite, and the country that reaches the asteroid first will have a gigantic supply of rocket fuel. Soon after its discovery, the United States found that the Soviet Union had just begun Project Borite, a space program designed to send cosmonauts to the asteroid in a spaceship called Pavlov II.

Naturally, the U.S. started its own program, known as Project ABC. The plan of this project, which is also called the American Borite Connection, is a simple one. First, a robot ship will be sent to the asteroid, after which nuclear warheads will propel the asteroid towards earth. If all goes well, it will land somewhere in northern Greenland, not far from the north pole. Even though some of the borite will burn up in the earth's atmosphere, most of it will make it safely to the surface. Greenland's ice cap will quickly freeze this "meteor" and prevent the rest of the borite from burning.

OBJECTIVES

How does our example relate to teaching through text? In the remainder of this chapter, you will learn to

1. differentiate rote drill from higher-level practice activities;

2. state two essential rules governing the impact of practice;

3. describe and implement various methods of reinforcing content vocabulary;

4. describe and implement various activities for using extended writing to reinforce and deepen content understanding;

5. adapt a variety of reinforcing game formats for use in your own teaching specialty; and

6. explain how bridging and review offer opportunities to reinforce earlier material while introducing new material.

DRILLING VERSUS EXTENDING

How does a teacher tell when a particular segment of content—a unit, a lesson, a concept—has been "covered"? Does the fact that students appear to *understand* the content make it safe to move on to new topics? There is often substantial pressure to do so, but unless the teacher makes provision to reinforce the content, the student's situation will be little different from our opening scenario in which a new fact was encountered, understood, and then abandoned. Learning is reinforced whenever our experiences bring it to mind in meaningful ways.

Practicing for Reinforcement

One way of bringing content repeatedly to mind is through rote drill. Our second scenario is an example, one in which the learner repeatedly reviews the same factual information until it is easily recalled. There are several drawbacks to this kind of drill. It tends to be tedious. It emphasizes low-level cognitive skills, such as quick recall. Most important, it fails to recognize the interconnectedness of the content.

On the other hand, drill does work as a means of enhancing the retention of information. A crucial question for teachers is whether it is possible to derive the benefits of drill without incurring its negative side effects. The answer is yes. By designing activities in which the recall of information is integrated with its application at higher levels, teachers can ensure the repetition needed for retention while deepening understanding through higher-level thought. By higher level we mean activities that stress relationships between and among concepts and that require students to make inferences and reach defensible critical judgments.

Two Principles of Practice

Can such activities effectively incorporate lower-level drill? Again, the answer is yes. The two basic principles of effective practice, now thoroughly documented by research, apply not only to rote drill but to higher-order activities as well.

1. Guided practice precedes independent practice. After the introduction of new materials and skills, a teacher should provide opportunities for practice. Whether such practice includes the mere repetition of simple tasks or more advanced cognitive activities that *require* such tasks, practice opportunities must progress from a teacher-assisted situation to one in which learners undertake the tasks without help (e.g., Rosenshine, 1986). At two key points, the teacher must judge whether the students are ready to go on. One of these is the point between initial, direct instruction and guided practice. The second is between guided and independent practice. Proceeding to the next phase before readiness is achieved in the current phase will impair learning.

2. *Massed practice precedes distributed practice.* Practice opportunities should be especially frequent just after the introduction of new material. Extremely frequent practice opportunities are said to be *massed* and coincide roughly with the guided practice phase. As students become better prepared to undertake practice activities on their own, not only does the teacher's role diminish but the frequency of the activities declines as well. At this point, the activities are said to be *distributed*. That is, they occur periodically, after intervals during which newer content is introduced.

USING LITERACY TO REINFORCE AND EXTEND

What can teachers do to strengthen and deepen their students' understanding of content? While most teachers recognize the clear need to do so, they also feel frustration over curricular demands. There is always, it seems, another chapter to cover, another concept to introduce. The following suggestions can help.

1. *Distribute practice.* Remember that the frequency of activities does not need to be great once the students have initially grasped the content and have had some success in recalling and applying it.
2. *Give comprehensive exams.* Examinations that hold students accountable repeatedly for the same material compel them to distribute their review.
3. *Provide activities that link new content with old.* You can greatly increase the efficiency of practice by designing activities in which content previously taught is used with new material. This is usually not difficult because of the interconnectedness of the concepts.
4. *Provide activities that require higher-level skills.* When practice opportunities require students to apply and think about content, drill of individual facts will occur in meaningful contexts. The result will be learning that students not only recall but transfer, adapt, and apply.

Reading and writing are useful ways to implement the last two of these suggestions. The activities that follow use literacy to provide quality practice and extension in a manner that stresses conceptual linkages and causes information to be brought to mind repeatedly, though not in rote fashion. The notion of distributing practice in content so that students encounter it in higher and higher contexts is called the *spiral curriculum* (Bruner, 1960, 1964, 1966, 1971). That is, repeatedly meeting the same facts and concepts makes the curriculum circular, in a sense, but meeting them at higher levels converts the circle into a spiral. This powerful idea underlies all the techniques presented in this chapter. We begin by reexamining three of the approaches to vocabulary we introduced in Chapter 6.

Reinforcing Vocabulary

In designing reinforcement activities for newly introduced terms, teachers can easily incorporate some of the terms previously studied. The interconnectedness of content, the fact that new information and ideas build on an existing knowledge base, facilitates this practice. Teachers may object that precious time is wasted by rehashing old material. The rule of distributed practice suggests that the time is well spent, however, for integrating new and old vocabulary into the same activity makes the effort a time-effective one. Some of the approaches described earlier as ways of *introducing* vocabulary also have great potential for *reinforcing* it.

Feature Analysis   You will recall that feature analysis involves charts listing category members in the left-most column and differentiating features as headings of the other columns. Students can use the charts to compare and contrast concepts that belong to the same category. Compiling such a chart and then using it to make comparisons requires repeated attention to word meanings. The benefits of rote drill are evident without the tedium. Students review the concepts en route to higher-level accomplishments.

Feature analysis charts can contain previously introduced terms as well as new ones. In many cases, a chart completed earlier can serve as the basis of a new activity. Students first add the new category members, then chart their characteristics, and finally contrast them with the terms entered earlier. Charts used in this way underscore the *continuity* of content—its natural tendency to build on itself.

Figure 10.2 demonstrates how a teacher might return to the same feature analysis chart used in an earlier lesson to characterize governmental checks and balances. Initially, the chart addressed only those used by legislators. The expanded form includes devices used by all three branches. Note that the teacher has had to tell students to add a new column at the right of the original chart. This addition broadens the chart's scope to encompass the three branches.

Graphic Organizers   Like feature analysis, graphic organizers stress the interrelatedness of terms by presenting them in closely connected clusters. The diagrams highlight the most important relationship connecting the terms: time, place, subconcepts, and so on. Teachers can return to past organizers in the way we've described for feature analysis. Students begin with a previously completed diagram and a list of carefully selected new terms. Their task is to integrate the new words into the existing diagram.

Figure 10.3(a) and Figure 10.3(b) (p. 223) provide a before-and-after example of how this process works with a tree diagram. Expanding old diagrams in this way causes students to reconsider previous material (the intent of distributed practice) but does so in a manner

FIGURE 10.2

Sample feature analysis chart expanded to accommodate new content

(a) Initial form of the chart:

Checks and balances	Aimed at judiciary	Aimed at executive
Override vote	0	+
Confirmation	s	+
Impeachment trial	+	+

(b) The chart's expanded form:

Checks and balances	Aimed at judiciary	Aimed at executive	Aimed at legislature
Override vote	0	+	0
Confirmation	s	+	0
Impeachment trial	+	+	0
Veto	0	0	+
Construction	0	0	+
Appointment	+	0	0
. . .			

Note: A plus indicates a positive relationship; a zero indicates a negative relationship; "s" indicates the relationship sometimes exists.

that underscores meaning and aids the student in getting the "big picture" of how knowledge in a given content area is organized.

Sometimes the introduction of a new topic will make the use of a previous organizer seem irrelevant or unfeasible. The solution can lie in higher-level connections that link the topics and show students how seemingly unrelated prior material is in fact integrally connected. As an example, a biology teacher has used the graphic organizer depicted in Figure 10.4(a) (p. 224) to describe the hierarchical organization of the class, *Insecta*. She later employs a different diagram, the one in Figure 10.4(b), to present the organization of another class, *Arachnida*. By means of a bridging activity, she and the class combine the two organizers by adding a connecting higher-order concept. This is possible because both classes belong to the same phylum, *Arthropoda*. (This is only one sort of bridging device. We explain this topic in more detail later in the chapter.) The result is Figure 10.4(c).

List-Group-Label   We indicated in Chapter 6 that List-Group-Label is especially useful after material has been introduced. You will recall that in the initial stage, List, students brainstorm all the words they can think of that are associated with a given topic. The very nature of this task makes it likely that

FIGURE 10.3

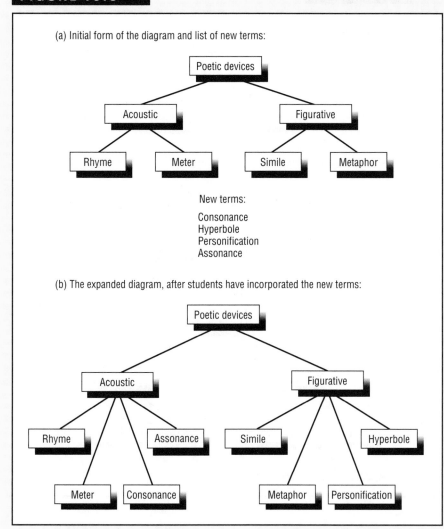

(a) Initial form of the diagram and list of new terms:

Poetic devices

Acoustic

Figurative

Rhyme

Meter

Simile

Metaphor

New terms:

Consonance
Hyperbole
Personification
Assonance

(b) The expanded diagram, after students have incorporated the new terms:

Poetic devices

Acoustic

Figurative

Rhyme

Assonance

Simile

Hyperbole

Meter

Consonance

Metaphor

Personification

Example of a tree diagram expanded to include new content

the terms they generate will include some from previous material. The teacher should be watchful, however, for opportunities to steer the discussion toward such terms if the students do not generate them spontaneously.

Additional opportunities to interject review of earlier terminology occurs in the third stage—Label. Overarching category designations may involve such terms. Moreover, once the category labels are applied, the teacher can suggest additional, previously encountered category members where appropriate.

Linking two graphic organizers with a higher-order concept

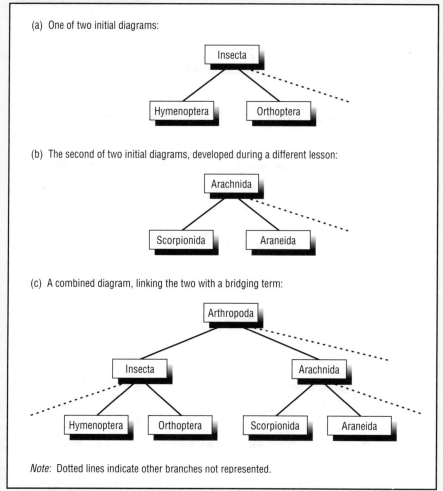

FIGURE 10.4

(a) One of two initial diagrams:

Insecta

Hymenoptera   Orthoptera

(b) The second of two initial diagrams, developed during a different lesson:

Arachnida

Scorpionida   Araneida

(c) A combined diagram, linking the two with a bridging term:

Arthropoda

Insecta   Arachnida

Hymenoptera   Orthoptera   Scorpionida   Araneida

Note: Dotted lines indicate other branches not represented.

Nested Lists   A natural offshoot of List-Group-Label is a newer technique introduced by Kirsch and Mosenthal (1990). Their notion of *nesting* (embedding lists within one another) requires students to seek out instances in which some categories are actually subsets of others. This might well occur as an additional step in a List-Group-Label activity when a number of student-generated categories are plainly visible on the chalkboard.

In Figure 10.5, students can combine three categories into a single system of nested categories by noting how they are interrelated. A teacher cannot always expect three such ready-made categories to occur so conveniently, however. Teachers must encourage students to ferret out nested relationships and then combine (or nest) the original lists accordingly.

FIGURE 10.5

(a) In this example, students complete List-Group-Label with the following lists (among others) appearing on the board:

Types of Government	Democracies	Kingdoms
Democracy	United States	Saudi Arabia
Kingdom	France	Jordan
	Great Britain	
	Germany	
	Japan	

(b) The students continue by nesting these lists into the following:

Types of Government
    Democracy
        United States
        France
        Great Britain
        Germany
        Japan
    Kingdom
        Saudi Arabia
        Jordan

Using nested lists as an extension of List-Group-Label

You may have noted that nested lists bear a close similarity to graphic organizers. In fact, they represent an alternate way of conveying the information contained in a tree diagram. Figure 10.6 illustrates how the nested lists of our example can be translated into graphic form. Pointing out this relationship to students and affording them opportunities to convert one form to the other is a good idea.

Sentence Formation   Another way to stress interconnections among content vocabulary is to provide students with sets of two or more terms and require that they be combined in a sentence or paragraph that focuses on their relationship. This technique is an excellent means of (1) reviewing previous vocabulary while emphasizing links with new terms and (2) taking advantage of writing as a means of refining and elaborating each student's content knowledge.

This activity can vary considerably in sophistication depending on which terms are included in a given set and how many terms are used. Figure 10.7 illustrates how progressive the difficulty and complexity can become. This is a good reason to start simply, providing only two terms and requiring a single sentence. You will need to prepare students for more complex tasks involving three or more terms. These tasks also present good opportunities for collaborative efforts among students.

FIGURE 10.6

Nested categories
represented in a tree
diagram (see Figure 10.5)

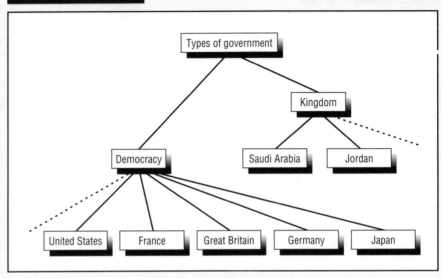

FIGURE 10.7

Sample sentence
formation tasks

1. *Example with 2 terms:*
   real numbers
   rational numbers
   Possible response: Every rational number is a real number.

2. *Example with 3 terms:*
   real numbers
   rational numbers
   integers
   Possible response: All integers are both rational and real numbers.

3. *Example with 4 terms:*
   real numbers
   rational numbers
   integers
   prime numbers
   Possible response: All prime numbers are integers, which in turn are always
   both rational and real numbers.

Sentence Verification   The reverse of the sentence formation exercise we have just described involves providing students with ready-made sentences that express relationships among two or more of the concepts being studied. Royer, Greene, and Sinatra (1987) have suggested this as a method of assessing comprehension. In their approach, students must classify each sentence as "old" (representing material from the text) or "new" (involving inferences based on text material).

Sentence verification also offers an excellent opportunity to reinforce content learning. We suggest a modification of the original technique for use in reinforcement activities.

1. Begin by listing key vocabulary from the current unit.
2. Add closely related terms from earlier units.
3. Select a number of sentences containing the new terms from the reading material.
4. Rewrite some of the sentences, expressing the same meaning in a different way.
5. Rewrite others so that their meaning is no longer true.
6. Write some original sentences that link the new and old terms in meaningful ways. Include a few false statements.
7. Write original sentences that express inferences about the content. The inferences may be altogether certain or merely probable. Again, include some that are false.
8. Ask students to classify each sentence as true, possibly true, or false.

This is an open-book exercise and should encourage students to look for more than the literal match of the sentences. Verbatim sentences are included, to be sure, but along with inferences, paraphrases, and logical links with previous material. Figure 10.8 provides examples of each of the sentence types based on the Pluto passage from Chapter 7.

Extended Writing Activities

A recurrent theme of this book is that providing students with opportunities to write about content will deepen and refine their understanding. Postdiscussion writing activities are ideally positioned to make this happen; they come *after* the initial direct instruction in new material and *after* some of the students' difficulties with the material have been remedied by discussion. Here and in Chapter 9 we have already described some of the brief writing activities students might undertake, such as composing questions and constructing sentences that link technical terms.

To read means to borrow; to create out of one's readings is paying off one's debts.
Georg Christoph Lichtenberg

FIGURE 10.8

Sentence verification
examples

Exact sentence (from the "Pluto" passage of Chapter 7):
  The telescopic image of Pluto is generally indistinguishable from that of a faint star.

Paraphrased version:
  Through a telescope, Pluto resembles a star.

False version:
  Pluto's image is much brighter than that of most stars.

Original sentence linking old and new terms (Let's assume Venus has already been studied.):
  Pluto's image is much dimmer than that of Venus.

Original sentence expressing an inference:
  Pluto cannot be seen without a telescope.

There is nothing to write about, you say. Well then, write and let me know just this—that there is nothing to write about.
  Pliny, the Younger

Extended writing serves the same goal of deepening understanding but on a larger scale. Here, students have the chance to draw on many aspects of what they know—including knowledge from other content areas—in creating a written product that represents how they have mentally constructed their content knowledge. Below, we offer a few examples of such activities.

Encyclopedia Entries   Give students a concept (a key word or phrase) and ask them to compose an encyclopedia entry for that term. Be careful to specify what you expect such an entry to contain. Examples of real entries can be helpful in providing students with an idea of the format and content of this type of writing. Do not use entries covering the term itself, however. The students must decide what information to include and how to convey it succinctly to an encyclopedia user, who is typically in search of a rapid introduction to the topic.

Writing encyclopedia entries is an excellent collaborative activity. One student might serve as editor, assigning subsections and expediting their completion. Another student could construct figures, tables, and diagrams while still others compose the subsections.

Process Descriptions   Studying processes allows students to summarize them, step by step; this activity helps the students crystallize their conceptualization of how the processes occur. Applications arise in many subject areas. They abound in the physical sciences (e.g., evaporation, digestion, erosion, life cycles, solar formation, the scientific method itself) but also occur in such widely diverse areas as language arts (the writing process and library research procedures, for example), mathematics (steps to follow in solving a particular type of problem, proving a theorem, creating a geometric construction, etc.), and social studies (how a bill becomes a law, naturalization, colonization, election procedures, etc.).

An especially good way to present the task of process writing is to show students a diagram of the process. A time line, especially a flowchart, is suitable for this purpose. Ask students to convert the diagram to words—to describe in prose what the diagram denotes. A hidden benefit of this activity is that it underscores for students how graphic organizers work.

Writing for Contrast and Synthesis   There is much to be gained from writing about, or in response to, a single source, such as a textbook selection, book, essay, or article. In many subjects, however, it is important to expose students to multiple sources and to ask that they either contrast them or integrate them into a single, coherent statement on a given topic. Both tasks require (1) access to multiple sources, (2) the ability to read each one critically and with a specific purpose in mind, and (3) the capacity to quote or paraphrase selectively to achieve that purpose.

Students should begin with a limited number of sources. If they are unfamiliar with this sort of writing, the teacher might actually prescribe the specific sources. However, those selected by students themselves are apt to be more meaningful and motivating.

Students just beginning to write for such purposes will need plenty of help. Synthesis or contrast writing is a high-level cognitive task and should be modeled like any other. Showing students finished examples of writing can be effective, of course, but it is not enough. You must demonstrate the *process* as well as the *product*. Begin by selecting a topic together with two or more sources that treat the topic. Tell how you found the sources. Introduce the students to each source. (They will not necessarily need to read each one in detail.) Point out information in the sources that is related to your purpose. For example, if your goal is to contrast conservative and liberal approaches to the environment, proceed through each source until you reach suggested actions and their justification. A good method is to make transparencies of the source material, highlighting points with a marker as you move through it with the class. Next, discuss how you would plan the organization of your essay. Constructing an informal outline, perhaps with student input, can be beneficial. Finally, distribute copies of the actual written product, allowing students to read and emulate it.

At all times, stress the procedure as a general one, independent of a specific topic. The danger in using just one example is that students may overgeneralize its elements. Therefore, use more than one. Start fresh with a new—and ideally quite different—illustration. When students possess both written products, point out their similarities (resulting from the same basic writing/thinking process) and their differences (resulting from the specific nature of the two topics).

By selecting topics with immediate relevance to course material, you can ensure that modeling this process will do double duty—not only showing students how to proceed but also instructing them in the content contained in the examples themselves! Once they begin their own projects, this activity is well suited to meaningful review of facts and concepts in the context of a higher-level task.

Writing from Scenarios   You can encourage students to view content from novel perspectives and to apply it to realistic situations by suggesting a set of circumstances, or a scenario, together with a specific writing task. Here are some examples from a variety of content areas:

- *Business:* Give students a warranty and a hypothetical case involving a defective product. They are to become dissatisfied consumers. Ask them to compose a letter to the dealer asking for a replacement or a refund. Insist that they cite the warranty appropriately.

- *Social Studies:* Place students in the role of the current president and ask that they write a State-of-the-Union address. Numerous sources should be used. Note that in real life, this speech is produced by a coordinated team, not by the president acting alone. A collaborative activity may be appropriate.

- *Science:* Ask students to play the role of scientist by predicting the results of an experiment of their own design. Have them write a proposal including background information (what they currently know), their hypothesis, and the proposed method. Having them perform their experiment at school may not be feasible. However, they could send the proposal to an industry scientist or to a professor in the appropriate field and ask for a projection of what would happen. The cover letter communicating their request would constitute yet another writing opportunity!

- *Mathematics:* Ask students to become "math reporters" who research and report on real-world math applications. They can begin with the *Reader's Guide to Periodical Literature* in the school library and use "mathematics" as a descriptor. What they discover will probably surprise them and may help solve a thorny problem for math teachers: convincing apathetic students that mathematics has relevance to their lives.

- *Literature:* Ask students to select an author they have studied, preferably on more than one occasion, and then to "become" that author. They are to compose an original work imitating their chosen author's style.

- *Art:* First, ask students to choose both a noted artist and one painting by that artist. They are then to role-play the artist and assume that a fine arts magazine editor has asked for an "explanation" of the painting, touching on such questions as why certain colors were selected, why the objects in the painting are arranged as they are, and so on.

- *Physical Education:* Ask each student to select a strategy, play, or formation associated with a given sport. Their task is to describe and defend their selection, contrasting it favorably with alternatives.

- *Music:* Suggest that each student select a popular song and then write out the lyrics. This process will require them to give ample attention to rhyme schemes, refrains, and other literary elements since the lyrics are essentially a form of poetry (see McKenna, 1977c). They are then to describe how the musical elements of the song (pitch, speed, rhythm, instrumentation, etc.) reinforce the message conveyed by the lyrics.

Activities with Game Formats

Our experience is that many content teachers tend to be skeptical about activities that resemble games. A common objection is that they represent a waste of time. Ensuring that practice with skills and concepts is an integral part of the activities should counter such an objection, however. Another complaint is that the competition inherent in all games tends to reinforce differences between the academic haves and have nots—differences that may already be painfully apparent to the latter students. To reduce this tendency teachers should (1) use games sparingly, as a means of introducing variety into instruction; (2) use formats that involve elements of chance as well as skill; (3) make certain that a variety of skill levels is represented in the game, making success possible for all students; and (4) employ formats that encourage team play so that individuals are not readily isolated as deficient. The formats that follow meet all four of these criteria.

Quiz Bowl In Quiz Bowl, teams of four students vie in responding to questions over factual content. An electronic buzzer system that identifies the first to "buzz in" while locking out others is helpful though not essential. (Production of such a system is cheap and makes a good science project, one you might suggest to a colleague.) The format used for years by NBC's weekly *College Bowl* program entails toss-up questions, worth 10 points, and bonus questions, worth varying numbers of points. Toss-ups are clear-cut, single-answer queries. The student who buzzes in must answer the question without the help of teammates. A student may interrupt the teacher-moderator if she or he infers the rest of the question, but there is a five-point penalty if, after interrupting, the student gives a wrong answer. The question is then repeated in its entirety for the other team. When the student is wrong but has not interrupted, no penalty is assessed. The other team does receive a chance to respond, however. When a toss-up is correctly answered, that student's team receives a chance to answer a bonus question. The team works together to answer these questions, which, while factual, may involve lists, have multiple parts, or comprise a sequence of clues (the more clues the team needs, the fewer the points awarded). The team routes answers to bonus questions through a captain, who is the official spokesperson for the team and must quickly decide differences of opinion among team members.

Quiz Bowl can easily promote motivational practice in content. Some suggestions for enhancing its effectiveness include the following:

1. Make certain that each team has a balance of students in terms of ability. Strive for parity.

2. Ask students to write questions (an interesting writing activity) for later use in Quiz Bowl. Use these questions (perhaps with a little editing) along with those you write yourself. By asking students to write their names on the questions, you can ensure that a particular item is used only when its author is not a member of one of the teams.

3. Determine whether an organized Quiz Bowl system exists on an interschool basis. If so, your class sessions might be linked to qualification trials for interschool competition. Note that the format we described above is for the original NBC version. It may differ from local adaptations.

Concept Bingo   Based on the ordinary bingo format, Concept Bingo begins with a list of 25 new terms written on the board. The teacher instructs students to create a 5-×-5 grid and to write the words, one by one in any order, in each of the grid's squares. Prior to the game, the teacher should have written each word and its definition on an index card. The teacher shuffles the cards and reads aloud one definition at a time (but not the word!). Students find the word matching the definition and cover it using small scraps of paper, paper clips, or anything handy. Winning occurs as it does in regular bingo. Note that every student will have a play for every definition the teacher reads. The difference is in the random arrangement originally chosen by the student. This element of luck is important, for it helps disguise the fact that some students may be learning the word meanings at a slower rate than others. They will not be embarrassed because all the students realize that there is a large chance factor involved.

Richardson and Morgan (1990) recommend that each winning student read aloud the words that constitute the win so that the teacher can validate the victory by rereading the definitions as the student says each word. In this way the word-meaning pairs are reinforced yet again and an opportunity for questions is created. Richardson and Morgan also note that variations are possible. For example, the 25 "words" used might be chemical symbols; instead of definitions the teacher might read facts specific to each element or compound symbolized.

Dictionary Challenge   Not only do you review selected vocabulary but you also expose students in passing to a host of other terms with Dictionary Challenge. You can use an ordinary dictionary, but it is preferable to locate one dictionary specific to your teaching specialty. The game involves a small group of students so that several games may be going on at once in the same classroom if all students are to participate. Provide students with a lengthy list of content terms. Include previous terms and, if you wish, even terms they have yet to encounter. You may place the list on the board, on a transparency, or on paper so that students can refer to it during the game.

Each round begins with one student secretly choosing a term from the list, looking it up in the dictionary, and then reading (1) the definition given *or* (2) the definition of another term from the dictionary. The other student must decide whether the definition read aloud is true or false. When the student holding the dictionary finishes, the others simultaneously signal "true" or "false." The dictionary holder receives one point for each of the students who were fooled. The book then passes from one student to the next around the circle. When it has made one full rotation, the game is over. It is important to devise a system that compels students to signal their beliefs simultaneously so that some are not tempted to wait and see how a superior student responds.

This game does more than provide an entertaining review. It also exposes students in a nonthreatening way to a multitude of content-specific terms. Imagine how many definitions a student may browse through while looking for a distractor to read aloud.

We suggest that a content dictionary is a good resource to keep in your classroom for a number of other purposes. If you are not familiar with one, consider the following examples from a variety of areas:

Dictionary of Accounting (MIT Press, 1985).

Dictionary of Alcohol Use and Abuse (Greenwood, 1985).

Dictionary of Animals (Arco, 1984).

Dictionary of Automotive Engineering (Society of Automotive Engineers, 1989).

Dictionary of Biology (McGraw-Hill, 1985).

Dictionary of Business and Economics (Free Press, 1986).

Dictionary of Chemical Terms (McGraw-Hill, 1986).

Dictionary of Computer Terms (Barron, 1989).

Dictionary of Composers (Taplinger, 1981).

Dictionary of Earth Sciences (Rowman, 1983).

Dictionary of Geology (Penguin, 1973).

Dictionary of Law (HarperCollins, 1982).

Dictionary of Mathematics Terms (Barron, 1987).

Dictionary of Medical Terms (Barron, 1989).

Dictionary of Painting (Philosophical Publishing, 1958).

Dictionary of Philosophy (International Publishing, 1985).

Dictionary of Physical Sciences (Rowman, 1983).

Dictionary of Physics (French and European Publications, 1982).

Dictionary of Plant Names (Timber, 1985).

Dictionary of Politics (Free Press, 1974).

Dictionary of Psychology (Dell, 1985).

Dictionary of Soccer (Cool Change Publishing, 1989).

These are only examples and exclude entire categories of dictionaries, such as those devoted to foreign languages. If you fail to find one suitable to your teaching area, consult *Books in Print*, Title or Subject volumes, under the heading "Dictionary." You will find many that are too technical (and too expensive!) for use in this and related activities, but many, including those above, are affordable and contain a great deal of age-appropriate material.

Crossword Puzzles   A game that works well as a reinforcement activity is the traditional crossword puzzle. This format stresses word meanings as an individual activity that can be completed outside of class. All students are likely to be familiar with the format so that little explanation is necessary. Crosswords also provide an excellent method of reinforcing old and current vocabulary in the same exercise.

A few additional suggestions will add variety to the games you produce. You can spice up a puzzle by adding a few extra words that are relevant to your class (e.g., students' names, the school mascot, etc.). Also, do not feel constrained to use only formal definitions as clues. Use related facts and details occasionally that suggest some of the words without actually defining them.

A drawback to the creation of crossword puzzles is the time required on the part of the teacher. Two recommendations can help. First, use computer software to generate puzzles. If you're not familiar with how such programs work, you'll be amazed at how quick and convenient they can be. We'll return to this topic in Chapter 14. Our second suggestion is nontechnological. Create a square grid for use as a master and, once you've decided on the arrangement of words, darken the unused squares with a felt marker. This method is not nearly so quick as using a microcomputer but it eliminates using a ruler to construct each puzzle from scratch.

REINFORCING THROUGH DIRECT INSTRUCTION

One of the most efficient ways to reinforce content, once covered, is to refer to it again while introducing new material. Among many teachers, there is an unfortunate tendency to compartmentalize content into segments that are all but abandoned on completion. In other words, teachers assume that once a unit is over, it's time to move on. This may be a consequence of planning in units, but it is not an unavoidable one.

We have discussed ways of reinforcing multiple units of content simultaneously *after* direct instruction in new material. We turn now to methods of reinforcing prior content *during* new direct instruction, beginning by reconsidering Figure 4.3. That figure depicts the three phases of the Explicit Teaching Model. It is easy to conclude that the final phase (practice) must be completed before new direct instruction is attempted, as suggested by Figure 10.9(a). We have attempted to demonstrate that this is not the case, however,

FIGURE 10.9

(a) The basic model:

Readiness for Unit 2	Direct Instruction over Unit 2	Practice on Unit 2	Readiness for Unit 3

(b) Modifying the practice phase:

Readiness for Unit 2	Direct Instruction over Unit 2	Practice on Unit 2 primarily with some practice on Unit 1	Readiness for Unit 3

(c) Modifying all phases:

Readiness for Unit 2 including review of or references to Unit 1	Direct Instruction over Unit 2 with appropriate references to Unit 1	Practice on Unit 2 primarily with some practice on Unit 1	Readiness for Unit 3 including review of or references to Units 1 & 2

Building extra practice into the Explicit Teaching Model

by suggesting methods for simultaneous practice in multiple objectives. The result is the time frame shown in Figure 10.9(b). Here, some of the practice over Unit 1 is delayed until the practice phase of Unit 2. That is to say, the practice over Unit 1 is distributed.

We now consider a second way of reinforcing previous material—by calling attention to it during the readiness or direct instruction phase of a subsequent unit. The timing of this approach is depicted in Figure 10.9(c). Two important techniques useful in referring to previous material while conducting instruction in new material are review and bridging. Let's look at each.

Review

We introduced the idea of review in Chapter 5 as a means of building the background students will need for a particular reading assignment. The role of initial review can be broader, however, and is not limited to lessons that center around assigned reading. Review is effective in the readiness phase of any lesson. Reviewing underscores the connectedness of content and encourages students to learn new content by integrating it with their existing knowledge. It also allows a lesson to begin with a feeling of student success and recollection, a warm-up for the actual agenda.

Bridging

Bridging is the act of specifying logical connections between new and previous material. Review provides one opportunity for a teacher to bridge, by linking new ideas and concepts with those recently studied. Bridging need not be a part of review, however. It can occur during the direct instruction phase or at any other appropriate juncture. Bridging is effective when a logical connection with *any* earlier material (not just the material that has been most recently covered) becomes possible. Unlike review, which is an appropriate way to begin almost any lesson, bridging must wait until an adequate foundation of content knowledge has been established. That is, there must be something to which to bridge.

Bridging can take many forms but two seem especially useful. One involves the teacher's use of earlier content to make a comparison. For example, a history teacher in the midst of discussing World War II will have numerous opportunities to compare the circumstances with those of World War I (covered earlier in the course). These comparisons not only strengthen the students' conceptual framework for the Second World War, but they provide a quick, distributed review of the earlier material as well.

The second means of bridging goes a step beyond a mere comparison. Where appropriate, the teacher offers an overarching fact or principle that links the elements being compared. Our history teacher might begin by comparing

Reviewing the old while introducing the new may bring to mind the distinction between recitation and discussion (Chapter 9). The idea was similar: Discussions that include *some* factual questions provide for review *and* extension during the same lesson.

the Allied and Axis Powers of World War II with the Allied and Central Powers of World War I. One of the similarities—that Britain and United States were allied in both causes—might form the basis of a transcendent fact: that these two countries have been allied for well over a century in what Churchill called the "Grand Alliance." Stating this bridging fact before covering World War II would have less impact because it would lack that very powerful example. Similar occasions arise in the sciences, as when numerous experiments or subprocesses can finally be linked by more general principles. The big picture becomes clear.

All this is not to say that bridging cannot occur in advance, as a way of setting the stage for what is to come. Mention of the Grand Alliance during a discussion of World War I might well serve to enhance students' appreciation of events in that war. Bridging, however, is retrospective. Even if the Alliance were mentioned before, it should be reintroduced later.

Bridging is a relatively new target for researchers, but the investigations conducted to date have provided evidence of its effectiveness in developing comprehension at higher levels (e.g., White, Hayes, & Pate, 1991).

SUMMARY

Practice is an essential ingredient of content learning. To be effective, practice need not consist of rote drill of factual information. Providing students with opportunities to use content knowledge in meaningful ways, ways that often involve literacy, serves to reinforce basic facts. Practice should progress from a guided to an independent condition and from an intensive, massed schedule to a distributed, periodic one.

Some of the vocabulary techniques useful in introducing new terms can also serve to reinforce them. These include feature analysis, graphic organizers, and the List-Group-Label technique. A good way to extend the last of these is by using nested lists. Other activities entailing brief written exercises include sentence formation and its reverse, sentence verification. More extensive writing activities are also appropriate and many are possible. We examined here activities that engage students in the writing of encyclopedia entries, process descriptions, contrasts and syntheses of material from multiple sources, and compositions based on various scenarios. This chapter also explored the limited use of game formats for reinforcement and extension, though several cautions and criteria were noted. We described examples that met all the criteria.

Finally, we introduced two methods of reinforcing previous content in the midst of directly teaching new material. These were reviewing, just prior to the new instruction, and bridging, which entails making logical connections between previous and current facts and concepts.

GETTING INVOLVED

1. Build a unit for teaching students to write for the purpose of synthesizing or contrasting sources (choose one skill or the other). Begin by selecting two topics, for your goal will be the creation of two examples. For each topic, select two sources for the sake of simplicity. Make sure the sources are relatively easy to comprehend. Also, avoid sources and topics that will soon be dated (current events, etc.). In that way, you will ensure that the unit will be useful regardless of when you teach it and irrespective of the textbook you may be using. Last, you will need to construct the written examples themselves, making certain to target appropriate levels of difficulty and prior knowledge. In other words, aim for considerate writing.

2. Choose a topic that will not be readily outdated and that is apt to be included in any textbook used in your teaching specialty. Compile a list of closely related terms associated with the topic you've chosen. Then compose sentences that express relationships among the terms. These relationships should be altogether true, probably true, or false. Your sentences can form the basis of a sentence verification exercise for eventual use with your students. Your list of words, of course, will be useful in the reverse activity, sentence construction.

SECTION....................five

More Ways to Facilitate Learning through Text

In the final four chapters, we address a number of new issues, including study skills, the needs of special learners, motivating students, and microcomputer applications.

The subject of study skills is vast. We intentionally limit the focus of Chapter 11 to those skills and strategies that are most useful to content literacy *and* most easily addressed by content specialists in the course of subject matter instruction. The four areas that meet our requirement are note taking, review and homework, test taking, and strategies for helping students with independent reading.

Belinda Lazarus brings to Chapter 12 the expertise of a special educator who is able to look at the problems of special students from a highly practical perspective. She offers a variety of ideas for addressing their needs in your classroom. These include working with special educators, adapting materials and the tasks you require of special students, and altering teaching methods.

Chapter 13 examines one of the most neglected areas in content literacy: student attitudes. We begin by providing an understanding of motivation (in a way that may be useful in other contexts) and examine a quick method of determining specific areas of student interest *within* your subject specialty. We then turn to methods of improving student attitudes toward content literacy.

Our discussion of microcomputer applications in Chapter 14 is an extension of the ideas we offer on attitude building. Certainly the uses of micros we present have that potential. More important, however, we argue that technology offers novel ways to improve content literacy dramatically.

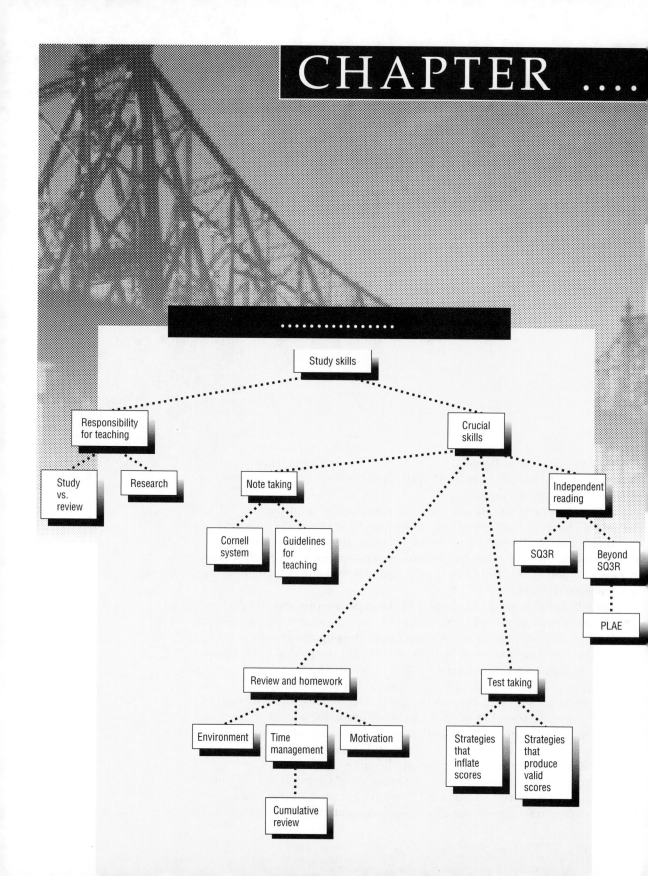

CHAPTER ....

Study skills

Responsibility
for teaching

Study
vs.
review

Research

Crucial
skills

Note taking

Cornell
system

Guidelines
for
teaching

Independent
reading

SQ3R

Beyond
SQ3R

PLAE

Review and homework

Environment

Time
management

Motivation

Cumulative
review

Test taking

Strategies
that
inflate
scores

Strategies
that
produce
valid
scores

ELEVEN

Study Skills:
Encouraging Independence
in Content Literacy

Children have to be educated, but they have also to be left to educate themselves.

Ernest Dimnet, The Art of Thinking

As a successful college student, you are undoubtedly able to apply a variety of skills in learning whatever your courses may require. These skills include the ability to take notes during lectures, to read certain assignments without benefit of an introduction, to review for tests, and to take tests with an awareness of how they are typically designed. Odds are, no one directly taught you these skills. You probably acquired most of them through trial and error, refining them through application in secondary classrooms. Your success in developing good study techniques on your own may have led you to a common assumption that such techniques do not need to be taught, that they are somehow self-evident. For various reasons, however, many students fail to acquire adequate study skills. Some students are so constrained by limited decoding ability that the notion of productive study is only a distant goal. For others, the trial-and-error process may never have produced the right formulas for success. Still others are unwilling to try different approaches and are locked by habit into ineffective methods.

In this chapter we strive for a balance between two conflicting demands. One is the need to convey content knowledge and understanding. The time required to do so leaves little extra for lessons in how to learn. At odds with this demand is the reality that, unless they receive guidance in effective study, many students will not acquire the intended content. This amounts to a paradox—a "Catch 22"—that we address and, we hope, resolve.

OBJECTIVES

The main goal of this chapter is to present methods of integrating study skill instruction into content teaching. In this way, the demand for extra time is minimized and students can see how the skills should be used with actual course material. To accomplish this goal we focus on several objectives. Specifically, your reading of this chapter should enable you to

1. define the term *study*;

2. discuss the issue of who is responsible for teaching study skills;

3. identify the study skills most important in content coursework generally;

4. further identify those skills most important in your own teaching specialty; and

5. describe methods of integrating instruction in these skills into content instruction.

In addition, this chapter is rather unusual in that it gives you a chance to judge your own study techniques as a college student. Reading it should enable you to

6. undertake independent reading assignments more effectively; and

7. improve your test performance by means of (a) better methods of review and (b) more knowledgeable approaches to taking examinations.

RESPONSIBILITY FOR TEACHING STUDY SKILLS

In Chapter 1, we discussed the objections usually voiced by content teachers to the suggestion that they play an active role in developing content literacy in their students. Three important objections included the inability to contend with student deficiencies, the suspicion that literacy activities will demand too much class time, and a denial of any real need for instruction in this area. These objections are likely to be even stronger in the matter of study skills, which are often viewed as naturally developing without direct instruction.

If you have not yet taught, we can probably do little to convince you that such skills do not automatically accrue as students pass upward through the secondary grades. You will need to experience the situation for yourself, firsthand. What we *can* do is equip you with a knowledge of the most important skills and with methods of instilling them that do not greatly intrude on instructional time. We begin by considering exactly what it means to study.

Study versus Review

By *study* we mean "the process of learning the content of printed materials without direct assistance" (Miller & McKenna, 1989, p. 281). This definition is intentionally broad and exceeds the common view that study is the same as review (as in "studying" for a test or "studying" a list of facts until you remember them). Our definition applies to any activity in which the student must learn without help. One such activity is review, to be sure, but there are others. They include (1) reading materials that have not been introduced and for which a student may lack adequate background, (2) taking notes that capture the organization and content of lectures, and (3) taking tests intelligently by avoiding unnecessary pitfalls. We could extend this list considerably, but our aim is to focus on skills that are central to success in content subjects. Even these few examples, however, suggest that study is far more than review. It entails a set of skills for learning independently.

What the Research Suggests

It is probably natural for teachers, who tend to be good students and who have rarely received instruction in how to study, to assume that their students do not need direct instruction in study skills (Gall, Gall, Jacobsen, & Bullock, 1990). Not surprisingly, teachers rarely teach these skills. Durkin (1978–1979) spent over 7,000 minutes observing reading and content lessons in the intermediate grades and witnessed no study skill instruction at all. The fact that many students do not automatically develop these skills was documented by Thomas and Rohwer (1986), who investigated the use of four important skills among students at three age levels (see Table 11.1).

The realization that teachers must teach study skills comes at a time when the psychology of learning suggests that students must be actively engaged with content in order to learn it. As Gall and his associates (1990) put it, "Educators are seeing more clearly than ever that the student is not a passive recipient of the teacher's instruction, but an active participant in it" (p. 6). Study skills, by their very nature, require active participation.

You may suspect that a reasonable way of instilling good study skills is to teach them as a part of a reading or language arts course. Indeed, this is the approach used most often with deficient college freshmen. While it can be effective, there are drawbacks, especially with less mature and less academically able students in the middle and secondary grades. One problem is that it is up to the student to transfer study strategies learned in an abstract form, independent of any specific content subject, to day-to-day classroom situations. This transfer may be difficult because of differences in the materials

Table 11.1
Use of Four Study Skills at Various Age Levels

Use of Study Skills by Middle- to High-Ability Students at Different Levels of Schooling

Study Skill	Percentage of Students Using Skill		
	Junior High School	*Senior High School*	*College*
Taking notes on assigned readings	31%	40%	43%
Taking notes when teacher emphasizes point in class	50%	71%	92%
Making up questions to guide reading	15%	5%	3%
Making charts, graphs, or other pictures to represent important ideas or events	8%	9%	9%

Source: *From* Tools for Learning: A Guide to Teaching Study Skills *(p. 4) by M. D. Gall, J.P. Gall, D. R. Jacobsen, and T. L. Bullock, 1990. Alexandria, VA: Association for Supervision and Curriculum Development. Copyright 1990 by the Association for Supervision and Curriculum Development. Reprinted by permission of the Association for Supervision and Curriculum Development.*

used and in the requirements of individual courses. Anderson and Armbruster (1984), in their summary of research on study skills, concluded that the most effective approaches to study are those best matched to the criteria that a particular teacher would use to assess performance. For example, a student might be ill advised to concentrate on mnemonic strategies for detailed facts when the instructor will administer essay examinations. A student enrolled in a study skills class may therefore learn too many techniques, or the wrong techniques, to be able to apply them appropriately to a specific course. This observation prompted Schmidt and her colleagues (Schmidt, Barry, Maxworthy, & Huebsch, 1989) to suggest that only one educator is in an ideal position to develop the right skills in the right place at the right time: the content teacher. Laframboise (1986–1987) reached the same conclusion based on research.

When the content teacher selects a set of study skills to emphasize, he or she can ensure that those skills are geared to the requirements the teacher has established for the students. And there is a second, equally powerful advantage. By showing how the skills work with actual course material (not "canned" commercial material), the teacher further ensures that the students will be able to apply the skills in the context of *that* course. True, the students may acquire the skills in the abstract so that they can apply them elsewhere or on other occasions, but this is a by-product. The primary concern of the content teacher is met—students can apply the skills to the task at hand.

As one example, Stoodt and Balbo (1979) found that when content teachers took a little time to teach appropriate study skills, using their own materials as the basis, their students demonstrated significantly better comprehension and learning. However, it is not enough to insist that teachers provide instruction in how to study. Showing them how to provide that instruction is just as important (Armbruster & Anderson, 1981). It is to that goal that we devote the remainder of this chapter.

NOTE TAKING

Good students concur in their belief that note taking is worthwhile. Psychologists differ, however, as to exactly how notes help us learn. One view is that the *process* of taking notes (selecting, condensing, organizing, paraphrasing, and so forth) assists us in integrating the new material into memory. Another view holds that it is in the *product*—the written notes themselves—that the real value lies, as an aid to later review.

Anderson and Armbruster (1991), in examining research into the matter, found mixed evidence for the process view but strong and consistent support for the product theory. We suspect that, under the right conditions, both factors play a role in effective note taking.

Students can take notes over lectures or written materials. Because we have already discussed ways to guide students in writing while reading (Chapter 8), we focus here on note taking during lectures. Let's begin by inspecting one of the most popular techniques yet developed.

The Cornell System

Walter Pauk, of the Cornell University Reading Research Center, has developed over the course of several years a system of note taking that incorporates a number of sensible ideas (Pauk, 1988). Students use ruled paper with an especially wide left margin (2 inches or so). If they begin with ordinary notebook paper with a 1-inch margin, Pauk encourages them to draw a new vertical line and to use this as the margin. During class, the students take notes only to the right of the line. Soon after class, while memory is fresh, they rewrite their notes onto paper that is similarly ruled. This is the time to improve legibility, rephrase certain points, add remembered details, insert punctuation, number subpoints, and so forth. When the revision is complete, the wide left-hand margin comes into play. Here the students write headings, symbols, questions, short phrases, and other cues that might help them categorize and remember the material on the right of the line. Thinking of these cues, of course, is a good way to arrive at an understanding of how the content is organized. Later review consists of covering the right-hand portion of each page while using the left-hand cues to help recall the material. Research suggests that the Cornell System is effective (Anderson & Armbruster, 1991; Jacobsen, 1989).

Teaching Note Taking

Norm Stahl and his colleagues (Stahl & King, 1984; Stahl, King, & Henk, 1991) advocate the Explicit Teaching Model for showing students how to take notes. You will recall from Chapter 4 that this approach first involves modeling the technique for students and then allowing them to practice it while the teacher monitors and reinforces. A lesson deliberately devoted to note-taking instruction may sound inappropriate to a content classroom, but two advantages make the idea appealing. First, note taking need not be the sole objective. You can teach whatever material you normally would while using it as a vehicle to convey note-taking skills. Second, there is no need for students to transfer a set of skills learned elsewhere (in a reading class, perhaps) to the content setting. Stahl, King, and Henk (1991) warn of the reluctance of some students to risk trying a new technique when grades are at stake. Encouraging that technique yourself, while modeling it with your own materials, can help overcome this reluctance.

Modeling good notes can begin with a brief introduction to the Cornell System or an adaptation of it. Teaching note taking yourself is efficient because every example then comes from current content. Using the chalkboard or overhead projector as you lecture means showing students precisely how the notes should look at each point. During the important last step of filling in the left margin with cues, you can soon begin to seek input from students.

Using the Cornell System as a means of organizing the notes overall is a good beginning. However, you must make additional points and use other techniques if you hope to change the habits of your students significantly. The following recommendations come from two recent sources in which teams of investigators have looked carefully at research.

1. Take stock of your students' note-taking abilities early by collecting notebooks and examining their written products (Anderson & Armbruster, 1991).
2. Lecture at a reasonable rate for novice note takers and construct model notes over important content on the chalkboard or overhead projector as you speak (Anderson & Armbruster, 1991).
3. Pause frequently to allow students to process what you've said more fully as they write (Anderson & Armbruster, 1991).

4. Encourage students to be alert for definitions and examples as they listen (Gall et al., 1990).

5. Teach useful abbreviations, including not only standard ones (such as *w/o* for *without*) but those that students should "coin" on the spot (such as *phot.* for *photosynthesis*) (Gall et al., 1990).

6. Encourage students to paraphrase rather than strive for verbatim transcriptions (Gall et al., 1990).

7. Stress the need to look for cues the teacher provides that certain material is important. "Examples of such signals are emphasis words (e.g., 'the chief cause was ... '), transitions (e.g., 'now let's look at ... '), enumerations (e.g., 'there are five characteristics of ... '), repetitions ('let me remind you that ... '), as well as nonverbal movements and gestures" (Gall et al., 1990, p. 97).

To these suggestions we add three more:

8. Encourage students to use an informal outline format in which they indent to show subpoints and examples. Indention is an age-old trick of note taking for it provides a good visual organizer without the need to write anything additional. Figure 11.1 presents examples of notes actually taken by an A student and a C student over the same lecture in a seventh-grade social studies class. Note the organizing use of indention that is beginning to develop in the notes of the superior student.

9. Consider giving grades on the notes themselves as an added inducement to students to take them effectively.

10. As you monitor and reinforce students' efforts to practice their note taking, make transparencies of selected student notes to use as examples (anonymously, of course) with the class as a whole.

One of the best methods of encouraging good note taking is by administering tests that have a reasonable basis in the notes taken (Anderson & Armbruster, 1991). This policy leads to better review habits and to better performance on tests. We now look at each of these two study skills in turn.

REVIEW AND HOMEWORK

Note taking and review are naturally linked. You will recall that an important way notes help students is as an aid during review. Not surprisingly, Hartley and Davies (1978) observed that teaching note taking is most effective when notes make review easier. The guidelines suggested in the previous section are a first step, but teachers

Memory is a net; one finds it full of fish when he takes it from the brook; but a dozen miles of water have run through it without sticking.
Oliver Wendell Holmes, Sr.

FIGURE 11.1

Sample lecture notes produced by two seventh graders over the same material

SOURCE: Courtesy Andrea Matthews, Henry County Junior High School, Georgia.

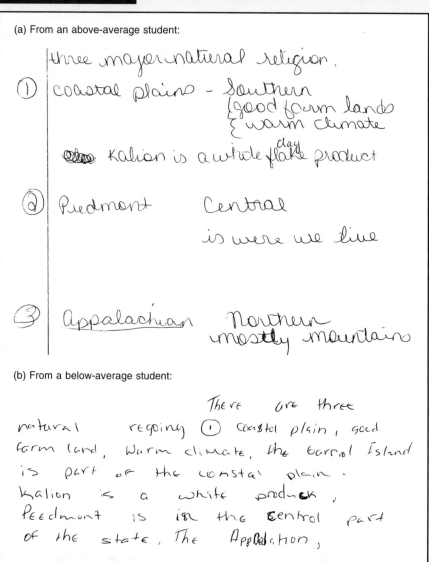

(a) From an above-average student:

three major natural religion.

① coastal plains - Southern
{good farm lands
{warm climate

~~elea~~ Kalian is a white flake product (clay)

② Piedmont   Central
                is were we live

③ Appalachian   Northern
                 mostly mountain

(b) From a below-average student:

There are three natural regoing ① Coastal plain, good farm land, Warm climate, the barrol Island is part of the constal plain. Kalion is a white product, Peedmont is in the central part of the state, The Appalation,

must attend to the review habits of students and be ready to provide direct instruction when necessary.

Environment

A traditional suggestion is to study in the same place each time and to use that place for nothing else. The rationale is that conditioning will cause the student to anticipate studying on arrival at the designated place. There are difficulties with this suggestion, however. To begin with, a long history of research does not support the practice (Risko, Alvarez, & Fairbanks, 1991). Moreover, the suggestion is often unattainable for disadvantaged individuals. It is better to advise students to seek out a place that is as free from distractions as possible. According to most studies, music and television qualify as distractions under most circumstances (Risko et al., 1991). This finding does not mean that students must envelop themselves in cryptlike silence to be successful. It does mean reducing distractions as much as possible, including friends, media, and the temptation of pastimes. Where cramped quarters and the sounds of television and siblings cannot be entirely escaped, a student can still largely avoid them by the use of earplugs or a headset tuned to "white noise."

Time Management

In terms of habit formation, it is probably more effective to begin at the same time each night rather than reserving an exclusive place. To avoid fatigue, students might try dividing time allocated for review and homework—after school and before bed, for example (not just after dinner). Gall and his colleagues (1990) recommend dividing complex tasks, such as writing a report, into manageable components (gathering information, making an outline, etc.).

> I *took a speedreading course and read* War and Peace *in two minutes. It's about Russia.*
>
> *Woody Allen*

Research argues against advising students to maintain a rigorous schedule (Risko et al., 1991). More effective is advising them to set priorities for each session in advance—deciding what it is reasonable to try to accomplish (Gall et al., 1990). Where deadlines are the same, it may be wise to begin with the most difficult subject first, when the student is freshest. This policy is contrary to human nature, however, and must be consciously instilled. Another helpful suggestion is to think ahead to predictable distractions and to schedule easier subjects for these times. A student who must study in the same bedroom with her sister, whose boyfriend calls dutifully each night at nine, would do well to schedule routine tasks for that time. As Nell (1988) observed, the more difficult the reading, the more susceptible we are to distractions.

Cumulative Review   One of the most important aspects of time management is the need for periodic review (e.g., Gall et al., 1990). In Chapter 10, we stressed the effectiveness of distributing practice. Our focus was on lesson planning that leads to distribution, but the same principle applies to review. Consider the actual case of Bill, an average student who entered a twelfth-grade botany class and was elated to discover that there would be no textbook. Tests would be based on notes alone. By the end of the first 50-minute period, however, Bill's elation had turned to dismay. He had taken five pages of notes. Afraid to allow his notebook to accumulate untouched until the first exam (Bill's usual m.o.), he reviewed that day's notes after school. The next day, burdened with an additional five pages, Bill thought it prudent to review again. This time, however, instead of reviewing only the second day's installment, he began with the previous day's notes. Each day he repeated this cumulative process, always starting with the very beginning of his notebook. His initial suspicion that this practice would soon require inordinate amounts of time was quickly dispelled. He found that he zipped rapidly through earlier material, which had become quite familiar to him. Bill's botany teacher used a combination of short quizzes and lengthy exams that together totaled 1,200 points by the end of the course. Bill, who had been a B-minus student, missed 10!

Motivation

A teacher cannot guarantee that students will review independently, regardless of what steps he or she may take to do so. And after all, independent study is essentially a matter of self-discipline and maturity. On the other hand, teachers may be able to marshal two sources of motivation that are present even when the teacher is not: the student and the parents.

Encourage students to set short-term goals for a study session and to reward themselves when they accomplish those goals. Zimmerman and Pons (1986) observed that high-achieving high school students tended to apply self-administered rewards and punishment far more frequently than low achievers. For example, a student may wish to watch a favorite sitcom at 8:30 and may use this as an incentive for finishing a given segment of homework by this time. Failure to do so means missing the show.

Enlisting the aid of parents, while occasionally difficult, is often worth the effort. Many cooperative parents are unaware of specific ways they may be able to contribute to the development of good study habits in their children. Gall and his associates (1990) offer some suggestions in Figure 11.2.

TEST TAKING

Is it advisable to teach students how to take tests? Millman, Bishop, and Ebel (1965) defined *test wiseness* as the "capacity to utilize the characteristics and formats of the test and/or the test taking situation to receive a high score. Test wiseness is logically independent of an examinee's knowledge of the subject matter" (p. 707). Deliberately setting out to instill test wiseness in one's students has long been decried as bad practice (e.g., Hoffman, 1962). Millman and associates (1965), however, argue that test wiseness actually reduces measurement error. The logic here is that if students are equally test wise, so that no one has an unfair advantage, differences in performance must be attributable to varying degrees of content understanding. Accordingly, present-day authorities often recommend teaching students to be test wise (e.g., Wark & Flippo, 1991).

FIGURE 11.2

Teachers should send letters or newsletters to parents asking them to help their children develop time management skills. The following are examples of ways that parents can help:

a. *Providing study time.* Duckett recommends that parents provide a scheduled time for home study, with a definite beginning and end, and ensure that distractions and noise are kept to a minimum during that time. Quarg suggests that parents have children put aside one to two hours each night for studying. Parents should keep demands for home chores and family activities reasonable.

b. *Monitoring study.* Parents can make sure students complete assignments and, if necessary, help them schedule time for working on assignments.

c. *Modeling time management.* Parents can demonstrate and model techniques they use for managing their own time—for example, their system for keeping track of appointments.

d. *Providing tools for time management.* Parents should consider buying their children a daily schedule book, a "To-Do" pad, or an assignment book, or perhaps helping children construct their own. They should also make sure that each child has an accurate watch and, if necessary, an alarm clock.

e. *Rewarding good time management.* Parents can praise or reward students for completing assignments and getting to class on time.

Ideas for involving parents in shaping study habits

SOURCE: From *Tools for Learning: A Guide to Teaching Study Skills* (p. 78) by M. D. Gall, J. P. Gall, D. R. Jacobsen, and T. L. Bullock, 1990, Alexandria, VA: Association for Supervision and Curriculum Development. Copyright 1990 by the Association for Supervision and Curriculum Development. Reprinted by permission of the Association for Supervision and Curriculum Development.

Our position is more moderate. We suggest that there are two major strategies for helping students take tests. One type increases the student's chance to respond correctly when he or she does not know the answer. An example is the suggestion that true/false items containing an absolute term (such as *always* or *never*) are generally false. An answer of "false" to these items will often be correct. The second type of strategy allows the student to make a better score by being more efficient and logical. For example, the advice to skip harder questions the first time through a test is an effective strategy for managing time and reducing anxiety; however, it does not reward ignorance.

We recommend that teachers adopt a three-part policy. First, they should teach students strategies that promise to make their test taking more efficient and to display their achievement to best advantage. Second, they should become aware of techniques calculated to improve scores in the absence of achievement. Finally, they should not teach these strategies but should instead construct tests that are impervious to their use. Let's look at each type of strategy more closely.

Strategies That Inflate Scores

Objective tests present many pitfalls for the novice test writer. Even professional test developers frequently fall victim to them, as witnessed by studies in which students given only the questions (not the passages) from

FIGURE 11.3

Sample test
items containing
grammatical clues

(a) Option *a* cannot be right because of a subject/verb disagreement:

Teachers should avoid multiple-choice options that
  a. is absurdly true.
  b. have opposite meanings.
  c. grammatically agree with their stem.
  d. are only a few words long.

(b) Option *b* cannot be right because its first word cannot follow the article *an*:

In writing multiple-choice tests, teachers should avoid an
  a. option that is absurdly false.
  b. distractor that is too short.
  c. item with only one correct answer.
  d. answer that may relieve anxiety through humor.

standardized reading comprehension tests do significantly better than chance (e.g., see Tuinman, 1971). Our listing of some of the more common errors is by no means complete, but it should help you become aware of numerous traps. Remember, we offer these guidelines for *constructing* tests and not as a curriculum for students who will be *taking* them. The idea, of course, is that even students familiar with the techniques will be unable to apply them.

1. Avoid using two multiple-choice options with essentially the same meaning. Test-wise students know that neither can be correct. Yet it is tempting, after constructing two good distractors, to concoct a third by paraphrasing one of the other two (Wark & Flippo, 1991).

2. Avoid creating two options with opposite meanings. Logic tells the test-wise student, who may know nothing of the idea being tested, that one of the two options must be wrong.

3. Avoid options that are absurdly false. One justification for the occasional use of this practice is that it may relieve anxiety through humor. On the other hand it increases the odds of a correct response through sheer guessing and should be employed sparingly.

4. Avoid options that disagree grammatically with their stem. Two errors are especially common: (a) subject-verb disagreement and (b) inappropriate presence of *a* or *an*. (See Figure 11.3.)

5. Avoid "hiding" the correct option in the B or C position. Instructors often suspect that when the correct option is either first or last (in the A or D positions), it is overly "exposed" (Wark & Flippo, 1991). Test-wise students exploit this practice, however, by guessing B or C far more frequently than A or D.

6. Avoid using the absolutes *always* and *never* in false statements. If, on the other hand, you can use them in true statements, all the better.

Strategies That Produce Valid Scores

When students employ test-taking strategies that are inefficient or illogical, their poor performance may be the result of their defective technique, which may in turn mask their real ability. Creating *positive test wiseness* by instilling strategies that enable students to show what they know is not difficult. It requires briefly but repeatedly discussing the strategies before tests. It requires discussing them again when you distribute the corrected exams for review. That's it. The strategies are simple enough that little set-aside time for direct instruction is needed. These techniques are good examples of the content area teacher's being the right person for the job since no transfer is required. The following are some strategies that underly positive test wiseness:

1. Encourage students to read all multiple-choice options before responding.
2. Encourage students to skip harder items and return to them later.
3. Encourage students to use the process of elimination in responding to different multiple-choice items.

(Note: The first three suggestions are based on McClain's observation, 1983, that better students employ them much more often that average students.)

4. Teach students to be alert for "Type K" multiple-choice items (those that contain options involving other options—for example, "all of the above," "none of the above," "a and c above"). The best strategy for responding to such items is to realize that the options must be treated as individual true/false items. The student must first determine the truth of each stand-alone option (that is, each option that does not refer to any others), and then consider the alternative/s that do refer to other options.
5. Encourage students to change their answers on reconsideration whenever closer inspection suggests a change. The widespread notion that one's first impression is best is a myth that runs counter to a large and consistent body of research (see Lynch & Smith, 1975; Wark & Flippo, 1991).
6. Stress the importance of time management. Students should note the time regularly and adjust their pace as needed. One usually thinks of running short of time as the inevitable result of poor management, but in reality the opposite is often true, especially for poor students, who find testing unpleasant and rush through, squandering precious time (Gall et al., 1990).
7. Regarding essay tests, Gall and colleagues (1990) have crystallized a number of studies into four succinct suggestions: "(a) Read the question carefully; (b) jot key words and phrases next to the question and use

them to outline the answer; (c) make the answer appropriate in length; and (d) review the answer for clarity, grammar, and spelling" (p. 188).

8. Readence, Bean, and Baldwin (1989) offer an additional suggestion for approaching essay questions: Pay close attention to the verb. This word invariably suggests how a student should organize a response.

We suspect that even the most strident opponent of teaching test wiseness could live with these two sets of suggestions for (1) making tests immune to negative test-wise strategies while (2) helping students to demonstrate their understanding by better managing their time and thought. It is certainly clear that teachers cannot afford scrupulously to avoid discussing tests. Convincing research has long told us that learning improves when students know how they will be measured (Anderson & Armbruster, 1984). Such knowledge helps them take the right kind of notes and review in appropriate ways. It makes good sense to confront the issue of testing proactively, equipping students with test-taking skills and preparing them thoroughly for each exam by means of in-class review and a written study guide. The story related in Figure 11.4 suggests how convincing a little positive experience can be.

STRATEGIES FOR INDEPENDENT READING

We have organized this text around the vital need to prepare students for reading assignments, to provide guidance during reading, and to extend comprehension following reading. In short, comprehension is better

FIGURE 11.4

A tale of "accidental" review

SOURCE: From *I Hate School: How to Hang In and When to Drop Out* (p. 92) by C. G. Wirths and M. Bowman-Kruhm, 1987, New York: Harper & Row.

There's a good story about a guy who planned to cheat on a history test. He decided to write all the main ideas and dates down on a sheet of paper and hide it in his inside jacket pocket. When he had finished writing it all down, he realized the paper was way too big to go in his pocket, so he got a smaller piece. This time he used many abbreviations and he skipped information that he realized he already knew. Boy, was he disgusted when he found he still had a paper so big it would be obvious he was concealing something. This time he used a really small piece and abbreviated everything—skipping lots of stuff that by now he knew.

The next day he tucked the paper in his jacket, and went off to school. During the morning he put his jacket in his locker to be sure nothing happened to it. Unfortunately, just before history class he was talking to a girl and forgot to get his jacket. His teacher would not let him leave.

Scared, he looked at the test, and to his astonishment it didn't look too hard. He answered all he could and passed with a respectable C+. Why? His repeated writing and reviewing as he prepared his cheat materials was the ideal way to study.

Cheating is cheating. There is no way that it is right. In the long run you will get caught and you will be the one hurt. Don't do it.

when certain activities occur before, during, and after reading. When a teacher gives the same assignment to an entire class, he or she organizes these activities on a classwide basis. For example, the same background-building techniques or the same content literacy guide would precede a textbook chapter to be read by all students. But what about reading selections that students select individually? Because a teacher cannot possibly provide background, set purposes, and so on for such reading, the student must do without the benefits of a DRA, DR–TA, KWL, or relevant explicit instruction. The student who encounters an encyclopedia entry while doing a report, selects a book as part of a project, or reads a magazine article while researching a term paper must rely on strategies previously learned for approaching these tasks. Unfortunately, many students fail to attain the goal of *strategic reading*—selecting and using strategies depending on the reader's purposes and the material to be read. In this section we will explore some ways of moving students toward this goal.

> I *read part of it all the way through.*
> *Samuel Goldwyn*

SQ3R

Robinson (1946) offered an effective technique to help readers approach reading assignments without assistance. SQ3R consists of five steps:

1. *Survey.* The reader looks over the entire selection before reading, noting subheadings, diagrams, captions, and possibly the summary.
2. *Question.* The reader converts each subheading into a question, perhaps by marking on the text.
3. *Read.* The reader approaches each section by noting the question fashioned from the subtitle. The question provides a focus for reading the section.
4. *Recite.* Before proceeding to the next section, the reader again considers the question and inwardly "recites" the answer. If the reader is unable to construct a reasonable answer, selective rereading may be needed.
5. *Review.* After completing the entire selection, the reader reflects on the questions again and also considers main ideas learned from the reading.

The similarity between SQ3R and the Directed Reading Activity is apparent. Because a teacher is unavailable to provide background, students acquire it through surveying the selection. They develop questions from subheadings in lieu of a content literacy guide. In place of discussion, they both ask and answer these questions. To be sure, these devices are no substitute for expert guidance, but they go far toward enhancing comprehension. Figure 11.5 illustrates the relationship between SQ3R and the first four steps of the DRA.

A limitation of SQ3R is that it requires direct teaching and extensive practice. Research has shown that simply mentioning the steps and hoping for

FIGURE 11.5

A comparison of SQ3R and the DRA

SOURCE: From *Teaching Reading in the Elementary School* (p. 288) by J. W. Miller and M. C. McKenna, 1989, Scottsdale, AZ: Gorsuch Scarisbrick. Copyright 1989 by Gorsuch Scarisbrick. Reprinted by permission.

Steps of the DRA		Steps of SQ3R
1. Background	⟵⟶	Survey
2. Purpose	⟵⟶	Question
3. Reading	⟵⟶	Reading
4. Discussion	⟵⟶	Recite
		Review

the best is not enough to assure that students will acquire a reading strategy of this kind (Caverly & Orlando, 1991). On the other hand, teachers can do much to provide extensive practice opportunities with SQ3R by relating it to textbook assignments. Once students have become familiar with content literacy guides, teachers can introduce a new type of guide based on SQ3R. After introducing the five steps together with an example based on the chapter the students have just read, the teacher distributes an SQ3R worksheet. Like other literacy guides, the worksheet compels the student to interact with the text and to write information and responses. The chief difference is that the worksheet requires students to generate questions from subheadings. Gall and his associates (1990) offer an example of a completed SQ3R worksheet, which appears in Figure 11.6.

Beyond SQ3R

When it was introduced in 1946, SQ3R represented a novel approach to strategic reading. More recently, its usefulness in some situations has led educators to regret its limitations in others. For example, the approach does not work with material that lacks subtitles. Moreover, the subtitles may at times fail to address a student's purposes in reading. It is not surprising that SQ3R led to a spate of adaptations. By 1982, Walker was able to list 39 (each known by an acronym).

PLAE　　This trend suggests that, to be effective, students must be able to apply a variety of techniques, depending on their purposes and the nature of the material. Simpson and Nist (1984), responding to the inability of any single strategy to be effective on all occasions, suggested a method for making students consciously select the strategies they use. In PLAE (Preplan, List, Activate, Evaluate), the student begins by examining the task at hand

FIGURE 11.6

Name _Jackie Jefferson_

Course _Social Sciences I_

Date _October 15, 1989_

Textbook _The Metropolitan Community_

Chapter _3_   Pages _47-61_

I.   SURVEY the chapter (take about 5 to 10 minutes). As you survey the chapter, answer the following questions.

A. What is the title of the chapter? _The World and the U.S._

B. Is there a chapter summary at the beginning or end of the chapter? _YES_
   On what page(s) is this summary located? ___47___ Be sure to read any summary information.

C. What are the main subheadings in this chapter? Please list them below:
   1. _Globes and maps show places on the earth_
   2. _Directions and the poles_
   3. _The equator and the hemispheres_
   4. _Map symbols_
   5. _Countries in North America_
   6. _Learning More About Maps: What scale means/measures_
   7. _How maps show distance_
   8. _____

D. Please describe one or two illustrations, graphs, charts, pictures, or cartoons that stood out as you surveyed the chapter.

   Page 58 shows an actual size drawing of an ice cream cone and a scale drawing of it

E. Are there study questions listed at the end of the chapter? _YES_
   If so, be sure to read them.

F. Are there key vocabulary words listed at the end of the chapter? _NO_
   If so, be sure to read them.

(continued)

Example of an SQ3R worksheet

SOURCE: From *Tools for Learning: A Guide to Teaching Study Skills* (pp. 130–132) by M. D. Gall, J. P. Gall, D. R. Jacobsen, and T. L. Bullock, 1990, Alexandria, VA: Association for Supervision and Curriculum Development. Copyright 1990 by the Association for Supervision and Curriculum Development. Reprinted by permission of the Association for Supervision and Curriculum Development.

G. Can you describe in one or two brief sentences what this chapter will be about?

It will tell me how maps are used to show what the world and different countries look like.

II. QUESTION yourself about the chapter by turning the major subheadings that you listed in part I-C into questions. Use who, what, where, when, why, and how when developing your questions.

1. *How do globes and maps show places on the earth?*
2. *What do directions and poles show us?*
3. *What are equators and hemispheres?*
4. *What is the purpose of map symbols?*
5. *What are the countries in North America?*
6. *What are scales, and what are they used for?*
7. *How do maps show distance?*
8. _____

III. READ one major subheading area of the chapter at a time and then RECITE the answer(s) to the question(s) you asked for each major subheading in section II.

A. Answer question 1 from section II, using one or two sentences.

Globes and maps help us learn geography and how to find places on our planet. They do this by: categorizing land and water separately and labeling each country and each body of water.

B. Answer question 2 from section II, using one or two sentences.

Directions and poles are north, south, east, west, NE, SW, etc. They help us locate places on a map or globe.

(continued)

C. Answer question 3 from section II, using one or two sentences.

Equators and hemispheres divide the earth in half. The equator is an imaginary line around the middle of the earth, and the north and south hemi-spheres are what make up each half.

On the back of this page, answer the rest of your subheading questions.

IV. REVIEW the entire chapter by going back through the chapter and outlining the main points. Your main points come from the headings, main ideas, and key words.

A. Globes and maps
 1. globes are three-dimensional
 2. maps are two-dimensional
 3. help us locate bodies of water, countries, cities, and land forms
B. Directions and poles
 1. N, S, E, W
 2. in between directions: NE, SW, etc.
 3. north and south poles
C. Equator and hemispheres
 1. equator splits earth in half
 2. north and south hemispheres
 3. Make it easier to locate places on map or globe

to determine what must be accomplished. The student then mentally lists strategies that may be useful and uses (activates) one or more that seem best suited to accomplishing the desired purposes. Finally, the student evaluates whether the purpose has in fact been achieved and, if not, what other strategies might be used to achieve it. Not surprisingly, research has shown that PLAE works (Nist & Simpson, 1989).

At the heart of the technique is the notion that superior students have a variety of strategies at their command and are capable of selecting those that are best suited to a given situation. Content teachers can move their students toward this point first by seizing opportunities to build their ability to take notes, review, take tests, and read independently, and second by encouraging them to become cognizant of how and when they employ these skills. Wade, Trathen, and Schraw (1990) found that it is probably best not to be overly prescriptive in how students should study. Let them experiment with techniques until they identify those that are most comfortable. This policy is consistent with the reasoning behind PLAE.

SUMMARY

Study involves learning independently the content of printed materials. While numerous skills are involved, some are best taught by content teachers, who are in a position to demonstrate their use with course materials. Centrally important are the ability to take notes, to review, to take tests, and to read independently using purposeful strategies. These abilities receive little attention from teachers, who often assume that students will develop them naturally. Research, however, suggests that teachers must directly instruct students in the use of these skills.

Note taking aids learning by the mental involvement needed in taking the notes and also by their use during review. Content teachers can develop note-taking skills in their students by modeling them during content lectures. The Cornell System provides a good basis from which to begin teaching, but other guidelines are also important. These include (1) assessing students' note-taking abilities, (2) speaking at a slow rate, (3) pausing often, (4) stressing definitions and examples, (5) teaching abbreviations, (6) encouraging the use of paraphrase, (7) helping students focus on cues the teacher provides, (8) recommending indention as a means of organizing, (9) giving grades on notes, and (10) preparing transparencies from actual examples of students' notes.

When reviewing or doing homework assignments, superior students seek a relatively quiet environment. They also manage their time by setting priorities, avoiding early fatigue, and motivating themselves. Cumulative review can be an especially effective way to ensure long-term retention.

Whether to teach test wiseness is a controversial issue. Our suggestion is to teach those techniques that contribute to valid test scores and to construct tests that are immune to techniques that tend to inflate scores. Teachers should avoid (1) distractors with similar meanings, (2) options with opposite meanings, (3) absurdly false options, (4) options that disagree grammatically with their stem, (5) hiding the correct choice in the B or C position, and (6) absolutes in true/false items. At the same time, they should teach students (1) to read all options before responding, (2) to skip harder items till last, (3) to use the process of elimination, (4) to use true/false strategies with "Type K" items, (5) to change answers when it seems warranted, (6) to manage their time, (7) to read essay questions carefully, jotting down key words and producing an answer of appropriate length and clarity, and (8) to pay special attention to the verb in an essay question.

Numerous strategies for independent reading are available. Most are adaptations of SQ3R (Survey, Question, Read, Recite, Review), which provides some of the benefits of a DRA in the absence of a teacher. SQ3R is limited, however, and superior students must be able to call on other strategies when their purposes or the material requires them.

GETTING INVOLVED

1. Use yourself as a guinea pig. Select one or more of the note-taking and review techniques discussed here that you do not already use in your own approach to college coursework. Try out each technique and judge for yourself whether you want to encourage your students to employ it. We suggest you keep an informal log as you begin to use the method you've chosen. Record any problems you may experience in getting used to it, any modifications you may develop, and of course any evidence you may gather of its effectiveness in helping you retain course material.

2. Compare a sample of your own lecture notes with the guidelines recommended in the Cornell System. Which of the guidelines do you follow? With which ones is your own system at odds? In these cases, can you give reasons (other than habit) in defense of your approach over the Cornell System?

3. Here's an action research project to try with your students. Select a unit that contains factual information for students to remember. If you have two sections of the same course, use a carefully distributed review schedule with one of the classes. We suggest 10 minutes, one day a month, for five months. The last 10-minute review should occur just prior to a quiz over the unit. On the day that this class undertakes its last 10-minute review, conduct a 50-minute review with the other class. (This will be the *only* review this class will receive.) Both classes will have participated in the same total amount of review when you administer the quiz. Judge for yourself whether distributing review had an effect on the class average for the quiz. If you do not teach two sections of the same course concurrently, you can still perform the experiment by comparing a current class with one that will take the course the next time you teach it. In either case, you'll need to use classes that in your judgment are of relatively comparable ability.

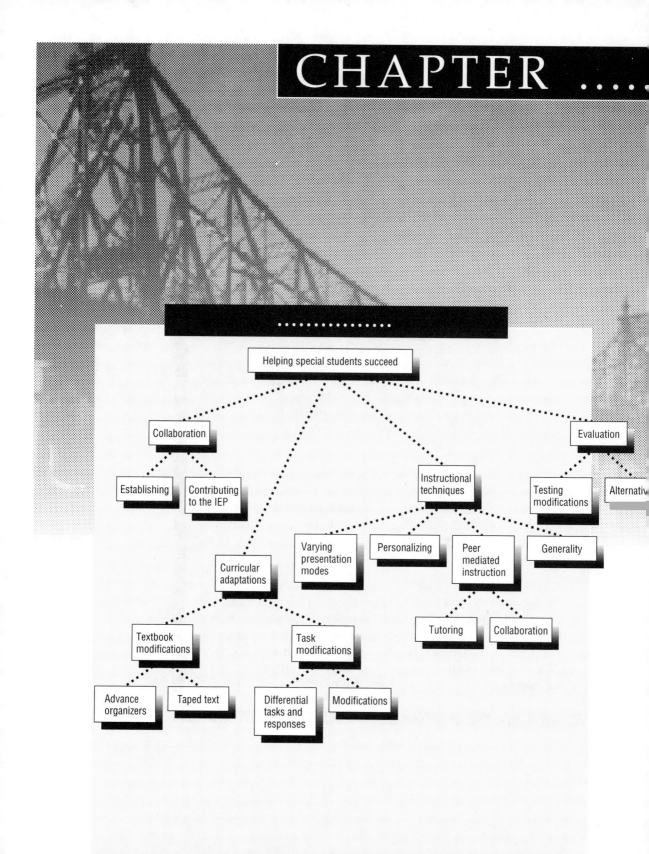

TWELVE

Teaching Students with Special Needs

Belinda D. Lazarus
University of Michigan at Dearborn

I*n the middle of every great difficulty lies opportunity.*

Albert Einstein

Diversity characterizes the student population of most classrooms. For years, classroom teachers have considered a variety of individual differences and skill levels in developing instructional objectives and activities that meet the needs of students exhibiting a wide range of cultural, economic, and experiential backgrounds. The integration of handicapped students into the regular classroom further diversifies the group and challenges teachers to reach beyond traditional instructional techniques in order to accommodate students with learning problems.

While numerous students have special needs, this chapter focuses on the educational needs of mildly handicapped (MH) students. The MH population includes students with learning disabilities, behavior disorders, mild mental retardation, and speech/language disorders. The techniques offered in this chapter can be used separately or together with handicapped and nonhandicapped students alike, regardless of their skill levels.

OBJECTIVES

After studying this chapter, you should have a working familiarity with a variety of instructional techniques that meet the needs of MH students while improving access to information for all the students in your classes. You should be able to

1. compare and contrast expected behaviors of nonhandicapped adolescents with the actual behaviors of MH adolescents;

2. describe the rationale for including MH students in the regular classroom;

3. describe ways to establish and maintain collaborative relationships with special educators;

4. contribute to the development of the Individualized Education Program for MH students in your classes;

5. develop and use curricular and instructional modifications to accommodate a variety of individual needs within large group settings;

6. vary modes of evaluation to measure comprehension of content while controlling for skill deficits; and

7. provide differential practice and review for groups containing students who function on a variety of knowledge levels.

THE BASIS FOR REGULAR EDUCATION INTEGRATION

Classroom teachers often wonder, "With all the responsibilities teachers have, why do I have to contend with handicapped learners in my classes? How can I be expected to teach handicapped learners when I lack the specialized materials and training I need? Why aren't regular classroom teachers ever consulted BEFORE handicapped students are placed in their classrooms?" Questions like these arose from a general misunderstanding of the intent of Public Law 94-142 (The Education for All Handicapped Children Act of 1975) and other special education legislation designed to provide a free and appropriate education for all handicapped children. Regular *and* special educators initially interpreted the provisions of P.L. 94-142 from an exclusionary perspective, and many classroom teachers breathed a collective sigh of relief as handicapped learners were transferred to special education classrooms staffed by teachers with "specialized training" seasoned with a touch of "magic."

However, after nearly two decades, initial predictions of significant skill gains, normalization through remediation of skill deficits, and the eventual return of "cured" MH students to the regular classroom remain an unfulfilled promise. To date, special education "pull-out" programs have failed to produce enduring skill gains that transfer across settings (Stainback & Stainback, 1984; Will, 1986), adequate preparation for postsecondary education or employment (Gartner & Lipsky, 1990), and the social and self-management skills needed to establish and maintain the personal and professional relationships needed by adults (Gresham, 1981, 1984). To the contrary, the isolation and individualization in pull-out programs frequently cause increased passivity, impulsivity, and "learned helplessness" in MH students (Hallahan & Reeve, 1980). Recent studies also show that MH and nonhandicapped learners exhibit similar skill gains from the same kinds of instruction (Haynes & Jenkins, 1986; Wang & Walberg, 1988).

The failure of special education instruction to meet the expectations of parents, educators, and handicapped learners has generated numerous controversies. The most recent, a Regular Education Initiative (REI) promoted by prominent special educators, calls for a reintegration of MH students into the regular classroom. However, in spite of many similarities shared by MH and nonhandicapped students, one glaring fact remains: Most MH students, especially at the secondary level, have severe deficits in one or more academic and/or social skill areas.

BEHAVIORAL CHARACTERISTICS OF ADOLESCENTS

At a time when youth attempt to apply basic skills accumulated throughout grammar school, assert their independence, and explore the limits of convention, MH students lack the academic skills and social awareness needed to succeed. Adolescents are expected to forge new and mature relationships and accept their individual sexuality. However, MH students cling to immature behavior patterns, consistently overestimate the acceptability of their academic and social behaviors (Bruininks, 1978; Bryan, 1982), remain emotionally dependent on adults, and attribute their shortcomings to external sources of control (Polloway, Smith, & Patton, 1984).

Table 12.1 compares the expected academic and vocational behaviors of adolescents with the actual behaviors that are commonly observed in MH adolescents.

In addition to the behaviors listed on Table 12.1, teachers frequently cite MH students' lack of basic academic and social skills; poor handwriting, spelling, and listening skills; disorganization; irresponsibility; attention deficits; and disruptive behaviors as common complaints (Gresham, 1984; Hallahan & Reeve, 1980; Wiens, 1983). Further, studies show that MH students have a high rate of absenteeism (Schultz, Tucker, & Turnbull, 1991) and a higher dropout rate (31% versus 25%) than their nonhandicapped peers (Rumberg, 1987); they require counseling for emotional problems at a rate that is three times higher than that of nonhandicapped students (Gresham, 1981). However, many mildly handicapped students are also gifted in one or more academic or artistic areas and receive special education and gifted services in their respective school districts (Lazarus, 1989a; Whitmore, 1986)! But, as perplexing and contradictory as MH students may seem, many strategies help them succeed in regular classroom settings.

HELPING MILDLY HANDICAPPED STUDENTS SUCCEED

Several strategies exist to help MH students gain skills in regular-curriculum content courses. The following sections organize techniques into three categories: collaboration among regular and special educators, curricular adaptations, and instructional techniques. Each of the

Table 12.1		
Comparison of Expected and Exhibited School Behavior of Handicapped Adolescents		
	Expected Adolescent Behavior	**Exhibited Adolescent Behavior**
School	good listeners	low achievers
	good readers	few basic skills
	good writers	5th grade—reading, writing
	self-controlled	6th grade—math
	independent	inactive learners
	initiators	low motivation
	organized	low self-esteem
	accumulators of	high off-task behaviors
	academic credits	increased behavior problems
	test takers	poor test takers
Work	good listeners	occupationally immature
	good readers	immature social perceptions
	good writers	problems—interpersonal
	self-controlled	relationships
	independent	poor social skills
	initiators	
	good speakers	

Source: *Courtesy Timothy Heron.*

techniques recommended has been field tested and shown to be effective with MH students in regular classroom settings.

All the techniques may be used as presented, combined, or adapted to suit the needs of a particular class or student. However, a few general considerations will enhance their utility. First, apply the techniques as inconspicuously as possible. No one likes to stick out like a sore thumb. So, when possible, make accommodations available to all students. For example, if content literacy guides are made available for the MH students in your classes, make them available to everyone. Second, rethink your usual approach and try to incorporate accommodations as efficiently as possible. Consider task demands, the student composition of the class, and available resources. Third, try a variety of approaches. If one does not yield the desired results, try another one. Fourth, access as many materials and human resources as are available in your school. Paraprofessionals; special educators; reading, language, and math specialists; student assistants; volunteers; and parents (especially parents of the MH students) are frequently willing to share their time and resources to offset some of the extra work and materials needed to develop accommodations.

Collaboration among Regular and Special Educators

As increasing numbers of MH students are integrated into regular-curriculum content courses, collaboration among regular and special educators fulfills a pivotal role in moving MH students into and maintaining them within the regular classroom. Idol-Maestas, Nevin, and Paolucci-Whitcomb (1984) describe such collaboration as interactions among educators for the purpose of solving a mutual problem. They suggest that, to enhance collaborative efforts, teachers first establish equality by listening, respecting, and learning from each other. They must recognize that each collaborator views the problem from a different perspective. They must therefore provide reinforcing feedback to each other and use a data-based approach to evaluate the effectiveness of strategies devised by the collaborators.

Joint undertakings stand a better chance when they benefit both sides.

Euripides

Collaborative approaches offer several advantages to regular classroom teachers. Special education teachers have a wealth of information about the MH student's achievement levels, reinforcer preferences, academic and social strengths and weaknesses, and approaches to independent and group tasks. Second, special educators are frequently willing to share ideas, materials, and resources (e.g., computer programs, paraprofessional time, etc.). This can be a two-way street, in addition. Just as White and Jordan (1986) argued that adult educators should use reading materials that stress careers (so that mature students could learn something useful as they learn to read), content area teachers might offer their own textbooks to special educators and to reading specialists for use in developing reading proficiency. Third, special educators usually share a close relationship with parents and can help regular educators establish functional relationships with the parents. On the other hand, regular educators can provide information about the social and academic task demands of the classroom, realistic estimates of the time and resources they can devote to the MH student, and the levels of academic performance of the other students in the class. Together, the regular and special educator can use each other's knowledge to develop Individualized Educational Programs (IEPs) that incorporate support strategies needed by the MH students.

Contributing to the IEP

Many regular educators complain that their ideas and concerns are not considered in the development of the IEP. Conferences are scheduled at times that are inconvenient for regular educators to attend and, in some cases, MH students are placed in regular classes before the teachers are prepared to receive them. However, P.L. 94-142 specifically states as a *minimum* requirement that the extent of the handicapped student's participation in regular-curriculum classes must be addressed in the IEP. Unfortunately, this minimum requirement is often interpreted too narrowly, and simplistic statements like "mainstreamed for science" are listed. As one science teacher put it, "A more accurate statement would be, 'Johnny can't read, write, or find my room consistently, but we're putting him in your room anyway.' " This remark reveals the legitimate frustrations teachers feel when their ideas and concerns are bypassed.

However, content teachers armed with a few tips can have their concerns addressed by the IEP. First, a "rough" draft of the IEP is usually written before the actual IEP meeting with the parents. As a result, a meeting with the special educator while the rough draft is being developed allows the content teacher to request support and suggest an evaluation schedule and criteria to monitor the MH student's progress in the regular classroom setting. Through collaboration, educators develop and write into the IEP the kinds of support needed by the MH student and by the person/s responsible for the support. Figure 12.1 shows a model of a typical IEP with a section marked "extent of participation in the regular classroom." These spaces are usually small; however, an addendum may be added if extra space is needed. For example, in this section of the IEP the teachers may write, "mainstreamed for science with the following support from special education personnel: help with reading assignments and homework, oral readers for tests, provision of a 10-minute review time, and use of paraprofessional by the science teacher as needed not to exceed 2 hours per week." The teachers can designate virtually any kind of support. This flexibility is most likely to benefit all concerned (students and teachers alike) when a collaborative effort is used.

Another section of the IEP specifies the goals and objectives that guide the MH student's instruction. Goals and objectives must be developed for all the subjects addressed in the special education setting. However, they are not for the exclusive use of special educators. Regular educators may add goals and objectives that address regular classroom demands. Figure 12.2 depicts the typical goals and objectives section of the IEP and lists objectives addressing the concerns of the regular classroom teacher.

With a little foresight, planning, and assertiveness, regular educators can have their concerns addressed in the IEP. The following sections describe a variety of techniques that may be used to accommodate MH students in regular-curriculum classes. While these techniques require some extra effort, the work may be shared and the responsibilities designated on the IEP.

Curricular Adaptations

Comprehension begins with access to information through various modes. Reading assignments, class discussions, and lectures represent a common mode of transmitting information in content courses. In fact, Putnam, Deshler, and Schumaker (in press) found that content teachers devote 48 percent of each class period to lectures based on reading assignments. As a result, high school

FIGURE 12.1

FIGURE 12.1

Circle one:
Initial IEP
Reviewed IEP

SCHOOL YEAR
INDIVIDUALIZED EDUCATIONAL
PROGRAM (IEP)

White: County Office
Yellow: Permanent Record
Pink: Teacher
Gold: Parent

Name _____ Birthdate _____ Age _____ Grade _____

Address _____ Phone _____

Parents/Guardians _____

Address _____ Phone _____

School/District of Residence _____ County _____

School/District/Agency Providing Program _____ County _____

_____

I. Specific special education program/placement and type(s) of services:
   (Include grade, date to be initiated and anticipated duration.)

_____

II. Extent of participation in regular education program:
   (include grade and support services needed from special education and support
   services personnel.)

_____

III. If initial placement, indicate previous grade, building, program:

_____

IV. Statement of present levels of educational performance:
   (Include assessment strategies, scores, and dates.)

Cover page of an Individualized Educational Program (IEP) with space indicated for extent of participation in the regular curriculum

FIGURE 12.2

Page of an Individualized
Educational Program
(IEP) listing goals
and objectives that
address the concerns
and responsibilities of
the special and regular
education teachers.

page 2 of 5

GOALS *To improve study skills.*

OBJECTIVES	MATERIALS	STAFF	EVALUATION
1. When provided with guided notes, student will take notes during lecture with 100% accuracy.	guided notes & transparencies	science teacher	visual inspection 3 times a week
2. After each lecture, student will review guided notes for 10 minutes.	completed guided notes.	special education aide	observation; timer; review tally
3. When a chapter test is read for the student, he will write the correct response 80% of the time.	test made by science teacher	special education teacher	grading by science teacher

students need reading, note-taking, and study skills to benefit from instruction. Unfortunately, MH and remedial students often have limited reading and language skills that prevent them from benefiting from several primary sources of learning from the start. Several curricular adaptations improve access to information and help bypass reading and language deficits experienced by low-achieving students.

Textbook Modifications   The textbook remains a standard tool in secondary classrooms. Studies show that textbooks are often poorly organized, written on a readability level that is above the grade level of students using the textbook, and contain misleading or even inaccurate charts, figures, and diagrams (Kantor, Anderson, & Armbruster, 1983). After evaluating textbooks on the basis of structure, coherence, unity, and audience appropriateness, Kantor and associates (1983) characterized many of the texts as "inconsiderate" to the reader (see Chapter 5). They estimated that secondary-level texts were appropriate for only the top 50 percent of the students using the book. Needless to say, sometimes even the best readers experience difficulties with reading assignments. Mildly handicapped students lack the basic vocabulary needed to read assignments independently, fail to activate prior knowledge relating to the assignment, and often give up in frustration before they have finished the first page.

However, several textbook modifications help compensate for the skill deficits of MH and remedial students. You read about one such adaptation, the use of marginal glosses, in Chapter 5. Two additional modifications are fairly simple and effective for MH students with visual processing problems. The first involves highlighting topic sentences, key terms and definitions, and other important information with a pastel-colored, felt tip marker. It is especially helpful to color-code related concepts and include a key explaining the color-coding system. For example, all topic sentences might be highlighted in yellow, terms and definitions in pink, and important information (e.g., people, dates) in green. The second modification requires a photocopying machine with an enlarging option. First, photocopy each page of the reading assignment and then enlarge each photocopy as much as possible. A print size that is at least as large as the print used in primary picture books works best, so the original photocopies may need to be cut in half before enlarging. This is a good assignment for an aide or paraprofessional.

Tape-recorded textbooks are also a popular accommodation offered to MH students. However, students need both good listening skills and supplements to the recordings if they are to derive maximum benefit from tape-recorded texts. Essentially, providing MH students with a tape recorder and a verbatim recording of the reading assignment does little to improve the student's comprehension of content (Schumaker, Deshler, & Denton, 1982). However, (1) listening to taped readings while following along with the textbook and (2) beginning taped readings with a review of previous readings appear to help some MH students (Rivers, 1980). While limited research exists regarding the effectiveness of taped text material, Deshler and Graham (1980) maintain that in taping content material, several elements must be considered:

1. Instructional goals and objectives must be identified.
2. Specific aspects of the text relating to the objectives should be considered.
3. When the entire reading is not recorded, a summary or outline of the entire reading should be provided for students to lend a context to the major concepts that are recorded.
4. Important concepts should be differentiated from unimportant and distracting details.

5. Emphasis on maps, tables, charts, chapter titles, and headings should be considered.

6. A marking system that coordinates text with recordings to prevent students from getting confused or lost should accompany each recording.

Schumaker and associates (1982) contend that recordings that are organized to emphasize active student participation and followed by direct instruction that reviews important concepts result in significant achievement gains in MH students. To relieve the teacher, peer tutors, paraprofessionals, or trained volunteers may provide the direct instruction review.

If you will carefully consider the six recommendations of Deshler and Graham above, you will see that departures from a word-for-word oral reading of the text are often in order. This is why the content teacher is the best possible person to do the recording. Consider a few possibilities. The teacher can judiciously skip extraneous material in the same way that a selective guide might advise readers to do (see Chapter 8). Likewise, the background of the content teacher enables her or him to paraphrase difficult prose, to restate and summarize main ideas, and to interject additional facts and observations that may enhance comprehension. Moreover, the teacher can embed writing tasks, questions to think about, and other directive remarks at key points in the material. In short, the taped version can incorporate most of the advantages of a content literacy guide, marginal notes, and other background-building devices.

The fact that the content teacher is the one individual with adequate expertise to skillfully create taped versions of text assignments may present a depressing prospect. You cannot safely relegate the task to a paraprofessional or a gifted student. There are, however, some compensating advantages. First, taping affords a marvelous opportunity to become acquainted with your own text. When you prepare content literacy guides, you will rely on the same sorts of analysis (which portions to direct students to skip, which questions to pose, etc.), so that no additional effort is required. Second, you need only one version. Once finished, the tape becomes a resource for as long as the materials will be assigned, and dubbing to make multiple copies is easy. Third, if you teach in a setting large enough that other teachers are assigning the same materials, collaboration becomes possible. If, for example, three teachers use the same text, each of them must record only a third of the material. Even if you teach in a smaller setting, you can readily locate colleagues in other schools who use the same text. The publisher's area sales representative can help, as can your membership in state organizations associated with your content area.

Another recommendation, graphic organizers, might be characterized as a textbook supplement—one with enormous potential to help MH and remedial readers. According to Torgesen and Kail (1985) and Wong (1978), MH students are passive learners who do not automatically organize concepts and integrate information with existing knowledge. To address these deficits, Tobias (1982) suggests techniques that increase the organizational salience of the content and require overt responses from students. You will recall from Chapter 6 that graphic organizers are a visual and verbal representation of key terms and concepts that can be organized in many ways. You learned that a variety of terms are used to describe these diagrammatic displays of information (e.g., semantic maps, flow charts, tree diagrams, etc.). The common thread linking these visual-verbal representations is the use of words or statements that are connected graphically in a meaningful way. While numerous forms of graphic organizers have proven effective with nonhandicapped students, organizers that are laden with a large number of words and minimal directional indicators (arrows, lines connecting concepts, etc.) often confuse MH and other low-achieving readers.

Two kinds of graphic organizers appear to benefit MH and remedial students the most. Each contains simple vocabulary, requires students to supply at least some of the information, and projects unmistakable visual symbols depicting the linkage among and between information. Figure 12.3 depicts a graphic organizer that addresses the Civil War in a comparative organization. Lines connect related information and arrows indicate comparisons between paired aspects of the Civil War. Key terms are provided at the bottom of the page. The graphic organizer shown in Figure 12.4 (p. 275) describes "growing a garden." Information is organized hierarchically and comparatively with lines and arrows depicting relationships and comparisons. As the authors suggested in Chapter 6, the organizers shown in Figures 12.3 and 12.4 have been tested as postreading devices. They can, however, be used either before or after reading.

In a series of three studies with learning disabled, remedial, and nonhandicapped secondary students, Horton and Lovitt (in press) found that the use of comparative and hierarchical models of graphic organizers as postreading activities improved *all* the students' average test scores. Several suggestions specific to the needs of MH and remedial students can improve the effectiveness of graphic organizers. The following are derived from research by Horton and Lovitt (and others) on graphic organizers:

1. Train students to use graphic organizers. Explain the purpose, organization, and student behaviors needed to use the graphic organizer.
2. Keep the vocabulary and structure simple. Too many words and symbols confuse or intimidate low achievers.
3. Include information that is essential to understanding the important concepts, relationships, and objectives of the reading.
4. Provide opportunities for students to respond and receive corrective and reinforcing feedback. Blank spaces and an answer key are ways to transform graphic organizers into active learning opportunities.

FIGURE 12.3

An example of
a comparative
graphic organizer

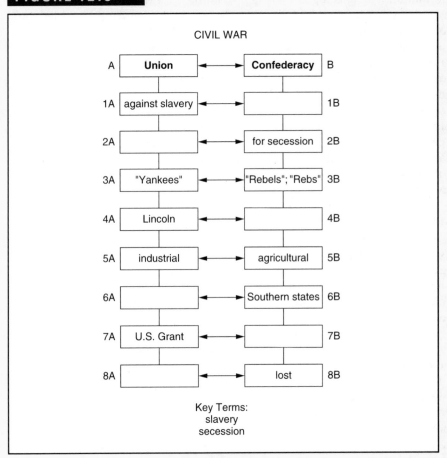

5. Choose a format that corresponds to the structure of the information (e.g., Figures 12.3 or 12.4).

6. Choose reading material that is poorly organized in the text or has proven to be otherwise difficult for students to understand.

A final textbook adaptation, rewriting, is one that I cannot in good faith recommend. Rewriting textbooks to reduce their readability level represents an accommodation that appeals to the "common sense" of most educators and has repeatedly been recommended for low-achieving students (e.g., Osterlag & Rambeau, 1982; Wright, 1982). This modification originated with the practice of comparing the readability levels of textbooks based on formulas (see Chapter 3)

FIGURE 12.4

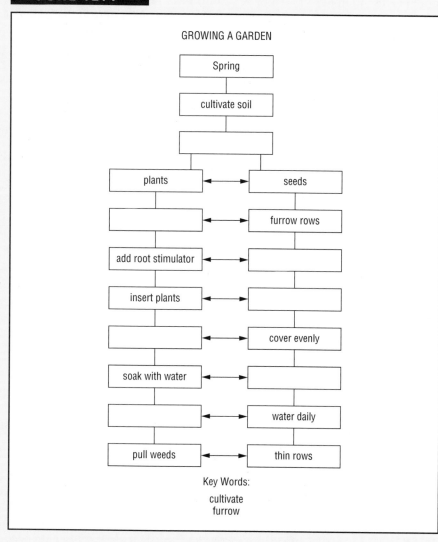

An example of a combination hierarchical-comparative graphic organizer

with the reading levels of students as measured by standardized tests. Following this logic, a textbook written on a twelfth-grade level and used by a student with a fifth-grade instructional level would be seven grades too advanced for the student. However, the practice of comparing readability levels with reading achievement scores is similar to comparing apples with pastrami. Often, little agreement exists among the various readability formulas when they are used on the same passage or among achievement scores earned by students on different tests (Eaton & Lovitt, 1972; Lovitt, Horton, & Bergerud, 1987). Further, research at the Center for the Study of Reading at the University of Illinois suggests that condensing or altering passages on the basis of readability formulas may seriously distort the logical relationships among parts of the text, disrupt the presentation of ideas, and make it difficult to convey the meaning of the original content (Davison, 1984). Fry (1989), author of one of the most widely used formulas, has warned that suggesting the necessity for rewriting a text is a blatant misuse of the formulas, which are designed merely to predict the difficulty of text that already exists. Rewriting textbooks requires expertise and an unreasonable amount of teacher time. Moreover, it does not appear to benefit students. As a result, the time devoted to rewriting textbooks in an effort to reduce readability is better spent on techniques that take less time and have consistently proven effective.

Task Modifications   Instead of modifying the text, another means of adapting the curriculum to meet the literacy needs of MH students is by modifying the tasks these students are asked to perform. Potential task modifications assume as many forms as the multitude of available task options. Lewis and Doorlag (1991) describe four general categories of task modification:

1. change the criteria for successful performance in terms of quantity, speed, and/or accuracy
2. change the task characteristics
3. break the task into component subtasks
4. select an alternate task

They caution teachers to offer alternative tasks only when students are unable to benefit satisfactorily from modifications of the tasks required of other members of the class.

While teachers can apply the four task modification categories, alone or in combination, to any task, several specific modifications have proven effective with MH, remedial, and nonhandicapped students. Three techniques—task differentiation, differentiated responding, and guided notes—frequently allow MH students to participate in class activities with their classmates, gain needed skills, and compensate for skill deficits.

Task differentiation rests on the assumption that students comprising a group operate on different knowledge levels ranging from simple recall through complex application of basic information to solve a variety of problems. For example, proficient learners usually recall or recognize countless basic skills with the ease and accuracy needed to apply the information to a variety of problem-solving situations. However, MH students struggle with recollection of the basic information (e.g., math facts, sight words) needed to accomplish higher-level tasks (e.g., problem solving, comprehension). As a result, tasks that require the recall and practice of basic information pose as great a challenge to MH students as problem-solving tasks pose to proficient learners.

Task differentiation may be group oriented or applied with individuals. For group projects, such as panel presentations, teachers might assign each individual in the group specific tasks according to his or her knowledge level. While MH students may be asked to gather factual information pertaining to the group's topic, proficient learners may be assigned the task of evaluating and synthesizing the information. For individual tasks such as book reports, MH students may be directed to focus their report on specific aspects of the book such as character development, sequence of events, or a summary of the plot. In each instance, MH students engage in the same task on a different, more skill-appropriate level.

Differentiated responding capitalizes on a multitude of oral, written, and gestural response modes to provide MH students with the opportunity to "show what they know" without the confounding influence of a weak response mode. For example, just as a teacher would not expect a blind student to copy information from the chalkboard, MH students with weak fine motor skills should not be expected to handwrite reports. Many MH students exhibit favored and weak response modes. However, as Table 12.2 demonstrates, many alternatives exist. The oral, written, and gestural response and presentation modes listed in Table 12.2 represent a variety of options that teachers may offer students or use themselves in presenting content.

Chapter 8 introduced you to *guided notes,* a skeleton outline containing the main ideas and key terms of a presentation and spaces for students to write related and subordinate information. Guided notes facilitate note taking from lectures and reading assignments (Lazarus, 1988). While useful with nonhandicapped students, this technique has special applications with MH learners. In two separate studies conducted in regular-curriculum science and social studies classes, Lazarus (1991; in press) showed that the use of guided notes to facilitate note taking and review significantly improved both MH and nonhandicapped students' scores on chapter tests completed in the regular class setting. In each study all students were given copies of guided notes and the teacher lectured and led class discussions based on reading assignments. Student copies of guided notes (Figure 12.5, p. 279) contained many blank spaces that students completed as the teacher lectured and showed the completed copies of the guided notes on transparencies (Figure 12.6, p. 280).

Teachers participating in the studies discovered that the easiest and most efficient way to develop guided notes was first to highlight the main ideas and key terms in their lecture notes with transparent markers so secretaries and paraprofessionals could word process the student copies. They then used a different color to highlight the information needed for the completed copy transparencies. Finally, they added the information to the student copy and saved the completed notes on a computer disk. Teachers, paraprofessionals, and secretaries responding to a "consumer satisfaction" survey reported that developing the guided notes took about one hour per week each for the teacher

| | Table 12.2 | Listing of Alternative Response and Presentation Modes That May Be Used by Students and Teachers |

Oral	Written	Gestural
Oral presentations to small group or class	Graphs	Pointing
Tape-recorded summaries	Charts	Charades
Role playing	Flowcharts	Pantomime
Debates	Collage	Signalling/ cueing
Media presentations	Puppets	Manipulatives
Narrative drawings	Journals	Response boards
Team discussions	Highlighting or underlining	Experiments
Committee meetings	Word processing	Nodding or shaking head
Peer tutoring	Guided notes	Blinking
Choral responding	Advanced organizers	Smile/frown
Dramatic presentations/ interpretations	Transparencies	
Guessing games	Drawings/paintings	
Trials	Genealogical charts (story character genealogy)	
Storytelling	Graffiti	
Interpretive readings	Bulletin boards	
Interviewing	Posters	
Oral test responses/ presentations	Newsletters	
Simulations	Critiques	
Brainstorming	Puzzles/games	
Demonstrations	Poems	
	Riddles	
	Chalkboard	
	Letters	
	Workbooks	
	Programmed instruction	
	Dialogues	

FIGURE 12.5

Chapter 20   REVIEW TALLY

CELL REPRODUCTION

I. All life starts out as a _____ .

    A.   - - - - ->

    B.

II. _____ are formed by _____

    _____ .

III. Two types of cell division

    A. *Mitosis—*

        1. _____ is used for replacement of:

            a.

            b.

            c.

            d.

            e.

        2.

        3.

Student copy of guided notes with cues and review tally

and the word processor. Further, each staff member indicated that the time and resource expenditures were reasonable. Students reported that using the guided notes was fun and prevented them from losing their place during lectures.

In developing and using guided notes, Lazarus (1988) suggests:

1. Include at least the main ideas and key terms on the student copies.
2. Provide guided notes for everyone in the class.
3. Use a consistent format that closely parallels the lecture, reading assignment, and/or content to be learned.
4. Show complete copies of the guided notes on transparencies.
5. Periodically evaluate the students' guided notes; and, most important,
6. Train the students to use the guided notes for review. After each review the student places a check in the Review Tally.

FIGURE 12.6

Example of transparencies with completed guided notes that correspond with the student's copies

Chapter 20

CELL REPRODUCTION

I. All life starts out as a *single cell*.
    A. Single cell – – – – –> Millions of cells
    B. Humans have millions of cells.

II. *New cells* are formed by *cell division*.

III. Two types of cell division
    A. *Mitosis* — process of cell division in which 2 cells are formed from 1 cell
        1. *Mitosis* is used for replacement of:
           a. red blood cells
           b. skin cells
           c. muscle cells
           d. root tips
           e. leaf cells
        2. Before cells divide, the cell parts are copied, so the result is 2 identical cells.
        3. Mitosis is a series of steps.

Instructional Techniques

Over the last two decades research on teaching effectiveness has coalesced into a body of knowledge highlighting specific teacher behaviors that improve academic achievement. In addition to identifying behaviors such as teacher selection, pacing, and monitoring of activities, this body of knowledge substantiates what effective teachers have known all along: What teachers *do* in the classroom affects what students learn! Unfortunately, the current trend in many states toward alternative teacher certification evolved from the notion that knowledge of content is more useful than the instructional strategies used to teach the content. Very little research supports the contention that knowledge of content takes precedence over knowledge of effective teaching techniques.

The following section describes four specific strategies that promote skill gains for MH and remedial students in regular-curriculum classes. These research-based techniques are (1) varying modes of presentation, (2) personalizing the learning environment, (3) using peer-mediated instruction, and (4) programming for generality. Each technique benefits nonhandicapped students while accommodating MH students.

Varying Modes of Presentation.   Presenting information in a variety of ways simultaneously provides students with multiple exposures to information and helps meet individual needs within a group setting. Table 12.2, described in the preceding section, contains modes of presentation that may be used or adapted to suit many curricular needs. For example, a lecture accompanied by transparencies and demonstrations might be tape-recorded during the presentation for future review. The transparencies could be posted on a bulletin board and the demonstration left on display for future reference. Without significantly adding to the teacher's workload, these techniques access auditory, visual, and kinesthetic modalities and provide enduring sources for students to refer to after the presentation.

Personalizing the Learning Environment   Most MH students repeatedly experience rejection and isolation from peers *and* teachers. As a result, they may engage in behaviors that disrupt the learning process to attract attention. Adelman (1971) suggests that personalizing the learning environment to create the perception that the MH student is receiving the teacher's personal and undivided attention promotes the positive classroom climate and feelings of acceptance needed to maintain MH students' focus on academics.

At first glance, personalization may sound like an impossible goal. Fortunately, three simple techniques help personalize the MH student's learning environment. First, seating MH students as close as possible to the teacher and source of instruction appears to increase their productivity and accuracy (Heron & Harris, 1987). Second, providing a personalized teacher model for the student to imitate improves the acquisition and maintenance of skills (Blankenship, 1978; Cooper, Heron, & Heward, 1987). A personalized model requires the teacher first to perform the desired academic or social response for the MH student individually and then to watch the student imitate the teacher. Blankenship (1978) found that the personalized modeling approach involved an average of only 35 seconds per day per MH student. Finally, providing MH students with immediate, corrective, and reinforcing feedback by using prearranged gestural cues (nods, smiles, hand-signals, etc.) and/or self-correcting materials promotes task persistence and the development of independent work habits.

Using Peer-mediated Instruction   Perhaps the greatest and most readily available resource in classrooms is the students themselves. Peer-mediated instruction provides individualized instruction in an efficient manner, frees the teacher to spend more time on planning, and benefits all students by providing additional practice and the motivation to independently seek information to answer questions and defend their positions (Custer & Osguthorpe, 1983; Lovitt, 1977). Further, peer-mediated instruction challenges students to assume some of the responsibility of learning, can be structured to provide students with numerous opportunities to respond and receive immediate feedback, promotes social interactions among students, and increases academic performance across a variety of academic domains (Maheady & Harper, 1987; Maheady, Sacca, & Harper, 1988).

Peer tutoring is the most widely recognized form of peer-mediated instruction. Tutoring may use same-aged or cross-aged student pairs to teach each other in a reciprocal manner. To develop a systematic peer tutoring program, you must first select the information to be learned by the students. Tutoring lends itself to practice of factual information, such as names, vocabulary words, and so on. Once you've identified the content, you can implement well-established guidelines with your students. Heward, Heron, and Cooke (1982) developed a field-tested classwide peer tutoring training manual that thoroughly describes the following elements of an effective peer tutoring program:

1. Pretest students and pair them according to similar skill levels.
2. Devote three to five 30-minute sessions to training students.
3. Use direct instruction strategies to teach each component of tutoring (e.g., model the behaviors, provide guided practice, and provide independent practice).
4. Include prompting, praising, testing, and recording of results as basic components of the program.
5. Provide students with two pocket folders, notecards, pencils, and any other material needed to conduct the tutoring.
6. Schedule tutoring for 20 to 30 minutes per session.
7. Circulate around the room during tutoring sessions to monitor task persistence and provide feedback.
8. Use a timer to monitor time and to signal changes in tutoring activities.

While peer tutoring involves one-to-one interactions, peer collaboration allows small groups of students to work together on a common assignment. Peer collaboration represents a variation of what has come to be called *collaborative consultation* and rests on the assumption that each contributor offers different skills, interests, and perspectives to accomplish a mutual task. Unlike other small-group approaches (e.g., cooperative learning), student training focuses on collaboration skills. Once students learn to collaborate, group members control task assignments within the group and the teacher monitors task persistence, provides guidance, and serves as a resource for students.

Johnson and Johnson (1984) describe four general skills that students need to learn before using peer collaboration. A brief description of the skills follows.

1. forming skills: management skills needed to organize the group and establish acceptable behavior norms
2. functioning skills: behaviors needed to complete tasks and maintain effective working relationships
3. formulating skills: behaviors needed to understand, analyze, and retain information
4. fermenting skills: behaviors needed to reconceptualize material, locate information, and draw conclusions (See Johnson & Johnson, 1984, for specific examples of skills in each general skill area.)

Programming for Generality   As passive learners, MH students seldom generalize skill gains to similar situations, settings, and individuals (Donahoe & Zigmond, 1990). As a result, social and academic skills gained in special education settings may not transfer to the regular classroom. Fortunately, MH students can be trained to transfer skills across a variety of environmental factors (Cooper et al., 1987; Stokes & Baer, 1977).

A *technology of generality* based on numerous studies offers several time-tested techniques to promote generality. Once again, collaboration among special and regular educators identifies skills to program for generality and the appropriate techniques to use. First, teach enough examples of the desired skill to ensure acquisition. The number of examples needed varies with the complexity of the task and with student characteristics. Second, use a variety of trainers and settings to teach the same skill in the same way. This strategy communicates to students that many academic and social skills remain constant regardless of the setting or individuals present (e.g., 2 + 2 is always 4, "please" and "thank you" function with bus drivers as well as teachers). Third, while teaching skills, vary environmental conditions in a controlled and systematic manner, such as changing noise and activity levels, so students learn to function under a variety of conditions. Fourth, reinforce skill gains with reinforcers that are available in many different environments (e.g., praise, "free time"). Finally, the simple act of telling students where and when generalization of a particular skill might be appreciated often yields the desired results. For example, a teacher might advise students that, although the lunchroom is noisy and less structured than classrooms, teachers and cooks alike appreciate "thank you's." However, while in the midst of a football play, a "thank you" may generate an undesirable consequence.

EVALUATING STUDENT PROGRESS

Classroom teachers express numerous concerns about evaluating MH students' performance in regular-content courses. Teachers worry about the fairness of making test modifications, assigning grades derived from modified or alternate evaluation methods, and the perception that MH students receive a "watered down" curriculum that gives them an unfair advantage over the other students and that calls for a "watered down" test. At this point in the chapter, you can probably guess that such concerns reflect a misinterpretation of the spirit of integration. Namely, while most students benefit from teaching strategies that address individual needs, few students, MH or otherwise, benefit from a diluted curriculum. This standard applies to evaluation practices as well as curriculum content.

Testing

Written tests represent a common form of evaluation used by teachers responsible for numerous students. Unfortunately, many MH and other low-achieving students perform poorly on written tests. Basic skill deficits and poor self-management skills confound their efforts to communicate skill gains (Wood & Miederhoff, 1988). According to Wood and Miederhoff (1988), MH students often know the correct answers to test questions, but either they do not understand the directions or they fail to comprehend the questions. Wood and Miederhoff suggest that effective test construction begins with clear directions for taking the test. They offer the following suggestions:

1. Provide an example of how the student is to respond. For example:
   Directions: Circle the best answer.
   Example: Who wrote *Paradise Lost?*
   1. Jon Brown
   2. John Milton
   3. Thomas More

2. Keep the directions simple.
3. Have directions written on the test *and* read them orally.
4. Place the directions at the beginning of each separate test section.
5. Make sure students clearly understand the directions. As students begin to take the test circulate around the room and check the first few responses made by students.

Numerous test modifications allow MH students to take the same test as their classmates regardless of each student's particular disability. Vogel and Sattler (1981) and Lazarus (1989b) list the following modifications:

1. Allow for untimed tests.
2. Allow an oral reader for objective exams.
3. Allow the students to take the test alone with a proctor and to give oral responses.

4. Provide clarification and oral rephrasing of questions to bypass vocabulary, syntactic, and comprehension deficits.

5. Allow students to use calculators, dictionaries, and other resource books during exams.

6. Provide scratch paper and lined paper to aid students with poor handwriting skills.

7. Provide alternatives to computer scored answer sheets (e.g., allow students to circle or underline the correct answer).

8. Give the test page by page over a longer period of time.

9. Enlarge the print and shorten the number of lines on the MH student's test.

These suggestions can be modified and combined in many situations and can be offered to any student (not just MH students) needing extra consideration. Further, allowing students to correct tests for a better grade transforms testing into a learning experience.

Alternative Methods of Evaluation

When modifications of the test given to the entire class do not compensate for skill deficits or disabilities, alternative methods of evaluation may allow MH students to demonstrate their levels of skill acquisition. Once again, the response modes listed in Table 12.2 offer a variety of ways to evaluate student progress. In many cases drawings, demonstrations, oral reports, and other alternatives can be used to assess the same information contained in a test. However, when an alternative method is used, the teacher should make arrangements with the MH student privately to avoid embarrassing the student or, better yet, should offer the alternative to the whole class.

SUMMARY

As an increasing number of handicapped students are integrated into regular-curriculum classes, educators need to reconceptualize their roles as teachers. Handicapped students present a shared responsibility among regular and special educators responsible for their academic and social growth. As a result, collaboration, cooperation, and curricular and instructional modifications can transform conventional teaching strategies into opportunities to create and use different approaches that may benefit all students.

Only the imagination limits the types and number of task and instructional modifications that teachers can use. Task modifications involve either changing an existing assignment or making an appropriate substitution. Instructional modifications offer opportunities to experiment with different presentation and response modes, to involve students in their own learning, and to offer students a variety of activities to gain and practice new skills in a variety of situations.

Modifications in evaluation practices include techniques to control for students' disabilities or skill deficits while enabling them to demonstrate skill mastery. Alternatives to tests present another method of assessing student progress. In many cases, when teachers use modified or alternative evaluation strategies students not only respond to the evaluation but also gain skills during the evaluation.

Overall, the inclusion of handicapped students in regular education settings poses numerous challenges for teachers to meet. However, the teachers' challenges pale in comparison to the day-to-day challenges handicapped students face in a classroom full of demands that are just beyond their reach. Fortunately, the things that teachers do can tilt the scale for a handicapped student and teach that student far more than the basics.

GETTING INVOLVED

1. At the beginning of the school year you wrote a note to the special education teachers in your building requesting participation in the development of IEPs for any handicapped students who will be mainstreamed into your history class. As a result, you are attending your first team meeting to discuss the inclusion of a 16-year-old behavior-disordered student in your seventh-period class. What kinds of information will you request from the team? What kinds of information can you share? What kind of support might you request from the special education teacher and other school personnel?

2. Carl, a 15-year-old boy in your natural science class, reads independently at a fourth-grade level and experiences difficulties with written language. Describe five accommodations you might offer Carl. What involvement would you request from special education and other special services personnel?

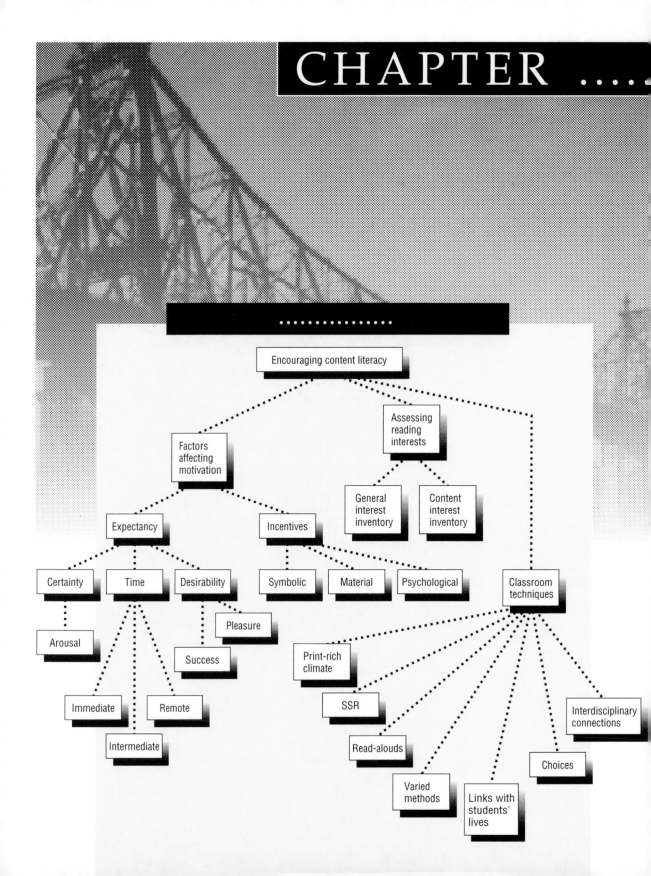

Encouraging content literacy

Factors affecting motivation

Assessing reading interests

Expectancy

Incentives

General interest inventory

Content interest inventory

Certainty

Time

Desirability

Symbolic

Material

Psychological

Classroom techniques

Arousal

Pleasure

Success

Print-rich climate

Immediate

Remote

SSR

Interdisciplinary connections

Intermediate

Read-alouds

Varied methods

Links with students' lives

Choices

THIRTEEN

Student Attitudes:
Encouraging Content Literacy

Knowledge which is acquired under compulsion obtains no hold on the mind.

Plato

As you begin this chapter, pause for a moment to consider *why* you are reading it. Is it because we have aroused your curiosity to the point that you want to learn more in general about content literacy? Could it be that you have specific instructional questions that you think might be addressed in this chapter? Or is it that your instructor will hold you accountable for the chapter on an exam? Perhaps you've read an account of the topic by other authors and wish to contrast their views with ours. Whatever the case, you *are* reading it, and this is evidence that some factor or set of factors is causing you to do so. Had they not existed, you would at this moment be doing something other than reading Chapter 13.

Effective teachers know something about how these factors operate and are able to translate them into instructional practice. The result is improved learning for good and poor readers alike (Clary, 1991) and, in addition, better attitudes toward the subject matter and toward literacy activities related to it.

OBJECTIVES

This chapter describes the basic principles of motivation and suggests ways of making those principles work for you in the classroom. When you have read it, you should be able to

1. describe the basic factors that affect motivation;

2. create a literate classroom climate conducive to positive attitudes;

3. implement a program of voluntary reading related to your subject area;

4. undertake thematic planning as a means of stressing the interconnectedness of content;

5. suggest alternatives to traditional book reports; and

6. modify your teaching in other ways to encourage reading, writing, and thinking about content.

FACTORS THAT AFFECT MOTIVATION

All human behavior is the result of factors that operate both within us and within our environment. These are often complex and may interact with one another in complicated ways. Knowing something about them, however, helps make student behavior more predictable and more productive. In this section, our discussion is rather general, even though our aim is to apply the principles of motivation to content literacy. Our treatment is general because the same principles underlie *all* behavior, not just that related to reading and writing. This means that they apply to other aspects of your teaching.

Expectancy

The probability that we will behave in a particular way depends to a large extent on the results we expect. Expectations have three characteristics that influence how they affect behavior. The first characteristic is *certainty*—the individual's notion of how likely an outcome is. The second is *time*—the prediction of when the outcome will occur. The third characteristic is *desirability*—the estimation of how appealing the outcome will be.

Certainty   A student begins any task with an idea of what will happen in the process. Sometimes the student is virtually certain of what will occur, as when she opens her book and finds pages filled with print. At other times, a student may be far less certain, such as during the first class session with a new teacher. When actual events are similar to what the student expects, the level of *arousal,* or alertness, is apt to be low. When, however, expectancies are vague to begin with (during the first day with a new teacher, for example) or when real occurrences are different from the student's expectations, arousal increases.

When a teacher skillfully arranges for student expectancies to be slightly thwarted, the result can be heightened arousal, attentiveness, and curiosity. Changes in classroom routine, variations in methods of instruction, and the occasional use of novel approaches and topics are ways of ensuring that student expectancies are not always confirmed.

Time   Students also have some notion of when outcomes will occur. Whether they expect a given event to happen soon may have a great effect on the role that event will play in their decision making. For convenience, we can describe expectancies in relation to time as immediate, intermediate, and remote. *Immediate expectancies* involve outcomes in the near future. As a result of reading this chapter, for example, you may expect to do well on a test. *Intermediate expectancies* concern outcomes that are slightly more distant. Because you believe that reading the chapter will help you on the test, you also expect to do well in the course. In other words, you recognize that there is a link between your reading now and the letter grade you will ultimately receive, even though those two events may not occur in quick succession. *Remote expectancies* involve outcomes that we project for the relatively distant future. You have probably thought, for example, how passing this course will contribute to earning a degree or certificate, which in turn may mean a job, salary schedule advancement, and so forth. Without necessarily verbalizing these outcomes, you are nevertheless able to relate remote results to the reading of this chapter.

The effect of intermediate and remote expectancies on behavior depends in part on the maturity and foresight of the student. Because these outcomes do not occur quickly, they lack the reinforcing power of immediate results. For this reason it is more effective (with some students) to remind them of an upcoming test than to warn them they may not get into college without an understanding of a given unit, lesson, or concept.

Immediate expectancies are sometimes at odds with intermediate and remote ones. You may be tempted by a chocolate sundae because of your immediate expectancies concerning how it will taste. However, the intermediate expectancy of gaining weight and the remote expectancy of health risks due to fat and cholesterol may be enough to inhibit you. Whenever there is a mixture of desirable and undesirable expectancies, an *approach/avoidance* situation occurs. When the pluses and minuses are nearly equal, temporary indecision and even anxiety may result. Usually, however, the scales quickly tip one way or the other. One of the most effective approaches to motivation is to add positive expectancies when the thinking of students is dominated by undesirable predictions. How to do so is the principal aim of this chapter.

Desirability   Another useful way of classifying expectancies is to distinguish between the *expectancy of success* and the *expectancy of pleasure*. Psychologists generally refer to the latter as *valence,* which is roughly equivalent to "appeal." Expectancy of success and valence are related but they are not the same. It is easy to imagine wishing to do sometime even though we suspect we may fail (high valence, low expectancy of success). You can also name an endless assortment of tasks you could easily accomplish but have little desire to do (low valence, high expectancy of success). Figure 13.1 depicts the four combinations of high and low valence and expectancy of success. A teacher's goal must be high levels of each. When this situation occurs, students will be likely to engage in the behavior. We have devoted most of this book to methods of increasing a student's expectancy of success. We turn now to ways of increasing valence.

FIGURE 13.1

The relationship of valence to expectancy of success

SOURCE: From *Teaching Reading in the Elementary School* (p. 266) by J. W. Miller and M. C. McKenna, 1989, Scottsdale, AZ: Gorsuch Scarisbrick. Copyright 1989 by Gorsuch Scarisbrick. Reprinted by permission.

		Valence	
		High	Low
Expectancy of Success	High	The student wants to succeed and expects to.	The student knows that he or she can succeed but does not care.
	Low	The student wants to succeed but does not expect to.	The student doubts that he or she can succeed but does not care.

Incentives

An incentive is any inducement or reward used to encourage a particular behavior. It can be *symbolic* in nature (the honor roll, letter grades, etc.) *material* (food, privileges, and so forth), or *psychological* (praise, teacher approval, self-satisfaction, etc.). By using incentives, the teacher acknowledges that an academic task has little valence for students. The incentive presents a desirable expectancy to counterbalance the undesirable outcome students may project, such as boredom, frustration, or fatigue.

Though incentives can be very effective, their use is somewhat controversial. Some educators equate incentives (especially the material kind) with bribes that cause students to learn for the wrong reasons. Defenders of incentives counter that if a learning task has intrinsic appeal, students will eventually come to recognize it. The challenge is giving students enough experience to make a judgment. Incentives can help persuade them to participate.

Using incentives requires no special talent, but a few simple guidelines can make them more effective.

The well-meaning people who talk about education as if it were a substance distributable by coupon in large or small quantities never exhibit any understanding of the truth that you cannot teach anybody anything that he does not want to learn.

George Sampson

1. *Use a variety of incentives.* Try to match the incentive with the required task. Avoid overuse of the same incentive. Brainstorming a list like the one in Figure 13.2 is a good first step.

2. *Individualize incentives.* Not all incentives work equally well with all students. Some may shun public praise, for example, while others thrive on it. Be alert to the effects an incentive has.

FIGURE 13.2

Material:
  food
  privileges
  field trips
  reading (SSR)
  being read to (read-alouds)

Symbolic:
  grades
  distinctions
  awards

Psychological:
  oral praise
  written praise
  nonverbal positives (smiles, gestures, etc.)
  calls or letters to parents

A partial list of incentives available to classroom teachers

3. *Don't use incentives when they're not needed.* When motivation is already adequate, it is pointless to use incentives. In fact, it can even be counterproductive by creating an expectation of external rewards that did not exist before.

4. *Provide the incentive as soon as possible after the desired behavior.* Reinforcement by incentives works best when the reward follows the targeted behavior quickly. Even major incentives like a party or a field trip should follow soon after the attainment of the goal.

ASSESSING READING INTERESTS

Many students harbor negative attitudes toward content assignments and schooling in general. The reasons are many and include a history of frustration due to poor reading ability, a failure to perceive the relevance of content, and poorly designed instruction. The total of a student's past experiences contributes to an overall attitude toward the subject area in general. In discussing her preferences, a student may state that she likes social studies, dislikes math, can take or leave science, and so forth. In other words, students have an overall attitude toward content subjects, and it is easy to assume that that attitude may extend to any content task related to the subject. McKenna (1986) asked middle-grade and secondary students with reading problems to rate each of the core content areas as possible reading interests. These topics were interspersed among a total of 44 varied reading interests. Not surprisingly, the students rated the traditional subjects quite low. Science, for example, was ranked 44th out of 44 choices!

We suggest, however, that it would be a mistake to conclude that the attitude of these students toward reading within the field of science was uniformly negative regardless of the specific subtopic. There may well be areas *within* science that they viewed much more favorably. In psychological terms, these areas may have had a higher valence than the subject area as a whole. Discovering these existing interest areas within a field of study is therefore a first step toward encouraging more content reading. When such interests exist, incentives are unnecessary.

Teachers can rapidly assess interests by means of an inventory. Two types are in common use. A *general interest inventory* presents a wide range of topics not confined to a given content area. General inventories may be of interest to language arts teachers, who often wish to encourage reading by offering an array of subjects. A *content interest inventory* also presents a list of topics but all of them derive from the same subject area. The content inventory gets past a student's general attitude toward the subject by breaking it down into subtopics. The students in McKenna's study (1986) might have rated the following science-related subtopics much higher than their overall rating of science per se:

- mysteries science cannot explain
- Viking's trip to Mars: pictures and account
- evolution versus creationism
- the Manhattan project: building the first atomic bomb

The content interest inventory treats a subject like science not as one topic but as many. By using it teachers recognize that a student's interest may not be uniform across an entire subject. Identifying possible interests within the broader subject is an activity that is highly worthwhile.

Constructing a Content Interest Inventory

To produce a good content inventory, you must possess an adequate working knowledge of your subject together with an idea of what reading materials are available to students within that subject. The following guidelines can help.

1. Make a list of interesting subtopics. The key word is *interesting*. You must attempt to outguess your students by predicting aspects of your subject matter that may have built-in appeal. One finding of the McKenna study (1986) may offer some help. He observed that the unusual or strange aspects of virtually any subject tend to give it appeal. Be on the lookout for the unusual aspects of your own subject area—aspects that many content teachers ironically avoid.

2. Identify materials for each area. Make sure you can deliver to goods! There is little reason to assess the extent of a student's interest in a given area if you cannot place in that student's hand corresponding materials. These can include books (fiction and nonfiction), magazine articles, newspaper articles you have collected, and so forth.

3. Add a few blanks at the end of the inventory. In many respects, a content interest inventory is like an election ballot. You are asking students to vote for their preferences. Like any ballot, an inventory should provide for write-ins. Inspecting what students may write on these blanks can give you an idea of topics you may not have thought of when you constructed the inventory. In fact, students' suggestions may cause you to revise the inventory before using it again.

4. Word process the inventory. Revisions are easy when you produce the instrument on a computer. You can quickly remove unpopular topics and add write-ins that appear often. With repeated use you can see your inventory evolve into a well-designed opinionnaire.

5. Decide how students will respond. The simplest format is a checklist. Students simply check the topics they prefer and make no marks next to those they aren't interested in. Unfortunately, this system is too crude to provide much information about how strong an interest may be. We recommend a rating scale format in which students respond to each topic by indicating the *degree* of their interest. While many scale formats are common, one suggested by Readence, Bean, and Baldwin (1989) is easy to grasp and has a natural appeal for students. Simply direct them to assign "letter grades" to each of the inventory's topics. A grade of *A* indicates strong interest, a *B* moderate interest, a *C* relative indifference, a *D* dislike, and an *F* strong dislike.

Administering a Content Interest Inventory

Giving the inventory is simple and requires little time. At the beginning of a term, it provides an excellent opportunity to discuss the subject area in general and apprise students of some of its more interesting dimensions. When you give your inventory, keep the following guidelines in mind.

1. Make your purpose clear. Tell students that the inventory is not a test and that there are no right or wrong answers. Point out that there is not even a way of tallying the results to produce a score. Make it plain that you do not care how they respond as long as they answer sincerely. You might suggest that you would be rather surprised if anyone were to rate all the categories highly. Most important, communicate the true purpose of the inventory, which is to enable you to suggest materials corresponding to those topics the students rate favorably.

2. Read the inventory aloud as students respond. This practice ensures that even poor decoders can respond sincerely, provided they can follow along while you read. It also affords an opportunity to elaborate informally on certain topics and to suggest an example or two of what you have in mind.

Interpreting the Results

Topics receiving a grade of *A* are pure gold. In them you have managed to uncover a potential source of subject matter curiosity and excitement. For some students, of course, *A*s will be few in number or nonexistent. You will have to rely on grades of *B* or below in these cases. In other words, where there is no primary interest area, one that is strong relative to the other areas is the best you can hope for. Be prepared to recommend materials corresponding to the strengths you have identified. Later in this chapter we will discuss methods for providing students with the opportunity to read such materials.

There is also a way to quantify the results of the inventory and to produce a single score representing overall interest in reading about the content area. Even though the letter grades cannot be directly summed, they can be converted to numerical values in the same way that grade point averages are determined. An *F* would receive zero points, a *D* one point, a *C* two points, and so forth. By adding these numbers for all topics and dividing by the number of topics, you can produce a student's average rating based on the same scale used to compute grade point averages. An average could in fact be interpreted in roughly the same way, with values above three indicating a strong general attitude and a healthy breadth of interests. While these averages are of little diagnostic value, you can use them to gauge your own success in fostering an interest in your subject area. By averaging these scores for an entire class, and by giving the inventory a second time at the end of the term, you will be in a position to make a pre/post comparison.

PROMOTING CONTENT LITERACY IN YOUR CLASSROOM

The remainder of this chapter presents a variety of techniques for fostering positive attitudes toward literacy activities, reading in particular, related to your subject area. Some of the techniques involve activities while others amount to no more than slight modifications in your style of teaching. Together they represent an extensive array of possibilities. One word of caution, however: while there are many techniques, there are no guarantees. We would invite you to read, sample, and implement with your own students. See for yourself which of these approaches produces the best result *for you*.

Creating a Print-Rich Environment

A subtle way to promote literacy is to immerse your students in surroundings that are rich in print. Perhaps the best way is to bring books related to your subjects into the classroom. These books might include some that belong to you personally as well as school library books. Consider establishing a "branch" library in your classroom, a system in which the books are officially checked out to you but are then rechecked to individual students or simply used within the classroom. Keep in mind that paperbacks are far more inviting than hardbound editions. They are less intimidating to students, less like textbooks in appearance, and often smaller and embellished with cover art. Fader and Shaevitz, in their classic *Hooked on Books* (1966), suggest displaying the books so that the covers are visible. An old wire rack from a drug store is ideal for this purpose, but other methods are equally acceptable. You can, for example, simply place the books on a shelf so that they lean against the back wall, their covers in full view. Fader and Shaevitz compared booksellers, who display books in this manner, with librarians, who typically shelve books so that only the spines are visible in an effort to conserve space. Booksellers, whose livelihood depends on attracting readers, tend to have greater success than librarians in luring consumers to their product.

Even the walls of your classroom can encourage content literacy. Line them with book jackets, posters, mounted articles, and selected student work. An appealing extra touch is the display of quotations related to your area. A thought-provoking "Quote of the Day," written in a conspicuous spot at the front of the room, can serve as an interest-grabbing sponge activity as students file into class. With a little foresight, you can often find quotations that bear on the day's lesson. Any book of quotes can become a content literacy resource, as the examples in Figure 13.3 (p. 298) show. Quotations have two characteristics that arouse interest: They are brief and they are carefully crafted to convey an insight. You can test the value of our suggestion to use them by asking yourself whether your own reading of this text hasn't been drawn irresistibly toward the quotable nuggets we've deliberately buried throughout it for effect! Our point is that there are many ways to create what Clary (1991) has called "an atmosphere that shouts the importance of reading" (p. 343).

In Chapter 6 we suggested using quotations that had the form of false definitions as a means of introducing new vocabulary. Our suggestion here is much more general. Quotations can always be used to enliven content.

Give Students a Chance to Read

You cannot expect students to become content literate unless you give them opportunities to explore the subject area through print. Textbook assignments are not enough. Students occasionally need time to browse wherever their inclinations lead them and to do so in an atmosphere free of accountability and restraint.

Content Area SSR   A systematic way of providing this sort of reading time is *sustained silent reading* (SSR). Hunt (1967) originally intended the technique for building *general* reading interest and for providing additional practice in *general* reading skills. But SSR holds immense potential for content literacy. By defining acceptable materials as any that relate to your area, you can ensure that SSR will broaded students' encounters with the discipline.

The advantages of content area SSR are persuasive. It extends understanding by offering new contexts for some of the very concepts students are studying. Its timing is flexible so that teachers can use it without observing rigid time demands. It uses choice as a motivator, for even though

FIGURE 13.3

Examples of
brief, provocative,
content-specific quotations

Science

In science, all facts, no matter how trivial or banal, enjoy democratic equality.
　　—Mary McCarthy

The physicists have known sin; and this is a knowledge which they cannot lose.
　　—J. Robert Oppenheimer

Children are the only true scientists.
　　—R. Buckminster Fuller

Mathematics

There is no royal road to geometry.
　　—Euclid

A man has one hundred dollars and you leave him with two dollars, that's subtraction.
　　—Mae West

They say there is divinity in odd numbers, either in nativity, chance, or death.
　　—Shakespeare

Language Arts

Literature is the art of writing something that will be read twice; journalism what will be grasped at once.
　　—Cyril Connolly

Prose,—words in their best order; poetry,—the best words in their best order.
　　—Samuel Taylor Coleridge

All books are either dreams or swords.
　　—Amy Lowell

Social Studies

Half a truth is better than no politics.
　　—G. K. Chesterton

The worst thing in this world, next to anarchy, is government.
　　—Henry Ward Beecher

Ballots are the rightful and peaceful successors to bullets.
　　—Abraham Lincoln

the selections are limited to the confines of a subject area, the options are still plentiful. It is appealing because the teacher does not hold students accountable for what they read. This policy conveys the powerful lesson that there are times when reading, even content area reading, is done for pleasure. Finally, SSR offers a subtle but effective reward that teachers can use in good conscience to reinforce achievement and encourage reading at the same time. Imagine the effect of telling students that if they complete an assignment successfully and efficiently, they may participate in SSR for the final 10 minutes of class. The thought of students working industriously for the privilege of reading further in the same general area is greatly satisfying.

SSR is not a highly structured technique. Teachers can adapt it easily to meet their needs, particularly in content settings. A few basic guidelines, however, can mean the difference between an effective program and a relative waste of time.

1. *Make the purposes of SSR clear.*   Describe the procedure before you begin. Emphasize that the point is to give the students an opportunity to pursue their own interests within the subject area. Make it plain that there will be no reports to write, no questions to answer, no follow-up of any kind. The idea is to explore, sample, and browse.

2. *Define acceptable materials.*   Making an assortment of content-related reading materials available in your classroom is a good first step toward defining what is acceptable and what is not. However, do not limit students to these materials alone. Invite them to explore the field on their own. Such an invitation will mean spelling out what you will permit, and you'll need to think through this issue relative to your own instructional philosophy.

3. *Encourage students to select materials in advance.*   You cannot depend on every student's having appropriate materials prior to each SSR session, even when you have announced the session in advance. One of the many benefits of stockpiling reading matter in your classroom is that it becomes a convenient SSR resource for these students. Begin a session by allowing one minute to find something to read if necessary. Trips to the library or locker will not be needed.

4. *Announce the time limit.*   Tell students at the beginning of each session how much time you have set aside for SSR. Start with five minutes or so until students become comfortable with the routine. You may later wish to increase the length of sessions gradually. Some teachers use a spring-driven kitchen-type timer, but a wall clock will do. On those occasions when SSR is the last activity of the class period, the bell serves as a signal to stop.

5. *Prohibit studying.*   SSR is not a study hall. Its success depends on making time available for free reading within your subject area. Using the time to complete assignments defeats this purpose.

6. *Enforce silence.*   A quiet environment is essential if SSR is to work. Deal with disruptions by ending the session and returning to more structured activities. The culprits will soon get the message.

7. *Participate in SSR yourself.*   If reading is really worth doing, model it by using the SSR session to extend your own content reading. If you subscribe to a professional journal, this may be a good time to look through the latest issue. If you're currently engrossed in a new book in your area bring it with you to school and bring it out of hiding for SSR.

8. *Avoid accountability.*   One of SSR's most appealing traits is that students are not required to report on, discuss, or be tested over what they read. Don't spoil this positive feature by asking them to do any of these.

9. Link SSR to the content interest inventory. Try to ensure the availability of materials that correspond to each of the subtopics on your content interest inventory. Use the inventory results to make suggestions to students who seem indifferent or hesitant to choose. Do not be overly prescriptive, however. Suggest, but don't push.

Read Aloud to Your Students

Researchers have amply documented the value of reading aloud to young children. But what about students in middle grade and secondary content classes? Can teachers justify the time needed to read selections aloud in class? The answer, we believe, is a qualified yes. When selections are relatively brief and when they are carefully chosen to emphasize current topics, they can add variety, stimulate enthusiasm, and model the importance of literacy without diverting excessive time away from direct instruction.

Read-alouds often conjure thoughts of short stories and novels, but nonfiction can be just as viable. Consider a few examples:

- A newspaper article on cancer research appears the week before a teacher begins a health unit on the subject of cancer. She reads selected portions at the beginning of the unit.
- An article in *Sports Illustrated* details how modern advances in protective gear now reduce the chances of football injuries. A coach reads it aloud to his team just before equipment is distributed during late summer practices.
- A mathematics teacher, looking for a fresh approach to teaching percentages to a "practical math" class, brings the sports page of the morning paper and reads the won-lost records of various teams, asking students to compute their winning percentages.
- A history teacher reads the accounts of President Zachary Taylor's exhumation. The articles lead naturally into a unit on the Civil War.
- A sociology teacher leads off a discussion of marriage with recent selections from "Dear Abby."
- A civics teacher reads aloud two recent syndicated columns taking opposite sides of a current issue.

This does not mean that fiction has no place in content classrooms. Our history teacher might have read selections from *Gone with the Wind,* and our sociology teacher might have read aloud from Isaac Asimov's "robot" novels, detailing how different social systems arose on various fictitious planets and why.

Read-alouds offer a valuable flexibility in planning for stimulating instruction. They afford an excellent way to introduce an objective by focusing students' attention and thoughts. They can emphasize the contemporary import of content whenever the sources are news reports and current articles. You can even use read-alouds to fill up an odd moment pleasantly or to reward students for their efforts in class assignments. (Here is yet another way of using reading as a reward!)

Vary Your Teaching Methods

We have discussed how creating slight differences between what students expect to happen and what actually happens tends to increase arousal. The key word is *slight.* Major unannounced departures from classroom routine can be disruptive and even anxiety provoking. When the routine is constantly varied in small ways, however, students are apt to become more attentive because of the uncertainty of their expectancies (Mathison, 1989).

An important way to create small deviations is by varying the methods you employ. This is one reason we have deliberately introduced a variety of techniques for building background knowledge (Chapter 5), for introducing technical vocabulary (Chapter 6), and so on. By adding these techniques to your teaching repertoire, you are in a much better position to select for variety. If you used a graphic organizer to introduce terms for the previous unit, use feature analysis for the next one. If you feel you've fallen into a rut with the DRA, try KWL for a change.

In Chapter 1, we referred to the movie *Teachers,* which contains a number of insights into the instructional issues educators face. An amusing example of what can happen when variety is all but eliminated involves a teacher nicknamed "Mr. Ditto." You will note in Figure 13.4 that the nickname is an apt one.

FIGURE 13.4

"Mr. Ditto" had perfected his classroom routine to the point at which students knew precisely what to do at all times. As they entered the classroom, they took a copy of the day's assignment from one tray and worked on it independently until the bell signaled the end of the period. They then dropped it into an adjacent tray on their way out of the room.

Mr. Ditto meanwhile sat at his desk in the back of the room while his students worked away, their backs toward him. Mr. Ditto never spoke, nor was there need to. Every student knew the general routine, and the details were self-explanatory. Mr. Ditto would occasionally nod off, but who wouldn't now and then after engineering such a beautiful system?

One day tragedy struck. Mr. Ditto succumbed to a heart attack. He had been dutifully manning his post at the rear of the room when it happened. It was several hours later, however, before anyone noticed he was dead!

The story of Mr. Ditto

Look for Links with the Lives of Students

Researchers have observed that the most successful teachers consistently point out to students how new material relates to their lives (e.g., Hunter & Russell, 1977; Rosenshine, 1986). This is not always an easy task. When the topic in health class is pregnancy or when the introduction of the electoral process in civics coincides with student council elections, the linkage is natural. (You should point it out no matter how obvious it seems, however!) But when the topic in algebra is the quadratic formula, the task of relating your objective to students' perceptions of relevance is more demanding. Resourcefulness and creativity are occasionally required.

No barrier of the senses shuts me out from the sweet, gracious discourse of my book friends. They talk to me without embarrassment or awkwardness.
Helen Keller

When you can see no persuasive connection, two suggestions might help. One is to remind students of an in-school, short-term, academic purpose, such as an upcoming exam. A statement like "Today's lesson will be very important for Friday's quiz" will at least have a motivational effect on students who are achievement conscious. The second suggestion is to ask students why they think a particular objective is important to them. Some teachers find this strategy risky since it may invite negative responses, but if students do announce that they see no utility in a given lesson, they are merely saying aloud what they already think. If, however, even one student can suggest something positive, it may well have a ripple effect among the other class members and give you an idea for an effective purpose statement the *next time* you teach the same lesson.

Provide Choices Wherever Possible

We have discussed the fact that any proposed task has an inherent valence, or appeal. This quality will differ from one student to the next and is usually difficult to predict with certainty. Affording a choice of assignments will permit students to select the option with the highest personal valence. The key is to extend choices that *all* lead to the objectives you have targeted. A math teacher may feel comfortable asking students to compute any 10 of the 30 problems at the end of a chapter, even in the knowledge that many will select those that seem easiest to them. On the other hand, the problems may not uniformly reflect the content of the chapter, but the teacher might still be able to make choices available without compromising the objectives. For example, the teacher might ask students to "work any 5 of the first 10 problems and any 5 of the last 20," or to "work number 7 and any 9 of the remaining ones."

There are two additional benefits of choice that are more difficult to quantify. One is that power transfers from the teacher to the student whenever alternatives are offered. By being empowered to choose, students may develop a more positive outlook toward the climate of a class and may consequently take greater responsibility for their own learning. The second benefit is equally subtle. By offering choices, the teacher compels students to make those choices. This urges their active engagement with the content as they weigh, consider, and ultimately select. The math teacher who tells students to select any 10 of 30 problems virtually assures that they will *read* all 30!

Look for Interdisciplinary Connections

When students can see how content in one area relates to the concepts and ideas of other areas, their understanding is broadened and, equally important, they are more likely to perceive its significance. Indicating connections across content areas is therefore an additional way of demonstrating the purpose for learning it. These connections can be very motivational.

In middle schools, *thematic planning* by teams of teachers aims at showing students how content actually transcends the boundaries of traditional subject areas (Cooter & Griffith, 1989). The team might, for example, coordinate the start of a unit on percentages in math with the calculation of election results in social studies and calories in health. A short story studied in language arts might have references germane to a science or history unit so that these teachers can refer to the story in their own lessons while the language arts teacher references the links with history and science as the story is discussed. Such connections allow an additional (and extremely effective) means of reinforcing content—reciprocally.

What about circumstances in which team planning is not the norm? Even if you plan and teach in relative isolation, interdisciplinary links are still possible. For example, you can examine what is required in language arts and look for connections with your own units. You can suggest titles of fiction that are especially relevant to the topics in your course. You can use literature as a change of pace whenever you find a good link. Finally, you can form your own "team" by identifying even one colleague in another area with whom you can compare curricula in a quest for cross-references.

More Ideas

Mathison (1989) has listed some of the most frequently recommended ideas for stimulating interest in content area reading. We have discussed nearly all of these at various points in this text, but now is an ideal time to review them. Mathison's list includes

1. using analogies (Chapter 5)
2. relating personal anecdotes (Chapter 5)
3. disrupting students' expectations (Chapter 13)
4. challenging students to resolve a paradox (Chapter 9)
5. introducing novel and conflicting information or situations (Chapter 9)

> That which any one has been long learning unwillingly, he unlearns with proportionable eagerness and haste.
> William Hazlitt

SUMMARY

Several factors influence whether students will be motivated to undertake literacy tasks. One is their expectancies about the nature of these tasks. An important aspect of these expectancies is the degree of certainty in students' minds. Relative uncertainty can lead to heightened arousal and is a useful motivator. A second aspect involves the time at which students expect outcomes to occur. Immediate expectancies usually have greater motivational power than intermediate or remote expectancies. Desirability is a third characteristic of expectancies and is termed *valence.* One method of motivating students to undertake tasks with low valence is to use incentives, or rewards. Symbolic, material, and psychological incentives couple, in the student's mind, a desirable expectancy with one that is less desirable (performing the task itself). Teachers should vary and individualize incentives. They should avoid using them when they are not needed, and when they do use them they should try to apply them as soon as possible after the desired behavior.

Content teachers should attempt to identify areas within their subject that may hold strong appeal (valence) for students. A content interest inventory is an assessment tool that asks students to rate subtopics that might be appealing. A teacher can construct such an inventory by first listing potentially interesting subtopics and then identifying available reading materials associated with each. Some blanks for "write-in" suggestions make a nice addition. Teachers who word process the inventory find revising it convenient. Students can respond in numerous ways, but one of the best is by indicating letter "grades." Reading the inventory aloud while students mark their responses helps ensure that reading problems do not interfere. Topics awarded a grade of *A* are useful to know in recommending materials for further reading.

Various teaching techniques can improve student attitudes toward content literacy. Creating a classroom environment rich in print is a good start. Providing time on occasion to read further within the subject area without accountability is helpful, and sustained silent reading (SSR) is a proven structure for developing such a program. Reading aloud to students is also remarkably effective and can be done quite flexibly. Varying instructional methods is another means of arousing interest, one that requires no departure from direct instruction time. Motivational teachers also look for links between content and its impact on the lives of students. Making these links clear to students can be quite effective. Giving students choices, especially where reinforcement activities are concerned, is another subtle means of motivation and can usually be done without compromising instructional objectives. Looking for interdisciplinary connections is one more way of stressing the importance of content. Emphasizing these connections invites collaborative planning and can lead to mutual reinforcement of colleagues' instructional objectives.

GETTING INVOLVED

1. Construct a content interest inventory. You will need to examine your teaching specialty closely, noting aspects that are likely to have special appeal for students. Remember to look for the unusual aspects of your area. That is, do not merely break down the general subject area into its typical components. Try to identify intriguing subtopics that students will not be likely to know about themselves.

2. Compile a list of fiction related to your area. Your school library media specialist can help. Aim for appropriate difficulty levels and lengths. Then assemble the books, whether you check them out, order them with school funds, or acquire your own copies. Finally, read them yourself, however quickly, so that you can make informal recommendations for SSR and so that you can reference appropriate titles as you teach.

3. Identify periodicals that relate to your area. Student-oriented magazines are available in most subjects, and it is worthwhile to learn about those related to your own area. Find out which of these are available in the school library and investigate the possibility of moving all but the most recent issues into your room. These periodicals will make an excellent resource for content area SSR. Olson, Gee, and Forester (1989) offer many other practical suggestions for incorporating content-specific magazines into classroom instruction.

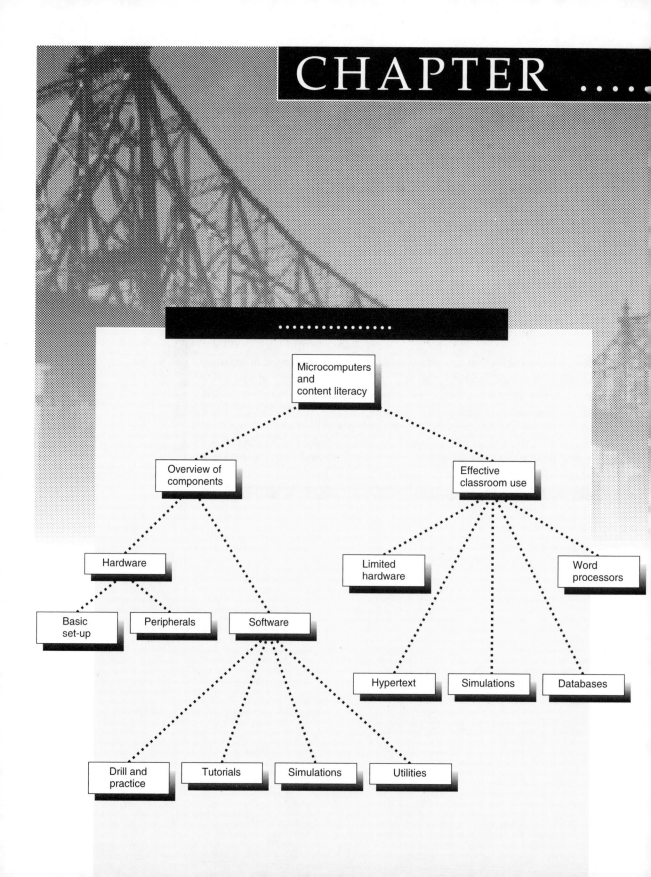

CHAPTER .....

Microcomputers and content literacy

- Overview of components
  - Hardware
    - Basic set-up
    - Peripherals
    - Software
      - Drill and practice
      - Tutorials
      - Simulations
      - Utilities
- Effective classroom use
  - Limited hardware
  - Hypertext
  - Simulations
  - Databases
  - Word processors

FOURTEEN

Computers: Frontiers of Content Literacy

With technology changing our lives so quickly, it seems difficult to think that computers will not be a part of schools in the future.
Robert Rickelman and William Henk

When microcomputers first appeared in American classrooms in the mid 1970s, their reception was mixed. While many teachers embraced micros as a long-awaited innovation, others were skeptical. Some thought that the prospect of "teaching machines," first raised in the 1950s, had finally materialized as a sinister threat to their very jobs (Rickleman & Henk, 1989). Some were reluctant to get their feet wet and delayed involvement as long as possible. Some were put off by logistical problems, such as access to hardware and the scarcity of quality software.

When lukewarm research findings on the effectiveness of computer-assisted instruction (CAI) began to emerge, many of these teachers were relieved. The computer revolution seemed over: The computers had lost. A core of enthusiasts remained, but the groundswell of early interest had dissipated. Historically, this has been precisely the fate of numerous educational trends and innovations. It is now clear, however, that microcomputers and related technology are not typical of previous innovations and will not share their fate. Consider the following facts:

1. Hardware costs continue to decline and, while considerable, no longer pose the severe limitation they once did.
2. The availability of quality software has vastly increased in virtually all content fields.
3. Computers, unlike most other educational innovations, are irreversibly linked to changes in the workplace and at home. Computers are everywhere and affect nearly all aspects of our lives.
4. The prospect that computers will replace teachers is now regarded as virtually nonexistent.

5. Most schoolchildren now reach the middle and secondary grades having acquired relatively good competence in keyboarding. Many are familiar with the operation of hardware and with the design of many forms of software.

6. New approaches to the ways in which computers and related hardware present textual material and permit students to interact with it now offer exciting possibilities for deepening their understanding and extending their thinking.

This chapter is framed by three beliefs. The first is that microcomputers and related technology can truly enhance student learning when they are creatively and prudently put to use by content specialists. The second is that their prevalence in American classrooms will greatly increase over the next decade, so much so that a working understanding of how to use them in teaching will be virtually indispensable. The third is that effective ways of integrating micros into instruction are still being pioneered and that there is still much to learn.

OBJECTIVES

The aim of this chapter is to give you an overview of microcomputer applications in content classrooms. Of particular importance are ways of encouraging content literacy through technology (see Figure 14.1). Specifically, your reading should enable you to

1. suggest trends documenting the growing importance of computers in education;

2. enumerate the most common kinds of peripherals and describe their uses;

3. recognize the traditional types of software together with their advantages and limitations;

4. describe strategies for coping with limited hardware;

5. define *hypertext* and describe its advantages for good and poor students; and

6. recognize innovative approaches to teaching with databases, simulations, and word processors.

HARDWARE: THE BASICS AND BEYOND

In the 1990s nearly everyone is familiar with the standard set-up of a microcomputer: A central processing unit (cpu) is linked to a keyboard and

FIGURE 14.1

"I DON'T GET IT! THEY MAKE US LEARN READING, WRITING AND ARITHMETIC TO PREPARE US FOR A WORLD OF VIDEOTAPES, COMPUTER TERMINALS AND CALCULATORS!"

Changing views
of "the basics"

SOURCE: Cartoon
by H. L. Schwadron,
October 1990, *Phi
Delta Kappan, 72,* p.
123. Copyright 1990 by
the *Phi Delta Kappan.*
Reprinted by permission
of the Phi Delta Kappan
and H. L. Schwadron.

to a monitor. The keyboard accepts input from the user while the monitor permits the user to review both input and output. These three components may be separate pieces of hardware linked by cables. In many cases the cpu and keyboard are housed together, as in the older line of Apple computers. Sometimes the monitor and cpu are together, as in the Macintosh line. In some models, called laptops, all three components are permanently combined in a single device. These three elements are so vitally necessary for nearly all users that we think of them as one unit—the minimum any user needs.

However, there are numerous attachments in addition to these basic components that make possible a wide range of applications. These "extras" are called *peripherals,* and some of them are doubtless already familiar to you. A *printer* produces tangible output, a "hard" copy of what one sees on the monitor screen. A *mouse* permits the user to move about the screen and work with its contents more flexibly than the keyboard alone.

Other peripherals are less common and make possible an exciting variety of specialized applications. A *modem* (short for *modulator-demodulator*) connects micros at distant locations or to large *mainframe* computers. A *video disk player* allows software to combine stored video material with the operation of the

FIGURE 14.2

Typical components of a
microcomputer system

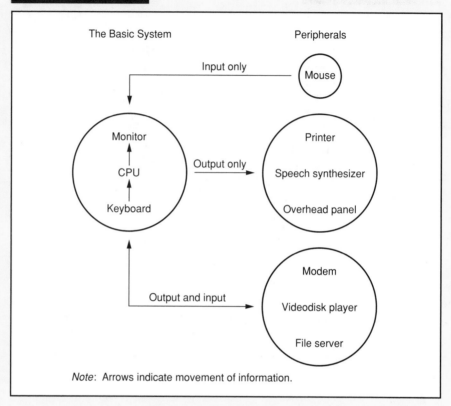

Note: Arrows indicate movement of information.

computer. A *speech synthesizer* produces humanlike voiced output when appropriate. A *file server* allows numerous computers to be networked together so that software can be stored in a central location and a teacher can look in on individual students as they work. An *overhead panel* allows a teacher to project and enlarge the monitor image using an ordinary overhead projector and screen.

Figure 14.2 summarizes the components we have just discussed. Keep in mind that the peripherals included are not a comprehensive listing but involve those that teachers most often use.

SOFTWARE: KINDS AND CHARACTERISTICS

Software consists of self-contained sets of potential commands organized for some specific purpose. Such commands, when activated at the appropriate time, may tell the computer to print a document, perform a computation, produce an image on the monitor screen, or a host of other possibilities. Most software is stored on disks and is "loaded" into the working memory of the cpu whenever it is used.

Traditional categories of educational software provide a useful frame of reference for envisioning how microcomputers can enhance instruction. Be aware, however, that boundaries defining the basic types are beginning to blur as new uses are discovered and new types developed.

Drill-and-Practice Software

Most of the software currently available to teachers provides students with opportunities to practice skills or reinforce knowledge recently acquired. Such programs have an obvious place in the Explicit Teaching Model but are also suitable for use in the later phases of other global designs. As their name implies, drill-and-practice programs operate on the assumption that direct instruction has already occurred. The software does not provide for new learning but complements what the teacher has already introduced.

Drill-and-practice software bears an obvious similarity to the traditional workbooks and rote assignments teachers have often assigned to provide for practice and reinforcement. Not surprisingly, the term *electronic workbook* has been used to criticize the most tedious of these programs. In their simplest form they are easy to develop but laborious to use.

Drill-and-Practice	
Nature and Purpose:	Reinforces previous learning by providing structured practice. Sometimes employs game format.
Advantages:	• Gives students immediate feedback
	• Can record student performance
	• Can provide positive reinforcers, such as graphics
	• Can be appealing to students, especially when game formats are used
Limitations:	• May fail to improve on tedious workbook format
	• May tempt some teachers to assume that such software is adequate for introducing new material

On the bright side, drill-and-practice software has distinct advantages when well designed. Most important, it offers immediate feedback about accuracy. The timing of feedback has repeatedly proved to be a critical element of instruction (Kulik & Kulik, 1988), and micros deliver it with breathtaking speed. Drill-and-practice systems can also record student results for later reference. They can provide both verbal and graphic reinforcers for good performance. They can even offer practice opportunities in arcade-style game formats that encourage self-competition. (One software producer has described such programs as "arcademic"!)

Tutorials

Some programs have a more ambitious design and attempt to introduce new material directly. Such software is as close as programmers have come to true teaching machines. Anyone familiar with their design realizes at once, however, that teachers have little to fear. Often the user must already possess a relatively strong background in related content and must also be a self-disciplined, independent learner. In short, the student who is capable of learning from a text without teacher assistance is the most likely candidate for tutorial software. Such students are few in number.

Tutorials	
Nature and Purpose:	Designed to provide direct instruction in new material
Advantages:	• Material can be sequenced in progressive difficulty
	• Can provide immediate feedback
	• Can adjust level of instruction based on a student's performance
	• Can record student's performance
	• Can provide interesting reinforcers
Limitations:	• Best suited to tightly ordered curricula such as mathematics
	• Require self-discipline and good independent learning skills
	• Require some background in the content for best results

Tutorials do offer advantages, however. First, they can present material in a sequence progressing in difficulty. When a student experiences problems, the program may move to an easier level. This advantage is clearly stronger for well-ordered subjects like mathematics than for content that is not tightly progressive in nature. Tutorials also have some of the advantages of drill-and-practice software: They provide immediate feedback; they allow monitoring and record keeping; and they serve as interesting reinforcers.

Simulations

Some programs attempt to place the student in a position to apply content under relatively realistic circumstances. In other words, they simulate a real-world situation and provide an opportunity for students to interact as they might in the real world. The advantages of simulations are numerous. To begin with, they are quick and provide instant feedback along with an endless number of second chances. They are also cheaper than the real thing since no materials are needed. They allow potentially dangerous situations, such as experiments in chemistry and physics, to be undertaken safely. They even allow students to control processes they could never influence in real life.

Simulations

Nature and Purpose:	Create realistic depiction of real-world events or processes. Used to test predictions and to help students become familiar with important processes.
Advantages:	• Quicker than the real process • Good approach to dangerous or costly processes (e.g., chemical reactions) • Can be used before, during, or after direct instruction • Are now used frequently in the workplace so that simulations are in this sense "real" experiences after all • Tend to create curiosity, even suspense • Encourage students to hypothesize
Limitation:	• Never equivalent to the real thing involving hands-on experience

Todd Balf describes his experience with SimEarth, a program that simulates biological and planetary evolution:

> Here's what I did in the driver's seat. I caused mass extinctions. I turned rain forests into tundra. I cooked up atmospheres that made life on Venus look agreeable. For days I found no evolutionary takers for sentience. Didn't anybody want intelligence? It took me a week to create even a ramshackle civilization, and when I did, it was peopled by what appeared to be rainbow trout who labored an unfathomable sixty hours a week and endured a quality of life my computer said was hellish. In one careless instance, I left my planet unattended for a critical few billion years. When I returned to the keyboard, "Toddland" had exploded in a pyrotechnic head-on with the red giant we know as the sun. I was reminded of what I already knew: I'm no God. (1991, p. 36)

From an instructional standpoint, simulations allow flexibility in planning since they can be used not only during direct instruction of new material but afterward as a means of extending and reinforcing. Teachers can even introduce them prior to instruction as a way of focusing students' thoughts and piquing curiosity. Finally, simulations are rapidly (and ironically) becoming actual experiences because of their use in the workplace. In other words, to expose students to simulations is no longer to use an artificial approach since simulations themselves are so often a part of our approach to inquiry.

On the downside, simulations are never equal to the real thing. They do not provide tangible experiences with such things as scientific equipment, artifacts, people, and places. On the other hand, they tend to prepare students well for such "real," hands-on experiences. And even if such encounters never occur, we believe the advantages of simulations outweigh the shortcomings.

Utilities

Some programs are designed primarily for out-of-class uses. These utilities are the workhorses that allow a teacher to prepare for instruction more effectively. Word processors make test and hand-out development more efficient. Data bases store class records conveniently and make monitoring student performance easier. Desktop publishing software enables teachers to prepare banners, posters, notices, newsletters, and the like with ease and professionalism.

These are some of the traditional uses of utilities—the uses originally intended by software developers. However, in classrooms across America utilities are coming out of hiding. Their "behind-the-scenes" uses are as viable as ever, but teachers are beginning to recognize their worth as classroom

---

Utilities

Nature and Purpose:	Assist the user accomplish a specific task. Word processors and data bases are primary examples.
Advantages:	• Can do "double duty" both in and out of the classroom • Encourage thinking and writing about content
Limitation:	• Require careful planning since they are not primarily intended as instructional software

---

software as well. They now perform double duty for many educators, serving as utilities outside of class and as instructional software in class. The prevalence of utility software in the workplace makes their new classroom applications even more fitting, and we address two of their major instructional uses later in this chapter.

USING MICROS EFFECTIVELY

Isaac Asimov (1974), well-known science and science fiction writer, told of his visit a few years ago to a conference on educational technology. At a presentation on the subject of cassettes, the speaker outlined new developments in both the audio and video varieties. This set Asimov speculating about trends in the field. What would the *ultimate* cassette be like? What qualities would it possess? Having tuned out the presenter, he began to list mentally all the characteristics that he believed cassettes should ideally afford their users. His list makes sense. In an energy-conscious era, they should require little or no power. Cumbersome cassette players should not be needed. In fact, Asimov argued, the user should need no equipment at all. Unlike present-day cassettes, the ultimate should move at a variety of speeds without distortion. Moreover, the user should be able to look back or skip forward easily and without delay. Perhaps of most importance, the ultimate cassette would not transmit the same images and impressions to everyone. Rather, each user would come away with an individual experience, one in keeping with personal background and experience. Asimov's point (have you guessed it?) was that the "ultimate" cassette, one possessing all these qualities, already exists. It is, of course, a book!

> The book is here to stay. What we're doing is symbolic of the peaceful coexistence of the book and the computer.
> Vartan Gregorian, president of the New York Public Library, on the computerization of the card catalogue

Reflecting on Asimov's clever argument, we might conclude that technology offers nothing that traditional printed materials do not already offer in a near-perfect way. We agree that books are, in may ways, difficult to beat when teachers use them prudently. There are, however, advantages technology offers that books simply cannot match. Each passing year brings new developments with implications for the classroom that are hard to grasp fully.

No one completely realizes the educational potential of microcomputers. This is true in part because of rapid changes in hardware that have left many teachers in a state of "future shock." Another reason has been the equally rapid development of high-quality educational software. We have been obliged to discard many of the negative judgments made more than a decade ago concerning some of the first programs to appear on the market, programs that were often poorly conceived. Yet another reason is that reliable research on educational use is both scant and extraordinarily difficult to design and conduct (Reinking & Bridwell-Bowles, 1991). Nevertheless, sound advice *can* be offered to teachers for making the most out of micros. Advice based on what we now know about effective instruction can help you put the use of computers into perspective and enable you to see how your own teaching can benefit by making micros an important part of the way you teach. We now offer specific suggestions for integrating micros into the framework of content instruction, with special emphasis on their role in developing content literacy.

Contending with Limited Hardware

Although the cost of microcomputers is diminishing, American schools still suffer from a painful ratio of students to machines. Moreover, many of the models now found in schools have been outdated by the industry (Mecklenburger, 1990). An early idea for contending with too few machines was to corral them into a single lab to be used on a limited basis requiring advance scheduling. Fortunately, this practice has largely given way to a policy of placing computers inside classrooms, even if only one unit is available to an entire class. On the other hand, our visits to content classrooms confirm that one or two computers often go unused despite their availability. When asked why, teachers typically explain that the poor student-to-micro ratio still prohibits any worthwhile use. We disagree and now offer a few ways of making better use of one or two classroom computers.

Use Display Panels   Try conducting lessons by projecting the output of a single machine for all to see. An overhead display panel will allow you to integrate any piece of software into direct instruction. Interaction with the program can become a group activity, and you can encourage student input at key points.

Allow Students to Work in Teams   A cluster of students working on the same project or task will require only one machine. All group members will be able to see, and the computer will in many cases help to focus the group's effort and keep students on task. A traditional four-student cooperative learning group is only one way of facilitating collaborative use of a micro. Many grouping arrangements are possible depending on the nature of the task.

Individualize through the Micro   Given a variety of software, students can pursue an assortment of objectives on an individual basis. Weaker students can obtain additional practice and assistance. Superior students can extend their understanding of content on their own. Equitable access to hardware is an important consideration, however. Computers used only for remedial aid are unfairly denied to abler students. On the other hand, allowing students to use the micro as a reward for finishing other work will place less able students at a disadvantage. Equity of access is a goal requiring careful planning and consciously developed policy.

Changing How We Think about Print

Our experience with books and other printed materials has led most of us to a long-standing assumption that text is essentially linear in nature. That is, it proceeds from a beginning to an end in a straight-line fashion. Were it not for the practical necessity of arranging print to fit onto pages, we could easily envision a book as a single line miles in length. But even in the oldest books this linear organization is not always the case. A footnote or trip to the index, for example, may take us off on a momentary tangent. Newer books, particularly textbooks, include many elements that depart from the linear flow of print. Sidebars, graphs, charts, embedded definitions, marginal glosses, and the like were discussed in Chapter 5 as methods of making books more useful and comprehensible. While there is still linear movement from page to page and chapter to chapter, there are now apt to be many departures from that mile-long line of print we envisioned a moment ago!

The Promise of Hypertext   The view of text as not merely linear but as a network of potential pathways to be followed however the reader chooses is known as *hypertext*. We have just described how improvements in textbook design make hypertext easier to envision and use. Actually, hypertext has always existed in the form of outside sources conceptually linked and accessible through such activities as library use. What the computer adds is immediacy and convenience of use. Moreover, it makes students aware of choices they might not be able to envision on their own.

Blanchard and Rottenberg (1990) describe a scenario in which social studies students are to analyze the westward movement of settlers in the United States:

> A master menu allows students to select from these topics: (1) general information, (2) political forces, (3) economic issues, (4) international issues. The learner selects general information and, among many icons, sees an icon for a Conestoga wagon. The selection of this icon accesses a videodisk image of a wagon complete with digitized audio of the wagon wheels rolling over the prairie. A new set of icons accompanying the video image allows the user to select a pop-up text superimposed on half of the visual image explaining how the wagons were designed to withstand the westward trip. Using a mouse pointer and clicking when the cursor is over boldfaced words in the text, the user can display a glossary text that defines the word, shows a graphic of it, and, if requested, an audio reading of it. The flexibility in "navigating" through such a learning environment is almost limitless. (p. 657)

Imagine a more comprehensive system, one in which pictures, sound recordings, footage stored on videodisk, and other nonprint materials could be accessed by the micro. Such a system is an expansion of hypertext known as *hypermedia*. While some hypermedia systems require linkage with videodisk players, the cost of this hardware has dropped considerably in recent years. Blanchard and Rottenberg offer an example of an inexpensive hypermedia program called *Culture 1.1*. In Figures 14.3 and 14.4, they illustrate one of the "tangents" made possible by this sort of software.

Hypertext and Authoring Software   Gates (1988) argues persuasively that the true power of hypertext is that it reflects how people really think. We do not think in linear fashion (the way a book is laid out) but range back and forth among a myriad of associations, connections, and possibilities. Of great potential are "authoring" programs that enable teachers to customize their content in a hypertext format. IBM's *Linkway*, for example, permits the integration of text with graphics, pictures, FM-quality music, voice synthesis, and full-motion video. But even without the broad multimedia dimensions, a few basic features demonstrate the utility of such software, especially for less able students. Consider a teacher who enters a reading assignment into a hypertext system. Students who later read the selection may have options like these at their fingertips:

- a built-in glossary to instantly provide definitions of technical terms when needed

FIGURE 14.3

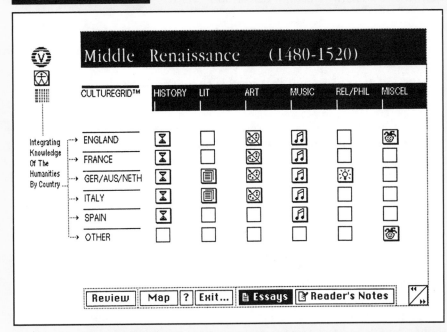

Selecting essays in the cultural grid for history of England in *Culture 1.1*.

SOURCE: From "Hypertext and Hypermedia: Discovering and Creating Meaningful Learning Environments" by J. S. Blanchard and C. J. Rottenberg, 1990, *The Reading Teacher, 43,* p. 660. Copyright 1990 by the International Reading Association. Reprinted by permission of Cultural Resources, Inc., 7 Little Falls Way, Scotch Plains, NJ 07076, and the International Reading Association.

FIGURE 14.4

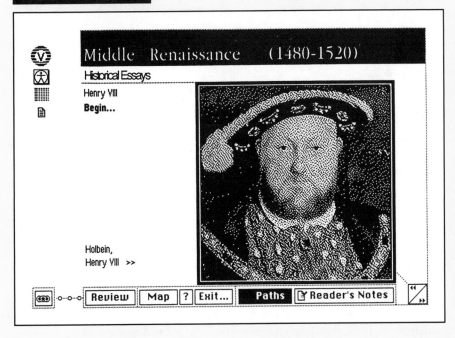

The result: *Culture 1.1* yields a visual of Henry VIII.

SOURCE: From "Hypertext and Hypermedia: Discovering and Creating Meaningful Learning Environments" by J. S. Blanchard and C. J. Rottenberg, 1990, *The Reading Teacher, 43,* p. 661. Copyright 1990 by the International Reading Association. Reprinted by permission of Cultural Resources, Inc., 7 Little Falls Way, Scotch Plains, NJ 07076, and the International Reading Association.

- a speech synthesizer to pronounce single words or read entire paragraphs aloud
- a restatement feature that reveals simplified versions of difficult sentences or paragraphs on demand

It is likely that middle- and secondary-level textbooks will soon begin to make hypertext versions available. This will eliminate the need for authoring by teachers and will make feasible at last a means of stimulating the brightest students and helping the most troubled at the same time.

Letting Simulations Make Content Come Alive

Simulations create the illusion that some process or scenario is actually happening. Because of this they involve an element of unpredictability that builds interest and even suspense. Because simulations are interactive, calling on students to make decisions at crucial points, they naturally encourage student involvement in active learning.

Because simulations are so much a part of present-day industry (think of flight simulators, economic forecast models, engineering design software, and the like), it is tempting to dismiss simulations as too technical and scientific for most classroom uses. It is certainly true that science teachers have many simulations from which to choose. *Three-Mile Island,* for example, places the student in complete control of a nuclear power plant. Numerous chemistry programs allow chemicals to be realistically mixed and processed without danger or expense. But educational simulations are now available in virtually all other content fields as well. A few examples from other core subjects will illustrate their range.

Imagine yourself on a Conestoga wagon heading west with other pioneers. Your very life might depend on the decisions you make concerning food supply, route, and so on. MECC's *Wagon Train 1848* creates precisely this simulated learning adventure, designed for cooperative learning groups. *What If?*, from MacMillan/McGraw-Hill, provides some 20 social simulations in which problems like these are presented:

- How shall we finance continued space exploration?
- Should we raise the minimum wage for American workers?

The program lists alternatives and allows students to interview various individuals. After they choose their course of action, likely results are projected. *Decisions, Decisions: The Environment,* from Tom Snyder Productions, presents a single scenario in which the student assumes the role of mayor of a small mining town faced with a growing water pollution dilemma. Four advisers are available to assist, but their counsel is often at odds. Stanton (1991) observed that when using these programs in his own social studies classes the students and their discussion remained the focal point. The software merely facilitated the flow of ideas.

MECC's *Probability Lab* is a math package that simulates coin flips, wheel spins, card draws, dice rolls, marble draws, and number picks. Students can predict the result and compare their hypothesis with the simulation. The computer's ability to make random choices means that the result of "flipping a coin" is not a foregone conclusion. This program, for example, can simulate up to one million consecutive flips, and the results will not be fully known until the millionth trial!

In literature, an entirely new genre has emerged in which students don the role of a principal character and make decisions as the plot proceeds. Such simulations, known as interactive fiction or text adventures, permit the same story to be experienced many times with different outcomes. In a series of programs known as *Zork,* for example, the students find themselves near an abandoned house that lies over a subterranean maze. The labyrinth contains both treasure and danger. The more sophisticated simulations, like *Zork,* do not present multiple-choice options but require the student to enter sentence-long commands that are "parsed" by the machine to determine their meaning. An actual dialogue transpires between the students and the software. It is hard to imagine a closer link between reading and writing. While it may appear that interactive fiction is limited to a single student user, Layton (1987) reported asking groups of students to make the decisions collaboratively.

Because they involve prediction, simulations are well suited to the DR–TA global plan. Hypothesizing is apt to be more frequent than in an ordinary DR–TA, but some reading is inevitable and the same instructional steps are pertinent.

Using Data Bases to Encourage Thinking

A data base stores information in such a way that it can be searched and sorted to meet the user's purpose. Books and libraries can be thought of as nonautomated data bases. Their use, however, is usually more time-consuming and restrictive than that of their electronic counterparts. Consider a simple filing system (many commercial versions are available) that a student has tailored for storing information about minerals. The headings for each mineral entered into the data base might include

NAME:
COLOR:
HARDNESS:
TEXTURE:
USES:
U.S. RANGE:

Once information about a number of minerals has been stored in the data base, the student can sort through it to solve a variety of research problems. The software can produce printed "reports" according to the student's specifications. In the previous example, a student could use the data base to create a feature analysis chart in which various minerals were listed in the left-hand column while the characteristics (color, hardness, etc.) formed the other column headings.

Many data bases come complete with built-in information. Some of these allow editing and expanding while others do not. Atlas data bases, for example, allow students to access maps and related geographical information. World almanacs have been computerized. Entire dictionaries and encyclopedias are stored on compact disks, which vastly increase the amount of data the micro can access (see Melnick, 1991). Other media are sometimes incorporated, as in the case of National Geographic's *Mammals.* Here, information about 200 animals is stored, including 155 vocalizations, 700 still photos, 450 maps, and 45 motion clips. The entire holdings of the National Gallery of Art in Washington, DC, have now been stored on a single CD, accessible by artist, period, country, and other categories. As these examples make clear, the range of available data bases is already stunning and continues to grow.

Like simulations, data bases encourage prediction. However, they are more commonly used as a tool for sorting and compiling information in order to answer specific questions. A filing system, like *Appleworks* or *Bank Street School Filer,* is therefore a natural candidate for the KWL lesson format. But instead of reading printed materials to discover the answers, students use the data base.

The availability of data bases by no means suggests that reading is unnecessary. Students read continually as the software is used and when the results are generated. Moreover, there are ample opportunities to link other kinds of literacy activities to data base research. Layton and Irwin (1989) offer the following example:

> Suppose you were to enter a classroom where the students are using the computer to study sports. As you arrive, the teacher explains that several days ago the class made a list of all the sports they knew. They also developed a series of questions that would apply to many sports, and these were translated into fields for a database form:

Name of sport:	Type (individual
Number of players:	or team):
Size of playing	
area:	Equipment:
When originated:	Where originated:
Famous past player:	Famous current player:

Now teams of students are busily gathering data about sports of their choice, using magazines, reference materials, and newspapers. Because the students are searching for specific information, they are skimming and taking notes. One team is at the room's one microcomputer, typing information about soccer. Another team is looking at a printout of countries of origin and is planning to make a map display. Two other students are using a printout about lawn bowling to write a descriptive article for the school newspaper.

Students, including reluctant learners, are actively involved in reading and writing. Problems of finding appropriate software and time for every student to use the computer are alleviated as students use printed materials and electronic technology in meaningful ways. (p. 724)

Developing Content Writing with Word Processors

One area in which research into the educational use of micros has been especially encouraging is the word processor (Root, 1988). When students use micros to prepare reports, journals, and other written documents, they tend to produce better written products. While many questions remain unanswered, such as the effects of social interaction among students and which instructional practices work best with word processing (Cochran-Smith, 1991), teachers in all fields should consider word processing software in conjunction with student writing opportunities.

Word processing has a number of qualities that contribute to its success. It emphasizes the interconnectedness of reading and writing (Shaver & Wise, 1991). It leads to a neatly printed, pride-inspiring final product (Wepner, 1990–1991). It permits students to publish their own "books," which can be a highly motivating undertaking, especially in the middle grades (Stratton & Grindler, in press). It encourages revision since changes do not require extensive recopying. It offers assistance with mechanics (especially spelling) and even matters of style and expression.

Student-oriented word processors make possible an additional advantage for teachers. They allow embedded messages to be stored at strategic points in order to offer on-the-spot guidance to student writers. Prompted writing might involve reminders of important considerations, suggestions about organization, and so forth.

While any commercial word processing package will suffice, some are designed for business use and might overpower students. Software written especially for student use is abundant, of course, but all educators should know about the availability of a *free* word processor, developed by educators for shared use. This is FrEd Writer (Free Education Writer) and is available from Computer Using Educators (CUE, P.O. Box 271704, Concord, CA 94527-1704). It offers all the advantages one usually expects in a basic package, including prompted writing options. (For a discussion of FrEd Writer, see Starshine, 1990.)

SUMMARY

The use of microcomputers in American classrooms holds great promise for developing content literacy. A number of factors suggest much greater use in the near future. These include (1) declining hardware costs, (2) increasing availability of high-quality software, (3) increasing presence of computers at home and in the workplace, (4) widespread realization that computers pose no threat to teachers, (5) growing computer competence among children reaching the middle and secondary grades, and (6) new approaches to how computers can represent text and make it usable.

A basic understanding of both hardware and software is necessary for planning instruction that effectively integrates micros. Indispensable hardware components include the central processing unit (cpu), the keyboard, and the monitor. In addition, peripherals greatly extend the range of computer applications. These include the printer, mouse, modem, videodisk player, speech synthesizer, file server, and overhead panel.

Traditional categories of software provide a useful frame of reference, but the distinctions are frequently lost when one type is used for a variety of classroom purposes. Drill-and-practice software provides students with opportunities to reinforce and extend learning that has already occurred. Tutorials, on the other hand, introduce new material directly. Simulations recreate real-world situations so as to encourage decision making and prediction. Utilities (word processors, data bases, etc.) were originally designed for out-of-class use but have recently entered the classroom because of their capacity to stimulate thinking and improve content-related writing.

Even though the expense of hardware may mean that only one or two machines are available in a classroom, there are ways to use them effectively. The overhead panel enables all students to see the output of a single machine, for example. Grouping students into teams allows hardware to be used collaboratively. Careful scheduling can also make one or two micros available to individual students according to their needs.

One of the most important changes in the way we think about computers and print involves hypertext. Software based on hypertext allows students to branch out into related topics, seek help with vocabulary and word pronunciation, ask for an oral reading of sentences or longer units, and so forth. By viewing text as a network of possible pathways, we shed the limiting assumption that it is strictly linear, proceeding from page to page from start to finish. Hypermedia is a natural extension of this idea to include access to nonprint sources, such as pictures, film, and audio recordings. Certain software makes it possible to customize one's own materials into a hypermedia system.

Simulations are not limited to scientific and technical settings. They are now available in nearly all content subjects. In social studies, for example, they may present students with problem scenarios, In mathematics, they may enable experiments with concepts like probability. In literature, interactive fiction and text adventures allow students to take an active part in what they read.

Data bases enable students to sort through information and note category relationships: They can be used as research tools to solve specific problems. Some data bases are built from student input, then used interactively. Others, like atlases, encyclopedias, and dictionaries, come ready-made. The latter now include ambitious hypermedia software.

Word processors encourage writing in content areas by producing an attractive finished product, by offering help with mechanics, and by making revision easier. Research suggests that word processors do tend to improve the quality of student writing. Word processing software designed for student use allows teachers to prompt writing by embedding messages at key points. FrEd Writer is an especially useful public domain word processor available free to teachers.

GETTING INVOLVED

1. Select a software title from among those mentioned in this chapter. Locate a review of it in a source like *Electronic Learning, The Computing Teacher, Technology and Learning, T.H.E. Journal,* or another of the many computer-related education journals. Other sources, more comprehensive and convenient than journals, include *Software Reviews on File* and *Datapro Directory of Microcomputer Software.* Both of these publications are frequently updated. Once you have located a review, read it critically and make a judgment about whether the program seems likely to enhance your students' learning.

2. Reviews are fine but they do only a fair job of showing you what a program is really like. If you're relatively new to micros as instructional tools, find a machine and software related to your teaching specialty. A school setting and a university micro lab are likely places to look. Then explore the software firsthand, trying to place yourself in your students' shoes. If you have read a review, to what extent do you agree with the reviewer?

REFERENCES

Adams, M. J. (1990). *Beginning to read: Thinking and learning about print.* Cambridge, MA: MIT Press.

Adelman, H. (1971). The not so specific learning disability population. *Exceptional Children, 37*(7), 528–533.

Alpert, B. R. (1987). Active, silent and controlled discussion: Explaining variations in classroom conversations. *Teaching and Teacher Education, 3,* 29–40.

Alvermann, D. E., & Boothby, P. R. (1983). A preliminary investigation of the differences in children's retention of "inconsiderate" text. *Reading Psychology, 4,* 237–246.

Alvermann, D. E., Dillon, D. R., & O'Brien, D. G. (1987). *Using discussion to promote reading comprehension.* Newark, DE: International Reading Association.

Alvermann, D. E., & Swafford, J. (1989). Do content area strategies have a research base? *Journal of Reading, 32,* 388–394.

Anderson, T. H., & Armbruster, B. B. (1984). Studying. In P. D. Pearson (Ed.), *Handbook of reading research.* White Plains, NY: Longman.

Anderson, T. H., & Armbruster, B. B. (1991). The value of taking notes during lectures. In R. F. Flippo & D. C. Caverly (Eds.), *Teaching reading and study strategies at the college level* (pp. 166–194). Newark, DE: International Reading Association.

Armbruster, B. B., & Anderson, T. H. (1981). Research synthesis on study skills. *Educational Leadership, 37,* 154–156.

Armstrong, D. P., Patberg, J. P., & Dewitz, P. (1988). Reading guides—Helping students understand. *Journal of Reading, 31,* 532–541.

Armstrong, D. P., Patberg, J. P., & Dewitz, P. (1989). Using reading guides to improve comprehension in literature classes. *English Quarterly, 21,* 233–246.

Aronson, E., Stephan, C., Sikes, J., Blaney, N., & Snapp, M. (1978). *The Jigsaw classroom.* Beverly Hills: Sage.

Asheim, L. (1987). *The reader-viewer-listener.* Washington, DC: Library of Congress.

Asimov, I. (1974). The ancient and the ultimate. *Journal of Reading, 17,* 264–271.

Aukerman, R. C. (1972). *Reading in the secondary school.* New York: McGraw-Hill.

Ausubel, D. (1960). The use of advance organizers in the learning and retention of meaningful verbal material. *Journal of Educational Psychology, 51,* 267–272.

Balf, T. (1991). A touch of genesis. *American Way, 24*(20), 36, 38, 43–44.

Barrett, T. C. (1972). Taxonomy of reading comprehension. In *Reading 360 Monograph.* Lexington, MA: Ginn.

Barron, R. F. (1969). The use of vocabulary as an advance organizer. In H. L. Herber & P. L. Sanders (Eds.), *Research on reading in the content areas: First-year report.* Syracuse, NY: Syracuse University, Reading and Language Arts Center.

Baumann, J. F. (1984). Implications for reading instruction from the research on teacher and school effectiveness. *Journal of Reading, 28,* 109–115.

Bean, T. W., & Steenwyk, F. L. (1984). The effect of three forms of summarization instruction on sixth graders' summary writing and comprehension. *Journal of Reading Behavior, 16,* 297–306.

Berman, S. (1987, Summer). Beyond critical thinking: Teaching for synthesis. *Educators for Social Responsibility: Forum 6,* 1–2.

Betts, E. A. (1946). *Foundations of reading instruction.* New York: American Book Company.

Binkley, M. R. (1988). New ways of assessing text difficulty. In B. L. Zakaluk & S. J. Samuels (Eds.), *Readability: Its past, present, and future* (pp. 98–120). Newark, DE: International Reading Association.

Blanchard, J. S., & Rottenberg, C. J. (1990). Hypertext and hypermedia: Discovering and creating meaningful learning environments. *The Reading Teacher, 43,* 656–661.

Blankenship, C. S. (1978). Remediating systematic inversion errors in subtraction through the use of demonstration and feedback. *Learning Disabilities Quarterly, 1,* 12–22.

Boggs, S. T. (1972). The meaning of questions and narratives to Hawaiian children. In C. B. Cazden, V. P. John, & D. Hymes (Eds.), *Functions of language in the classroom* (pp. 299–327). Prospect Heights, IL: Waveland.

Bormuth, J. R. (1967). Comparable cloze and multiple-choice comprehension test scores. *Journal of Reading, 10,* 291–299.

Bormuth, J. R. (1969). Empirical determination of instructional level. In J. A. Figurel (Ed.), *Reading and realism: Conference proceedings of the International Reading Association* (Vol. 13, part 1). Newark, DE: International Reading Association.

Bos, C. S., & Anders, P. L. (1989a). *The effectiveness of interactive instructional practices on content area reading comprehension.* Paper presented at the meeting of the American Educational Research Association, San Francisco.

Bos, C. S., & Anders, P. L. (1989b). Developing higher level thinking skills through interactive teaching. *Journal of Reading, Writing, and Learning Disabilities International, 4,* 259–274.

Bottom line: Basic skills in the workplace, The. (1988). Washington, DC: U. S. Department of Education.

Bransford, J. D., & Johnson, M. K. (1972). Contextual prerequisites for understanding: Some investigations of comprehension and recall. *Journal of Verbal Learning and Verbal Behavior, 11,* 717–726.

Britton, J. B., Burgess, T., Martin, N., McLeod, A., & Rosen, H. (1975). *The development of writing abilities (11–18).* London: Macmillan.

Bromley, K. (1985). Precis writing and outlining: Aids to learning content materials. *The Reading Teacher, 38,* 406–411.

Brophy, J. (1986). Principles for conducting first grade reading group instruction. In J. V. Hoffman (Ed.), *Effective teaching of reading: Research and practice* (pp. 53–84). Newark, DE: International Reading Association.

Brophy, J., & Evertson, C. (1974). *The Texas Teacher Effectiveness Project: Presentation of nonlinear relationships and summary discussion.* Austin, TX: Research and Development Center for Teacher Education. (ERIC Document Reproduction Service No. ED 099 345)

Brown, D. S. (1988). Twelve middle-school teachers' planning. *Elementary School Journal, 89,* 69–87.

Bruininks, V. L. (1978). Actual and perceived peer status of learning disabled students in mainstream programs. *Journal of Special Education, 12*(1), 51–58.

Bruner, J. (1960). *The process of education.* Cambridge, MA: Harvard University Press.

Bruner, J. (1964). The course of cognitive growth. *American Psychologist, 19,* 1–15.

Bruner, J. (1966). *Toward a theory of instruction.* Cambridge, MA: Harvard University Press.

Bruner, J. (1971). *The relevance of education.* New York: Norton.

Bryan, T. H. (1982). Social skills of learning disabled children and youth: An overview. *Learning Disabilities Quarterly, 5*(4), 323–333.

Carlsen, W. S. (1991). Questioning in classrooms: A sociolinguistic perspective. *Review of Educational Research, 61,* 157–178.

Carr, E., & Ogle, D. (1987). K-W-L plus: A strategy for comprehension and summarization. *Journal of Reading, 30,* 626–631.

Caverly, D. C., & Orlando, V. P. (1991). Textbook study strategies. In R. F. Flippo & D. C. Caverly (Eds.), *Teaching reading and study strategies at the college level* (pp. 86–165). Newark, DE: International Reading Association.

Clark, C., & Yinger, R. (1979). Teachers' thinking. In P. L. Peterson & H. J. Walberg (Eds.), *Research on teaching: Concepts, findings, and implications* (pp. 231–263). Berkeley, CA: McCutchan.

Clary, L. M. (1991). Getting adolescents to read. *Journal of Reading, 34,* 340–345.

Cochran-Smith, M. (1991). Word processing and writing in elementary classrooms: A critical review of related literature. *Review of Educational Research, 61,* 107–155.

Connolly, P. (1989). Writing and the ecology of learning. In P. Connolly & T. Vilardi (Eds.), *Writing to learn mathematics and science* (pp. 1–14). New York: Teachers College Press.

Cooper, J. O., Heron, T. E., & Heward, W. L. (1987). *Applied behavior analysis.* Columbus, OH: Merrill.

Cooter, R. B., Jr., & Griffith, R. (1989). Thematic units for middle school: An honorable seduction. *Journal of Reading, 32,* 676–681.

Corbeil, J.-C. (1986). *The Facts on File visual dictionary.* New York: Facts on File Publications.

Countdown 2000: Michigan's action plan for a competitive workplace. (1988). Lansing, MI: Governor's Cabinet Council on Human Investment.

Crawley, S. J. (1988). Using semantic mapping to help students organize social studies text. *Journal of the Middle States Council for the Social Studies, 10,* 24–29.

Cunningham, D., & Shablak, S. L. (1975). Selective reading guide-o-rama: The content teacher's best friend. *Journal of Reading, 18,* 380–382.

Cunningham, J. W. (1982). Generating interactions between schemata and text. In J. A. Niles & L. A. Harris (Eds.), *New inquiries in reading research and instruction: Thirty-first yearbook of the National Reading Conference* (pp. 42–47). Washington, DC: National Reading Conference.

Custer, J. D., & Osguthorpe, R. T. (1983). Improving social acceptance by training handicapped students to tutor nonhandicapped students. *Exceptional Children, 50*(2), 173–174.

Dahlberg, L. A. (1990). Teaching for the information age. *Journal of Reading, 34,* 12–18.

Darch, C. B., Carnine, D. W., & Kameenui, E. J. (1986). The role of graphic organizers and social structure in content area instruction. *Journal of Reading Behavior, 18,* 275–295.

Davey, B. (1983). Think-aloud—modeling the cognitive processes of reading comprehension. *Journal of Reading, 27,* 44–47.

Davison, A. (1984). Readability—appraising text difficulty. In R. C. Anderson, J. Osborn, & R. J. Tierney (Eds.), *Learning to read in American schools: Basal readers and content texts.* Hillsdale, NJ: Lawrence Erlbaum.

deBono, E. (1985). *Six thinking hats.* Boston: Little, Brown.

Dennis, L., McKenna, M. C., & Miller, J. W. (1989). Project READ:S: Effective design for content area reading. *Journal of Reading, 32,* 520–524.

Deshler, D. D., & Graham, S. (1980). Tape recording educational materials for secondary handicapped students. *Teaching Exceptional Children, 12,* 52–54.

Diehl, W., & Mikulecky, L. (1980). The nature of reading at work. *Journal of Reading, 24,* 221–227.

Dillon, J. T. (1984). Research on questioning and discussion. *Educational Leadership, 42,* 50–56.

Dillon, J. T. (1985). Using questions to foil discussion. *Teaching and Teacher Education, 1,* 109–121.

Dinnel, D., & Glover, J. H. (1985). Advance organizers: Encoding manipulations. *Journal of Educational Psychology, 77,* 514–521.

Dole, J. A., & Niederhauser, D. S. (1990). Students' level of commitment to their naive conceptions and their conceptual change learning from texts. In J. Zutell & S. McCormick (Eds.), *Literacy theory and research: Analyses from multiple paradigms: Thirty-ninth yearbook of the National Reading Conference* (pp. 303–310). Chicago: National Reading Conference.

Donahoe, K., & Zigmond, N. (1990). Academic grades of ninth-grade urban learning disabled students and low achieving peers. *Exceptionality, 1,* 17–28.

Duffelmeyer, F. A. (1985). Teaching word meaning from an experience base. *The Reading Teacher, 39,* 6–9.

Duffy, G. G., & Roehler, L. R. (1987). Improving reading instruction through responsive instruction through elaboration. *The Reading Teacher, 40,* 514–515.

Duffy, G. G., Roehler, L. R., Sivan, E., Rackliffe, G., Book, C., Meloth, M. S., Vavrus, L. G., Wesselman, R., Putnam, J., Bassiri, D. (1987). Effects of explaining the reasoning associated with using reading strategies. *Reading Research Quarterly, 22,* 347–368.

Durkin, D. (1978–1979). What classroom observations reveal about reading comprehension instruction. *Reading Research Quarterly, 14,* 481–533.

Earle, R. A. (1969). Developing and using study guides. In H. L. Herber & P. L. Sanders (Eds.), *Research in reading in the content areas: First year report* (pp. 71–92). Syracuse, NY: Syracuse University.

Eaton, M., & Lovitt, T. C. (1972). Achievement tests vs. direct and daily measurement. In G. Semb (Ed.), *Behavior analysis and education* (pp. 78–87). Lawrence: Kansas Department of Human Development.

Edwards, A. D., & Furlong, V. J. (1978). *The language of teaching.* London: Heinemann.

Edwards, P. R. (1991–1992). Using dialectical journals to teach thinking skills. *Journal of Reading, 35,* 312–316.

Fader, D. N., & Shaevitz, M. H. (1966). *Hooked on books.* New York: Berkley Publishing Corp.

Farrell, R. T., & Cirrincione, J. M. (1986). The introductory developmental reading course for content area teachers: A state of the art survey. *Journal of Reading, 29,* 717–723.

Festinger, L. (1957). *A theory of cognitive dissonance.* New York: Harper & Row.

Frager, A. M. (1984). How good are content teachers' judgments of the reading abilities of secondary school students? *Journal of Reading, 27,* 402–406.

Fry, E. (1981). Graphical literacy. *Journal of Reading, 24,* 383–390.

Fry, E. (1989). Reading formulas—maligned but valid. *Journal of Reading, 32,* 292–297.

Gall, M. D., Gall, J. P., Jacobsen, D. R., & Bullock, T. L. (1990). *Tools for learning: A guide to teaching study skills.* Alexandria, VA: Association for Supervision and Curriculum Development.

Gardner, M. K., & Smith, M. M. (1987). Does perspective taking ability contribute to reading comprehension? *Journal of Reading, 30,* 333–336.

Gartner, A., & Lipsky, D. K. (1990). New conceptualizations for special education. In S. B. Sigmon (Ed.), *Critical voices on special education: Problems and progress concerning the mildly handicapped.* Albany: State University of New York Press.

Gates, B. (1988). Computers in schools, today and tomorrow. *T. H. E. Journal, 16,* 14–15.

Gillespie, C. (1990–1991). Questions about student-generated questions. *Journal of Reading, 34,* 250–257.

Good, T., & Brophy, J. (1991). *Looking in classrooms* (5th ed.). New York: HarperCollins.

Graves, D. (1983). *Writing: Teachers and children at work.* Portsmouth, NH: Heinemann.

Gray, W. S. (1969). *The teaching of reading and writing: An international survey.* Paris: United Nations Educational, Scientific, and Cultural Organization.

Gresham, F. M. (1981). Social skills training with the handicapped: A review. *Review of Educational Research, 51,* 139–176.

Gresham, F. M. (1984). Social skills and self-efficacy for exceptional children. *Exceptional Children, 51,* 253–261.

Guthrie, J. T. (1983). Equilibrium of literacy. *Journal of Reading, 26,* 668–670.

Guthrie, J. T. & Kirsch, I. S. (1984). The emergent perspective on literacy. *Phi Delta Kappan, 66,* 351–355.

Hallahan, D. P., & Reeve, R. E. (1980). Selective attention and distractability. In B. K. Keogh (Ed.), *Advances in special education* (Vol. 1, pp. 141–181). Greenwich, CT: JAI Press.

Hartley, J., & Davies, S. K. (1978). Note-taking: A critical review. *Programmed Learning and Educational Technology, 15,* 207–224.

Hayakawa, S. I. (1939). *Language in thought and action.* New York: Harcourt Brace Jovanovich.

Hayes, D., & Tierney, R. (1982). Developing readers' knowledge through analogy. *Reading Research Quarterly, 17,* 256–280.

Haynes, M. C., & Jenkins, J. R. (1986). Reading instruction in special education resource rooms. *American Educational Research Journal, 23,* 161–190.

Henk, W. A. (1981). Effects of modified deletion strategies and scoring procedures on cloze test performance. *Journal of Reading Behavior, 13,* 347–357.

Henk, W. A., & Selders, M. L. (1984). A test of synonymic scoring of cloze passages. *The Reading Teacher, 38,* 282–287.

Herber, H. L. (1978). *Teaching reading in content areas* (2nd ed.). Englewood Cliffs, NJ: Prentice-Hall.

Heron, T. E., & Harris, K. C. (1987). *The educational consultant: Helping professionals, parents and mainstreamed students* (2nd ed.). Austin, TX: Pro-Ed.

Heward, W. L., Heron, T. E., & Cooke, N. (1982). Tutor huddle: Key element in a classwide peer tutoring system. *The Elementary School Journal, 83*(2), 114–123.

Hill, M. (1991). Writing summaries promotes thinking and learning across the curriculum—but why are they so difficult to write? *Journal of Reading, 34,* 536–539.

Hoffman, B. (1962). *The tyranny of testing.* New York: Collier.

Holbrook, H. T. (1984). Prereading in the content areas. *Journal of Reading, 27,* 368–370.

Hollingsworth, S., & Teel, K. (1991). Learning to teach reading in secondary math and science. *Journal of Reading, 35,* 190–194.

Holmes, B. C., & Roser, N. L. (1987). Five ways to assess readers' prior knowledge. *The Reading Teacher, 40,* 646–649.

Holt-Reynolds, D. (1991, December). *Directed reading strategies and how preservice teachers decide they are unnecessary: Exploring the effects of personal histories.* Paper presented at the meeting of the National Reading Conference, Palm Springs, CA.

Horton, S. V., & Lovitt, T. C. (in press). Construction and implementation of graphic organizers for academically handicapped and regular secondary students. *Academic Therapy.*

Howie, S. H. (1990). Adult literacy in a multiliterate society. *Journal of Reading, 33,* 260–263.

Hunt, L. C., Jr. (1967). Evaluation through teacher-pupil conferences. In T. C. Barrett (Ed.), *The evaluation of children's reading achievement.* Newark, DE: International Reading Association.

Hunter, C. S., & Harman, D. (1979). *Adult illiteracy in the United States: A report to the Ford Foundation.* New York: McGraw-Hill.

Hunter, M., & Russell, D. (1977). How can I plan more effective lessons? *Instructor, 87*(2), 74–75, 88.

Idol-Maestas, L., Nevin, A., & Paolucci-Whitcomb, P. (1984). *Facilitator's manual for collaborative consultation: Principles and techniques.* Reston, VA: National RETOOL Center, Teacher Education Division, Council for Exceptional Children.

Irvin, J. L., & Connors, N. A. (1989). Reading instruction in middle level schools: Results of a U.S. survey. *Journal of Reading, 32,* 306–311.

Jacobsen, D. R. (1989). *The effects of taking class notes using the Cornell Method on students' test performance in note-taking quality.* Unpublished doctoral dissertation. University of Oregon, Eugene.

Johnson, D. D., & Pearson, P. D. (1984). *Teaching reading vocabulary* (2nd ed.). New York: Holt, Rinehart and Winston.

Johnson, D. D., Pittelman, S. D., Toms-Bronowski, S., & Levin, K. M. (1984). *An investigation of the effects of prior knowledge and vocabulary acquisition on passage comprehension* (Program Report 84–5). Madison: Wisconsin Center for Education Research, University of Wisconsin.

Johnson, D. D., Toms-Bronowski, S., & Pittelman, S. D. (1982). *An investigation of the effectiveness of semantic mapping and semantic feature analysis with intermediate grade level children* (Program Report 83–3). Madison: Wisconsin Center for Education Research, University of Wisconsin.

Johnson, D. W., & Johnson, R. T. (1984). *Cooperation in the classroom.* Edina, MN: Interaction Book Company.

Johnson, D. W., & Johnson, R. T. (1989). *Cooperation and competition: Theory and research.* Edina, MN: Interaction Book Company.

Kantor, R. N., Anderson, T. H., & Armbruster, B. B. (1983). How inconsiderate are children's textbooks? *Journal of Curriculum Studies, 15,* 6–72.

Kazemek, F. E. (1988). Necessary changes: Professional involvement in adult literacy programs. *Harvard Educational Review, 58,* 464–487.

Kinney, M. A., & Harry, A. L. (1991). An informal inventory for adolescents that assesses the reader, the text, and the task. *Journal of Reading, 34,* 643–647.

Kintsch, W., & van Dijk, T. A. (1978). Toward a model of text comprehension and production. *Psychological Review, 85,* 363–394.

Kirby, D., & Liner, T. (1981). *Inside out.* New York: Boynton-Cook.

Kirsch, I. S., & Jungeblut, A. (1986). *Literacy profiles of America's young adults.* Princeton, NJ: National Assessment of Educational Progress.

Kirsch, I. S., & Mosenthal, P. B. (1990). Understanding documents: Nested lists. *Journal of Reading, 33,* 294–297.

Klare, G. R. (1988). The formative years. In B. L. Zakaluk & S. J. Samuels (Eds.), *Readability: Its past, present, and future* (pp. 14–34). Newark, DE: International Reading Association.

Konopak, B. C., Martin, S. H., & Martin, M. A. (1987). An integrated communications arts approach for enhancing students' learning in content areas. *Reading Research and Instruction, 26,* 275–289.

Kulik, J. A., & Kulik, C. C. (1988). Timing of feedback and verbal learning. *Review of Educational Research, 58,* 79–97.

Laframboise, K. L. (1986–1987). The use of study techniques with young and less able students. *Journal of Reading Education, 12*(2), 23–31.

Langer, J. A. (1981). From theory to practice: A prereading plan. *Journal of Reading, 25,* 152–156.

Langer, J. A. (1986a). *A sociocognitive perspective on literacy.* (ERIC Document Reproduction Service No. ED 274 988)

Langer, J. A. (1986b). *Literate communication and literacy instruction.* (ERIC Document Reproduction Service No. ED 276 020)

Lapp, D., Flood, J., & Farnan, N. (1989). *Content area reading and learning: Instructional strategies.* Englewood Cliffs, NJ: Prentice-Hall.

Layton, K. (1987). Interactive text adventures. *Media and Methods, 23*(4), 14–16.

Layton, K., & Irwin, M. E. (1989). Enriching your reading program with databases. *The Reading Teacher, 42,* 724.

Lazarus, B. D. (1988). Using guided notes to aid learning disabled students in secondary mainstream settings. *The Pointer, 33,* 32–36.

Lazarus, B. D. (1989a). Developing assessment profiles for gifted learning disabled students. *Journal of Reading, Writing, and Learning Disabilities International, 5*(3), 235–246.

Lazarus, B. D. (1989b). Serving learning disabled students in postsecondary settings. *Journal of Developmental Education, 12*(3), 2–7.

Lazarus, B. D. (1991). Guided notes, review, and achievement of learning disabled adolescents in secondary mainstream settings. *Education and Treatment of Children, 14,* 112–128.

Lazarus, B. D. (in press). Guided notes, supervised review, and achievement of mildly handicapped students. *Teaching Exceptional Children.*

Lazarus, B. D., & McKenna, M. C. (1991, April). *Guided notes: Review and achievement of mainstreamed LD students.* Paper presented at the meeting of the Council for Exceptional Children, Atlanta.

Leinhardt, G. (1983). *Routines in expert math teachers' thoughts and actions.* Paper presented at the meeting of the American Educational Research Association, Montreal.

Levine, K. (1982). Functional literacy: Found illusions and false economies. *Harvard Educational Review, 52,* 249–266.

Lewis, R. B., & Doorlag, D. H. (1991). *Teaching special students in the mainstream.* New York: Macmillan.

Lilly, M. S. (1986). The relationship between general and special education: A new face on an old issue. *Counterpoint, 6*(1), 10.

Lipson, M. Y., & Wixson, K. K. (1991). *Assessment and instruction of reading disability: An interactive approach.* New York: HarperCollins.

Lovitt, T. C. (1977). *In spite of my resistance—I've learned from my children.* Columbus, OH: Merrill.

Lovitt, T. C., Horton, S. V., & Bergerud, D. (1987). Matching students with textbooks: An alternative to readability formulas and standardized tests. *B.C. Journal of Special Education, 2*(1), 49–55.

Lunstrum, J. P. (1981). Building motivation through the use of controversy. *Journal of Reading, 24,* 687–691.

Lynch, D., & Smith, B. (1975). Item response changes: Effects on test scores. *Measurement and Evaluation in Guidance, 7*(4), 220–224.

Lynch, D. J., & McKenna, M. C. (1990). Teaching controversial material: New issues for teachers. *Social Education, 54,* 317–319.

Maheady, L., & Harper, G. F. (1987). A classwide peer tutoring program to improve spelling test performance of low income, third- and fourth-grade students. *Education and Treatment of Children, 10,* 120–133.

Maheady, L., Sacca, M. K., & Harper, G. F. (1988). Classwide peer tutoring with mildly handicapped high school students. *Exceptional Children, 55*(1), 52–59.

Manzo, A. V. (1968). *Improving reading comprehension through reciprocal questioning.* Unpublished doctoral dissertation, Syracuse University.

Manzo, A. V. (1969). The ReQuest procedure. *Journal of Reading, 2,* 123–126.

Manzo, A. V., & Manzo, U. C. (1990). *Content area reading: A heuristic approach.* Columbus, OH: Merrill.

Margolis, J. (1990, June 25). Jimmy! This is cricket? Coming to terms with a confusing foreign game. *Chicago Tribune,* Section 3, p. 7.

Margosein, C. M., Pascarella, E. T., & Pflaum, S. W. (1982, April). *The effect of instruction using semantic mapping on vocabulary and comprehension.* Paper presented at the meeting of the American Educational Research Association, New York.

Marshall, N. (1989). The students: Who are they and how do I reach them? In D. Lapp, J. Flood, & N. Farnan (Eds.), *Content area reading and learning: Instructional strategies* (pp. 59–69). Englewood Cliffs, NJ: Prentice-Hall.

Martin, M. A., & Konopak, B. C. (1987). An instructional investigation of students' ideas generated during content area writing. In J. E. Readence & R. S. Baldwin (Eds.), *Research in literacy: Merging perspectives: Thirty-sixth yearbook of the National Reading Conference* (pp. 265–271). Rochester, NY: National Reading Conference.

Martin, M. A., Konopak, B. C., & Martin, S. H. (1986). Use of the guided writing procedure to facilitate comprehension of high school text materials. In J. A. Niles & R. V. Lalik (Eds.), *Solving problems in literacy: Learners, teachers, and researchers: Thirty-fifth yearbook of the National Reading Conference* (pp. 66–72). Rochester, NY: National Reading Conference.

Mathison, C. (1989). Activating student interest in content area reading. *Journal of Reading, 33,* 170–176.

McClain, L. (1983). Behavior during examinations: A comparison of A, C, and F students. *Teaching of Psychology, 10*(2), 69–71.

McKenna, M. C. (1976). Synonymic versus verbatim scoring of the cloze procedure. *Journal of Reading, 20,* 141–143.

McKenna, M. C. (1977a). Reading viewed as the result of writing. *Reading Horizons, 17,* 264–267.

McKenna, M. C. (1977b). Searching for roots—of words. *Teacher, 95*(2), 93, 96, 99–101.

McKenna, M. C. (1977c). Songs for language study. *Audiovisual Instruction, 22*(4), 42.

McKenna, M. C. (1978). Portmanteau words in reading instruction. *Language Arts, 55,* 315–317.

McKenna, M. C. (1983). *The Stein and Day dictionary of definitive quotations.* New York: Stein & Day.

McKenna, M. C. (1986). Reading interests of remedial secondary school students. *Journal of Reading, 29,* 346–351.

McKenna, M. C., & Layton, K. (1990). Concurrent validity of cloze as a measure of intersentential comprehension. *Journal of Educational Psychology, 82,* 372–377.

McKenna, M. C., & Robinson, R. D. (1980). *An introduction to the cloze procedure: An annotated bibliography* (2nd ed.). Newark, DE: International Reading Association.

McKenna, M. C., & Robinson, R. D. (1990). Content literacy: A definition and implications. *Journal of Reading, 34,* 184–186.

McLeod, M. A. (1981). *The identification of intended learning outcomes by early childhood teachers: An exploratory study.* Unpublished doctoral dissertation, University of Alberta.

Mecklenburger, J. A. (1990). Educational technology is not enough. *Phi Delta Kappan, 72,* 104–108.

Melnick, S. A. (1991). Electronic encyclopedias on compact disk. *The Reading Teacher, 44,* 432–434.

Mikulecky, L. (1990). Literacy for what purpose? In R. L. Venezky, D. A. Wagner, & B. S. Ciliberti (Eds.), *Toward defining literacy* (pp. 24–34). Newark, DE: International Reading Association.

Miller, G. R., & Coleman, E. B. (1967). A set of 36 prose passages calibrated for complexity. *Journal of Verbal Learning and Verbal Behavior, 6,* 851–854.

Miller, J. W., & McKenna, M. C. (1989). *Teaching reading in the elementary school.* Scottsdale, AZ: Gorsuch Scarisbrick.

Millman, J. C., Bishop, C. H., & Ebel, R. (1965). An analysis of test wiseness. *Educational and Psychological Measurement, 25,* 707–727.

Moore, D. W., & Readence, J. E. (1980). A meta-analysis of the effect of graphic organizers on learning from text. In M. L. Kamil & A. J. Moe (Eds.), *Perspectives on reading research and instruction: Twenty-Ninth Yearbook of the National Reading Conference* (pp. 213–218). Washington, DC: National Reading Conference.

Moore, D. W., Readence, J. E., & Rickelman, R. J. (1989). *Prereading activities for content area reading and learning* (2nd ed.). Newark, DE: International Reading Association.

Morine, G. (1976). *A study of teacher planning* (BTES Tech. Rep. 75-11-6). San Francisco: Far West Laboratory for Educational Research and Development.

Myers, J. W. (1984). *Writing to learn across the curriculum.* Bloomington, IN: Phi Delta Kappa.

Nagy, W. E., & Anderson, R. C. (1984). How many words are there in printed school English? *Reading Research Quarterly, 21,* 304–330.

Nagy, W. E., & Herman, P. A. (1984). *Limitations of vocabulary instruction.* Technical Report No. 326. Urbana, IL: University of Illinois. Center for the Study of Reading. (ERIC Document Reproduction Service No. ED 24898)

Nell, V. (1988). *Lost in a book: The psychology of reading for pleasure.* New Haven, CT: Yale University Press.

Newmann, F. M., & Oliver, D. W. (1970). *Clarifying public controversy: An approach to teaching social studies.* Boston: Little, Brown.

Nist, S. L., & Simpson, M. L. (1989). PLAE, a validated study strategy. *Journal of Reading, 33,* 182–186.

Ogle, D. (1986). K-W-L: A teaching model that develops active reading of expository text. *The Reading Teacher, 39,* 564–570.

Olson, M. W., Gee, T. C., & Forester, N. (1989). Magazines in the classroom: Beyond recreational reading. *Journal of Reading, 32,* 708–713.

Orr, E. W. (1987). *Twice as less: Black English and the performance of black students in mathematics and science.* New York: Norton.

Osterlag, B. A., & Rambeau, J. (1982). Reading success through rewriting for secondary LD students. *Academic Therapy, 18,* 27–32.

Palincsar, A. S., & Brown, A. L. (1984). Reciprocal teaching of comprehension-fostering and comprehension-monitoring activities. *Cognition and Instruction, 2,* 117–175.

Paris, S. G., Wasik, B. A., & Turner, J. C. (1991). The development of strategic readers. In R. Barr, M. L. Kamil, P. B. Mosenthal, & P. D. Pearson (Eds.), *Handbook of reading research* (Vol. 2, pp. 609–640). White Plains, NY: Longman.

Pauk, W. (1988). *How to study in college* (3rd ed.). Boston: Houghton Mifflin.

Pearson, P. D., & Johnson, D. D. (1978). *Teaching reading comprehension.* New York: Holt, Rinehart and Winston.

Perfetti, C. A. (1991). *Subject matter text learning: Reading, knowledge, and texts.* Pittsburgh: Learning Research and Development Center, University of Pittsburgh.

Peterson, J., & Carroll, M. (1974). The cloze procedure as an indicator of the instructional level for disabled readers. In P. L. Nacke (Ed.), *Interaction: Research and practice in college-adult reading: Twenty-third yearbook of the National Reading Conference.* (pp. 153–157). Clemson, SC: National Reading Conference.

Peterson, J., Paradis, E., & Peters, N. (1973). Revalidation of the cloze procedure as a measure of the instructional level for high school students. In P. L. Nacke (Ed.), *Diversity in mature reading: Theory and research: Twenty-second yearbook of the National Reading Conference* (Vol. 1, pp. 144–149). Boone, NC: National Reading Conference.

Peterson, J., Peters, N., & Paradis, E. (1972). Validation of the cloze procedure as a measure of readability with high school, trade school, and college populations. In F. P. Greene (Ed.), *Investigations relating to mature reading: Twenty-first yearbook of the National Reading Conference* (Vol. 1, pp. 45–50). Milwaukee: National Reading Conference.

Piaget, J. (1952). *The origins of intelligence in children.* New York: International University Press.

Pittelman, S. D., Levin, K. M., & Johnson, D. D. (1985). *An investigation of the instructional settings in the use of semantic mapping with poor readers* (Program Report 85–4). Madison: Wisconsin Center for Education Research, University of Wisconsin.

Polloway, E. A., Smith, J. D., & Patton, J. R. (1984). Learning disabilities: An adult developmental perspective. *Learning Disabilities Quarterly, 7,* 179–186.

Prince, A. T. (1987). Enriching comprehension: A schema altered basal reading lesson. *Reading Research and Instruction, 27,* 45–53.

Putnam, M. L., Deshler, D. D., & Schumaker, J. B. (in press). The investigation of setting demands: A missing link in learning strategy instruction. In L. Meltzer (Ed.), *Cognitive, linguistic, and developmental perspectives on learning disorders.* Boston: Little, Brown.

Rankin, E. F., & Culhane, J. (1969). Comparable cloze and multiple-choice comprehension test scores. *Journal of Reading, 13,* 193–198.

Raphael, T. E. (1984). Teaching learners about sources of information for answering comprehension questions. *Journal of Reading, 27,* 303–311.

Raygor, A. L. (1977). The Raygor readability estimate: A quick and easy way to determine difficulty. In P. D. Pearson (Ed.), *Reading: Theory, research, and practice: Twenty-sixth yearbook of the National Reading Conference* (pp. 259–263). Clemson, SC: National Reading Conference.

Rayner, K., & Pollatsek, A. (1989). *The psychology of reading.* Englewood Cliffs, NJ: Prentice-Hall.

Readence, J. E., Bean, T. W., & Baldwin, R. S. (1989). *Content area reading: An integrated approach* (3rd ed.). Dubuque, IA: Kendall/Hunt.

Reinking, D. (1986). Integrating graphic aids into content area instruction: The graphic information lesson. *The Reading Teacher, 30,* 146–151.

Reinking, D., & Bridwell-Bowles, L. (1991). Computers in reading and writing. In R. Barr, M. L. Kamil, P. B. Mosenthal, & P. D. Pearson (Eds.), *Handbook of reading research* (Vol. 2, pp. 310–340). White Plains, NY: Longman.

Richardson, J., & Morgan, R. (1990). *Reading to learn in the content areas.* Belmont, CA: Wadsworth.

Richgels, D. J., & Hansen, R. (1984). Gloss: Helping students apply both skills and strategies in reading content texts. *Journal of Reading, 27,* 312–317.

Rickelman, R. J., & Henk, W. (1989). Reading and technology: Past failures and future dreams. *The Reading Teacher, 43,* 174–175.

Rinehart, S. D., Stahl, S. A., & Erickson, L. G. (1986). Some effects of summarization training on reading and studying. *Reading Research Quarterly, 21,* 422–438.

Risko, V. J., Alvarez, M. C., & Fairbanks, M. M. (1991). External factors that influence study. In R. F. Flippo & D. C. Caverly (Eds.), *Teaching reading and study strategies at the college level* (pp. 195–236). Newark, DE: International Reading Association.

Rivers, L. E. (1980). Use a tape recorder to teach basic skills. *Social Studies, 71*(4), 171–174.

Robinson, F. P. (1946). *Effective study.* New York: Harper & Row.

Robinson, R. D. (1991). *Teacher effectiveness and reading instruction.* Bloomington, IN: ERIC.

Robinson, R. D., & Good, T. L. (1987). *Becoming an effective reading teacher.* New York: Harper & Row.

Root, T. L. (1988). Using word processors with elementary students: Justifications and techniques. *Kansas Journal of Reading, 4,* 36–40.

Rose, B. (1989). Writing and mathematics: Theory and practice. In P. Connolly & T. Vilardi (Eds.), *Writing to learn mathematics and science.* New York: Teachers College Press.

Rosenshine, B. V. (1986). Synthesis of research on explicit teaching. *Educational Leadership, 43*(7), 60–69.

Royer, J. M., Greene, B. A., & Sinatra, G. M. (1987). The Sentence Verification Technique: A practical procedure for testing comprehension. *Journal of Reading, 30,* 414–422.

Rumberg, D. L. (1987). High school dropouts: A review of issues and evidence. *Review of Educational Research, 57*(2), 101–121.

Sarnacki, R. (1979). An examination of test wiseness in the cognitive test domain. *Review of Educational Research, 49,* 252–279.

Savage, J. F. (1983). Reading guides: Effective tools for teaching the gifted. *Roeper Review, 5*(3), 9–11.

Schatz, E. K., & Baldwin, R. S. (1986). Context clues are unreliable predictors of word meanings. *Reading Research Quarterly, 21,* 439–453.

Schmidt, C. M., Barry, A., Maxworthy, A. G., & Huebsch, W. R. (1989). But I read the chapter twice. *Journal of Reading, 32,* 428–433.

Schultz, J. B., Tucker, J. A., & Turnbull, A. P. (1991). *Mainstreaming handicapped students: A guide for classroom teachers.* Columbus, OH: MacMillan.

Schumaker, J. B., Deshler, D. D., & Denton, P. H. (1982). *An integrated system for providing content to LD adolescents using an audio-taped format.* (Research Report No. 66). Lawrence: University of Kansas Institute for Research in Learning Disabilities.

Schwartz, R. M. (1988). Learning to learn vocabulary in content area textbooks. *Journal of Reading, 32,* 108–118.

Schwartz, R. M., & Raphael, T. E. (1985). Concept of definition: A key to improving students' vocabulary. *The Reading Teacher, 39,* 198–205.

Searfoss, L. W., & Readence, J. E. (1989). *Helping children learn to read.* Englewood Cliffs, NJ: Prentice-Hall.

Shaver, J. C., & Wise, B. S. (1991). Literacy: The impact of technology on early reading. In B. L. Hayes & K. Campbell (Eds.), *Literacy: International, national, state, and local: Eleventh yearbook of the American Reading Forum* (pp. 139–145). Logan: Utah State University.

Shepherd, D. L. (1982). *Comprehensive high school reading methods* (3rd ed.). Columbus, OH: Merrill.

Shipman, P. (October 1, 1986). A culture divided by science. *Education Week, 6*(4), 24.

Simonini, R. C., Jr. (1966). Word-making in present-day English. *English Journal, 55,* 752–757.

Simpson, M. L., & Nist, S. L. (1984). PLAE: A model for planning successful independent learning. *Journal of Reading, 28,* 218–223.

Singer, H. (1975). The SEER technique: A non-computational procedure for quickly estimating readability level. *Journal of Reading Behavior, 7,* 255–267.

Skinner, B. F. (1981). How to discover what you have to say: A talk to students. *The Behavior Analyst, 4,* 1–7.

Slavin, R. E. (1988). Cooperative learning and student achievement. *Educational Leadership, 45*(2), 31–33.

Slavin, R. E. (1989–1990). Research on cooperative learning: Concensus and controversy. *Educational Leadership, 47*(4), 52–54.

Smith, C. C., & Bean, T. W. (1980). The guided writing procedure: Integrating content reading and writing improvement. *Reading World, 19,* 290–294.

Smith, F. (1988). *Understanding reading: A psycholinguistic analysis of reading and learning to read* (4th ed.). Hillsdale, NJ: Lawrence Erlbaum.

Spiegel, D. L. (1981). Six alternatives to the directed reading activity. *The Reading Teacher, 34,* 914–920.

Spiro, R. J. (1991, December). *Integrative reconciliation of paradigm conflict in reading: Joining multiple perspectives in reading research, in learning to read, and in preparing reading teachers for practice.* Paper presented at the meeting of the National Reading Conference, Palm Springs, CA.

Squire, J. R. (1983). Composing and comprehending: Two sides of the same basic process. *Language Arts, 60,* 581–589.

Stahl, N. A., & King, J. R. (1984). *Training and evaluating notetaking.* Paper presented at the meeting of the College Reading Association, Washington, DC.

Stahl, N. A., King, J. R., & Henk, W. A. (1991). Enhancing students' notetaking through training and evaluation. *Journal of Reading, 34,* 614–622.

Stahl, S. A., & Vancil, S. J. (1986). Discussion is what makes semantic maps work in vocabulary instruction. *The Reading Teacher, 40,* 62–67.

Stainback, W., & Stainback, S. (1984). A rationale for the merger of regular and special education. *Exceptional Children, 51*(2), 102–111.

Stainback, W., & Stainback, S. (1988). Educating students with severe disabilities. *Exceptional Children, 21*(2), 16–19.

Stanton, D. (1991). Social simulations. *Electronic Learning, 10*(7), 37.

Starshine, D. (1990). An inexpensive alternative to word processing—FrEdWriter. *The Reading Teacher, 43,* 600–601.

Staton, J. (1980). Writing and counseling: Using a dialogue journal. *Language Arts, 57,* 514–518.

Stauffer, R. (1969). *Directing reading maturity as a cognitive process.* New York: Harper & Row.

Stauffer, R. (1980). *The language experience approach to the teaching of reading* (2nd ed.). New York: Harper & Row.

Stedman, L. C., & Kaestle, C. F. (1987).   Literacy and reading performance in the United States, from 1880 to the present. *Reading Research Quarterly, 22,* 8–46.

Stein, H. (1978).   The visual reading guide (VRG). *Social Education, 42,* 534–535.

Stewart, R. A., & O'Brien, D. G. (1989).   Resistance to content area reading: A focus on preservice teachers. *Journal of Reading, 32,* 396–401.

Stokes, T. E., & Baer, D. M. (1977).   An implicit technology of generalization. *Journal of Applied Behavior Analysis, 10*(2), 349–367.

Stoodt, B. D., & Balbo, E. (1979).   Integrating study skills instruction with content in a secondary classroom. *Reading World, 18,* 247–252.

Strackbein, D., & Tillman, M. (1987).   The joy of journals—with reservations. *Journal of Reading, 31,* 28–31.

Stratton, B. D., & Grindler, M. C. (in press).   Discovering oneself: An important attribute in the middle school. *Middle School Journal.*

Taba, H. (1967).   *Teacher's handbook for elementary social studies.* Reading, MA: Addison-Wesley.

Taylor, D. (1989).   Toward a unified theory of literacy learning and instructional practices. *Phi Delta Kappan, 71,* 184–193.

Teale, W. H., & Sulzby, E. (1989).   Emergent literacy: New perspectives. In D. S. Strickland & L. M. Morrow (Eds.), *Emerging literacy: Young children learn to read and write* (pp. 1–15). Newark, DE: International Reading Association.

Thomas, D. A. (1989).   Reading and reasoning skills for math problem solvers. *Journal of Reading, 32,* 244–249.

Thomas, J. W., & Rohwer, W. D., Jr. (1986).   Academic studying: The role of learning strategies. *Educational Psychologist, 21,* 19–41.

Tierney, R. J., Readence, J. E., & Dishner, E. K. (1990).   *Reading strategies and practices: A compendium* (3rd ed.). Boston: Allyn & Bacon.

Tobias, S. (1982).   When do instructional methods make a difference? *Educational Researcher, 11,* 4–9.

Torgesen, J. K., & Kail, R. J. (1985).   Memory processes in exceptional children. In B. K. Keogh (Ed.), *Advances in special education: Basic constructs and theoretical orientations.* Greenwich, CT: JAI Press.

Tuinman, J. J. (1971).   Asking reading dependent questions. *Journal of Reading, 14,* 289–292, 336.

Tyler, R. W. (1950).   *Basic principles of curriculum and instruction.* Chicago: University of Chicago Press.

Vacca, R. T., & Vacca, J. L. (1989).   *Content area reading* (3rd ed.). Glenview, IL: Scott, Foresman.

Vacca, R. T., Vacca, J. L., & Rycik, J. A. (1989).   Text and context in content area reading: Planning and organizing successful learning environments. In D. Lapp, J. Flood, & N. Farnan (Eds.), *Content area reading and learning: Instructional strategies* (pp. 320–329). Englewood Cliffs, NJ: Prentice-Hall.

Vaughan, J. L., Jr. (1982).   Use the ConStruct procedure to foster active reading and learning. *Journal of Reading, 25,* 412–422.

Vogel, S., & Sattler, J. (1981).   *The college student with a learning disability: A handbook for college and university admission officers, faculty, and administration.* N.p. : Illinois Council for Learning Disabilities.

Wade, S. E. (1990).   Using think alouds to assess comprehension. *The Reading Teacher, 43,* 442–451.

Wade, S. E., Trathen, W., & Schraw, G. (1990).   An analysis of spontaneous study strategies, *Reading Research Quarterly, 25,* 147–166.

Walker, J. E. (1982).   Study strategies: Too many, too few . . . or just right? In D. R. Fleming (Ed.), *Proceedings of the Fifteenth annual conference of the Western College Reading Association.*

Wang, M. C., & Walberg, H. J. (1988).   Four fallacies of segregationism. *Exceptional Children, 55*(2), 128–137.

Wark, D. M., & Flippo, R. F. (1991).   Preparing for and taking tests. In R. F. Flippo & D. C. Caverly (Eds.), *Teaching reading and study strategies at the college level* (pp. 294–338). Newark, DE: International Reading Association.

Wedman, J., & Robinson, R. D. (1990).   Workplace literacy: A proposed model. *Adult Literacy and Basic Education.*

Wepner, S. B. (1990–1991).   Computers, reading software, and at-risk eighth graders. *Journal of Reading, 34,* 264–268.

White, C. S., Hayes, D. A., & Pate, P. E. (1991).   Bridging across instances of a concept in science instruction. In J. Zutell & S. McCormick (Eds.), *Learner factors/teacher factors: Issues in literacy research and instruction: Fortieth yearbook of the National Reading Conference* (pp. 263–268). Chicago: National Reading Conference.

White, R., & Jordan, W. (1986).   Vocational reading in adult education. *Adult Literacy and Basic Education, 10,* 90–100.

Whitmore, J. R. (1986).   Conceptualizing the issue of underserved populations of gifted students. *Journal for the Education of the Gifted, 10,* 141–153.

Wiens, J. (1983).   Metacognition and the adolescent passive learner. *Journal of Learning Disabilities, 16,* 144–149.

Will, M. C. (1986).   Educating children with learning problems: A shared responsibility. *Exceptional Children, 52,* 411–415.

Wirths, C. G., & Bowman-Kruhm, M. (1987).   *I hate school: How to hang in and when to drop out.* New York: Harper & Row.

Wong, B. (1978). The effects of directive cues on the organization of memory and recall in good and poor readers. *Journal of Educational Research, 72,* 32–38.

Wood, J. W., & Miederhoff, J. W. (1988). A model for adapting the teacher-made test. *The Pointer, 33*(1), 7–11.

Wood, K. D. (1988). Guiding students through informational text. *The Reading Teacher, 41,* 912–920.

Wright, J. D. (1982). The effect of reduced readability text material on comprehension and biology achievement. *Science Education, 66,* 3–13.

Yinger, R. J. (1980). A study of teacher planning. *Elementary School Journal, 80,* 107–127.

Zahorik, J. A. (1975). Teachers' planning models. *Educational Leadership, 33,* 134–139.

Zakaluk, B. L., & Samuels, S. J. (1988). Toward a new approach to predicting text comprehensibility. In B. L. Zakaluk & S. J. Samuels (Eds.), *Readability: Its past, present, and future* (pp. 121–144). Newark, DE: International Reading Association.

Zimmerman, B. J., & Pons, M. M. (1986). Development of a structured interview for assessing student use of self-regulated learning strategies. *American Educational Research Journal, 23,* 614–628.

INDEX